Ordination Reconsidered

The Biblical Vision of Men and Women as Servants of God

Bertil Wiklander

Ordination Reconsidered

The Biblical Vision of Men and Women as Servants of God

Newbold Academic Press

Author:
    Bertil Wiklander
Copy editor:
    Jonquil Hole
Graphic design:
    Any Kobel, Switzerland
Layout:
    CAB-Service, Germany
Printing:
    INGRAM

© Bertil Wiklander, 2015

Unless otherwise stated, biblical quotations are either the author's own translation or are taken from The New Revised Standard Version of the Bible, Anglicized Edition, copyright © 1989, 1995 by the Division of Christian Education of the National Council of the Churches of Christ in North America, and are used by permission. All rights reserved.

The opinions expressed in our published works are those of the author(s) and do not reflect the opinions of Newbold Academic Press or its Publishing Panel.

Except as otherwise permitted under the Copyright, Designs and Patents Act 1988 this publication may only be reproduced, stored or transmitted in any form or by any means, with the prior permission of the publisher, or in the case of reprographic reproduction, in accordance with the terms of a licence issued by The Copyright Licensing Agency. Enquiries concerning reproduction outside those terms should be sent to Newbold Academic Press, Bracknell, Berkshire, RG42 4AN, UK.

ISBN 978-0-9932188-4-2, Softcover
ISBN 978-0-9932188-5-9, e-Book

CONTENTS

CONTENTS		7
PREFACE		11
1. Introduction		15
1.1	What is Ordination?	16
1.2	Ordination and the Bible as the Only Creed	18
1.3	Church Debate, Study Committees, and Decisions	20
1.4	The Purpose of This Book	24
Part One: The Church		
2. Adventist Ordination – A Historical Review		25
3. The Issue of Women's Ordination		39
4. Ordination of Women in the Writings of Ellen White		53
5. What Does the Bible *Say* and What Does It *Mean*?		63
Part Two: The Bible		
6. The Mission of God		79
6.1	The Grand Central Theme of the Bible	79
6.2	The Creator Who Dwells with Human Beings	84
6.3	Man and Woman Created in the Image of God	86
6.4	Caretakers of the Garden of Eden – Husband and Wife	92
6.5	The Fall	104
6.5.1	The Promised Seed and the Protection of Marriage	106
6.5.2	Atonement and Priests	117
6.5.3	Patriarchy	123

7. The Mission of Israel		135
7.1 The Election of Israel		135
7.2 Ordination in the Old Testament		139
7.2.1 Assistants of Moses – Judges and Elders		141
7.2.2 The Consecration of Priests and Levites		141
7.2.3 The Commissioning of Joshua		144
7.2.4 The Concept of the Spirit in Leaders		146
7.2.5 Conclusions		147
7.3 The Absence of Female Priests		149
7.4 Women as Servants of God		154
7.4.1 Women in the Priestly Kingdom and Holy Nation		155
7.4.2 Husband-Wife Relationships		157
7.4.3 The Judges – Men and Women		162
7.4.4 The Nazirites – Men and Women		162
7.4.5 Women Proclaiming God's Word		163
7.4.6 Prophetesses and Leaders		164
7.4.7 The Sages – Men and Women		168
7.4.8 Conclusions		169
7.5 The Davidic Line		170
7.6 Summary		176
8. The Mission of Christ		179
8.1 Christ and the Kingdom of God		179
8.2 The Call to Become Part of the Kingdom Mission		183
8.3 Christ as High Priest		185
8.4 Humility and Submission as Christ's Kingdom Characteristics		186
9. The Mission and Ministry of the Church		189
9.1 Service-Ministry		195
9.2 Men and Women as Servants-Ministers of Christ		198
9.2.1 Disciples and Apostles		199
9.2.2 Female Disciples and Eyewitnesses to the Resurrection		203
9.2.3 The Women in the Johannine Writings		212
9.2.4 Elders		215
9.2.5 Servants-Ministers		217

	9.2.6	Women as Servants-Ministers	221
	9.2.7	Women as Apostles	226
	9.2.8	The Offices of Elder, Overseer, and Deacon	230
	9.2.9	The Gender of Overseers and Deacons (I Timothy 3.1-13)	239
	9.2.10	Women behind the Expansion of Early Christianity	248
9.3	Commissioning-Ordination in the New Testament		249
	9.3.1	The Silent Gospels	250
	9.3.2	The Origin of Christian Ordination	254
	9.3.3	The Proto-Ordination Texts	259
	9.3.4	The Commissioning of Women and Spiritual Gifts	285
	9.3.5	New Testament Ordination Terminology	290
	9.3.6	Conclusions	291
9.4	The Laying On of Hands		297
	9.4.1	Old Testament Usage	297
	9.4.2	New Testament Usage	300
9.5	The Meaning of Man as 'Head' and Woman in 'Submission'		308
	9.5.1	The Socio-Cultural Environment of Women in Paul's Writings	309
	9.5.2	The Word kephale in Ephesians 5.23 and I Corinthians 11.3	314
	9.5.3	Ephesians 5.21-33	325
	9.5.4	I Corinthians 11.2-16	349
	9.5.5	I Corinthians 14.33-40	369
	9.5.6	I Timothy 2.8-15	379
	9.5.7	Submission in the New Testament	396
	9.5.8	Conclusions	400

Part Three: The Biblical Vision for the Church

10. Men and Women in Pastoral Ministry and Leadership	403
10.1 'He Made Them to Be a Kingdom and Priests to Our God'	403
10.2 The Bible, the Church, and the Mission of God	435

APPENDIX Considerations for the Church in Its Ordination Policies	439
Abbreviations	443
Selected Bibliography	445

PREFACE

Unity and mutual understanding are essential in the Seventh-day Adventist Church, but so are truth and openness. As an expression of these long-held Adventist values, this book emanates from the conviction that Adventists can only deal appropriately with the issue of women's ordination by taking seriously *the primacy of the biblical foundation* and understanding the *meaning of the Bible as a whole* in its original languages and historical contexts.

The Bible constantly challenges its readers. It challenges the Church to reconsider its current theology and practice of ordination, and this book seeks to explain why.

My study was completed before the General Conference Session in San Antonio, Texas, where the Seventh-day Adventist Church decides on an important matter of policy concerning ordination. Regardless of the outcome of the decision, however, the Church worldwide will for a considerable time have to deal with the biblical issue of ordination and educate the members accordingly. This book is an attempt to provide valid guidance for this long-term endeavour of the Church.

As an issue in Adventism for nearly fifty years, ordination is usually addressed in collections of papers where each paper deals with a specific aspect of ordination. A significant exception is Viggo Norskov Olsen's *Myth and Truth about Church, Priesthood and Ordination* (1990). What is still missing, however, is a biblical theology of ordination based on the Bible *as a whole* and an application of biblical exegesis that *probes deeply into the meaning of the texts*. The present study aims to fill this need. The reader is invited not just to *read* but embark on a *study* of the biblical text. The fullness of the biblical teaching on ordination can only be found by getting rid of simplistic reading, superficial slogans and an undiscerning faith in tradition.

This book is a result of the intense study of ordination conducted by the General Conference of Seventh-day Adventists in 2011-2014. I was asked to do the research and draft the text for a study report by the Biblical Research Committee of the Trans-European Division. Being unanimously endorsed by the Division Executive Committee in November 2013, the report was submitted to the General Conference Theology of Ordination Study Committee and presented there in January 2014.[1] After my retirement on 1 August 2014, I spent considerable time deepening my research and refining the conclusions.

The responsibility for any deficiency in the text rests only with me. However, I reiterate my gratitude to the Division Biblical Research Committee for suggestions received in my initial research that formed the basis of the Report authorised in November 2013. The advice of Dr Laurence Turner and Dr Cedric Vine was highly valued. In particular, I thank Dr Ján Barna for his paper, now available in print,[2] which shaped my understanding of the biblical framework for a theology of ordination. My study also benefited from the reports and papers presented to the General Conference Theology of Ordination Study Committee and its final report published in June 2014.

I thank the Trans-European Division for various forms of encouragement and support, Mrs Jonquil Hole for her patient and

---

[1] 'The Mission of God through the Ministry of the Church: A Biblical Theology of Ordination – with Particular Attention to the Ordination of Women', A Study by the Biblical Research Committee of the Trans-European Division, November 2013 (*http://www.adventistarchives.org/gc-tosc*).

[2] J. Barna, 'Towards a Biblical-Systematic Theology of Ordination', 2014, pp. 97-112.

sensitive approach to the copy-editing, Newbold Academic Press and its chairman, Mr Manfred Lemke, for graciously taking on the publication, and Dr Ján Barna for suggestions that led to constructive improvements of the final manuscript.

May the reading inspire enthusiasm and commitment among men and women as equal participants in the mission of God in the world.

Stockholm
May 2015
Bertil Wiklander

CHAPTER 1
Introduction

The movement of Seventh-day Adventism began with a biblical vision of God's amazing future for the world and his people. More biblical discoveries followed. The Bible proved to be a repository of divine principles and visions discovered by deep study. All along, the movement had an openness to new light from the word of God:

> However long men may have entertained certain views, if they are not clearly sustained by the written word, they should be discarded. [...] We have many lessons to learn, and many, many to unlearn. God and heaven alone are infallible. Those who think that they will never have to give up a cherished view, never have occasion to change an opinion, will be disappointed. *As long as we hold to our own ideas and opinions with determined persistency, we cannot have the unity for which Christ prayed.*[1]

> When God's people are at ease, and satisfied with their present enlightenment, we may be sure that he will not favour them. It is his will that they should be ever moving forward, to receive the increased and ever-increasing light which is shining for them.[2]

---

[1] E. G. White, *Counsels to Editors and Writers*, 1946, p. 37 (the quotation is from *R&H*, 69:30, 26 July, 1892, p. 466; emphasis supplied).
[2] Ibid., p. 41 (from *Gospel Workers*, 1915, p. 300).

A vital, new vision was the discovery of Adventist identity and mission in the message of the three angels in Revelation 14.6-13.[3] God's people at the end of time were seen as active participants in his mission to 'every nation and tribe and language and people' while being identified as those who 'keep the commandments of God and the faith of Jesus'.

However, the book of Revelation also describes the people of God as 'a kingdom and priests to our God' (Revelation 5.10; cf. 1.5-6; 20.6). This is an important discovery in the context of the current Adventist deliberations concerning ordination and women's ordination in particular. In this book I will attempt to show that this description of God's people is in keeping with a consistent biblical vision of men and women in pastoral ministry. This vision challenges readers to re-think their concept of ordination and to make changes that will encourage and inspire men and women to take part in the mission of the church.

The Seventh-day Adventist Church is challenged today by the issue of ordination and whether or not it can accept a gender-inclusive pastoral ministry on biblical grounds.[4] This book is a fresh attempt to present and address this challenge. A brief orientation of the specific questions it seeks to answer is given in the following.[5]

1.1 What is Ordination?

In the Seventh-day Adventist Church today, ordination is a ceremony by which the community of believers formally authenticates God's call of a recipient individual to a special Christian service,

---

[3] Cf. B. Wiklander, 'The Mission of God and the Faithfulness of His People: An Exegetical Reading of Revelation 14:6-13', 2009.

[4] See, for example, J. Lorencin, *Priestly Ministry in the Old and New Testament: Should Women Be Ordained?*, 2012; M. Hanna and C. Tutsch, *Questions and Answers about Women's Ordination*, 2014.

[5] Cf. the vast collection of material at: '2013-14 GC Theology of Ordination Study Committee', The Seventh-day Adventist Church: Office of Archives, Statistics, and Research. *http://www.adventistarchives.org/gc-tosc*.

currently as pastoral gospel minister, local church elder, and deacon/deaconess. The recipient is a member of the priesthood of all believers by baptism into Jesus Christ. When God calls he also equips the recipient with the spiritual gifts needed for service. The ceremony adds no new spiritual quality or status but confirms the presence of spiritual gifts. It includes prayer for God's blessing and a traditional, collegial laying on of hands after certain biblical patterns. Ordination for the pastoral gospel ministry is reserved for men only, while women can be ordained as local church elders and commissioned as ministers.[6]

However, the biblical basis for ordination as practised by Seventh-day Adventists calls for thought. The concept of ordination is not clearly defined in the original Hebrew and Greek texts of the Bible and there is no command in the Bible to ordain individuals for a church office. What is often perceived today as a solid biblical teaching on ordination seems rather to be a temporary on-and-off practice that incorporates a rite of uncertain significance in the New Testament, such as the laying on of hands.

These observations take on even more significance in light of the history of the early Christian church. During the second century AD, the Christian church took over the pagan Roman practice of *ordinatio*[7] and merged it with the elements of prayer and the imposition of hands that were occasionally used by the New Testament church after Old Testament and Jewish models.[8] *The Apostolic Tradition* of Hippolytus

---

[6] *Seventh-day Adventist Minister's Handbook*, 2009, p. 85; *Seventh-day Adventist Church Manual*, 2010, pp. 33-34, 72, 77, 78-79; *Working Policy of the TED of Seventh-day Adventists*, 2012-2013 Edition, 2013, sections E 05, E 10, and L; cf. the 'Consensus Statement on the Theology of Ordination' in GC-TOSCR June 2014, pp. 20-21.

[7] For a detailed study of this development, see TED-TOSCR, 2013, section 4.1.5.

[8] See e.g. Acts 6.1-6; 13.1-3. Old Testament models may also have been imitated, e.g. Exodus 29/Leviticus 8; Numbers 8.5-22; 27.15-23. The relevant passages have been examined in some detail in chaps. 7 and 9 below.

of Rome (c. 170-235) is the earliest preserved example of a Christian ordination.[9] The Roman ordination theology that developed over the centuries differed significantly from the biblical principles associated with commissioning-ordination.[10]

In view of the pronounced Adventist adherence to the Bible in matters of faith and practice, valid reasons therefore exist for raising questions such as: What is biblical ordination? Are all parts of the Seventh-day Adventist practice of ordination truly biblical? Have any traces from the Roman ordination survived in the Adventist practice?[11] How far should the Seventh-day Adventist Church go in applying the principle of *sola scriptura* to the issue of ordination? Have Adventist believers locked themselves into a way of thinking about ordination that has more to do with their cultures and long-held traditions than with a plain 'thus saith the Lord'?

Adventism arose among people who questioned tradition and tested long-held opinions by the Bible. The current turmoil regarding ordination may serve as a reminder of this valuable heritage. It is a cherished thought in Adventism that 'we have nothing to fear for the future except as we forget the way the Lord has led us, and his teaching in our past history'.[12] Thus, going back to the Bible in order to get it right should be seen as an opportunity and not a threat.

1.2 Ordination and the Bible as the Only Creed

From its very beginning the Seventh-day Adventist Church has held high the principle of the Bible as the only creed. As one engages

---

[9] B. S. Easton, *The Apostolic Tradition of Hippolytus*, Cambridge University Press/Archon Books, 1962; cf. V. Norskov-Olsen, *Myth & Truth about the Church, Priesthood and Ordination*, 1990, pp. 149-151; TED-TOSCR, 2013, section 4.1.7.

[10] For further study of these developments, see TED-TOSCR, 2013, sections 4.1, 4.2 and 4.6.5.

[11] For an affirmation of this question, see TED-TOSCR, 2013, section 4.6.5.

[12] E. G. White, Letter 32, 1892 (published in *Life Sketches of Ellen G. White*, 1915 p. 196).

in the study of ordination, however, it is surprising to find that so little is said about it in the Bible and that what is said is rather ambiguous and leaves hardly any certainty.

At a closer look, there is no ready-made or unambiguous definition of ordination in the Bible. The passages that deal with appointments for leadership are strikingly few and some of them are ambiguous or incomplete (from our modern perspective).[13]

The terminology and origin of ordination raise further questions. Hebrew and Greek equivalents of the English noun 'ordination' are not found in the Bible. The verbs used in biblical Hebrew and Greek are not technical terms (which is the case with 'ordain' in modern English), but they have common meanings like 'make, choose, appoint, put, set' (see 7.2 and 9.3.5 below). The English terms 'ordain' and 'ordination' originated in Latin and in the context of concepts already applied in the administration of the Roman Empire.[14] Thus, the occasional New Testament examples of setting someone apart by the laying on of hands, which is not a defined ordinance in the Bible, became integrated in the more formal and strict Roman concept of ordination. This change was facilitated by the theology of the apostolic church fathers, especially Tertullian (c. 160-220) and Cyprian (c. 205-258), and was gradually integrated as a sacrament in the Roman Catholic Church.[15] The Protestant reaction to Roman Catholicism was then expressed in a multitude of different ways with various degrees of retention of elements from the Roman understanding of ordination.[16]

---

[13] Cf. N. Vyhmeister, 'Ordination in the New Testament?', 2002, pp. 24-27.
[14] See ibid.
[15] See V. Norskov-Olsen, *Myth and Truth about the Church, Priesthood and Ordination*, 1990, pp. 90-104, 149-152; TED-TOSCR, 2013, sections 4.1 and 4.2.
[16] V. Norskov-Olsen, *Myth and Truth about the Church, Priesthood and Ordination*, 1990, pp. 104-125, 149-164; TED-TOSCR, 2013, sections 4.4, 4.5, 4.6 and 4.7.

What the Bible is very clear about, however, is the spiritual calling and equipment with spiritual gifts for any ministry in the church. On this matter, the Bible has a lot to say. But on ordination by the laying on of hands, it is rather ambiguous or silent.

So, how did ordination enter a movement that claimed the Bible as its only creed? And what was the outcome in terms of a genuinely biblical form of ordination? I will seek to answer these questions in chapter 2 below.

1.3 Church Debate, Study Committees, and Decisions

In modern times, at least since the 1970s, the Seventh-day Adventist Church has grappled with the issue of women's ordination for the pastoral ministry. The historical roots of this challenge are examined in chapter 3 below. However, since the General Conference Session in Atlanta, 2010, the debate has taken place in the context of a quest for a biblical theology of ordination.

A special study committee appointed by the General Conference in October 2011 brought its report in June 2014.[17] It recommended a brief consensus statement on the biblical theology of ordination,[18] but the report on women's ordination was divided into three different views voted on in a secret ballot in the committee.

One group argued that the Bible does not permit ordination of women for the gospel ministry and that even the current church practices of ordaining women as local church elders and commissioning women for pastoral ministry should therefore be withdrawn (32 votes).[19] This group emphasised the biblical qualifications for ordination as found in I Timothy 3 and Titus 1 (especially the expression 'husband of one

---

[17] *General Conference Theology of Ordination Study Committee Report – June, 2014*, Silver Spring, MD: The General Conference of Seventh-day Adventists, 2014.
[18] Ibid., pp. 20-22.
[19] Ibid., pp. 25-60, 119-120.

wife')[20] and the fact that never in the Bible were women ordained as priests, apostles or elders.[21]

The largest group of the three demonstrated that the Bible says very little about Christian ordination and contains no objections to women's leadership roles but invites men and women to serve God who bestows his spiritual gifts without partiality: 'The biblical evidence is clear: there is nothing spiritually, ethically, or morally wrong with ordaining women to the gospel ministry' (40 votes).[22] This group emphasised the roles of female leaders such as Deborah, Huldah, Phoebe, and Junia, and biblical passages in Genesis 1-2 and Galatians 3.26-28 that stress the equality of all people in God's eyes. It showed that passages allegedly referring to an exclusive male leadership (e.g. Ephesians 5.21-33; I Corinthians 11.2-16; I Timothy 2.9-14) actually have the roles of husband and wife within marriage in mind, while giving counsel on how to deal with false teachings in the local church.[23] The much debated expression 'husband of one wife' in I Timothy 3.1-13 is not understood to mean that only a man can be an elder: 'The same phrase is used to refer to both deacons and elders (I Timothy 3.1, 12) and it is now clear that a woman can occupy the office of a deacon.[24] Therefore, although the phrase is certainly gender specific it is not gender exclusive because there were female deacons. The emphasis of the phrase is on moral purity rather than on gender (cf. 5.9). Within a prevalent cultural context of temple prostitution, Paul uses masculine language to present sexual purity

---

[20] Ibid., pp. 28, 36, 53. See, however, the exegesis in 9.2.9 below.
[21] Ibid., pp. 44-48. We will show in chapters 7 and 9 below that Old Testament priests were not ordained in a way that is relevant for the church – their office was hereditary, their installation in office was a ritual consecration and purification, and only the Levites received the laying on of hands, because they were to replace the firstborn of the Israelites. We will also show that no apostle, elder, deacon, or servant-minister was ordained by the laying on of hands in the New Testament.
[22] GC-TOSCR, 2014, pp. 62-97, 121-122 (the quotation is taken from p. 65).
[23] Ibid., pp. 73-78.
[24] See the examples given in ibid., pp. 84-87.

and monogamy as a qualification of deacons and elders whether they are men or women. Arguing that elders and deacons are to be sexually pure, this instruction identifies a moral attribute that also qualifies women since Paul also teaches that a faithful elder-widow is a "wife of one husband" or a "one-man woman" (I Timothy 5.9, ESV).'[25]

The third group affirmed 'the biblical pattern of male leadership, under the headship of Christ, in the office of the ordained minister', but did not see this pattern as 'a moral absolute or universal divine command, or of sacramental or salvific significance' – it is rather primarily meant to promote order in the church and further its mission'. Based on a wide range of biblical precedents, therefore, it was acknowledged that, 'in certain circumstances, God permits divine patterns for ecclesiastical organisation to be adapted or modified in order to promote the mission, unity, and welfare of the church' (22 votes).[26] Thus, the third group emphasised that God made exceptions, such as the case of granting Israel's desire for a king. Therefore, women's ordination is a matter of church policy and not a moral imperative and, consequently, the Seventh-day Adventist Church should allow each field to decide whether or not to ordain women.

Of those committee members who studied the Bible and the issue of women's ordination in 2011-2014, two-thirds (67.4%) recommended that each regional division should be given the right to determine its policy concerning a gender-inclusive ministry. Based on this Report, the General Conference Annual Council on 14 October 2014 voted to refer the question to the General Conference Session in San Antonio, Texas, 2-11 July 2015. The vote is recorded as follows: Whereas, The unity for which Jesus prayed is vitally important to the witness of the Seventh-day Adventist Church, and;

> Whereas, The Seventh-day Adventist Church seeks to engage every member in its worldwide mission to

---

[25] Ibid., p. 86.
[26] GC-TOSCR, 2014, pp. 98-116, 123-124 (the quotations are from p. 123).

make disciples of Jesus Christ among people from every nation, culture and ethnicity, and;

Whereas, Various groups appointed by the General Conference and its divisions have carefully studied the Bible and Ellen G White writings with respect to the ordination of women and have not arrived at consensus as to whether ministerial ordination for women is unilaterally affirmed or denied, and;

Whereas, The Seventh-day Adventist Church affirms that 'God has ordained that the representatives of His Church from all parts of the earth, when assembled in a General Conference Session, shall have authority'

Therefore, The General Conference Executive Committee requests delegates in their sacred responsibility to God at the 2015 General Conference Session to respond to the following question:

After your prayerful study on ordination from the Bible, the writings of Ellen G White, and the reports of the study commissions, and;

After your careful consideration of what is best for the Church and the fulfillment of its mission,

Is it acceptable for division executive committees, as they may deem it appropriate in their territories, to make provision for the ordination of women to the gospel ministry? Yes or No.[27]

The outcome of the work of the Theology of Ordination Study Committee in 2011-2014 is evidence that no solution has been found in the quest for a biblical understanding of ordination that allows men and women to serve God as equals. The purpose of the present book, therefore, is to propose a fresh solution.

---

[27] October 14, 2014, Edwin Manuel Garcia (ANN), 'News: Adventist Church Sets Vote on Women's Ordination for Next July', *http://news.adventist.org*.

1.4 The Purpose of This Book

This book examines the biblical view of ordination with particular attention to the issue of women's ordination. It does so as part of the historical quest for a biblical theology of ordination in the Seventh-day Adventist Church and hints at areas in the practice of ordination where the Church should seek a closer adherence to the Bible. I endeavour to show that, while there is no biblical prohibition against women's ordination, there is indeed a biblical vision of men and women in pastoral ministry and church leadership (summarised in 10.1 below).

There are certainly many reasons for the deadlock reported by the Theology of Ordination Study Committee (see 1.3 above). An important explanation is the way in which the biblical text has been perceived, read, and interpreted by Adventist scholars, and we will come back to that in chapter 5 below. Another explanation concerns the surprisingly simplistic and superficial understanding of Ellen White's position regarding women's ordination, which will be considered in chapter 4 below. Above all, however, what is still missing is a study of biblical ordination that is based on *a thematic concept of the Bible as a whole*, that proceeds with such openness that *the full meaning potentials of the texts are seen*, and that probes deeply and methodically enough into the *Hebrew and Greek originals* to allow for valid understandings in view of the *content, setting, purpose, and context* of the texts.[28] The outcome of such a systematic and exegetical approach is presented in chapters 6-9 below.

The purpose is ultimately to show a way for the Church out of its dilemma, to ensure a better understanding of the real issues, and to safeguard church unity (see 10.2 and the Appendix below).

---

[28] Cf. the statement by Ellen White: 'The most valuable teaching of the Bible is not to be gained by occasional or disconnected study. Its great system of truth is not so presented as to be discerned by the hasty or careless reader. Many of its treasures lie *far beneath the surface*, and can only be obtained by diligent research and continuous effort.' (*Education*, 1903, p. 123; emphasis added).

Part One: The Church
CHAPTER 2

Adventist Ordination – A Historical Review

The ordination issue in the Seventh-day Adventist Church began with its introduction in the Sabbatarian Adventist movement in the 1850s. In order to understand the current issue of Adventist ordination, it is important to acknowledge what happened when the Church was first organised. The things we learn from this review will prepare the way for Part Two: The Bible.

Beginnings in the 1850s

Some ten years before the conference organisation in 1861 and the General Conference in 1863, leaders of the Sabbatarian Adventists began to argue in favour of a recognised clergy.[1] The situation around 1850 was that some leaders had been ordained as ministers in their previous churches, following the patterns for ordination in the Christian Connexion (Joshua Himes, James White), Methodism (John Byington, Frederick Wheeler), and the Baptists (A. S. Hutchins).[2] But with growth came issues of unity, recognised leadership, and congregational needs of administering the church ordinances. However, the movement hesitated because of its strong anti-organisational position.[3] Yet James White and other leaders

---

[1] G. R. Knight, 'Early Seventh-day Adventists and Ordination', 1998; id., *Organizing to Beat the Devil: The Development of Adventist Church Structure*, 2001, pp. 15-66; D. J. B. Trim, 'Ordination in Seventh-day Adventist History', 2013. Cf. TED-TOSCR 2013, section 4.6.1.

[2] G. R. Knight, 'Early Seventh-day Adventists and Ordination', 1998, p. 105.

[3] This was a heritage from the Christian Connexion – a loose association of congregations formed in the US in 1810 from Baptists, Methodists and

believed that recognised ministers were necessary because the small Adventist congregations needed to know which travelling preachers they could trust. The challenge was how to introduce organisation and a formal practice of recognising ministers in a community that would not accept any new practice unless it was found in the Bible.

Ordinations began to take place for practical reasons before the Bible had been thoroughly studied. The known patterns of ordination from other churches were followed. The earliest evidence of a Sabbatarian Adventist ordination ceremony was that of Washington Morse in July 1851.[4] Ordination to the gospel ministry was practised among Sabbatarians in September 1853, when James White led out at a conference in Pottsdam and the congregation 'set apart our dear Br. Lawrence to the work of the gospel ministry, to administer the ordinances of the church of Christ, by the laying on of hands'.[5]

The ordination services were 'simple and straightforward'. The key elements were prayer and the laying on of hands of preaching brethren present, which was in harmony with the practices of the evangelical churches at the time.[6]

Three Offices Requiring Ordination

While the practice of ordaining gospel ministers began, by 1854 the *Review and Herald* also reported several ordination services of deacons. In January 1855, J. B. Frisbie pointed out the existence of 'two classes of preaching elders' in the New Testament – the 'travelling elders' and the 'local elders'. The former 'had the oversight over several churches as evangelical or travelling elders or bishops' (cf. II Corinthians 11.28). The local elders 'had the pastoral care and oversight of one church' (cf. Titus 1.5; Acts 14.23).[7] Frisbie then suggested that, following the

---

Presbyterians with the Bible as the only creed (ibid., pp. 101-103).
[4] Ibid., p. 106.
[5] [J. White], 'Eastern Tour', *R&H* 4:11, 20 September 1853, p. 85; cf. G. R. Knight, 'Early Seventh-day Adventists and Ordination', 1998, p. 106.
[6] G. R. Knight, 'Early Seventh-day Adventists and Ordination', 1998, p. 107.
[7] J. B. Frisbie, 'Church Order', *R&H* 6:20, 9 January 1855, p. 155.

Bible, the local Sabbatarian churches should have both elders and deacons in the local church (cf. I Timothy 13.1-13), letting the first have 'oversight of the spiritual, the other the temporal affairs of the church'.[8] This position was established in 1856.[9]

The Sabbatarians now had three offices for which ordination was practised: the gospel minister, the local church elder, and the deacon. This order was confirmed as the Seventh-day Adventist Church was organised in 1861-1863 and still remains. There is, however, no explicit biblical ground for ordination being attached specifically to these three offices. They are not mentioned in the New Testament as a set of leadership positions and nowhere is ordination stated as a condition for any of them. Instead, the practice of ordination for this set of offices can be traced back to the early Roman Catholic Church, where ordination was a condition for the overseer (*episkopos*), presbyter (*presbyteros*), and servant (*diakonos*).

James White's Biblical Basis for Ordination in 1853

In a series of four articles on 'Gospel Order'[10] in *Review and Herald* in December 1853, James White raised the issue of the biblical theology of ordination for the first time in Adventism.[11] The concept of 'gospel order' – at times referred to as 'Bible order' or 'church order' – was used by both James and Ellen White from at least as early as 1850.[12]

---

[8] Ibid.
[9] G. Land, *Historical Dictionary of the Seventh-day Adventists*, 2005, p. 218. See also G. R. Knight, *Organizing to Beat the Devil: The Development of Adventist Church Structure*, 2001, pp. 35-41.
[10] For the origin and meaning of this term, see TED-TOSCR, 2013, section 4.6.1, footnote 1196.
[11] See James White's series of articles on 'Gospel Order' in *R&H*, 4:22, 6 December 1853, pp. 172-173; 4:23, 13 December 1853, p. 180; 4:24, 20 December 1853, pp. 188-190; 4:25, 27 December 1853, pp. 196-197. The first article in the series was preceded by an article on 'Gospel Union' (*R&H*, 4:22, 6 December 1853, p. 172).
[12] G. R. Knight, *Organizing to Beat the Devil: The Development of Adventist Church Structure*, 2001, p. 35; cf. the survey on pp. 33-38.

In his third article James White's main reason for ordination rested on a biblical argument. The church was to be in compliance with 'the order of the gospel' (based on passages like Mark 3.14; Matthew 28.16-20; I Corinthians 12.28; Ephesians 4.11-16; I Timothy 4.14-16; II Timothy 1.6), and Jesus had 'commissioned'[13] his disciples to preach and baptize believers in his name (Matthew 28.19-20). Christ gave the same 'commission' to Paul (Galatians 1.11-12) and 'God has set some in the church, first apostles, secondarily prophets, thirdly teachers' (I Corinthians 12.28; cf. Ephesians 4.11-16). In view of the New Testament passages he concluded:

> From this we learn that the order of the gospel is that men who are called of God to *teach and baptize*, should be ordained, or set apart to the work of the ministry by the laying on of hands. *Not that the church has power to call men to ministry, or that ordination makes them ministers of Jesus Christ; but it is the order of the gospel that those who are called to the ministry should be ordained, for important objects.*[14]

Even in this brief summary, James White's thinking about ordination reveals his roots in the Christian Connexion, where he was ordained in 1843, and where many of the Sabbatarian Adventists whom he sought to convince originated. To the Connexionists, preaching and teaching required no ordination, for these were gifts of the Spirit founded on God's appointment. When White therefore says that those who are 'called of God to teach *and baptize* should be ordained', his Connexionist background shines through. Ordination was the church's public recognition and conferred especially the authority to administer the ordinances (baptism and holy communion), not merely preaching or teaching God's word.

---

[13] In his article on the gospel minister (*R&H* 4:24, 20 December 1853) James White tends to use 'commission' about the call of God and Christ, while 'ordain' is used in close adherence to the KJV.

[14] J. White, 'Gospel Order', *R&H* 4:24, 20 December, 1853, p. 189 (emphasis supplied).

Another Connexionist feature is the implied idea of Christ as Head of the church and the non-sacramental view of the laying on of hands.

James White's three *practical* reasons for ordination address 'the spiritual good of the flock' and the 'unity' of the church.[15] A minister needs the *approval* of ministerial colleagues and of the church. There is a need to secure *unity* in the church, which may be achieved by the laying on of hands on behalf of the church and as a united expression of the church. Ordination was a tool that *eliminated the influence of false teachers.*

According to James White, the Bible is the only basis for ordination. Reference is made to 'being ordained *according to the Word*'. The New Testament is the sole source of biblical guidance for ordination. The Old Testament consecrations for the inherited priesthood are completely ignored. However, no attempt was made to analyse the biblical texts or to go deeper into the original Greek version of the New Testament. One gets the impression that White uses 'ordination' as a well-known term that does not need any explanation to his readers. The use of the term 'ordain' is based on the King James Version of the Bible (from 1611) – the KJV is notorious for using the ecclesiastical term 'ordain' where the Greek text has many different common verbs meaning 'make' or 'set'.[16] The references to the *manner* of ordination were taken directly from the plain word of the old KJV translation in Acts 6.1-6; 13.3; I Timothy 4.14; II Timothy 1.6. Ordination as such is not White's key interest, but rather the biblical 'gospel order' established by God in his word and by Christ in his church, which, if the church follows it, will bring blessings, unity, fellowship, love, and strength to the church. It will, above all, protect the church from false and divisive teaching and forward the work of mission. Ordination maintains 'gospel order'.

---

[15] Ibid., pp. 188-189.
[16] See TED-TOSCR, 2013, section 4.5.4.

The fundamental condition of ordination is that of being called by God and Christ. The church does not have the power to *call* members to ministry, and neither the ordination ceremony nor the status of being ordained '*makes* them ministers of Jesus Christ'. The qualifications of an ordinand are therefore extremely important. The manner of ordination is 'being set apart to the work of the ministry by the laying on of hands' (I Timothy 4.11-16 and II Timothy 1.6), and the ritualistic or sacramental aspect of the imposition of hands is explicitly abrogated. The imposition of hands is performed on behalf of the whole church who in this way affirm the ordinand's divine calling and spiritual gifts, recognising him as a representative spokesperson of the church, sympathising with him and including him in prayer.

There are no references to biblical passages regarding the headship of males as opposed to females. It is simply implied that an ordinand is thought of as a male. Although White comments on each detail in I Timothy 3.1-7, he makes no reference to the phrase 'the husband of one wife' (3.2).

Ellen White shared her husband's general view of the need for ordination. Late in 1853, she wrote an article based on a vision received in September 1852. 'Gospel order' was endorsed as the church's way of undoing the damage done by unqualified ministers and the resulting confusion and disunion. She called attention to the New Testament church where 'God's solution was the setting apart of ministers by the laying on of hands'. In vision an angel told her that 'the church must *flee to God's Word* and become established upon gospel order'.[17] She referred to the apostolic example for the Adventist Church:

> Brethren of experience and of sound minds should assemble, and *following the word of God* and the

---

[17] E. G. White, *Supplement to the Christian Experience and Views of Ellen G. White*, Published on 1 January, 1854, Reprinted in: *Early Writings of Ellen G. White*, 1882, p. 99 (emphasis supplied).

sanction of the Holy Spirit, should, with fervent prayer, lay hands upon those who have given full proof that they have received their commission of God, and set them apart to devote themselves to His work.[18]

Ellen White's explicit appeal to the Bible is noteworthy. Historians recognise that 'the Sabbatarian leaders by the mid-1850s had no doubt as to the biblical validity of ordination'.[19] But Ellen White spoke, like her husband James, primarily about the biblical foundation of *gospel order*. In her 1854 article, she does not use the terms 'ordain' or 'ordination', but uses biblical expressions such as 'called', 'chosen', 'laying on of hands', 'receive one's commission from God', and 'set apart'. Ordained ministers are referred to in a biblical way as 'servants of God'.

Deep faithfulness to the Bible as the only creed, as demonstrated in the Christian Connexion, characterised James White's introduction of ordination in 1853. However, he used the King James Version (not the Greek original), simply quoting the KJV from a common-sensical literal reading, which was the generally accepted approach to the Bible text at this time[20] (without a deeper study of the Bible as a whole), and he was driven by practical needs to establish gospel order for the sake of mission. Consequently, some elements of church tradition were initially taken for granted by the Sabbatarians, especially the element of *the imposition of hands* (but its significance was not explained) and the view that the *ordinances* (baptism and holy communion) could only be administered by an ordained minister.[21] Later on, the Sabbatarians also accepted the idea of a certain *succession* of those who were laying

---

[18] Ibid., p. 101 (emphasis supplied); cf. G. R. Knight, 'Early Seventh-day Adventists and Ordination', 1998, p. 103.

[19] G. R. Knight, 'Early Seventh-day Adventists and Ordination', 1998, p. 104.

[20] See chapter 5 below.

[21] In his article of 20 December 1853, James White does not mention imposition of hands as part of Jesus' appointment of the twelve and only refers to this rite based on I Timothy 4.11-16 and II Timothy 1.6 (p. 189). He also makes a case for an ordained minister being the one that 'administers the ordinances of the gospel' (ibid.). Both these elements were

on hands, to which we will return in a moment,[22] and the (originally Methodist) idea of a period of *ministerial probation* before a person was ordained.[23] The early ordination ceremonies were characterised by a special out-pouring of the *Holy Spirit*, but essentially upon the congregation taking part and not merely the ordinand.[24]

It is noteworthy that 'the Sabbatarians must have had some underlying idea of apostolic succession, since the ones performing the initial ordinations were those who had already been ordained in other Protestant denominations'.[25] This idea of a succession was not specifically addressed by James White, although it may be vaguely hinted at in the New Testament (Acts 13.1-3 and the connection with 14.23; Titus 1.5). It is still being practised within the Seventh-day Adventist Church, for the only persons who can lay their hands on an ordinand for the gospel ministry are already-ordained ministers. However, we may well ask ourselves today if this is a biblical principle or a tradition from the post-biblical church.[26]

The Reliance on Church Tradition

A year after Ellen White's article on Gospel Order in 1854, in January 1855, J. B. Frisbie, who became an influential figure in the development of ordination among the Sabbatarian Adventists, published a lengthy article in the *Review and Herald* on 'Church Order'. Frisbie was ordained in the Methodist Church in 1846 and served as a Methodist minister until he joined the Sabbatarian Adventists in 1853.[27] This background made him more prone to

---

dominant in the Christian Connexion (TED-TOSCR, 2014, section 4.4.5).

[22] Cf. G. R. Knight, 'Early Seventh-day Adventists and Ordination', 1998, p. 111.

[23] Ibid., p. 108.

[24] The sweet 'melting' through the outpouring of the Spirit at ordinations was a phrase especially used by the Methodists in their encounters with God (ibid., pp. 107-108).

[25] Ibid.

[26] See TED-TOSCR, 2013, section 4.6.3.

[27] L. R. van Dolson, *Elder J. B. Frisbie – S.D.A. Pioneer in Michigan*, 1965, p. 5.

accepting ecclesiastical terminology for ordination and church offices, stemming from the roots of Methodism in Anglicanism.[28] Frisbie's article addressed a range of issues. Ordination was to him 'the separating act by which grace was imparted to do the work and office of a bishop'.[29] In a section with the title 'Gospel order in the ministry', Frisbie frankly declared that 'Christ chose his disciples, and ordained them' (which is what the KJV translation says in Mark 3.14, although the Greek text simply states that he 'made twelve'). Then he described how the church at Antioch 'laid their hands on' Paul and Barnabas, and termed this the 'ordination of Paul'.[30] Frisbie relied on a literal reading of the KJV which provided his final arguments, although none of his suggested readings noted here are actually stated in the biblical text.

Thus, ordination by prayer and the imposition of hands was an existing custom already practised when ordination became urgent among the Sabbatarians in the early 1850s. The underlying biblical interpretations in the examples given above were common in the Christian denominations from which the Sabbatarians had emerged. No exegesis was done on the Greek text and the Bible as a whole was not used as context. The generally accepted common-sensical literal reading of biblical texts was considered sufficient. The common practice of biblical interpretation included the proof-text method which allowed for free connections between texts with related topics or similar words, all facilitated by the King James Version, which excelled in using 'ordain' as the term for 'appoint', thus inviting the reader to connect passages that were in important ways quite different. Therefore, it is to be concluded that the early ordinations among the Sabbatarians in the 1850s were not based on a deep and comprehensive study of the Bible but were undertaken for practical reasons and in close keeping with the evangelical Christian tradition.

---

[28] See TED-TOSCR, 2013, section 4.4.2.
[29] J. B. Frisbie, 'Church Order', *R&H* 8:9, 26 June 1856, p. 70.
[30] Id., 'Church Order', *R&H* 6:20, 9 January 1855, p. 154.

The Threat of Ritualism and 'Incomplete Biblical' Foundation

When the Michigan Conference of Seventh-day Adventists was formed in October 1861, 'the process and meaning of ordination had been pretty well hammered out by the young church.'[31] The organising meetings of the Conference confirmed already-established practices. These practices became institutionalised by the General Conference of Seventh-day Adventists when it was organised on 21 May 1863. This ordination system is essentially the same that is used today.[32] The approach of the Sabbatarians was 'pragmatic and eclectic rather than built upon a tightly-reasoned theology of ordination'.[33] This is still the case in the Seventh-day Adventist Church, and, unfortunately, it has become a fixed tradition seen by many almost as a 'biblical doctrine'.

Despite Ellen White's constant warnings against 'formalism' in ordination,[34] a solemn ritual with spiritual and ecclesiastical significance developed – closely imitating the practice in other denominations. This element is not based on explicit biblical instructions and contains elements of Roman Catholic ordination.[35] The GC Session decision in 1879 is an example of this. In the following, some interpretative comments are included in brackets:

> We regard ordination as *a solemn and impressive ceremony* [a formal ritual], sanctioned by the Holy Scriptures and *indicating* [ordination's first symbolic meaning] *the setting apart, or separation, of the person receiving it from the body of believers with whom he has been associated* [separation of ordinand from the laity], *to perform the office to which he is ordained* [ministry is an institutionalised office and ordination gives access

---

[31] G. R. Knight, 'Early Seventh-day Adventists and Ordination', 1998, pp. 109-110.

[32] For an outline of the essence of the ordination system at the constituting session for the Michigan Conference in October 1861, see ibid., pp. 110-111.

[33] Ibid., p. 111.

[34] See, for example, the article on 'Gospel Order' printed in January, 1854, reprinted in *Early Writings*, 1882, p. 97: 'Formality should be shunned'.

[35] See TED-TOSCR, 2013, section 4.6.5; cf. section 4.2.

to it] and as *suggestive of the conferring of* [allusion to ordination as conferring spiritual gifts] *those spiritual blessings which God must impart to properly qualify him for that position* [suggests that God's qualification of a person for the position happens through the act of ordination]. (Emphasis supplied.)[36]

By about 1914, the role of ordination had developed into a central feature of the concept of 'ministry' in the Seventh-day Adventist Church. David Trim describes the view of ordination acquired over time as follows:

> In this system, moreover, the ceremony of ordination had central significance that was more than functional; *it verged on the ritualistic*. It was a key rite of passage which as well as recognising the Holy Spirit's calling of the individual also symbolised the *imparting of authority* to the individual by the Church. It was, consequently, an honour not accorded lightly. As the denomination developed and grew, the ceremony became more elaborate and what it symbolised seems to have developed, too. It was not sacramental, for Adventists never held that it was by going through ceremony that one received the spiritual gifts associated with and needed for ministry. However, the language used about it strongly suggests that the ceremony was seen as more than just an acknowledgement of a calling. Even if in a limited way, it *imparted a spiritual quality as well as ecclesiastical authority*, to those who underwent ordination.[37]

Based on his review of the history of Seventh-day Adventist theology and practice of ordination, Trim concluded that the Seventh-day Adventist understanding of ordination 'developed relatively quickly and then remained remarkably stable and consistent for at least the first half of our history'. He noted that early Adventists did

---

[36] Eighteenth Session, Twelfth Meeting, Nov. 24, 1879, 7 p.m. (GCSM 1863-88, p. 162).

[37] D. J. B. Trim, 'Ordination in Seventh-day Adventist History', 2013, p. 21 (emphasis supplied).

not theorise much about ordination: 'Their theology of ordination to some extent has to be worked out from their practice. Because of this, where our pioneers perpetuated attitudes and practices of other churches it is not always clear when they had first subjected them to scrutiny and decided to keep them because they were biblical, and when they simply were continuing in the ways they had been brought up to think and act.' While Adventists gave sustained critical attention to biblical passages on organisation during the 1850s, there is less evidence for why their practice evolved in the ways it did after 1863 and for the actions taken by GC Sessions of the 1860s, '70s and '80s. Trim therefore concludes that 'our founders were not impervious to the prejudices of the time and they may have not always realized how much they had inherited from the Christian past.' He suggests, finally, that 'one response to the history whose contours I have sketched out would be to say that *it is not biblical – or rather, is only incompletely biblical*.'[38]

Conclusions

Since the Seventh-day Adventist Church claims that the Bible is its only creed, David Trim's conclusions above should be taken very seriously and raise concerns. They invite the Seventh-day Adventist Church to seek to understand in what way its ordination practice is 'only incompletely biblical' and to identify how it was influenced by a Protestant-Christian tradition that – knowingly or unknowingly – held on to *parts of* the sacrament of ordination in the Roman Catholic Church.[39] Such an understanding would help the Church

---

[38] Ibid., p. 28 (emphasis added); cf. TED-TOSCR, 2013, section 4.6.3.

[39] The TED Biblical Research Committee has provided in its Report a comprehensive study of the history of ordination from the New Testament to our times (TED-TOSCR, 2013, chapter 4). It gives evidence of how the Sabbatarian Adventists were influenced by a Protestant-Christian tradition that held on to elements of the Roman Catholic ordination system. In light of a survey of Roman Catholic ordination, a summary of at least nine elements in Seventh-day Adventist ordination practices is given that should be evaluated with a view to making those practices more biblical (TED-TOSCR, 2013, section 4.6.5).

acknowledge where its ordination theology and practice need to be *reformed* in order to better reflect the theology and teaching of the Bible.[40] In the context of such a reform, the Church will also be able to better assess the issue of women's ordination in the light of the Bible rather than from its own church tradition.

If, on the other hand, it is argued that ordination is a practical matter that does not necessarily need to be proven by the Bible,[41] then even women's ordination should be determined by the Church on the same practical grounds. Objectives that James White sought to achieve by ordination in order to establish 'gospel order' in the 1850s, such as the unity and mission of the church (see the summary above), would then become fundamental also for the ordination of women.

Summing up, the practice of ordination entered the Seventh-day Adventist Church mainly as a practical initiative in order to safeguard the unity and mission of the Church. The theological concepts used were drawn from a few biblical passages according to the KJV which reflected an Anglican view of the church and the ordination of the clergy from 1611. The theology of ordination was not built on a thorough study of ordination in the Bible as a whole in the original languages. It was heavily influenced by the evangelical church traditions on ordination which the Sabbatarians were accustomed to.

The model of ordination introduced by James White served the Church well at the time. However, it was accepted without specific reflection on the role of women in ministry and ordination and without deep Bible study. The contemporary role of women in American culture in the nineteenth century was simply taken for granted and then further built upon as time went by. Today, this construct has become an impasse that threatens church unity, as the Church grapples with women's ordination.

---

[40] Cf. the suggestions in TED-TOSCR, 2013, section 4.6.5.
[41] For this view, see G. R Knight, 'Ecclesiastical Deadlock: James White Solves a Problem That Had No Answer', 2014; cf. TED-TOSCR, 2013, section 2.1.

Therefore, as pointed out in our Introduction above, what the Church needs now is a study of biblical ordination that proceeds from *a thematic concept of the Bible as a whole*, that maintains an openness of mind which enables us to see *the full meaning potentials of the biblical texts*, and that probes deeply and methodically enough into the *Hebrew and Greek originals* to allow for valid understandings in view of the *content, setting, purpose, and context* of the biblical texts. This is attempted in Part Two: The Bible (chapters 6-9 below).

CHAPTER 3
The Issue of Women's Ordination

The issue of women's ordination has been alive in the Seventh-day Adventist Church especially in the first and last decades of its history. In the following, it will be shown that the path of the Church regarding women's ordination has been decided largely on account of ingrained customs of the surrounding society, both in the American setting in the nineteenth century when the Church was organised and in recent decades. The lack of a comprehensive and penetrating study of the biblical texts is again coming to the forefront, and the present chapter therefore adds to the rationale for Part Two of this study: The Bible.

The North American Setting in the 1800s

In the early nineteenth century, women were often ordained in Protestant denominations in the United States. This was stimulated by societal changes. After the end of the American Revolution in 1783, the thoughts of equality and freedom expressed in the Declaration of Independence of 1776 promoted greater openness. Social factors caused an increase in public leadership roles for women and ordinations of women. There were 'increasing educational opportunities for girls; women's financial and legal independence from their husbands and fathers; better health care and decreased birth rates; skills gained by women from taking care of homes, farms, businesses, and communities in the absence of men during the Civil War; the lack of educated men available to serve the frontier church; and a growing sense among women that they had special gifts to use in service in the church, often born out of their experience in church missionary societies and in the social reform movements of the time'.[1]

In this context, the Society of Friends (Quakers) allowed women to serve as ministers in the early nineteenth century. The Primitive Methodist Church in Britain allowed female ministers in 1807. The Christian Connexion Church, an early relative of the Christian Church (Disciples of Christ) and the United Church of Christ, ordained women as early as 1810. In New England Clarissa Danforth became the first ordained woman in the Free Will Baptist denomination in 1815.[2] The early Sabbatarian Adventists came from these denominations.

Thus, James White and many others were familiar with women's ordination from their background.

Early Adventist Attempts to Include Women in Ministry

In the 1860s and 1870s, attempts were made in the Seventh-day Adventist Church to incorporate 'a caring, pastoral ministry' within the initial evangelistic perspective. It appears that 'women, as members of husband-wife evangelistic teams, performed such roles'.[3] And, gradually, women received recognition as licensed ministers.[4] Coming out of the Christian Connexion, where women played a significant role as preachers and teachers and some of them were even ordained, it is no surprise that James White considered the ministry of women important. He expressed the view that 'the minister's wife stands in so close a relation to the work of God, a relation which so affects him for better or worse, that she should, in the ordination prayer, be set apart as his helper'.[5]

---

[1] D. B. Hull, 'Women in Ministry: Nineteenth Century', 2004, p. 776.
[2] Cf. the review of women's ordination in the Christian Connexion in TED-TOSCR, 2013, section 4.4.5.4.
[3] B. Haloviak, 'A Response to Two Papers by David Trim', 2013, p. 2.
[4] Id., 'A Place at the Table: Women and the Early Years', 1995, pp. 29-32.
[5] J. White, 'Report from Brother White', *R&H* 30:09, 13 August 1867, p. 136.

However, in James White's 'mother church', the Christian Connexion, women's ordination was less controversial if it excluded responsibility for the administration of the ordinances. This was regarded as a male duty, because it had a 'priestly', representative function on behalf of the people before God, and, perhaps also because of the societal convention of male headship. Further, denominations organised as local churches with authority to make their own decisions for local needs would more easily accept women's ordination than those where a hierarchic structure entailed many different entities that had to take the same decision and apply the same practice everywhere.[6] Obviously, the issue of *authority* was an obstacle to women's ordination, because the patriarchal notion of male authority was still deeply rooted in society.

Similarly, in the Seventh-day Adventist Church the link between administering the ordinances and ordination for the gospel ministry impacted women's ordination. This link had no biblical foundation but was a heritage from the Baptists (although at times questioned there), Methodism, and Presbyterianism – all of them denominational fathers of the Christian Connexion.[7] However, the task of ministering the word of God remained open to women, because it was understood as a divine calling, and it was acknowledged that women also received this spiritual gift. (This remarkable fact did not lead to deeper theological reflection, however.) While Seventh-day Adventist women therefore were licensed ministers and served as preachers and teachers, the core issue for women's ordination to the gospel ministry was the ecclesiastical authority as 'head' that ordination was understood to convey by the Church. We have seen earlier in this chapter, however, that this headship concept was not based on biblical study but was simply taken for granted because of the long-standing Christian tradition of ordination and leadership practices. In view of these striking circumstances, the issue of women's ordination cannot

---

[6] TED-TOSCR, 2013, section 4.4.5.4.
[7] Ibid., section 4.4.5.

be properly addressed today unless the biblical teaching on ordination is taken into account without prejudice.

When the church organisation was established in 1863, the Church *confirmed* the distinction between ordained and licensed ministers. Many women worked as licensed ministers but were not ordained. Ordination had been given the role of separating men from women, mainly because of the (male) authority linked to ordination. However, the 1863 State Conference Constitution included the licensed minister within its definition of 'all ministers in good standing'.[8] Licensed female ministers were in other words accepted as 'ministers in good standing'. In the main, the office of the minister was that of an itinerant preacher and teacher of the Word, called and 'ordained' by Christ. This is how Ellen White understood her own ordination (see chap. 4 below).

A proposal from the so-called Resolution Committee discussed at the 1881 General Conference Session did recommend women's ordination, since several women were licensed ministers and had the gift of the Spirit to teach and preach the word.[9] The text discussed was:

> Females possessing the necessary qualifications to fill that position, may, with perfect propriety, be set apart by ordination to the work of the Christian ministry.[10]

This proposal was not voted by the Session, but it was not stricken in the minutes and was referred to the General Conference Committee of three men, where it was not acted upon.[11]

---

[8] B. Haloviak, 'A Response to Two Papers by David Trim', 2013, p. 3.

[9] As documented and outlined in D. J. B. Trim, 'Ordination in Seventh-day Adventist History', 2013, pp. 5-8.

[10] *R&H* 58:25, 20 December 1881, p. 392. Note the discussion regarding the divergent reports in the *Review* and *Signs of the Times*, in: B. Haloviak, 'A Place at the Table', 1995, p. 43, note 10; D. J. B. Trim, 'The Ordination of Women in Seventh-day Adventist Policy and Practice', 2013, pp. 9-10.

[11] Cf. the different opinions on how to interpret the sources in: B. Haloviak, 'A Place at the Table', 1995, pp. 32-33; D. J. B. Trim, 'Ordination in Seventh-day Adventist History', 2013, pp. 12-17; id., 'The Ordination of

One aspect that James and Ellen White had included in 'being set apart for the gospel ministry' was the 'gospel order' which implied 'formal organisation'. Thus, indirectly, they considered the ordained minister's position as being an authoritative one. Besides being based on their understanding of Scripture, this was also a heritage from the Christian Connexion and Methodism. However, there was an important distinction between the two. In the Christian Connexion the authority of the ordained minister derived from the authority of the Bible and the spiritual gift of God to preach and teach the Word. In the Methodist tradition, authority was connected with a formal hierarchical organisation and the office of the bishop.

Influences from the Methodist Concept of Ordination

J. B. Frisbie was one of the more influential Sabbatarians in the ordination debate in the 1850s. He was a former Methodist minister (ordained in 1846) who had joined the Sabbatarian Adventists in 1853.[12] A few years later he endorsed the view of the ordained minister's authoritative role but argued it along the lines of *office* and *hierarchy* rather than being spirit-filled in teaching and preaching the authoritative word of God. The thinking in the Church was therefore influenced on this point by the Methodist position, rather than that of the Christian Connexion which tended to oppose hierarchies. It should be noted that Methodism had grown out of Anglicanism, which preserved a good deal of the Roman understanding of ordination.[13]

Thus, in his 1856 article Frisbie suggested that ordination gave the authority to *ordain other ministers or elders*. This is hard to prove as a principle taught in the Bible, as we will see in chapter 9 below, but it was a key issue in the Methodist Church, coming out of the Anglican tradition with its apostolic succession and episcopal understanding

---

Women in Seventh-day Adventist Policy and Practice', 2013, pp. 8-12; B. Haloviak, 'A Response to Two Papers by David Trim', 2013, pp. 13-14. Cf. TED-TOSCR, 2013, section 4.6.3.2.

[12] L. R. van Dolson, *Elder J. B. Frisbie – S.D.A. Pioneer in Michigan*, 1965, p. 5.

[13] See TED-TOSCR, 2013, section 4.4.2.

of church leadership. Frisbie suggested yet another meaning of ministerial ordination, namely, that only an ordained minister had authority to *found new churches*. It was mentioned only in passing and was not taken up by the Adventists until the GC Session in 1866. It was then stipulated that *local churches were not fully organised until they had 'ordained officers'*, which confirmed Frisbie's earlier proposal. In other words, the identity of a local *church* was conditioned by *ordination*. There is, however, no biblical basis for this rule, but it complied with the Methodist understandings rooted in Anglicanism and ultimately going back to Roman Catholicism.

The Distinction between Clergy and Laity

The *authoritative* nature of the minister's office was emphasised still further over time. The Seventh-day Adventist Church's first formal statement specifically on ordination was adopted at the 1879 GC Session. It includes the observation that 'ordination signifies the setting apart, or appointment, of a person to some official position'. The resolution concluded: 'We consider it inconsistent for our conferences to grant credentials to individuals […] who have never been ordained or set apart by our people.'[14] Thus, ordination was definitively settled as necessary for a credentialed minister, which underlined the minister's *status*. Furthermore, a report was adopted at this Session which declared that it was the minister, rather than the elders or deacons, whose responsibility it was to 'set things in order in the church, give good counsel […] bring up the members to a proper standard […] and thus edify and build up the church'. Pastoring became described as 'the work of the ministry'. However, 'the effect of these trends was to start to differentiate pastors from parishioners in a way not true for most early Adventist ministers.'[15] The headship and authority of the ordained minister was emphasised *at the expense of the laity* who would lack such authority since they

---

[14] See the reference in D. J. B. Trim, 'Ordination in Seventh-day Adventist History', 2013, p. 13, footnote 67.
[15] Ibid., p. 13.

were not ordained. Not only the laity's but also the women's path to ordination was hampered by this development. Thus, the unbiblical separation of the ordained ministers from the laity – which had once developed in the Roman-Catholic Church[16] – became a tool that blocked the recognition of women as ordained gospel ministers.

The Handling of the 'Licensed Minister'

The institution of a licensed ministry was confirmed when the Seventh-day Adventist Church was organised in 1863. From the start it was emphasised that the right of licensed ministers (including women), even their duty, was to *preach*. At the 1878 GC Session, the purpose of a license was defined as that of 'preaching the third angel's message'. But licensed ministers had no right to administer the ordinances, ordain, organise churches, and so on. This strict regulation applied in the GC sessions of both 1879 and 1885. A report adopted in 1885 stated:

> It is well understood that a license from the conference does not authorise the licentiate to celebrate ordinances, to administer baptism, or to organise a church. And, therefore, if a local elder receives a ministerial license, it does not enlarge his sphere of action as an elder; it gives him no authority to celebrate the ordinances outside of the church of which he is acting as elder.[17]

Consequently, while the ordained local church elder could administer the ordinances in one local church at a time and could not organise a new church, the licensed minister (including women) could do none of that. Trim notes that the geographical (or quantitative) scope of the licensed minister's authority was more extensive than the elder's, but qualitatively it was much less.[18] The license was 'a recognition that

---

[16] For the development from Irenaeus to Tertullian and Cyprian, see D. Jankiewicz, 'The Problem of Ordination', 2013, pp. 15-22; see also TED-TOSCR, 2013, sections 4.1 and 4.2.

[17] Twenty-Fourth Session, 14th Meeting, 2 December, 1885 (GCSM 1863-88, p. 162). Emphasis in the original.

[18] D. J. B. Trim, 'Ordination in Seventh-day Adventist History', 2013, p. 19.

the licentiate had demonstrated a set of attributes, knowledge and/ or skills that warranted being given a place of trust and a ministerial role in the Church, one that was general, unlike that given to elders and deacons, who of course were restricted to a particular church. In particular, the licensed minister had demonstrated the ability, or potential, to preach and publicly proclaim biblical truth – but lacked the experience, expertise, achievements, or innate attributes regarded as necessary for ordination to take place.'[19]

In this way, ordination was made the tool by which women were separated from having equal access to the role of a gospel minister in the Church. However, these measures were *not founded on biblical principles*, but were motivated by Christian tradition, practical needs, and perhaps a good deal of patriarchal prejudice regarding women's proper place. In this historical context, therefore, the counsel of Ellen White regarding women in ministry and women's ordination is nothing less than revolutionary![20]

Thus, from a modest start that was mainly triggered by the practical need to deal with church order, ordination became an ecclesiastical tool that separated male from female ministers. Male ministers took positions of authority, while women were merely allowed to preach and teach because of their spiritual gifts. The issue of an alleged biblical teaching of male headship and female submission did not exist at the time. It was a commonly accepted societal pattern that women would not hold organisational authority. Since the position of an ordained minister had become an office of authority in the Church, women would not be considered. However, the entire construction of what ordination signified had developed from 1853 into a construction that was more based on church tradition than the biblical teaching.[21]

---

[19] Ibid.
[20] See TED-TOSCR, 2013, sections 4.6.2.3 and 4.6.2.4.
[21] The specific features are presented in TED-TOSCR, 2013, section 4.6.5.

The Debates and Changes in 1970-2014

There was little change in the policies regarding ordination in the first half of the twentieth century but a new era emerged in the 1970s. Beginning with a request to the General Conference in 1968 from the Finnish Union in what is today known as the Trans-European Division, pressure began to build in favour of women's ordination. In 1974 the GC Annual Council 'authorised the divisions in exceptional cases to allow the ordination of women as local church elders'.[22] Ten years later it was voted that 'divisions were free to determine their own policies regarding the ordination of women as local elders'.[23] In the meantime, a discussion had developed over ordination of women to the gospel ministry. Thus, in the mid-1980s the GC appointed study commissions to examine this issue, but no consensus was reached on how to understand the Bible and few world-church divisions would accept ordination of women to the gospel ministry. This had a significant impact on the outcome of the GC Session in 1990.[24]

Based on a report from the Commission on the Role of Women in the Church, the GC Annual Council in 1989 recommended to the GC Session in 1990 that, in view of the lack of consensus on the biblical teaching about ordination and the danger of disunity in the Church, women should not be ordained for the gospel ministry, but licensed or commissioned ministers, including women, would have the privilege of baptizing and performing marriages. The GC Session voted to accept these recommendations.[25]

The Report to the session delegates in 1990 included two items from the 1989 Annual Council decision:

---

[22] G. Land, 'Ordination', *Historical Dictionary of the Seventh-day Adventists*, 2005, p. 218.
[23] Ibid.
[24] Cf. R. R. Wisbey, 'SDA Women in Ministry 1970-1998', 1998, pp. 235-237.
[25] Ibid., pp. 238-245; cf. pp. 235-255.

1. While the Commission does not have a consensus as to whether or not the Scriptures and the writings of Ellen G. White explicitly advocate or deny the ordination of women to pastoral ministry, it concludes unanimously that these sources affirm a significant, wide-ranging, and continuing ministry for women which is being expressed and will be evidenced in the varied and expanding gifts according to the infilling of the Holy Spirit.

2. Further, in view of the widespread lack of support for the ordination of women to the gospel ministry in the World Church and in view of the possible risk of disunity, dissension, and diversion from the mission of the Church, we do not approve ordination of women to the gospel ministry.[26]

The lack of consensus regarding whether or not the Bible and Ellen White's writings '*explicitly*' advocate or deny the ordination of women to pastoral ministry' was one obstacle. This issue will be comprehensively considered in the remaining part of this book.

The second obstacle was that a majority of the world divisions strongly supported the policy stipulation that ordination to the gospel ministry is only *a worldwide recognition*. Since most divisions rejected women's ordination to the gospel ministry, a vote to accept it would therefore create 'disunity, dissension, and diversion from the mission of the Church'. But from where did this idea of a worldwide recognition of the ministerial ordination come? It certainly is not stated in the Bible. In fact, it goes back to the *Working Policy* 1930. It stated that 'ordination of the ministry is the setting apart of the man to a sacred calling, not for one local field alone, but for the entire Church'.[27] The biblical foundation for this rule from 1930 is hard to

---

[26] Tenth Business Session, 55th General Conference Session, Indianapolis, Indiana, 11 July, 1990. The text is reprinted in R. R. Wisbey, 'SDA Women in Ministry 1970-1998', 1998, p. 244.

[27] D. J. B. Trim, 'Ordination in Seventh-day Adventist History', 2013, p. 25 with reference to the *Working Policy* 1930, p. 71.

find. In the New Testament, the few examples we have of the laying on of hands for induction into a leadership responsibility always took place locally, by the local congregation, for local needs of ministry, and it is questionable if the Bible commands a dominance of the total church which restricts the local work of ministry, if it is guided by the Holy Spirit and locally approved. The worldwide recognition of ministerial ordination is therefore purely an ecclesiastical decision.

Probing further, the concept of a worldwide validity of the ordination to the gospel ministry touches on three areas:

1. The issue of transfers of ordination: This was an old ecclesiastical issue in the United States among Congregationalist or Associationist churches like the Free-Will Baptists and the Christian Connexion who did not have a hierarchical form of organisation.[28] As the world-wide work of the Seventh-day Adventist Church expanded, the transfer of an ordained minister needed to be worked out in a *practical* way that saved administrative work.

2. The issue of a hierarchical church organisation: The GC Session in 1879 had decided that in granting ministerial credentials, ultimate authority rests with the General Conference.[29] This meant that the General Conference was ultimately in charge of the ministerial ordination. Practically, however, it could not perform the act of ordination in every corner of the world, but this had to be delegated to unions, who had to be in close cooperation with their division which represented the General Conference in their area. On this point, the Church has moved away from the biblical ideal of letting the local congregation identify and affirm God's call to his servants through ordination. The concept of ordination has, just as it did in the Roman Catholic Church during the late Middle Ages, become detached from the priesthood of all believers in the local community and become linked to the *individual* who receives ordination because

---

[28] Cf. TED-TOSCR, 2013, section 4.4.4.
[29] D. J. B. Trim, 'Ordination in Seventh-day Adventist History', 2013, p. 22.

he is seen as someone receiving authority to perform the ordinances and to serve as a head in the church.[30]

3. The issue of authority: Since the ordained minister is seen as an authority in the Church, the transfer of the authority *linked to his person* through ordination from one world division to another becomes the responsibility of the 'highest' instance in the church organisation, that is, the General Conference. For a regional division or union to determine locally 'the good standing' of a transferred ordained minister, it would mean that the ecclesiastical authority given by the church entity that ordained him could be questioned by the receiving entity, thus leading to potential conflict. The worldwide recognition of an ordained minister – granted by the GC – takes care of that potential threat to unity. However, this is an ecclesiastical decision, not one that is based on the Bible. The biblical link between *the congregation* that bestows delegated authority upon the minister as their servant is lost. And there are other practical ways to manage the transfer of ordained ministers in a world-wide church, such as the 'service request' and the 'call' which are *initiated* by the recipient field, meaning that only those ordained ministers that are called by the receiving organisation can serve there.

In 1995 the GC Session considered a proposal from the North American Division 'to have divisions determine their own policies regarding the ordination of women as ministers'.[31] This would have allowed divisions to deal with the ministerial ordination of women as they had been allowed to do with the ordained local church elders and commissioned ministers. However, the matter was introduced as an issue of biblical theology, not an ecclesiastical and practical issue, and the Session declined the request.

---

[30] Cf. TED-TOSCR, 2013, section 4.2.4.
[31] G. Land, 'Ordination', *Historical Dictionary of the Seventh-day Adventists*, 2005, p. 219. Cf. R. R. Wisbey, 'SDA Women in Ministry', 1998, pp. 246-250.

The development from the GC Session in 2010 to 2014 has been briefly reviewed in section 1.3 above and will not be repeated here. But the Church is again faced with a choice. The issue of women's ordination to the gospel ministry will not go away. Settling it once and for all would allow the Church to concentrate on its mission and move forward.

Concluding Remarks

In much of the current church debate, the issue of women's ordination has been seen as one of *faithfulness to the Bible*. However, the Church in the past was not primarily driven by such faithfulness in developing its policies on ordination. As we have seen in chapter 2 above, pragmatic concerns were more fundamental.

The issue has also been seen as one of *unity* in the Church. However, recent developments show that uniformity in church policy regarding the ordination of women are no longer being upheld. Seventh-day Adventists have always accepted differences in policy between different parts of a very diverse World Church. The implication is that unity is defined as a unity of spirit and purpose, not as a uniformity of methods or actions.

Different points of view on women's ordination also arise within *different church cultures* in *different social contexts*. This compels the Church to apply biblical principles on how members relate to each other within the spiritual community (I Corinthians 12-13). After teaching the diversity of spiritual gifts, but the oneness of God and his appointment of various ministries, including leadership, the apostle Paul directs attention to 'a still more excellent way', i.e. the love of God in I Corinthians 13. He also says:

Colossians 3.12-14 As God's chosen ones, holy and beloved, clothe yourselves with compassion, kindness, humility, meekness, and patience. Bear with one another and, if anyone has a complaint against another, forgive each other; just as the Lord has forgiven you, so you must also forgive. Above all, clothe yourselves with love, which binds everything together in perfect harmony.

We noted earlier Ellen White's counsel not to define Church unity as 'viewing every text of Scripture in the very same light' and that 'nothing can perfect unity in the Church but the spirit of Christ-like forbearance'.[32] This is biblical, timely advice to the entire church body.

The debate on women's ordination has essentially demonstrated that the Church does not have the desired uniform understanding and that, in practice, it has agreed to disagree on this matter. The message to the Church is therefore to learn to live together with its differences 'in a more excellent way' and 'in the spirit of Christ-like forbearance', as both the Bible and Ellen White suggest.

Our review in the present chapter indicates that, regarding women's ordination, the Church still suffers from the lack of a comprehensive and penetrating study of the biblical texts. This is the rationale for what follows below in Part Two below: The Bible.

---

[32] E. G. White, *Manuscript Releases*, vol. 11, p. 266.

CHAPTER 4
Ordination of Women in the Writings of Ellen White

The wisdom and spiritual guidance of Ellen White (1827-1915) has always had a formative influence on Adventist thinking.[1] Participants in the church debate on women's ordination have consequently referred to her statements or lack of statements on this issue.[2] Her view of the ordination of women has been studied in detail by many.[3] Here we will make a very brief summary of the essential key points.

A Positive View of Women's Ordination

It is well-known to Seventh-day Adventists that Ellen White 'emphatically and repeatedly invited women to be trained and

---

[1] See D. Fortin, 'Ellen G. White's Role in the Development of Seventh-day Adventist Doctrines', *EGWE*, pp. 774-778. One of the Fundamental Beliefs of the Church concerns 'The Gift of Prophecy', which is recognised as being 'manifested in the ministry of Ellen G. White'. The relationship between her writings and the Bible is defined as follows: 'As the Lord's messenger, her writings are a continuing and authoritative source of truth which provide for the church comfort, guidance, instruction, and correction. They also make clear that the Bible is the standard by which all teaching and experience must be tested.' (*Seventh-day Adventist Church Manual*, 2010, p. 162.) See also 'The Role of Ellen G. White Writings in Doctrinal Matters', *Adventist Review* 157:41, 4 September, 1980, p. 15.

[2] Cf. D. Fortin, 'Ordination', *EGWE*, pp. 1011-1014.

[3] See, for example, D. Fortin, 'Ordination in the Writings of Ellen G. White', 1998; id., 'Ellen White, Women in Ministry, and the Ordination of Women', 2013; J. Moon, '"A Power That Exceeds That of Men": Ellen G. White on Women in Ministry', 1998 (the quotation in the title is taken from 'Words to Lay Members', *R&H* 79:34, 26 August 1902, pp. 7-8); TED-TOSCR, 2013, section 4.6.2; GC-TOSCR, 2014, pp. 87-92.

employed in various forms of ministry, and even to ordain some to these ministries'.[4] Denis Fortin says that the case for allowing the ordination of women today can be supported by carefully considering (a) Ellen White's thoughts on the role of women in the church, taken in its nineteenth-century context, (b) her understanding of the mission of the Seventh-day Adventist Church, (c) her counsels regarding ministry and its many functions taken in historical context, and (d) her non-sacramental understanding of ordination and early Seventh-day Adventist practice of ordination.[5]

Silence on Alleged Key Biblical Texts

Ellen White is completely *silent* on some key texts and concepts that have been used to prevent women from serving in ministry. In her days it was often considered inappropriate and indecent for a woman to speak in an assembly. Based on the traditional reading of passages like I Corinthians 14.34-35 or I Timothy 2.12, many objected to hearing women speak publicly at religious meetings. However, Ellen White never commented on these two key texts. This silence suggests that these passages should not be given any high profile as we discuss women's ordination today. White's male colleagues, however, did comment on these texts and sometimes referred to Galatians 3.28 to state that Paul's writing about women not speaking in public was within a cultural context that does not have universal application today. They also referred to many of Paul's female co-workers, stating the obvious conclusion that Paul was not speaking against women in ministry.[6]

Women's Involvement in All Aspects of Ministry

Ellen White advocated that women be involved in all aspects of service and ministry. When some men felt uncomfortable with women

---

[4] GC-TOSCR June 2013, p. 87. Cf. J. Moon, '"A Power That Exceeds That of Men": Ellen G. White on Women in Ministry', 1998; TED-TOSCR, 2013, section 4.6.2.

[5] D. Fortin, 'Ellen White, Women in Ministry, and the Ordination of Women', 2013, p. 1.

[6] GC-TOSCR, 2013, p. 88.

serving alongside their husbands, and being fairly remunerated for this work, she said: 'This question is not for men to settle. The Lord has settled it.' She added that God is calling women to engage in the ministry and in some instances they will 'do more good than the ministers who neglect to visit the flock of God'. She said: 'There are women who should labour *in the gospel ministry.*'[7]

Addressing a difficult situation in South Lancaster, Massachusetts, in 1879, she said: 'It is not always men who are best adapted to the successful management of a church. If faithful women have more deep piety and true devotion than men, they could indeed by their prayers and their labours do more than men who are unconsecrated in heart and in life.'[8] This statement includes women in management of a church.

In 1880 she invited youth to engage in literature evangelism because it can serve as a good education for 'men and women to do *pastoral labour*'.[9] In 1887 she discussed the need to provide good education to Adventist youth and advised administrators to train young women 'with an education fitting them *for any position of trust*'. In 1900 she continued to encourage women to do ministry: 'It is the accompaniment of the Holy Spirit of God that prepares workers, both men and women, to become *pastors to the flock of God.*'[10]

While being aware that there were limitations for what women could do in her time, she did not limit the options in ministry for women. *She never used the concept of male headship to limit women in ministry.* She encouraged women to be engaged in mission and do pastoral labour.

---

[7] E. G. White, 'The Laborer Is Worthy of His Hire'; Manuscript 43a, 1898, *Manuscript Releases*, vol. 5, pp. 324-327 (emphasis supplied)
[8] E. G. White to Brother Johnson, Letter 33, 1879, *Manuscript Releases*, vol. 19, p. 56 (emphasis supplied).
[9] E. G. White, *Testimonies*, vol. 4, p. 390 (emphasis supplied).
[10] Id., *Testimonies*, vol. 6, p. 322 (emphasis supplied).

A Biblical Understanding of Ordination

Ellen White understood ordination as an affirmation of *various functions*. She did not limit ministry to the traditional roles of the formally ordained – pastor, elder and deacon – but invited the Church to branch out into new forms of gender-inclusive ministry and to ordain people for these new roles. In 1908 she encouraged the mission of medical missionaries, i.e. physicians (including women) and said that it is 'largely a spiritual work' which 'includes *prayer and the laying on of hands*; he therefore should be as sacredly set apart for his work *as is the minister of the gospel*'.[11] Similarly, in 1895, she wrote about the work of lay people in local churches and said:

> Women who are willing to consecrate some of their time to the service of the Lord should be appointed to visit the sick, look after the young, and minister to the necessities of the poor. *They should be set apart to this work by prayer and laying on of hands.* In some cases they will need to counsel with the church officers or the minister; but if they are devoted women, maintaining a vital connection with God, they will be a power for good in the church. *This is another means of strengthening and building up the church. We need to branch out more in our methods of labour. Not a hand should be bound, not a soul discouraged, not a voice should be hushed; let every individual labour, privately or publicly, to help forward this grand work.* Place the burdens upon men and women of the church that they may grow by reason of the exercise, and thus become effective agents in the hand of the Lord for the enlightenment of those who sit in darkness.[12]

She understood ordination as an affirmation that served various functions and purposes. It was not a form of sacrament limited only to certain gender-specific functions. In a letter 'to the brethren' in 1904, she uses Isaiah 61.6 to unify clergy and laity, men and women

---

[11] Id., *Evangelism*, p. 546 (emphasis supplied).
[12] Id., 'The Duty of the Minister and the People', *R&H* 72:28, 9 July 1895, p. 434 (emphasis supplied).

in the church, and, perceiving them all as *one* in God's ministry, she invokes his promise through Isaiah as being fulfilled in the church, that all believers, men and women, are *priests* of the Lord and *ministers* of our God.[13]

Ellen White therefore maintained no distinction between clergy and laity in working for 'the uplifting of humanity'. She says that ordination does not make you 'God's messenger', but you are made God's messenger by 'God's Spirit working in you' as you 'taste that the Lord is gracious' and 'know his saving power'. Obviously, she has a dual concept of being called, appointed or ordained in the church, one that is *formal-ecclesiastical* and gives authority to administer the ordinances and to govern, and one that is *informal-spiritual* by the work of the Holy Spirit for doing all kinds of ministry.

In view of her statements, it is clear that 'church ordination is not a prerequisite to serve God, because it is the Holy Spirit who gives fitness for service to Christians who in faith are willing to serve'.[14] 'In fact, as in the case of Paul and Barnabas, ordination from above precedes ordination by the church' – Ellen White says that while 'Paul and Barnabas had already received their commission from God Himself', 'neither of them had as yet been formally ordained to the gospel ministry'.[15] This latter point strengthens the conclusion that she believed in two aspects of 'ordination' – one *spiritual* ordination or commissioning from God by the Holy Spirit, and one *formal* ordination from the church. This is how James White experienced his ordination in the Christian Connexion, according to his autobiography.[16] He was first called by God and sent as an itinerant preacher to various local churches in 1842-1843, and then in April

---

[13] This passage has been analysed in detail in TED-TOSCR, 2013, section 4.6.2.4.
[14] D. Fortin, 'Ordination in the Writings of Ellen G. White', 1998, p. 117 (referring to *The Acts of the Apostles*, 1911, p. 40).
[15] Ibid., p. 117 (referring to *The Acts of the Apostles*, 1911, pp. 160-161).
[16] J. White, *Life Incidents*, 2003, p. 104; cf. TED-TOSCR, 2013, section 4.4.5.3.

1843 he was formally ordained. This formal ordination gave him the authority to administer the ordinances on behalf of the church. The same view of ordination was revealed in his articles on 'gospel order and ordination' in December 1853.

How, then, did Ellen White relate these two concepts to each other? The *essential* 'ordination' was the first, the spiritual calling and commissioning by God. And this is how she understood her own ordination for the ministry. She was never ordained by the Seventh-day Adventist Church. It was not the order of the Church in her times to ordain women as gospel ministers, and she abided by that. She did however by vote receive an 'ordained minister's credentials' for many years from the Michigan Conference and later from the General Conference,[17] but without having been ordained by prayer and the imposition of hands. She accepted this credential (she could have refused it) but did not exercise the authority it gave her in full. She believed that God had *ordained* her to the prophetic ministry. In 1909, as she looked back at her experiences in 1844, she said: 'In the city of Portland, *the Lord ordained me as His messenger*, and here my first labours were given to the cause of present truth.'[18]

Thus, according to Ellen White, essential ordination is the same as commissioning. She has a non-sacramental understanding of the laying on of hands. Ordination is primarily a form of affirmation and commissioning to a task. Ordination and commissioning is the same thing.[19] This seems to have been her position as early as in 1854 when she made her first statement on ordination (see chapter 2 above). She exemplified this view in 1896 when she commented on John Tay's visit to Pitcairn in 1886:

> It has been a great mistake that men go out, knowing they are children of God, like Brother Tay, [who] went

---

[17] See, for example, the report in *R&H* 40:13, 10 September 1872, p. 102.
[18] E. G. White, 'Letter 138, 1909', quoted in A. White, *The Ellen G. White Biography*, vol. 6, The Later Elmshaven Years, 1905-1915, 1986, p. 211.
[19] GC-TOSCR, 2013, p. 90.

to Pitcairn as a missionary to do the work, [but] that man did not feel at liberty to baptize because he was not ordained. *That is not any of God's arrangements; it is man's fixing.* When men go out with the burden of the work and to bring souls into the truth, those men are ordained of God [even] if [they] never have a touch of ceremony of ordination. To say [they] shall not baptize when there is nobody else, [is wrong]. If there is a minister in reach, all right, then they should seek for the ordained minister to do the baptizing, but when the Lord works with a man to bring out a soul here and there, and they know not when the opportunity will come that these precious souls can be baptized, why he should not question about the matter, he should baptize these souls.'[20]

In this remarkable statement, the *real* ordination is God's prior call to service, that is, God's spiritual ordination or commissioning. This is what counts. The ordination ceremony by the church is simply an affirmation of God's call to ministry. Resorting to an ordained pastor for baptism is a matter of order and availability, but the ordinances are valid even though they are administered by someone who is not ordained by the church. Ellen White's *biblical* view of ordination means that women may be ordained by God to ministry, and the question the Seventh-day Adventist Church is asking itself today is if it can affirm this by granting women permission to be ordained and issued with an ordained minister's credentials.

Ordination Linked to Mission
Initially, ordination by the Church was closely linked to evangelism and the mission of God in the world. Ellen White was adamant about this all her life. She was passionate about saving the lost, and her letter to the brethren in 1901 is a brilliant example of this.[21] The link of ordination to mission is underlined by the practice of ordination in Adventist history. 'George Butler became president of the Iowa

---
[20] E. G. White, 'Remarks concerning the Foreign Mission Work', Manuscript 75, 1896 (emphasis supplied).
[21] See TED-TOSCR, 2013, section 4.6.2.4.

Conference in June 1865 but was ordained only on September 1867. Uriah Smith served as editor of the *Review and Herald* from 1855, and secretary of the General Conference from 1863. He was ordained in 1874.'[22] Thus, the Adventist pioneers did not assign to ordination the role of 'headship' in some kind of church hierarchy. You did not need to be ordained to be elected or appointed as a leader. Today, the Seventh-day Adventist Church practices a different view of ordination.

Ellen White encouraged women, 'in a society and context in which women were not encouraged to be active in society, because she believed in a broad gender-inclusive ministry to warn a dying world of Christ's soon coming.'[23] If Seventh-day Adventists want to follow her counsel, ordination must be connected with mission and spreading of the gospel, as part of the mission of God (see chapter 6 below), and not with a dogged defence of ancient patriarchal customs and a view of ordination that *reduces* it to a policy rooted in human traditions. Ellen White urged Adventists to branch out in many forms of ministry to achieve God's mission, and this included women who could occupy 'any position of trust'.

The Divine Mandate to Promote Women in Ministry

Ellen White considered the call to promote and encourage the participation of women in ministry, 'not merely as an option, but as *a divine mandate*, the neglect of which results in diminished ministerial efficiency, fewer converts, and "great loss" to the cause, compared with the fruitfulness of the combined gifts of men and women in ministry.'[24]

Concluding Reflections

Ellen White took the view that 'the organisational structure of the church could be modified, or perfected, if, under divine guidance,

---

[22] GC-TOSCR, 2014, pp. 91-92.
[23] GC-TOSCR, 2014, p. 92.
[24] J. Moon, '"A Power That Exceeds That of Men": Ellen G. White on Women in Ministry', 1998, p. 193 (emphasis supplied).

the membership and the leadership thought it should'. Thus, 'the adaptability, or the further perfecting, of church organisation is an important element to understand how early Seventh-day Adventists viewed the development of their own model of church governance'. With her understanding that 'church structures must reflect harmony and order and be adaptable to new needs, Ellen White believed the church can determine, through study of Scripture and the guidance of the Holy Spirit, which new ministries are beneficial to its ministry and who is to function as an officer in the church'.[25]

On one particular point, however, Ellen White was adamant, namely that *ordination must follow the Bible*. As we have seen in chapter 2 above, an angel told her in vision that 'the church must *flee to God's word* and become established upon gospel order'.[26] She also stated as a principle that the mode of ordination should '*follow the word of God*'.[27] Based on the few existing apostolic examples of laying on of hands in the New Testament, she constantly warned Adventists against 'formalism' in ordination.[28] She obviously saw no hindrance for women's ordination in view of the content and mandate of mission in the Bible.

For the 'ordinance' of ordination,[29] Ellen White had no access to a comprehensive and scholarly study of the Bible, but she was left with the scattered references to laying on of hands that she found in her New Testament. As a rule, the Adventist Church at the time of the pioneers 'accepted a set of distinctive doctrines based on their study of the Bible, and Ellen White's influence in these early years was limited to confirmation and clarification of these doctrines. Never was she

---

[25] D. Fortin, 'Ordination', *EGWE*, pp. 1012-1013.
[26] E. G. White, *Supplement to the Christian Experience and Views of Ellen G. White*, Published on 1 January, 1854, Reprinted in: *Early Writings of Ellen G. White*, 1882, p. 99 (emphasis supplied).
[27] Ibid., p. 101 (emphasis supplied); cf. G. R. Knight, 'Early Seventh-day Adventists and Ordination', 1998, p. 103.
[28] Note her statement that 'formality should be shunned' (ibid., p. 97).
[29] For her understanding of the concept of 'ordinance', see D. Fortin, 'Ordinances', *EGWE*, pp. 1010-1011.

the initiator of these doctrinal beliefs.'[30] Although the Church did not submit ordination to any thorough Bible study in her life time, it is striking that she built both ordination and women's ordination into her overall biblical understanding of the role of the church in the cosmic mission of God, especially the priesthood of all believers.[31]

Ellen White's *holistic* understanding of the Bible guided her towards a flexible and mission-oriented concept of ordination. For example, in her comments on the setting apart of the seven in Acts 6.1-6, she says that the apostles took 'an important step in the perfecting of gospel order in the church by laying upon others some of the burdens thus far borne by themselves'.[32] She noted that this 'perfecting of gospel order' was accomplished when 'the apostles were led by the Holy Spirit to outline a plan for the better organisation of all the working forces of the church'.[33] She added that 'later in the history of the church … the organisation of the church was further perfected, so that order and harmonious action might be maintained'.[34] Characteristically, she subordinates here the nature of ordination to the more important issue of order and harmonious action in the church.

---

[30] Id., 'Ellen G. White's Role in the Development of Seventh-day Adventist Doctrines', *EGWE*, p. 774.
[31] For a survey, see id., 'Ordination', *EGWE*, pp. 1011-1014.
[32] E. G. White, *The Acts of the Apostles*, 1911, pp. 88-89.
[33] Ibid., p. 89.
[34] Ibid., pp. 91-92.

CHAPTER 5
What Does the Bible *Say* and What Does It *Mean*?

It was clear from the beginning in the Sabbatarian Adventist Movement that the Bible is the basis for introducing ordination in the congregations.[1] Today the statement of *Seventh-day Adventist Fundamental Beliefs* declares that 'Seventh-day Adventists accept the Bible as *their only creed*', and the first statement of belief concerns the nature and authority of the Bible.[2] Therefore, any attempt to reach consensus on the theology of ordination begins and ends with the Bible, or, rather, with *the way we choose to understand it*.

Sola Scriptura

The principle involved in the Adventist view of the Bible is often referred to as *sola scriptura*. It is 'a principle of religious authority which gained great visibility during the Protestant Reformation', where it was employed to 'point to the Bible as the only normative authority for Christian belief and practice'.[3] However, the Protestant Reformers and their later followers applied *sola scriptura* with varying degrees of consistency.[4] The emphasis on the *authority* of Scripture has not provided the *means* of understanding the *content* of Scripture.

---

[1] Note the positions taken by James and Ellen White (TED-TOSCR, 2013, sections 4.6.1 and 4.6.2).
[2] *Seventh-day Adventist Church Manual*, 2010, p. 156 (emphasis supplied).
[3] K. Donkor, '*Sola Scriptura* Principle and the Reformation', 2012, p. 7.
[4] See TED-TOSCR, 2013, section 4.4. Cf. K. Donkor, 'Contemporary Responses to *Sola Scriptura*: Implications for Adventist Theology', 2013, pp. 5-8.

Instead, various presuppositions of interpretation have flourished over centuries, resulting in a multitude of approaches and outcomes.[5]

Interpretation Subject to the View of 'Bible' and 'Text'

Seventh-day Adventists would agree today that seeking to understand ordination requires a comprehensive study of the Bible, 'our only creed', 'the authoritative revealer of doctrines', and 'the trustworthy record of God's acts in history'.[6] However, inevitably, when reference is made to the Bible as the only authority, this needs to be accompanied by specific principles of interpretation[7] which should be made explicit and open to being tested.

Being aware of this need, the General Conference Annual Council adopted guidelines in 1986 for the interpretation of the Bible: 'Bible Study: Presuppositions, Principles, and Methods', the so-called *Rio Document*.[8] Although it was written some thirty years ago and as such does not address 'a whole new movement in biblical studies' which has emerged in the last few decades,[9] it remains appropriate for a biblical study of ordination.[10] At the GC-TOSC meeting on 23 July 2013, Jiři Moskala, Dean of the Seminary at Andrews University,

---

[5] Cf. the distinction between 'formal' and 'material' principles of theology and the issue of a painful pluralism of interpretations; see, for example, W. W. Whidden, '*Sola Scriptura*, Inerrantist Fundamentalism, and the Wesleyan Quadrilateral: Is "No Creed but the Bible" a Workable Solution?', 1997, especially pp. 214-215.

[6] *Seventh-day Adventist Church Manual*, 2010, p. 156.

[7] W. W. Whidden, '*Sola Scriptura*, Inerrantist Fundamentalism, and the Wesleyan Quadrilateral: Is "No Creed but the Bible" a Workable Solution?', 1997, pp. 211-226.

[8] Adopted by the General Conference Annual Council on 12 October 1986 and published in *Adventist Review* 164:4, 22 January 1987, pp. 17-20. The document is available at the web-site of the Biblical Research Institute: https://adventistbiblicalresearch.org/materials/bible-interpretation-hermeneutics/methods-bible-study. The 1986 Rio document is fundamental to Adventist biblical research and is often reprinted in books on principles of interpretation: see, for example, G. W. Reid (ed.), *Understanding Scripture: An Adventist Approach*, 2005, pp. 329-337.

[9] See K. Ahn ,'Hermeneutics and the Ordination of Women', 2013, p. 23.

[10] Cf. the comments and clarifications on the Rio Document in TED-TOSCR, 2013, chapter 2.

presented a paper that practically illustrates how the principles of the Rio Document apply to the issue of ordination in the Bible.[11]

However, although most presenters of papers to the GC-TOSC in 2012-2014 declared that they based their work on the principles of the Rio Document,[12] no consensus on women's ordination was eventually reached.[13] The principles of the Rio Document were understood and applied in different ways, leading to contrary interpretations of the same biblical texts. Clearly, something more profound than simply principles and methods of interpretation is involved here.

Ján Barna, Lecturer at Newbold College, in his published doctoral thesis (2012) gives the clue to what the deeper issue of interpretation is in the Church's grappling with the issue of women's ordination since 1973.[14] It has to do not primarily with methods or tools of exegesis but with the way in which the interpreters understand the functions of language, texts and meaning in texts,[15] i.e. *how they read the biblical texts as 'texts'*.

The Errors of the Traditional, Literalist, 'Plain-Reading' Approach

Barna's study reveals that many Adventist interpreters of biblical ordination, often without being aware of it, are influenced by an unreflected, taken-for-granted, traditional system of interpretation that has been common to American Pietistic Evangelicalism since the eighteenth century.[16] It has philosophical underpinnings from 'the positivist assumptions of the Scottish Common Sense Philosophy'[17]

---

[11] J. Moskala, 'Back to Creation: Toward a Consistent Adventist Creation – Fall – Re-Creation Hermeneutic', 2013. It is included in NAD-TOSCR, 2013 under the title: 'Back to Creation: An Adventist Hermeneutic', pp. 154-175.

[12] All papers are available at *http://www.adventistarchives.org/gc-tosc*.

[13] See GC-TOSCR, 2014.

[14] J. Barna, *Ordination of Women in Seventh-day Adventist Theology*, 2012.

[15] Ibid., pp. 291-311.

[16] Ibid., pp. 286-291.

[17] The Scottish philosopher Thomas Reid (1710-1796) developed a broad attempt in philosophy, theology, science, and the humanities, which had strong appeal in North America, to show the Christian faith to be reasonable in a world where empirical methods of knowing reigned. By

or the objectivist Baconian method in particular but also generally the Enlightenment's rationalistic framework'.[18]

This view takes the text as an objective entity that consists of clear statements of facts and propositional truth. The *referential* meaning of the text becomes dominant, i.e. its function of *referring* or *pointing* to objects, persons, or concepts.[19] The preferred way of reading and understanding the Bible therefore becomes the *literalist* approach. In principle, anything that will challenge the literal sense of the text is viewed with suspicion.[20] Thus, even though the Rio Document clearly includes the value of relating the Bible to the cultural setting of the texts,[21] the opponents of women's ordination will put this under serious suspicion.[22] (However, when it conveniently fits the pre-determined outcome set up by this kind of interpreter, adding elements to the literal text seems to be no problem.[23] An element of inconsistency is therefore very disturbing in this approach.)

In the *literalist* approach to textual interpretation, the *explicit* information in the text, or *what it says* word for word, is to be trusted. The *implicit* information or what the stated text was intended to *mean* is viewed with suspicion (unless it can be objectively seen in the text), because, it is alleged, the work of extracting the meaning from the text requires too much involvement of the interpreter and thus renders the interpretation subjective.

'common sense' he meant that 'people universally accept the data provided by the senses they share with all humans as reliable signs of external reality' (C. M. Berryhill, 'Common Sense Philosophy', *ESCM*, 2004, p. 230).

[18] Ibid., pp. 269-272, 290-291.
[19] Note the 'mimetic' (imitation) theories of text that became prominent in the nineteenth century (H. W. Frei, *The Eclipse of Biblical Narrative*, 1974, pp. 51ff., 86ff.). Cf. B. Wiklander, *Prophecy as Literature*, 1984, pp. 8-15.
[20] A very good example is position #1 in GC-TOSCR, 2014, pp. 25-60.
[21] 'Bible Study: Presuppositions, Principles, and Methods' (see footnote 145 above), section 4p.
[22] See GC-TOSCR, 2014, p. 30 and elsewhere in position #1.
[23] See e.g. GC-TOSCR, 2014, pp. 44-48, where almost every passage on ordination in the Bible is supplied with elements that are not there.

Although Seventh-day Adventist interpreters know very well that the biblical text is not verbally or literally *inspired*, thanks to the guidance by Ellen White,[24] many have adopted basically the same view of the text that was held by believers in verbal inspiration within American evangelicalism from the eighteenth century. They refuse to accept that, if inspiration affected the *thoughts* of the biblical writers and they 'expressed these in their own words' (as stated by Ellen White and the Rio Document),[25] we must understand the *meaning* of their texts as we normally understand the meaning of texts, i.e. with full recognition of explicit and implicit information, immediate and wider context, associations of words and phrases that were commonly accepted by the original users of the text. Each of these methods was endorsed by Ellen White.[26]

The literalist approach to interpretation takes for granted that the reader today will read a biblical text in the same way as the author originally intended it, just provided the reader has faith and collects the relevant data. In this scheme the reader's presuppositions do not even need to be considered, since it is assumed that every 'sane and unbiased person of common sense could and must perceive the same things'.[27] The questions of language, understanding and pre-understanding tend to be marginalised, or even ignored, by all methodologies that are shaped in some way by these common-sense assumptions.[28] This has several consequences, for example:

1. The literalist plain-reading approach will, if possible, minimize the crucial impact of interpretation created by the fact that the

---

[24] See the collection of material in G. R. Knight, *Reading Ellen White: How to Understand and Apply Her Writings*, 1997, pp. 105-112.

[25] 'Bible Study: Presuppositions, Principles, and Methods' (see footnote 145 above), section 2a, (2).

[26] See e.g. R. M. Davidson, 'Interpretation of Bible', *EGWE*, 2013, pp. 650-653.

[27] Quoted from G. M. Marsden, *Fundamentalism and American Culture*, 2006, p. 111.

[28] Cf. J. Barna, *Ordination of Women in Seventh-day Adventist Theology*, 2012, pp. 289-290.

original Bible texts exist in Hebrew, Aramaic and Greek, which makes the need for interpretation and translation inevitable.[29] They therefore hold on to traditional Bible translations, if they can.[30] The Rio Document, however, issues explicit warnings against building 'major doctrinal points on one Bible translation, stating that 'trained biblical scholars will use the Greek and Hebrew texts, enabling them to examine variant readings of ancient Bible manuscripts as well'.[31]

2. If they can, the literalists trust dictionaries and grammars of the biblical languages, as if the meanings these offer are solid and unchangeable, although all biblical scholars know that these tools are secondary reconstructions, reflecting scholarly interpretations over many hundreds of years, and are far from objective.[32]

---

[29] This is done even though the texts are being studied in the original languages. For example, when position #1 claims that 'the Bible was written for everyone', the implied point is that 'it does not leave us to wonder who should be ordained to the biblical leadership offices and whether women qualify for the offices of elder or minister' (GC-TOSCR, 2014, p. 31). Thus, the writers suggest that even the complex matter of ordination is clear in the available Bible translations that 'the common people' can access. In chapters 7 and 9 below, however, we will see how clear the original texts are on ordination. Clearly, Ellen White acknowledged that there are issues in the Bible that require deep and patient study and even her quoted words say in a balanced way that the Bible 'was written for the common people *as well as for scholars*'. That the Bible 'was written for everyone' does not mean that there are no issues of interpretation in the original languages. Even in dealing with these tasks, the scholars, too, have 'full access to the Bible and a Spirit-filled ability to understand it'.

[30] Thus, for example, position #1 persistently renders the translation of the crucial Greek word *authenteo* in I Timothy 2.12 as 'to have authority over a man', using the sense given by NKJV and NRSV as if it is set in concrete (GC-TOSCR, 2014, pp. 33-34). The truth is that this word, which is unique in the Bible, has to do with 'wielding domineering and controlling influence' (see 9.5.6 below). But the supporters of #1 do not even discuss the lexical sense of the Greek word.

[31] 'Bible Study: Presuppositions, Principles, and Methods' (see footnote 145 above), section 4, 'Methods of Bible Study', para. a.

[32] See, for example, the way in which position #1 addresses the Greek term *kephale* in I Corinthians 11.3 (GC-TOSCR, 2014, p. 55). That Walter Bauer in his *Greek Lexicon* does not include 'source' is taken as evidence that this sense does not exist. However, for a comprehensive review showing how flawed this argument is, see 9.5.2 below. Position #1 misses the point

3. The literalists believe that what the text *says* is what it *means*. However, human language may or may not express its intended meaning by what is said. If I say 'it is raining today', it may be a literal statement about the current weather, or it may be my way of saying that I will not mow the lawn today. In the same way, biblical phrases do not always mean what they say, and the way to understand them is to examine carefully the literary context, the historical situation, and the cultural setting, as is well outlined in the Rio Document.[33] If the interpreter fails to consider the total meaning in context, because as a matter of principle he will simply stick to the literal and stated proposition in the text, he may distort the meaning of the word of God.

4. Words, phrases and passages usually have a range of possible meanings and communicative intentions in themselves – that is simply what language is like. What helps to narrow them down to the essential ones is the literary context and the situational setting of the communication. The Rio Document points out: 'In order not to misconstrue certain kinds of statements, it is important to recognize that they were addressed to peoples of Eastern cultures and expressed in their thought patterns.'[34] 'In connection with the study of the biblical text, explore the historical and cultural factors. Archaeology, anthropology, and history may contribute to understanding the meaning of the text.'[35]

It is true that while the biblical text is expressed in the words of the human authors, the Bible has a universal message that transcends culture: 'Although it was given to those who lived in an ancient Near

---

concerning *kephale* in I Corinthians 11.3, namely that it is used as a play on words with the two senses of 'head of a person' and 'life source' in a context dealing with the origin of humanity (see K. Haloviak, 'Is *Headship* Theology Biblical?', 2013, p. 122; cf. section 9.5.4 below).

[33] 'Bible Study: Presuppositions, Principles, and Methods' (see footnote 145 above), section 4, 'Methods of Bible Study', paras. f, g, k, p.
[34] Ibid., section 4. 'Methods of Bible Study', para. p.
[35] Ibid., section 4, 'Methods of Bible Study', para. k.

Eastern/Mediterranean context, the Bible transcends its cultural backgrounds to serve as God's Word for all cultural, racial, and situational contexts in all ages.'[36] However, this rule of interpretation must not be applied as a blanket acceptance of any literal statement in the Bible as God's word to us. For example, the literal injunction in Leviticus 19.27 that 'you shall not round off the hair on your temples or mar the edges of your beard' has no significance for Christians today. The principle of interpretation is that a reasoned conclusion must be made from the context and the setting of the text.

What is overlooked in the literalist approach is the unavoidable interaction between the text and the reader and the fact that individual words and utterances in written texts receive their true meaning *from relations between signs in the written context and between people in the communicative setting.* The interaction between text and reader occurs both (a) in the *contemporary* situation when the Bible text is being read today, and (b) in the *historical* situation of the author communicating with his intended readers through the original text.[37]

While an exclusive emphasis on the contemporary reader/interpreter may lead to unwanted subjectivity and threaten the authority of the biblical text, as many Adventist authors have rightly pointed out,[38] the *interaction* of the text and the originally intended reader in interpretation remains vital. Adventist principles of biblical interpretation cannot ignore the reader, because, as Ellen White put it: 'A true knowledge of the Bible can be gained only through the aid of that Spirit by whom the word was given.'[39] It is, after all, *the reader* who is aided by the Spirit.

---

[36] 'Bible Study: Presuppositions, Principles, and Methods' (see footnote 145 above), section 2, par. 1, point 4.
[37] See B. Wiklander, *Prophecy as Literature*, 1984, pp. 34-38, 42-43.
[38] For example, N. R. Gulley, *Systematic Theology: Prolegomena*, 2003, pp. 612, 689.
[39] E. G. White, *Education*, 1903, p. 189.

Confrontation between Two Camps of Interpreters

The lack of Adventist consensus regarding women's ordination in the Bible depends to a large extent on a confrontation between two camps of Adventist scholars and church leaders: (a) those who are literalists and conclude that some passages in the Bible *literally pronounce* prohibitions against women's roles as heads in the church, which, they argue, includes their ordination, and (b) those who embrace all the options of studying the Bible outlined in the Rio Document as they seek to understand what the biblical text *means*.

Misuse of Ellen White: An Example

Those who advocate the plain-reading approach often refer to Ellen White in support of their view. However, their references do little justice to her counsel. A recent example may illustrate this point.

An Adventist News Network release on 24 September 2014 quoted an official spokesperson who encourages Seventh-day Adventists worldwide to 'earnestly *read what the Bible says* about women's ordination' and to 'rely upon the Holy Spirit's leading in our own Bible study as we review the *plain teachings* of Scripture'. Church members are 'urged to prayerfully read the [TOSC] study materials, available on the website of the Church's Office of Archives, Statistics, and Research', and they are encouraged to 'look to see how the papers and presentations were based on an understanding of a *clear reading* of Scripture'. The spokesperson goes on to say that 'the Spirit of Prophecy tells us that we are to *take the Bible just as it reads*'. A quote is then given from *The Great Controversy* to illustrate what Ellen White said about how to read the Bible: 'The language of the Bible should be explained according to its obvious meaning, unless a symbol or figure is employed.'[40]

---

[40] Id., *The Great Controversy between Christ and Satan*, 1911 (1st edn 1888), p. 599.

The central issue here is how we are to understand the *meaning* of Ellen White's statement from *The Great Controversy*. That determines the counsel given to 'take the Bible just as it reads'.

What Ellen White says in the entire chapter 'The Scriptures a Safeguard' is both appropriate and true.[41] She admonishes believers to hold on to God and his truth as revealed in the 'plain utterances of the Bible' in order to 'stand through the last great conflict'.[42] She says that God's people 'must understand the will of God as revealed in His word; they can honour Him only as they have a right conception of His character, government, and purposes, and act in accordance with them.'[43] She therefore urges that believers study the Bible to *find the truth for themselves*, rejecting the authority of men to tell them what the Bible says: 'It is the first and highest duty of every rational being to learn from the Scriptures what is truth. [...] With divine help we are to form our opinions for ourselves as we are to answer for ourselves before God.'[44] 'His soul's salvation is at stake, and he should search the Scriptures for himself.'[45] God's people are to give *the Bible alone* the authority to determine 'all doctrines', 'all reforms', 'any point of religious faith', 'any doctrine or precept':

> But God will have a people upon the earth to maintain the Bible, and the Bible only, as the standard of all doctrines and the basis of all reforms. The opinions of learned men, the deductions of science, the creeds or decisions of ecclesiastical councils, as numerous and discordant as are the churches which they represent, the voice of the majority – not one nor all of these should be regarded as evidence for or against any point of religious faith. *Before accepting any doctrine or precept, we should demand a plain 'Thus saith the Lord' in its support.*[46]

---

[41] Ibid., pp. 593-602.
[42] Ibid. p. 593.
[43] Ibid.
[44] Ibid., p. 598.
[45] Ibid.
[46] Ibid., p. 595 (emphasis supplied).

Because of its unique authority and the need for each believer to know for himself what is truth, God has made 'Bible truth' plain in his word. All that believers need to know about God – his character, government, and purposes, or about sin, salvation in Christ and a righteous life – all has been made plain in the Bible (cf. II Timothy 3.14-17).

Ellen White's emphasis on the 'plain' meaning opposes the attempts by some to distort and complicate Bible truth in a way that generates ignorance, uncertainty, scepticism and doubt. She says:

> The truths most plainly revealed in the Bible have been involved in doubt and darkness by learned men, who, with a pretence of great wisdom, teach that the Scriptures have a mystical, a secret, spiritual meaning not apparent in the language employed. These men are false teachers. It was to such a class that Jesus declared: 'Ye know not the Scriptures, neither the power of God.' Mark 12.24. *The language of the Bible should be explained according to its obvious meaning, unless a symbol or figure is employed.* Christ has given the promise: 'If any man will do His will, he shall know of the doctrine.' John 7.17. If men would but take the Bible as it reads, if there were no false teachers to mislead and confuse their minds, a work would be accomplished that would make angels glad and that would bring into the fold of Christ thousands upon thousands who are now wandering in error.[47]

Obviously, Ellen White addresses here a common practice among other Protestant Christian denominations in nineteenth-century America, namely 'the "allegorical", spiritualising methods still dominant in the church'.[48] This approach was particularly used in attacks against central Adventist doctrines. For example, in 1854, D. P. Hall wrote in the *Review and Herald* about a non-Adventist Christian minister who 'denied the literality and tangibility of

---

[47] Ibid., pp. 598-599 (emphasis supplied).
[48] M. E. Boring, 'Interpretation of the Bible', *ESCM*, 2004, p. 82.

everything taught in the Bible'.[49] Another Adventist leader, J. N. Loughborough, wrote about the same issue in 1855:

> The beauty of Divine Revelation has been shut away from the minds of the common people, by their being taught, and supposing that the Bible does not mean what it says, or that the sense of the scripture writers is not contained in the scriptures themselves, but that they are mystical and have a hidden meaning. If this be a fact, we inquire, How shall we arrive at just conceptions of the word and its true interpretation?[50]

It is clear, therefore, that Ellen White's statement, quoted from *The Great Controversy* in the news release, addressed a specific problem experienced in a particular situation and that she sought to correct an aberrant way of interpreting the Bible that threatened to completely undermine Bible truth. Like her, Loughborough considered this a danger particularly to 'common people', and he continues by clarifying what a 'plain reading of Scripture' should mean:

> We admit that figures are used, and explained, but must claim that *a plain statement should be understood the same as when made in any other book*. We can form no just conceptions of God's character as revealed in the word, if this be not the truth of the matter. If God had revealed his will in such a way that man cannot understand it, and then pronounced in that word condemnation and death to those who did not obey his will, we should at once conclude that he manifested none of the character the word represents him as possessing.[51]

The implication of what Loughborough says here is that 'a plain statement' is understandable and understood 'as when made

---

[49] *R&H* 6:17, 19 August 1854 cf. D. F. Neufeld, 'Biblical Interpretation in the Advent Movement', 1974, p. 119.
[50] *R&H* 7:34, 4 September 1855; cf. D. F. Neufeld, "Biblical Interpretation in the Advent Movement', 1974, p. 120 (emphasis supplied).
[51] Ibid.

in any other book'. This does not necessarily mean that it is the *literal* statement that the text *pronounces* that has priority, but the statement is to be understood as statements are normally understood in written texts and not as a symbol that is difficult to understand. As we acknowledge all her writings, this principle is acknowledged by Ellen White.[52] Against the dangers of the mystical or spiritualising meanings of Scripture used in attacking Adventist beliefs in the nineteenth century, Ellen White naturally advocated 'taking the Bible as it reads' or looking for the 'plain or obvious meaning'.

In the recent news release, however, her principle that 'The language of the Bible should be explained according to its obvious meaning', is not only taken out of context and without considering its historical setting, but is applied to the issue of ordination in the Bible. We will see in more detail later on that ordination is not an obvious matter of 'Bible truth', but a matter on which the Bible and Ellen White are rather silent. Moreover, the various statements in the news release quoted above instruct Adventists to look with favour to the position(s) that applies the *literalist* manner of interpretation.[53] However, we will see now that this mode of interpretation does no justice either to the word of God or to Ellen White.

Ellen White's statements in *The Great Controversy* were not meant to describe the full nature of the biblical text or define the total task of exegetical research which often includes grappling with complex theological issues in the original biblical texts. She was very much aware of the fact that *there are scriptural passages that are not clear: While some portions of the Word are easily understood, the true meaning of other parts is not so readily discerned*.[54]

Behind the words of the Bible there lies an additional significance that must be discovered. In reflecting on Christ as 'the truth' she says

---

[52] See R. M. Davidson, 'Interpretation of Bible', *EGWE*, 2013, pp. 650-653.
[53] See Position #1 in TOSCR, 2014, pp. 28-32. Cf. Position #3 (ibid., pp. 99-116).
[54] Id., *Testimonies to Ministers and Gospel Workers*, 1923, p. 107.

that 'His words are truth, and they have a deeper significance than appears on the surface'.[55] She therefore advocates 'close reading'[56] and 'careful thought as to the meanings of the sacred text'.[57] At times, *the Bible requires deep study and deep effort*:

> But the most valuable teaching of the Bible is not to be gained by occasional or disconnected study. Its great system of truth is not so presented as to be discerned by the hasty and careless reader. Many of its treasures lie far beneath the surface, and can only be obtained by diligent research and continuous effort.[58]

This means that, while being plain and transparent regarding faith and salvation or 'Bible truth', the Bible is far from plain at times, unless given 'diligent research and continuous effort'. The Bible is certainly clear about God and the reasons for trusting him in faith. But it is not always clear on every point and may require deep study, as the issue of ordination clearly demonstrates.

Ellen White advocated 'the plain teaching', the 'obvious meaning' or 'the plain words of God' in two contexts:

Firstly, the Bible reader should reject the 'mystical, secret, spiritual meaning', but symbols may occur if expressed in the text. The plain teachings of the word of God 'are not to be so spiritualised that the reality is lost sight of. Do not overstrain the meaning of sentences in the Bible. [...] Take the Scriptures as they read'.[59] Seeking the 'simplicity of truth', readers of the Bible will 'more surely comprehend its deep meaning'.[60]

Secondly, for the purpose of salvation, readers are to 'cling to the Bible as it reads', refraining from 'criticisms in regard to its validity,

---

[55] Id., *Christ's Object Lessons*, 1900, p. 110.
[56] Id., *Education*, 1903, p. 190.
[57] Id., 'Search the Scriptures', *R&H* 60:40, 9 October 1883, p. 625.
[58] Id., *Education*, 1903, p. 123 (emphasis supplied); cf. pp. 124, 189.
[59] Id., *Selected Messages*, vol. 1, 1958, p. 170.
[60] Id., *In Heavenly Places*, 1967, p. 139.

and obey the Word'. This counsel applies to readers who refuse to accept God's word by criticising its validity.

This sound advice, however, does not mean that all Bible texts are to be understood *literally*. There are symbolic, metaphorical and even allegorical passages in the Bible. As in all languages, the biblical languages contain words, phrases and motifs that had peculiar associations in the minds of the Near Eastern and Mediterranean peoples who used Hebrew, Aramaic and Greek. Thus, the Rio Document says: 'In order not to misconstrue certain kinds of statements, it is important to recognize that they were addressed to peoples of Eastern cultures and expressed in their thought patterns'.[61] Where this applies, appropriate exegesis must take that into account.[62]

Seeking to Understand What the Bible Means

Seeking to understand the sense of the text is always the aim of biblical exegesis. But this includes deep study of the meaning intended for the original, historical audience.

Bible study begins with what the text *says*, but it seeks to understand what the text *means*, using all the 'Methods of Bible Study' listed in the Rio Document and exemplified by Jiři Moskala.[63] Such study may at times result in an understanding that goes far beyond the initial literal reading. In that case, if the interpreter would have held on to the literal reading, the meaning of the biblical text, the word of God, would have been distorted.

This book will show that the study of biblical ordination presents unusual and difficult challenges. This is why consensus is so hard to reach. However, my proposition is that ordination in the Bible

---

[61] 'Bible Study: Presuppositions, Principles, and Methods' (see footnote 145 above), section 4, para. p.

[62] Note the many exceptions listed to the plain meaning of Scripture in R. M. Davidson, 'Biblical Interpretation', *HSDAT*, 2000, pp. 65-66.

[63] J. Moskala, 'Back to Creation: An Adventist Hermeneutic', 2013, pp. 154-175.

is preferably studied in the context of the overarching themes that bind the Bible together as a unit. As this approach is developed in the following, we will see that it places God and his mission at the centre of what ordination means. And women's ordination then becomes a matter of God, how he created man and woman, how he has called men and women as his servants in Israel and in the church, and his future for the human race.[64]

The present study applies a *text-oriented view of the Bible*. The reality of the Bible *text* and its full meaning potential as a fabric of signs that relate to each other and the external world in a given communicative situation is taken for granted.[65] The text contains a *blending of divine and human*, since God inspired the thoughts of authors who used their own words to express them.[66] The parts of the Bible text may be divided into *books and sections of books*, each arising in specific *historical and cultural* situations and worded originally in Aramaic, Greek or Hebrew. This means that we must consider both *the original and the universal reader* in the interpretation.[67] The books of the Bible were collected into a canon of sixty-six books, and God has a communicative purpose in *the Bible as a whole*,[68] which we may discern by understanding its overall theme. God's victory through the life, death and resurrection of *Jesus Christ* is the centre of the Bible.[69] These main features will be exemplified in the following as we deal with ordination in the Bible.

---

[64] For a similar emphasis, see R. L Dudley, 'The Ordination of Women in Light of the Character of God', 1998.
[65] For an example of this approach, see B. Wiklander, *Prophecy as Literature*, 1984.
[66] See TED-TOSCR, 2013, section 2.4.
[67] See ibid., section 2.5.
[68] See ibid., section 2.6.
[69] See ibid., section 2.2.

Part Two: The Bible
CHAPTER 6

The Mission of God

Most of us would agree that the Bible should be allowed to speak to us with its own voice regarding how the church should function. Thus, defining the overarching core theme of the Bible is the first instance where consensus should be sought. As a starting point, we need to understand the biblical perspective within which the biblical authors speak about appointments of the servants-ministers of God. What were their central themes? What did they teach about the church? How did they understand God's appointment of men and women to serve him through the church of Christ?

6.1 The Grand Central Theme of the Bible

Obviously, the overarching and core theme of the Bible as a whole is 'God, his nature, will and purpose'. He is the point of departure in Genesis 1.1, continues to be the centre throughout the biblical writings until his grace in Jesus Christ is shared with all his people in Revelation 22.21 as the Bible ends with a view to what God will do in the future. The Bible refers to God in active terms, such as (a) 'the kingdom or reign of God' (e.g. Psalms 90-106; Mark 1.14-15); (b) 'the love of God' (e.g. John 3.16); and (c) 'the presence and communion of God with his created beings' (e.g. Revelation 4.11; 21.1-4).

Each of these variants of the grand central theme of the Bible is however confronted with an opposite sub-theme, with darkness and evil. Thus, the kingdom of God is challenged in 'the great controversy', and God's response is 'the plan of redemption'. This plan may be traced in the Bible from beginning to end (e.g. Genesis 3.15; John 3.16; Romans 8; I Corinthians 15; Revelation 21-22). It focuses on God's faithfulness, love and care for all people and outlines his purpose to re-establish the broken relationship between God and man, using his people as an instrument of his mission.

This thematic structure is central to the Seventh-day Adventist understanding of the Bible as a whole.[1] It may be conveniently referred to as 'the mission of God'. This profoundly biblical theme[2] was central in Ellen White's theology.[3] She pointed out that each passage of Scripture must be understood in the light of the Bible's multifaceted 'grand central theme, of God's original purpose for the world, of the rise of the great controversy, and of the work of redemption'.[4] Within this 'room' we may understand how the biblical authors organised their instructions regarding the people of God and his call to service.

'The mission of God' expresses the central and important biblical truth that God is revealed in Scripture as 'personal, purposeful and goal-orientated'.[5] This revelation is conveyed in a narrative of God's actions in human history, beginning with 'the God of purpose in creation'. It then moves on to the human rebellion against that purpose, but most of the story concerns God's redemptive purposes in human history. It finishes with the 'hope of a new creation' at the end of time.[6] Thus, 'the biblical worldview locates us in the midst

---

[1] See, for example, Fundamental Belief # 8 in: *Seventh-day Adventist Church Manual*, 2010, p. 157.
[2] See C. J. H. Wright, *The Mission of God: Unlocking the Bible's Grand Narrative*, 2006; A. Rodriguez (ed.), *Message, Mission and Unity of the Church*, 2013; J. Barna, 'Towards a Biblical-Systematic Theology of Ordination', 2014, pp. 101-105.
[3] TED-TOSCR, 2013, section 4.6.2.1.
[4] E. G. White, *Education*, 1903, p. 190; cf. pp. 125-126.
[5] C. J. H. Wright, *The Mission of God: Unlocking the Bible's Grand Narrative*, 2006, p. 63.
[6] Ibid., pp. 63-64.

of a narrative of the universe behind which stands the mission of the living God'.[7]

Understanding the Bible as the Story of the Mission of God

Seeing the Bible as a unified whole from the perspective of the mission of God gives us a key to understanding the central role of God when the biblical authors speak about appointments of his servants-ministers from Genesis to Revelation. This 'missional hermeneutic'[8] means that we seek to read any part of the Bible while relating it to one or more of the following biblical concepts:

- God's purpose for his whole creation, including the redemption of humanity and the creation of the new heavens and the new earth.

- God's purpose for human life in general on the planet and of all the Bible teaches about human culture, relationships ethics, and behaviour.

- God's historical election of Israel, their identity and role in relation to the nations, and the demands he made on their worship, social ethics, and total value system.

- The centrality of Jesus of Nazareth, his messianic identity and mission in relation to Israel and the nations, his cross, and resurrection.

- God's calling of the church, the community of believing Jews and Gentiles who constitute the extended people of the Abraham covenant, to be the agent of God's blessing to the nations in the name and for the glory of the Lord Jesus Christ.[9]

This approach to biblical commissioning-ordination puts God at the centre while helping us see the variations he has stipulated in advancing his mission at various times and in various circumstances.

---

[7] Ibid., p. 64.
[8] For this expression, its source and implications, see ibid., pp. 33-69.
[9] I follow here Wright's points as they are worded in ibid., pp. 67-68.

Ordination in the Context of 'God with a Mission'[10]

The biblical stories of God's appointments of his servants-ministers in the context of 'the mission of God' includes 'narrowing' thematic elements, such as the human fall, the election of Israel and the Davidic royal line, in which God adapts his plan to a given reality but pursues his original purpose. Above all, the Bible assigns to the mission of God a set of themes in which God's mission is being carried out on the basis of the death and resurrection of Christ. The mission of the church is part of the mission of Christ, which is part of the mission of God.[11]

Ordination in this context is God's appointment, blessing, and equipment of his servants-ministers to achieve his mission in the created but fallen world. This is expressed particularly in his act of creation, the moderation of his creative acts after the human fall, and in his direct calling of prophets and prophetesses (i.e. with or without any other human endorsement). God's ordination in this sense, therefore, is the prior act behind all ordinations of servants-ministers who carry out his will according to the Bible.

Ordination in the Context of 'Humanity with a Mission'[12]

The mission of God unfolds in various major dimensions of mission that flow throughout the Bible. Humanity initially receives its divine mission in creation. It is a delegated authority to man and woman to 'fill the earth and subdue it; and have dominion over' the rest of creation (Genesis 1.28). This is moderated by parallel commands 'to work … and to take care of' the Garden (Genesis 2.15). The implication is that 'to be human is to have a purposeful role in God's creation', for the care and keeping of creation is our human mission given by God.[13] The earth and the heavens belong to

---

[10] Ibid., pp. 62-65.
[11] Ibid., pp. 65-67; J. Barna, 'Towards a Biblical-Systematic Theology of Ordination', 2014, pp. 101-109.
[12] C. J. H. Wright, *The Mission of God: Unlocking the Bible's Grand Narrative*, 2006, pp. 65, 397-453.
[13] Ibid., p. 65.

God who made them (Deuteronomy 10.14; Psalm 24.1; Job 41.11). Thus, 'God is the earth's landlord and we are God's tenants'.[14]

From this perspective, ordination of humanity, as man and woman, is God's act at the creation and his moderating acts after the human rebellion. Because God continues his mission through humanity, despite the human fall, he is however compelled to adapt to human frailty, such as the institution of patriarchy. This aspect is studied in some detail in the remaining part of this chapter.

Ordination in the Context of 'Israel with a Mission'[15]

Against the background of human sin and rebellion in Genesis 3-11, Israel enters the scene as the result of God's call of Abraham in Genesis 12. Israel was called to be God's light to the nations (Isaiah 42.6; 49.6; 60.3; Acts 13.47) and to function as the channel for God's blessing of the nations.

Ordination in this context must take into account the various roles of leadership which were needed in Israel in order to keep the people together with its families and tribes, and to accomplish God's aim of keeping the covenant with Israel as 'a priestly kingdom and a holy nation' (Exodus 19.6). These aspects of God's mission are further examined in chapter 7.

Ordination in the Context of 'Jesus with a Mission'[16]

Jesus enters the people of Israel with a clear sense of mission. In God's declaration at the baptism of Jesus, he combines the identity of the servant figure in Isaiah (Isaiah 42.1) and the Davidic messianic king (Psalm 2:7). The mission of the 'Servant of the Lord' was to restore Israel to their God and to be the agent of God's salvation to the ends of the earth (Isaiah 49:6). The mission of the Davidic king was to rule over a redeemed Israel (Jeremiah 33:14-17) and to receive the nations as his heritage (Psalm 2:8).[17] Thus, because of the victorious

---

[14] Ibid., p. 397.
[15] Ibid., p. 65.
[16] Ibid., pp. 65-66.
[17] Ibid., p. 66.

faithfulness of Jesus to God's will and mission, even unto death, the mission of God reaches its climax in the mission of Christ.[18]

Commissioning-ordination in this context concerns how God called and sent Jesus Christ. At the most important level, the manner of this act is hidden in the mystery of the Godhead. However, at the textual level in the Bible, we detect certain parallels between the installation of the messianic king in Israel and the events of the baptism of Jesus, his resurrection, and ascension to God. Furthermore, God's installation of Christ as high priest suggests another connection with the idea of commissioning-ordination. These matters are further explored in chapter 8.

Ordination in the Context of 'the Church with a Mission'[19]

The mission that Jesus entrusted to the church was directly rooted in his own identity, passion, and victory as the crucified and resurrected Messiah, sent by God. The members of the church are to be witnesses of Jesus Christ who reveals the mind of God (Luke 24.45-57; Acts 1.8), thus fulfilling God's command to Israel, in order that the world may know God (Isaiah 43.10-12).[20]

Ordination in this context means that God (through Christ) calls, equips, and blesses a man or a woman for servanthood or ministry. In some way, however, this divine calling and the spiritual gifts bestowed on an individual need to be acknowledged by the church body where Christ is the Head. How this was done according to the New Testament is the object of study in chapter 9.

6.2 *The Creator Who Dwells with Human Beings*

The Bible reveals God as Creator, King and Sustainer of the world. His kingdom is eternal (Psalm 145.13; Daniel 4.34) and, through creation 'in the beginning', it includes the earth with humankind put

---

[18] Ibid.
[19] Ibid., pp. 66-67.
[20] Ibid., p. 66.

in charge of its living creatures (Genesis 1.1-2.4a). The created earth is God's dwelling place with humankind (2.4b-25). *Dwelling* with the humans, his aim is to *relate* to them in loving communion and *co-operate* with them in governing and caring for the earth.

The peace of God's kingdom on earth is however lost through the human Fall (Genesis 3). Yet God's purpose does not change. His *purpose* remains the same, but his *mission* now becomes one of restoring his kingdom and dwelling place (Revelation 21.1-5). This theme is emphatically underlined across the Bible as a whole.[21] Each biblical passage may be read as a variation of this theme.

There is a certain *order* in the kingdom of God, maintained by him and rooted in his infinite love and wisdom. Part of this order is, for example, God's commissioning of man and woman to rule the earth (Genesis 1.26-28); their caretaking of the Garden of Eden where God dwells (2.8-14); the prohibition not to eat of the tree of the knowledge of good and evil (2.15-17) that preserves the distinction between God and man (cf. 3.22-23); and the marriage relationship between man and woman as equal partners (2.18-25).

Instructions in the Bible regarding the order of the kingdom of God are based on the foundational nature of Genesis 1-3. Even the appointment for pastoral ministry 'is primarily about church order and should reflect the principles of order that rule the cosmic kingdom of God'.[22] *Any discussion of biblical ordination must therefore begin with Genesis 1-3.*

The passages in Genesis 1-3 define in general terms God's plan for men and women as his servants-ministers before and after the Fall. We find here the biblical foundation for 'the relationship between man and woman and what God expected of them'.[23] We will see how the passages in Genesis 1-3 indicate that *man and woman were*

---

[21] See, for example, Genesis 14.22; Exodus 20.8-11; Psalms 104; 148; Isaiah 45.12, 18; Mark 13.19; Colossians 1.16; Revelation 4.11; 10.6.
[22] GC-TOSCR, 2014, p. 68.
[23] Ibid., p. 69.

created equal and that neither of them was placed under the authority of the other.[24] Christ urged his followers to return to this ideal.

The Hebrew text in Genesis 1-3 has a long history of interpretation that has impacted Bible translations, dictionaries and grammars, creating very old and deeply rooted traditions of interpretation. Beginning with the Greek translation of the Old Testament, the Septuagint, and at each point in time over more than two millennia, the contemporary view of the roles of men and women influenced the interpretation. In the following, attempts will be made where possible to transcend these traditions in order to understand the original text.

6.3 Man and Woman Created in the Image of God

The creation account shows God creating the earth in six days and completing his creation by resting on and blessing the Sabbath day (Genesis 1.1-2.4a). As we engage more deeply with the meaning of the text, it is clear that the created earth is ordered and made into a dwelling place for God with the humans, which in biblical times was always known as a 'sanctuary' (Psalm 78.69). Reading the text with the eyes of the original or intended readers, we may conclude that, while the creation account places primary emphasis not on space but on *time*,[25] even by resting on the seventh day God dwells with man on earth as if it is a sanctuary, for 'in the ancient world, the "rest" of the gods was always in a temple; in fact, temples were built with the purpose of the deity resting in them'.[26] The seventh day

---

[24] Cf. the extensive study in TED-TOSCR, 2013, section 3.1.1.
[25] Note 'in the beginning' (Genesis 1.1), creation of light producing the day/night cycle (1.3-5), creation of luminaries for signs/festivals/days/years (1.14-19), the seventh day made holy (2.2-3); W. Vogels, 'Cultic and Civil Calendars of the Fourth Day of Creation', 1997.
[26] J. H. Walton, 'Creation in Genesis 1:1-2:3 and the Ancient Near East', 2008, p. 60; J. D. Levenson, 'The Temple and the World', 1984, pp. 275-298; V. Hurowitz, 'I Have Built You an Exalted House', 1992.

rest, therefore, acknowledges God as the Lord and King of the world, which functions as his holy and cosmic sanctuary.[27]

Man and woman are created 'in the image of God' (Genesis 1.26-28). The biblical text does not state explicitly what 'in his image' means but does provide some hints. Firstly, 'If humans are in God's image then there must be some analogy between God and humans. One such analogy is provided in 1.26b, with its granting of dominion over creation.'[28] This dominion is given to man and woman *as equals*.

Secondly, reading Genesis 1.26-28 in the light of Psalm 8 and the common use in Old Testament contexts of 'have dominion, rule' (Hebr. *radah*) for kings and rulers,[29] being created 'in the image of God' means that, as equals, men and women assume the function of servants of God and his governors of the world.[30]

Thirdly, Genesis 1.26-28 implies that man and woman are to function as *mediators* between God and the created world.[31] The author did not need to state this in the text, because the intended readers would supply this information from the manner in which a 'ruler' was understood in the historical setting of the text. A royal-priestly function was associated with the concept of kingship. It would be attached to the idea of man and woman being created 'in

---

[27] For this reason, Genesis 1.1-2.4a has been understood as being 'composed along the lines of a temple dedication ceremony in which, over a seven-day period, the functions of the cosmic temple are initiated and the functionaries installed' (J. H. Walton, 'Creation in Genesis 1:1-2:3 and the Ancient Near East', 2008, p. 61).

[28] L. Turner, *Genesis*, 2000, p. 24.

[29] See e.g. Psalm 72.8; 110.2 [v. 3 in the Hebrew text]; Isa. 14.6; 41.2; Ezekiel 29.15; cf. H. J. Zobel's conclusion that 'most of the texts using *rdh* appear to be concentrated' in 'statements concerning kings' (H. J. Zobel, '*radah*', *ThDOT*, vol. 13, pp. 332-333).

[30] Cf. the widespread ancient Near Eastern concept of the 'image of God' as the 'king, son, authorised representative, governor, or deputy of God' (H. Wildberger, '*tselem*/Abbild', *THAT*, vol. 2, cols. 559-561).

[31] J. Barna, 'Towards a Biblical-Systematic Theology of Ordination', 2014, pp. 101-102. For details, see section 3.1.1.1 in TED-TOSCR, 2013.

the image of God' and commissioned as governors and rulers (cf. the priest-king Melchizedek in Psalm 110 and Genesis 14.18).[32]

Thus, man and woman are not only co-dwellers with God but commissioned for a royal-priestly role: 'They are seen as "priests" – mediators who are to mediate God's presence and who are to rule as "royals", representing God's good rule to the creation on earth.'[33] The image of God 'designates the royal office or calling of human beings as God's representatives and agents in the world' and 'grants authorised power to share in God's rule or administration of the earth's resources and creatures'.[34] While the Bible teaches that 'all things are [God's] servants' (Psalm 119.91), this cosmic rule of God was to be *mediated* through man and woman, who carry the image of God 'in order to represent and mediate the divine presence on earth'.[35]

In Genesis 1.1-2.4a this *mediation* is not understood in the later sense of bringing atonement for sin by offering sacrifices, but rather in a general way as (a) *communicating* God's will to the created world and the needs of the world to God, and (b) *representing* God to the world and the world to God. The mediating function of man and woman derives from their standing between God and the world as *servants-ministers of God*. His kingdom is present in their ministry – they are priests serving him (cf. Revelation 5.10).

The Analogy between Creation and Sanctuary

Certain structural and linguistic features in the creation account in Genesis 1.1-2.4a are paralleled in the account of the construction of the sanctuary in Exodus (Exodus 25-31, 35-40), for example:[36]

---

[32] For an orientation on this concept, see R. Abba, 'Priests and Levites', *IDB*, vol. 3, p. 882.

[33] J. Barna, 'Towards a Biblical-Systematic Theology of Ordination', 2014, p. 101. See also R. J. Middleton, *The Liberating Image: The Imago Dei in Genesis 1*, 2005, pp. 87-90.

[34] R. J. Middleton, *The Liberating Image*, 2005, p. 27.

[35] Ibid., p. 87.

[36] This was first observed by J. Blenkinsopp ('The Structure of P', 1976, pp. 275-292) and has been confirmed by later research – see e.g. F. H. Gorman, Jr, 'Priestly Rituals of Founding: Time, Space, and Status', 1993, pp. 47-64;

1. Similarly to the creation of heaven and earth, God's purpose in making Israel build the sanctuary is that he 'may dwell among them' (Genesis 2.2-3, 8-14; 3.8; Exodus 25.8; cf. Revelation 21.1-5).

2. The instructions to Moses regarding how to build the sanctuary remind the reader of the seven days of creation. Six times God's instructions to Moses begin with 'the Lord said/spoke to Moses' (Exodus 25.1; 30.11, 17, 22, 34; 31.1), but the seventh time, which concludes the sequence, God emphatically commands Moses to speak to the Israelites: 'You shall keep my sabbaths, for this is a sign between me and you throughout your generations, given in order that you may know that I, the Lord, sanctify you. […] You shall keep the sabbath, because it is holy for you; […] It is a sign for ever between me and the people of Israel that in six days the Lord made heaven and earth, and on the seventh day he rested, and was refreshed.' (Exodus 31.12-14, 17).[37] Here the construction of the sanctuary is explicitly linked with the creation text in Genesis 1.1-2.4a.

3. In the Pentateuch certain formulae organise and give emphasis to specific portions of the work. Putting together the 'conclusion formula' ('X finished his work') and the more solemn and elaborate 'execution formula' ('X did according to all that God had commanded him'), we find that *special prominence* is given to the *creation of the world* (Genesis 2.1) and the *construction of the sanctuary* (Exodus 39.32; cf. 40.33).[38]

4. The *language* in the creation story and the story of the construction of the sanctuary shows distinct similarities: Genesis 1.31/Exodus 39.43; Genesis 2.2/Exodus 40.33; Genesis 2.3/Exodus 39.43; and Genesis 2.1/Exodus 39.43.[39]

J. H. Walton, *The Lost World of Genesis One: Ancient Cosmology and the Origins Debate*, 2009, especially pp. 78-92.

[37] The structure is noted, for example, in W. Vogels, 'Cultic and Civil Calendars of the Fourth Day of Creation', 1997, p. 178.
[38] J. Blenkinsopp, 'The Structure of P', 1976, pp. 278, 280.
[39] Ibid., p. 280.

5. *Thematically*, in both contexts, the Sabbath serves as the climax and the Spirit of God functions as the mover.[40]

The similarities and links noted here strengthen the impression that the created earth serves as a sanctuary in Genesis 1.1-2.4a and that the building of the sanctuary is devoted to the Creator, the Lord and King of the universe who wishes to dwell among men. (The implied sanctuary symbolism in 1.1-2.4a is further underlined in Genesis 2.)

The priestly function implied in 'the image of God' influences how we understand the relationship between the Creation, the Fall, and God's plan of redemption in the Bible as a whole. R. J. Middleton summarises this relationship as follows: 'In the cosmic sanctuary of God's world, humans have pride of place and supreme responsibility, not just as royal stewards and cultural shapers of the environment, but (taking seriously the temple imagery) as priests of creation, actively mediating divine blessing to the non-human world and – in a post-fall situation – interceding on behalf of a groaning creation until that day when heaven and earth are redemptively transformed to fulfil God's purpose for justice and *shalom*. The human vocation as *imago Dei* [image of God] in God's world thus corresponds in important respects to Israel's vocation as a "royal priesthood" among the nations (Exodus 19.6).'[41] This vocation is then assumed, in Christ, by the new Israel, the Christian church (I Peter 2.4-9).

Thus, the Hebrew text in Genesis 1.1-2.4a is worded in such a way that it elicits associations with temple imagery. Such imagery was not only widespread in the ancient Near East and is evidenced across the entire Bible, but it is central in John's vision of the final outcome of the great controversy in the book of Revelation.

---

[40] Ibid., pp. 281-282.
[41] R. J. Middleton, *The Liberating Image: The Imago Dei in Genesis 1*, 2005, pp. 89-90.

The description of God's people, men and women, as *priests* who *serve* God as *ministers* is vital at certain peaks in the structure of the book of Revelation (1.4-6; 5.9-10; 20.6). As John describes God who is 'making all things new' (Revelation 21.5), i.e. creating a new heaven and a new earth, he alludes to Genesis 1.1-2.4a. The home of God, where he dwells with human beings, is described as a sanctuary that comes down upon the newly created earth. It is where the nations come together for worship and to bring him glory (Revelation 21.1-4, 9-27).

This temple imagery is alluded to in Genesis 1.1-2.4a by the common linguistic feature of 'associative meaning'. Well-known concepts in the original setting of the text remind the intended readers of the implied sanctuary symbolism. This is however hidden to most modern readers and needs to be supplied through an exegesis of the Hebrew and Greek texts. *The priestly role of man and woman in the created world is implied in the text.*[42]

God's Commissioning-Ordination of Man and Woman

God's commissioning-ordination of man and woman as his servants-ministers in the created world proceeds in four steps:

1. *Decision* and *Announcement of Intent* (Genesis 1.26) – formally marked as collective acts of God: 'Let us make humankind in our image, according to our likeness; and let them have dominion over the fish of the sea, and over the birds of the air, and over the cattle, and over all the wild animals of the earth, and over every creeping thing that creeps upon the earth.'

2. *Appointment* (Genesis 1.27): 'So God created humankind in his image, in the image of God he created them; male and female he created them.'

3. *Blessing* (Genesis 1.28a): 'God blessed them.'

---

[42] See C. J. H. Wright, *The Mission of God, Unlocking the Bible's Grand Narrative*, 2006, p. 415.

4. *Charge* and *Authorisation* (Genesis 1.28b): 'God said to them: "Be fruitful and multiply, and fill the earth and subdue it; and have dominion over the fish of the sea and over the birds of the air and over every living thing that moves upon the earth".'

While this pattern is adapted to the context of divine creation, it resembles a formal, royal-priestly-prophetic installation (cf. Genesis 41.37-45; Numbers 27.15-23; Jeremiah 1.4-19). God initiates the commissioning. Thus, *when God 'ordains' man and woman as his royal-priestly servants, their gender makes no difference – they are equals.* The equality between man and woman in Genesis 1.1-2.4a is underlined by the following features in the text: (a) 'man' being created as 'male and female'; (b) their creation 'in the image of God'; (c) their sharing in equal manner in the divine 'blessing'; (d) their common power to 'subdue' the earth; (e) their mutual assignment to 'rule' over the animals; and (f) their common vocation to be God's vice-regents on earth (1.26-21).[43]

6.4 Caretakers of the Garden of Eden – Husband and Wife

The thematic unit in Genesis 1-2 is held together by the *general* creation of the world (1.1-2.4a) and the *specific* creation of man and woman as husband and wife in the Garden of Eden (2.4b-25).[44] The equal installation of man and woman as *ministers* of God charged with the task of subduing and ruling the created world has been declared in 1.26-28. Their mediation of God's good government to the world and leading the world to have communion with him and worship him continues to be part of the divine order in Genesis 2. The Bible reader must not ignore the *continuation* of the functional role in which God *first* placed them: they are *his two equal servants-ministers* in a world functioning as his holy sanctuary, in his kingdom.

---

[43] Following G. F. Hasel, 'Man and Woman in Genesis 1-3', 1984, pp. 9-22.

[44] This concurs with the conclusions of G. F. Hasel ('Man and Woman in Genesis 1-3', 1984, pp. 9-22) and R. M. Davidson ('Headship, Submission, and Equality in Scripture', 1998, pp. 259-295).

Genesis 2.4b-25 endorses the male and female *equality* in their service as rulers-priests in 1.1-2.4a, but deepens their *unity* by developing the relational and intimate aspects of *marriage*. This motif was implied in the blessing and charge to be fruitful and increase in 1.28 but is now made explicit.[45]

Describing the first family in human history (2.24) and their innocent existence in God's Garden of Eden (2.25), the passage in 2.4b-25 also has a forward-looking function. It provides the background for the Fall and the expulsion from Paradise in Genesis 3, which in turn is the condition for the primeval history of humans in chapters 4-11 and then the ancestral history of Israel in the rest of the Pentateuch.

Genesis 2.4b-25 opens with the early conditions on earth as the setting of the creation of humankind. It has been pointed out that the Hebrew text consistently uses *ha'adam* with the definite article, which literally means 'the human' as a species, and that only in 2.23-25, because of the context, *ha'adam* ('the human') is specified as *'ish* ('male man') which is referring to the male human as distinct from the female.[46] Thus, there is no explicit statement in the text that defines the human that was created from the dust of the ground as a male (2.7).

The intention behind this silence is understood in light of 2.23 and 5.1-2. The words 'this one shall be called woman (*'ishah*), for out of man (*'ish*) this one was taken' (2.23) recognise that the human (*ha'adam*) is now created as male and female. The male human identifies himself as male only when he discovers his female human partner. Thus, the narrative is not really about how the male man is first created followed by the woman being created in order to 'help'

---

[45] G. F. Hasel says: 'The more extensive story of the creation of man and woman in Gen 2 does not stand in tension or opposition to [the equality between man and woman in Gen 1], but corroborates the compressed statements of Gen 1, complementing them with additional details' (ibid.).

[46] S. Tengström 'Man och kvinna i Genesis 2-3', 2005, pp. 281-285.

him. It is rather about the formation of a *human being* out of dust from the ground, and this human is then divided into two genders that are mutually related to each other (2.21-23) and are drawn to each other (2.24).

This understanding of *'adam* is supported by Genesis 5.1-2: 'When God created humankind (*'adam*), he made them in the likeness of God. Male and female he created them and named them 'Humankind' (*'adam*) when they were created.' Here, Hebrew *'adam* is not the male individual's proper name but means 'humankind' and has a dual reference, to man and woman. Both are created as humans in the image of God.

This dual reference in *'adam* – humankind including man and woman – needs to be kept in mind in Genesis 1-3 as a whole. As in many other languages, the masculine form may include men and women. The context will usually help the reader to decide the reference, but the dual meaning needs to be considered especially in 2.7-23.

Mankind's Ministry in the Garden of Eden
Humankind is created to 'serve' by working the ground from which the human was taken (2.4b-7), but God removes man from the ground and puts him to serve as caretaker of the Garden of Eden (2.8-15) – in some sense the Garden represents the created world that God commissioned mankind to govern in Genesis 1, but it is also God's dwelling place, his sanctuary. Thus, from the context, the function as caretaker of the Garden is a 'human' task and may include the woman who is as human as her male partner. This does not need to be stated or made plain in the text, because it has been emphatically said in 1.26-28, and the purpose of the story in 2.4b-25 is to present man and woman as husband and wife.

Parallel hints in the Hebrew text show that the arrangement of the Garden of Eden resembled the sanctuary in Israel. Since these have been set out in some detail elsewhere,[47] it is sufficient to reduce the following to a brief summary:

(a) 'Eden' as 'the Garden of God' is identified with the heavenly sanctuary in Ezekiel 28.13. (b) The Garden planted by God is in the east (Genesis 2.8) and entered from the east (Genesis 3.24), giving it the same orientation as the Old Testament sanctuary.[48] (c) The activity of 'planting' (*nata'*) is connected both with Eden and the sanctuaries (Genesis 2.8; Exodus 15.17; cf. I Chronicles 17.9). (d) The Menorah in Hebrew tradition symbolised the tree of life and this tree was placed in the midst of (*betok*) the Garden, while the living presence of God was in the midst of (*betok*) the sanctuary (Genesis 2.9; Exodus 25.8). (e) Cherubim guard the entrance to Eden (Genesis 3.24) and they also 'guard' the entrance to the holy of holies (Exodus 25.19; I Kings 6.24-27; Ezekiel 9.3). (f) Together, the Hebrew verbs with which God commissions humans in Genesis 2.15 (*'abad* 'to work', and *shamar*, 'to watch') are used only in sanctuary contexts within the Pentateuch (Numbers 3.7-8; 8.26; 18.7). (g) Precious stones, 'gold and onyx', which are mentioned in the Garden (Genesis 2.11-12), are also used extensively in sanctuaries (Exodus 28.15-29). (h) The river Gihon from Eden that waters the Garden (2:10) has parallels in sanctuary symbolism and is understood as flowing from the throne of God.[49]

These signals in the text suggest a sanctuary environment where God is present. 'The Garden of Eden becomes the blueprint for how the whole earth should be: a sanctuary where humans live with God'[50] (cf. the eschatological passage of Revelation 21.1-4).

---

[47] See R. M. Davidson, 'Should Women Be Ordained as Pastors? Old Testament Considerations', 2013, pp. 18-19; cf. J. Barna, 'Towards a Biblical-Systematic Theology of Ordination', 2014, p. 101.

[48] Exodus 27.13-16; 36.20-30; 38.13-18; Numbers 3.38; I Kings 7.21; Ezekiel 8.16; cf. Ezekiel 44.1; 47.1.

[49] Revelation 22.1-5; cf. I Kings 1.38-39; II Chronicles 32.30; Ezekiel 47.1-12; Zechariah 14.8; Psalm 46.5; John 7.37-39; Revelation 7.17.

[50] J. Barna, 'Towards a Biblical-Systematic Theology of Ordination', 2014, p. 102.

Man and woman are to function as 'rulers' representing the good rule of God before the created earth, and they are therefore acting in this thematic context as 'royals' who represent God.[51] By their life, work, nourishment, Sabbath rest, marriage and procreation, they are to *mediate* God's kingship and his presence with his created beings. Without distinction, man and woman are *God's servants or ministers in his kingdom*.

The Unity and Partnership of Man and Woman as Servants-Ministers

As God creates the woman, not of dust this time, but of man's own body (2.21-22), *both of them are defined by what they do and by their origin*. The man comes from the dust of the ground and his task is to till the ground; the woman comes from the man and her task is to partner with the man.[52]

As the man meets the woman, he acknowledges the fundamental unity in their origin and constitution (2.23). Both are created by and subordinated to God. Both are made of the same bones and flesh. The 'woman' is to be called *'ishah*, implying an addition of the feminine ending to the word for 'man' (*'ish*), which underlines their equality: they are the same in status, just male and female. It should also be noted that Hebrew *'ishah* means both 'woman' and 'wife', and both meanings may be intentionally included here.

In a concluding comment, the passage looks to the future of humanity and envisages that, literally, 'a man leaves his father and mother and clings to his wife, and they become one flesh' (2.24). Note the present tense (preserved in the NRSV) which applies the comment to the times of the author of the text.

The point in the Garden of Eden is that, in marriage, the woman 'supports' (*'azar*) the man, and the man is drawn to her in order to unite with her, and they become one flesh. We will see later on, in

---

[51] Ibid.
[52] L. Turner, *Genesis*, 2000, p. 29.

our comments on Genesis 3.16c-d, that this marriage rule is reversed after the Fall: the woman will then 'be drawn to' her husband, while he 'supports' her.

The crucial question for us at this point is: Has God instituted a different status between men and women in Genesis 2.4b-25? Some interpreters affirm this question, but *this does not do justice to what the biblical text says and means.* Let us consider each of these arguments.

Being Created First Implies No Priority

The order in which man and woman are created is an insufficient argument for male superiority before the Fall (Genesis 2.7, 22). On the contrary, 'retarding of woman's creation in Genesis 2 underlines how crucial she is'![53] Genesis 2.4b-25 follows an *inclusio* or 'ring construction', which is a common pattern in the Bible. Accordingly, the creation of man (*ha'adam*, 'humankind') at the beginning and the woman at the end of the passage 'correspond to each other in importance'.[54] The text underlines their equality by using 'the same number of words (in Hebrew) for the description of the creation of the man as for the creation of the woman'.[55] 'The movement in Genesis 2, if anything, is not from superior to inferior, but *from incompleteness to completeness*. Woman is created as the climax, the culmination of the story. She is the crowning work of Creation.'[56]

This conclusive argument from the context in Genesis 2.4b-25 fits the general pattern in the Bible. First and second in order is not a biblical criterion for headship and submission: Cain was born before Abel, but Abel's sacrifice was accepted by God (Genesis 4.1-5); Esau was born before Jacob, but Jacob carried the blessing and the promises of God to Abraham (Genesis 27-28); Jacob put Joseph's son Ephraim before Manasseh, although Manasseh was born first

---

[53] Ibid.
[54] R. M. Davidson, 'Headship, Submission, and Equality in Scripture', 1998, p. 261.
[55] Ibid.
[56] Ibid. (emphasis supplied).

(Genesis 48.8-20). And in the context of Genesis 1-2, the animals are created before man, and yet man has dominion over them (1.24-30). The view that the order of the creation of man and woman signifies a hierarchical ranking is the fruit of erroneously reading into the text what simply is not there. It violates even a 'plain-reading' philosophy of interpretation.

Two minor points in the alleged arguments for female gender submission in Genesis 2 relate to the priority of the man (understood as 'male') as speaking and being spoken to in the narrative.

Firstly, it is claimed by some that man's headship over woman before the Fall would explain why God addresses man (male), not woman, and why man (male), not woman, does the speaking in the narrative. Again, these points are built on a flawed reading of the text which fails to take into account the movement from incompleteness to completeness and climax in the narrative. Thus, when God speaks to humankind (*ha'adam*) in 2.15-18, it is part of the process of bringing man to realise his need for a partner who is like him.

When the human being has entered the Garden as its caretaker, it is only to be expected that God instructs him about his food (as in 1.29-30 where both man and woman are addressed). While allowing the humans to eat of all the trees in the Garden, God must also deal with the exception. His warning not to eat of the forbidden tree was crucial for *humanity* (*ha'adam*) to avoid transgression and to be free moral agents with the power of choice. But God's passing on of such knowledge to humankind before the creation of woman – at this point the man represents (an incomplete) humankind (*ha'adam*) – does not thereby imply male headship over the female partner who has not yet been created.

The point in the narrative is rather that knowledge of the prohibition is imparted to *humanity* in a creation process moving towards its climax. As a human being, the woman shows in 3.2-3 that she, too, possesses the divine knowledge given to humanity. God holds both man and woman equally accountable to obey the order of his kingdom (3.8-13, 16-19).

Secondly, the circumstance that only the man speaks in the passage (2.23) does not reveal his pre-Fall headship over Eve any more than only Eve speaking outside the Garden (Genesis 4) reveals Eve's headship over Adam after the Fall.[57] The man's speech in 2.23 is simply a response to God's act of bringing the woman to him in which he acknowledges the fundamental equality between the human genders.

Man and Woman Represent a Complete Humanity

Man is incomplete when alone (2.18), i.e. humanity is complete only when man and woman are joined. While Genesis 2.4b-25 presents this point with a view to marriage, Genesis 1.1-2.4a maintains male and female unity in representing God towards the created earth. Therefore, the Hebrew terms underlying the phrase that is often translated 'helper suitable for him' (2.18, 20) do not warrant the principle of man's headship and woman's submission. Rather, they refer to man's *dependence* on woman (she *partners* with him) and their mutual *suitability* for each other.

Therefore, the argument alleged by some that the woman is formed merely to be a 'helpmate' or assistant to cure man's loneliness (2.18-20) is flawed. The biblical text defines *lonely* man's creation as 'not good' (2.18). Although each step in God's creation is defined as 'good' (Genesis 1.4, 10, 12, 18, 21, 25, 31), the creation of man is *not completed* ('good') until man is created *as man and woman*. Thus, God's order in creation is *not established* until he has created mankind as male and female, both equally reflecting the image of God.

The text states literally in 2.18 God's purpose to 'make for man an *'ezer kenegdo* (KJV: 'a help meet for him'; RSV: 'a helper fit for him'; NASB: 'a helper suitable for him'). Bible readers have often assigned to these words an inferior or subordinate status of woman.

---

[57] Ibid., pp. 261-262.

For example, John Calvin understood that woman was a 'kind of appendage' and a 'lesser helpmeet' for man.[58] But this is not what the text says. Even some Bible translations have missed this point.

Two features are essential. Firstly, the translation of the Hebrew *'ezer* as 'help' and 'helper' is misleading. The English 'helper' suggests an assistant, a subordinate, an inferior, whereas the Hebrew word contains no such connotation. 'In fact, the Hebrew Bible most frequently employs *'ezer* to describe a superior helper – God himself as the "helper" of Israel. This is a relational term, describing a beneficial relationship, but in itself does not specify position or rank, either superiority or inferiority. The specific position intended must be gleaned from the immediate context, here the adjoining *kenegdo*.'[59]

Secondly, turning to Hebrew *kenegdo*, 'like him', it has been correctly noted that *neged* conveys the idea of 'in front of' or 'counterpart', and that a literal translation of *kenegdo* is: 'like his counterpart, corresponding to him'. Used with *'ezer*, 'this term indicates no less than equality: Eve is Adam's "benefactor/helper", one who in position is "corresponding to him", "his counterpart, his complement". Eve is "a power equal to man"; she is Adam's "partner".'[60]

Thus, the Hebrew terms underlying the phrase 'helper suitable for him' (2.18, 20) do not warrant man's headship and woman's submission. They refer to man's *dependence* on woman (she is his beneficial partner) and their mutual *suitability* for each other.

Created from Man's Rib: 'In All Things Woman Should Be Man's Equal'

Being created out of man's body does not imply woman's subordination to man, but the text uses this element to underline their complete *equality*, which is confirmed by man's acknowledgement of her being 'bones of my bones and flesh of my flesh' (2.23). They are

---

[58] Ibid., p. 262.
[59] Ibid.
[60] Ibid.

made of the same substance, namely *humanity*. However, in terms of the material they were originally made of, man is from dust (material) and woman is from man (living being). By their origin, the male is focused on the material aspect of creation and working the ground, while the woman is focused on the people aspect of creation and is equipped to care for the needs of other people. Thus, the equality of man and woman functions as a *complementarity*.

It cannot be denied that the existence of the woman was in some way derived from man. But derivation does not imply subordination. The man was also 'derived' – from the ground (2.7), but nobody would conclude that the ground was his superior. Woman is not man's rib. The raw material, not woman, was taken out of man, just as the raw material of man was 'taken' (3.19, 23) out of the ground. God 'made' the woman out of the man's rib, to indicate their similarity and equality. Thus, the Hebrew word for 'make' in 2.22 is *banah*, which means 'build', so the woman came into being out of God's artistic hands.[61]

The symbolism of the rib points to *equality*. By building woman from man's rib, God appears to be indicating the 'mutual relationship' and 'the inseparable unity' in which man and woman are joined. 'The rib means solidarity and equality.'[62] This understanding is confirmed by man's poetic exclamation when he sees woman for the first time (2.23): 'This at last is bone of my bones and flesh of my flesh!' This phrase indicates 'a person "as close as one's own body" and it denotes physical oneness and "a commonality of concern, loyalty and responsibility", but does not lead to the notion of Woman's subordination or submission to Man'.[63]

It is possible, but not necessary, that the reference to man's 'rib' from which God created woman is a way of saying that they stand side by side, i.e. neither of them being superior or inferior to the

---

[61] Ibid.
[62] Ibid., p. 263.
[63] Ibid., p. 263.

other. Ellen White writes: 'When God created Eve, He designed that she should possess neither inferiority nor superiority to the man, but that *in all things she should be his equal.*'[64]

The Naming of the Woman

It has been alleged by some that by giving woman the name 'woman' in 2.23, man proves his authority over the woman. However, this interpretation would violate the whole point that the man is making in this verse. The point of his naming her is not to mark his authority and her submission, but to celebrate that he now has a companion that corresponds to his own nature ('bone of my bones'). 'The act of naming in the Old Testament normally signifies the ability of discernment, i.e. he discerns her true identity (cf. Genesis 16.13).'[65]

It has also been pointed out that in Genesis 2.23 two 'divine passives' are used. The first one, she 'was taken from', indicates that it was God who performed the action. The second one, 'she shall be called', indicates that, after creating her, God, not the man, was the one who called her 'Woman' ('This one is called [by the Lord] Woman').[66]

Finally, the woman is not really 'named' here (that happens according to 3.20 after the Fall), but she is called *'ishah* which is only a generic identification and means that the feminine ending is added to Hebrew *'ish*, 'man'. This is verified in 2.24, which indicates that a man is to cling to his *'ishah* ('wife'). The 'naming' of 'woman' simply highlights the unity and equality between the two.

Thus, the 'naming' of 'woman/wife' in Genesis 2.23 does not concern male superiority, but expresses the man's/husband's *acceptance* of the woman/wife as an intimate and equal human partner with him.

---

[64] E. G. White, *Testimonies for the Church*, vol. 3, 1885-1909, p. 484 (emphasis supplied).
[65] GC-TOSCR, 2014, p. 71.
[66] Ibid.

Equality in Marriage

In a patriarchal society it was expected that the woman would 'cling to' the man, but in Genesis 2.24 man is to 'cling to' his wife. This is a way for the author to say that both are to cling to each other in equality. The intimate unity between man and woman in marriage is defined as 'becoming one flesh' (2.24), which means the equal joining of two persons as a whole, not just physically or sexually.

Summary

The picture of the relationship between the married man and woman according to God's ideal in Genesis 1-2 is one of unity and equality (a) in their origin from God and accountability to him; (b) in being created in his image; (c) in their role as sexual partners, multiplying and filling the earth with new human beings; (d) in their role of being rulers of the earth; (e) in their equal substance of human bones and flesh; and (f) in their mutual support and intimate relationship in marriage.

Thus, there is nothing in Genesis 2.4b-25 to indicate a hierarchical view of the genders. The man and the woman before the Fall are presented as fully equal, with no hint of headship of one over the other or a hierarchical relationship between husband and wife.[67] Rather than a hierarchy of genders, Genesis 2 describes an equality and complementarity of genders. The focus is not on headship and submission between male and female, but on the headship of God and the servanthood of man and woman together, as royal-priestly ministers to the one God who rules the world and dwells in his sanctuary, the Garden of Eden.

---

[67] R. M. Davidson, 'Headship, Submission, and Equality in Scripture', 1998, p. 264.

6.5 The Fall

Having introduced God's 'grand blueprint mission' (Genesis 1-2),[68] the Bible story then brings a change to the status and condition of humanity (Genesis 3). The theme of the mission of God turns its focus onto dealing with the Fall. Man and woman are now unable to provide what was originally expected of them. Man 'is not in a position to extend God's presence, because he is now hiding from it'.[69]

The serpent brings disunity between God and humanity. He convinces man and woman that they are not made for what God had told them, because, he says, they are actually equal to God, and, hence, their purpose and mission is higher than what God has ordained for them. The tragic consequences are that humanity abandons God's mission blueprint.[70]

Within this secondary and narrower context of the mission of God, the purpose is to 'undo the human-divine disunity'. Human existence continues with pain and toil leading to death, but God is faithful to his blessing upon man and woman (being created 'in his image') and provides them with some safeguards (Genesis 3.16-22).

The Promised Seed through the Woman

The key mission purpose of God is to address the power of evil brought by the serpent. At the very heart of his mission is the purpose stated in Genesis 3.15, where God presents 'an embryonic statement' about the woman's 'seed' (Hebrew *zera'*), i.e. an individual representing humanity, at first thought to be the patriarch Israel and his people but later acknowledged and proclaimed as Messiah-Christ and his people.

This promised 'seed' would come from the woman, who is not formally cursed in God's sentence of her (Genesis 3.16a-b). She will still give birth but it will be painful and hard. The human ability

---

[68] J. Barna, 'Towards a Biblical-Systematic Theology of Ordination', p. 102.
[69] Ibid.
[70] Ibid.

to procreate, which is now central to God's plan (because of the woman's promised seed), is guarded by their marriage which is based on the wife's 'longing desire for her husband' (3.16c) and his 'being responsible for and caring for her needs' (3.16d).

Thus, the woman's seed will defeat the serpent (representing the evil power opposed to God), his lies and what he brought to the world. The promised seed will restore the peace of God's kingdom. God will be present and made known in the world.

The Mission of God through a Broken Humanity

God's mission will now be channelled through *a broken humanity* for whom God cares. God underlines this by dressing man and woman after the Fall in garments of skin (3.21), which served as a special outward sign of the new reality that their priestly duty of mediation now also includes mediation for themselves and that their presence with God requires the sacrificed blood of offering animals that will vicariously die in their place (see 6.5.2 below). This priestly duty of bringing atonement is later picked up by Cain and Abel, Noah, Abraham and his descendants.[71]

The Fall impacts not only the conditions of life for mankind but also the human *relationships* (a) to God, (b) to the environment of the Garden of Eden, and (c) to each other. The order God instituted in Genesis 1-2 is fundamentally *changed*, but *not all is changed*.

Features that remain, although being set in a new context, are: (a) mankind's creation in the image of God, i.e. the divine royal-priestly calling to humans to *represent* him and *mediate* his presence and activities in the world; (b) God's commission to man and woman to be fruitful (life-giving) and subdue the earth (according to the order of God's kingdom); (c) God's blessing upon man and woman (life-giving and authorisation); (d) the egalitarian ideal for man and wife in marriage (cooperative interdependence); (e) the fundamental

---

[71] The general drift of this paragraph follows Barna (ibid. p. 102) but the content is adapted to the findings in TED-TOSCR, 2013, section 3.1.1.3.

distinction between divine and human as the basis for God's ethical boundaries in guiding human life (the law of creation). The aspect of *continuation* needs to be kept in mind at each point in the reading of the story of the Fall in Genesis 3, because the biblical text indicates that this is essential.

We will now focus attention on how the Fall impacts man and woman with respect to their royal-priestly commissioning and their egalitarian status.[72]

6.5.1 The Promised Seed and the Protection of Marriage

When the wife eats of the forbidden fruit and gives it to her husband, he is 'together with her' (3.6) and 'listens to her voice' (3.17).[73] He is as knowledgeable of God's prohibition as is his wife, and yet he, too, eats of the forbidden fruit. Later on, as he faces the consequences before God, he blames his wife, and indirectly blames even God, saying: 'The woman you put here together with me – she gave me some fruit from the tree, and I ate it' (3.12).

Being true to the biblical text, therefore, the immediate impression is that the husband was 'together with his wife' but blames her for *giving* him the forbidden fruit. His disloyal act of blaming her in order to excuse his own disobedience is not to be taken as a statement of what actually happened. Both of them were disobedient, are equally guilty, and suffer the consequences together.

The logical element of *consequence* keeps all the parts together in 3.14-24. At the same time, God is not only acting as a *judge* who

---

[72] For a consideration of the passage as a whole, see TED-TOSCR, 2013, section 3.1.1.3.

[73] Walter Vogels contends that culpability for the Fall should be assigned to both the man and the woman (W. Vogels, '"Her Man with Her" (Gen 3:6b)', 1997, pp. 147-160). Focusing on *'immah*, 'with her' in Genesis 3.6, he shows that in a majority of instances in the Hebrew Bible the analogous expression 'with him' means that someone supports the person in question, and that this understanding is confirmed by the whole Eden story and the larger biblical context.

punishes, but he is also a *caring provider*, fulfilling his blessing on man and woman in 1.28 and providing for man and woman certain safeguards in the midst of their misery.

In the punishment of the woman (3.16) no curse is formally expressed, suggesting that God's blessing that made her fruitful in 1.28 still stands. Although created in the image of God, she is given a toilsome pregnancy and childbirth as a *consequence* of disobedience. Some of what God instituted in Genesis 1-2 continues but it is marred by hardship.

Concerning the husband (3.17-19), God first gives the curse but it is a curse upon the ground and not upon the man himself. Indirectly, however, the *consequences* turn out to be a torment for him. He will work the ground in pain until he returns to dust (3.17b-19), which 'suggests that ultimately it is the earth that subdues the man'.[74] Thus, the charge to man and woman to subdue the earth in 1.28 is replaced here by the earth subduing humankind.

The Wife's Punishment and Protection in Genesis 3.16
In the central passage of Genesis 3.16, God's judgement upon the woman can be divided into the following four parts:

> I will greatly increase your painful labour (*'itsabon*) in childbearing (3.16a);
>
> with painful labour (*'etseb*) you will give birth to children (3.16b);
>
> yet your longing desire (*teshuqah*) will be for your husband (3.16c);
>
> and he will be responsible for (*mashal be*) you (3.16d).

Hebrew dictionaries offer 'pain' and 'toil' as senses for the synonymous terms *'itsabon* (3.16a) and *'etseb* (3.16b), but in view of the same term (*'itsabon*) in the husband's punishment ('in toil you

---

74 L. Turner, *Genesis*, 2000, p. 33.

shall eat of it all the days of your life', 3.17) and its meaning elsewhere in Genesis (cf. 5.29), 'painful labour' is a preferable translation.

The meaning of the last two enigmatic lines (3.16c and d) of the divine sentencing is crucial for a proper understanding of the nature of God's design for marital relationships.[75] It has been the subject of much discussion and different views have been advanced.[76]

Like the first two lines in 3.16a-b, the second two lines in 3.16c-d may be taken as a 'synonymous parallelism' – a standard feature of Hebrew poetic expression where the same thought is repeated but in a variant way. God is declaring that although the woman would have painful labour in childbirth – 'an ordeal that would seem naturally to discourage her from continuing to have relations with her husband'[77] – 'yet', God assures her, 'your longing desire will be for your husband'.

In line with this understanding, we must consider more closely the meaning of the Hebrew *teshuqah*, 'strong desire, yearning' (3.16). This word appears only three times in Scripture, but its only other occurrence in the context of a man-woman relationship is Song of Songs 7.11 [in the Hebrew text; 7.10 in NRSV]. Here, the Shulamite bride joyfully exclaims, 'I am my beloved's, and his desire (*teshuqah*) is for me'. Drawing on this biblical usage of *teshuqah* to indicate 'a wholesome sexual desire', 'the term appears to be employed in 3.16c to indicate a positive blessing accompanying the divine judgment'.[78]

Richard Davidson has appropriately pointed out in this connection: 'A divinely ordained sexual yearning of wife for husband will serve to sustain the union that has been threatened in the ruptured relations resulting from sin.'[79] He continues to say that 'if Genesis 3:16d is seen

---

[75] R. M. Davidson, 'Headship, Submission, and Equality in Scripture', 1998, p. 264.
[76] As summarised in ibid., pp. 264-269; id., 'Should Women Be Ordained as Pastors?', 2013, pp. 21-23.
[77] Id., 'Headship, Submission, and Equality in Scripture', 1998, p. 268.
[78] Ibid.
[79] Ibid. (emphasis supplied).

to be in close parallelism with 3:16c, the emphasis upon blessing as well as judgement seems to accrue also to man's relationship with his wife'.[80]

The painful childbearing and childbirth that God inflicts in his judgement of the woman is connected with the woman's 'longing' for her husband in two ways: (a) it *presupposes* her sexual desire which eventually brings her the painful labour of carrying and giving birth to children; and (b) it *results* in her needy desire to be provided for and sustained during many years of repeated childbirths until and beyond the time when she would turn unfruitful in old age.

Her husband, who works the cursed ground and provides for her, determines both his response to her longing for sexual attention and to her life-long need for protection, provision and care. In this dual sense, he is her 'master'.

It is relevant to note here that marriage in Old Testament times appears to have been based on the husband's provision of 'food, clothing and marital rights' (Exodus 21.10-11),[81] and in this sense the husband is his wife's caretaker, provider and lover (cf. Ephesians 5.21-33 and section 9.5.3 below).

The Role of the Husband in Genesis 3.16

In this context, we must consider more closely the sense and reference of the Hebrew verbal expression *mashal be*, translated here by 'he will be responsible for you' (3.16d). This expression is often translated 'rule over', probably under the influence of the Septuagint translation *kyrieuo*, which is somewhat mechanically used in the whole Septuagint for Hebrew *mashal be*, but with little regard for the fine nuances of the Hebrew verb.[82] There are certainly royal contexts where *mashal* is best translated 'rule' (e.g. II Samuel 23.3). However, there are clear nuances in the concept of *mashal* in the book

---

[80] Ibid.
[81] D. Instone-Brewer, *Divorce and Remarriage in the Bible: The Social and Literary Context*, 2002, pp. 8-11.
[82] W. Foerster, '*kyrieuo*', *ThDNT*, vol. 3, p. 1097.

of Genesis.[83] The English 'rule over' expresses a strong dominance and authoritative dominion over something, but with the Hebrew preposition *be* the verb *mashal* may also be used in a non-hierarchic sense. This depends on three circumstances:

1. The object of the verb: if it refers to something or somebody that is 'in need to be served', *mashal be* tends to have the sense of 'manage' or 'care for'.

2. The function of *mashal be* in its written context: if the verb expresses a positive and affirming action, its sense leans towards 'be responsible for, manage, take care of'.

3. The function of the verb in relation to the status of its agent in the context: if *mashal be* signifies an action undertaken *on behalf of* or *in the service of* somebody who is superior to the agent, its sense also leans towards 'be responsible for, manage, take care of', while 'rule over' would be appropriate for the master or king standing above him. Thus, for example, the verb is used in the following three contexts in Genesis, besides 3.16:

The first context is the 'responsibility' of sun and moon to 'care for' or 'be in charge of' (*mashal be*) the illumination upon the earth and 'serve as signs' for the separation of day from night in the service of their Owner/Creator (1.14-18). 'Rule over' does not appropriately convey the function of the sun and the moon which is rather to be found in serving the purpose of illumination and marking day and night.

The second context involves the function of Isaac's servant who 'is in charge of' or 'takes care of' (*mashal be*) all Isaac's possessions (24.2), where 'rule over' would be quite inappropriate.

---

[83] Cf. R. D. Culver who says in his article 'Mashal III' in *ThWOT*, vol. 1, p. 534: '*Mashal* usually receives the translation "to rule", but the precise nature of the rule is as various as the real situations in which the action or state so designated occur'.

The third context regards Joseph who is said to 'be in charge of (*mashal be*) all Egypt' (45.8, 26), where 'ruling over all Egypt' would be inappropriate, since Joseph was not the ruler, above Pharaoh, but he 'was put in charge of', 'took responsibility for', or 'governed the affairs of' the country *in the service of* Pharaoh (41.45) – note that 'with respect to the throne [Pharaoh] remained greater than him' (41.40).

As we widen the context of the use of *mashal be* in the Old Testament and the Qumran Texts, it is clear that it can also have a managerial sense of 'be in charge of, taking care of, and be responsible for'.[84] We therefore prefer to translate *mashal be* as 'be responsible for' with an implied nuance of 'take care of' or 'be in charge of', as a trusted servant cares for the possessions of his master.

Regardless of considerations regarding vocabulary, however, it is the use of *mashal be* in its context that must have the final word. The immediate context in 3.16 portrays God addressing the woman because of her transgression. Two statements are made – each in the form of a synonymous parallelism:

A.

a. I will greatly increase your painful labour in childbearing;

b. with painful labour you will give birth to children;

B.

c. yet your longing desire will be for your husband;

d. and he will be responsible for you.

---

[84] See Psalms 8.7; 105.21; cf. J. A. Soggin, '*mashal*/herrschen', *THAT*, vol. 1, col. 931; W. L. Holladay, *A Concise Hebrew and Aramaic Lexicon of the Old Testament*, 1976, s.v. *mashal*, p. 219. See also H. Gross, 'Mashal II', *ThDOT*, vol. 9, pp. 69-71; Gross notes that a related noun *memshalah* is found in the Qumran Texts in which 'the notion of management appears alongside that of dominion: 1QS 10:1; 1QH 12:6, 9; 1Q34 fr. 3 2:3' (ibid., p. 71). The view that *mashal* signifies an act of 'responsibility and care' has been argued, for example, in V. Norskov Olsen, *The New Relatedness for Man and Woman in Christ*, 1993, p. 55; R. M. Davidson, 'Headship, Submission, and Equality in Scripture', 1998, p. 268.

Part A expresses the same content in lines (a) and (b) regarding the woman's punishment by painful labour in childbearing and childbirth. This punishment is connected with God's initial command to 'be fruitful and multiply and fill the earth and subdue it' and his blessing of them (1.26). The purpose of God's command remains and salvation will be brought by the woman's seed (3.15), but the punishment consists in painful labour. This may *threaten* continued procreation in that the wife might fear the pain and the hardship of pregnancy and refuse to be intimate with her husband. She will now also need special support during childbearing, childbirth, and thereafter.

Thus, in section B, God acts as a caring provider, intent on accomplishing his plan for humanity. He introduces an antithesis ('yet')[85] which safeguards procreation. The wife's (positive) 'longing desire' for her husband will lead to sexual intimacy and pregnancy, and the husband's responsible provision and care for her will support her during childbearing and childbirth.

Thus, part B expresses two contrasting statements with the same purpose, namely to protect the marriage and care for the 'woman's seed'. Line c refers to the woman's longing need for her husband, and line d to the man's satisfaction of those needs and his responsible care for his wife.

This understanding of 3.16 is compatible with a certain structural pattern of the punishment/remedy of the humans in 3.16-19. God inflicts painful and hard labour on both man and woman – on the woman as she provides human life through childbearing and childbirth (3.16a-b) and on the man as he provides bread to sustain life (3.17-19). Thus, God's speech to the woman in 3.16c-d forms a remedial *bridge* between the woman's and the man's punishments.

---

[85] The conjunction *waw* in 3.16c functions as a signal of an antithesis, as, for example, in Genesis 17.21 and 19.19: W. Gesenius & E. Kautzsch, *Gesenius' Hebrew Grammar*, 1978, p. 485.

It puts a remedy in place that joins 3.16-19 into a coherent whole following an A-B-B-A pattern:

A   Punishment: The woman's painful labour in childbearing and childbirth (3.16a-b)

    B Remedy: Her longing desire will be for her husband (3.16c)

    B¹ Remedy: He will be responsible and care for her (3.16d)

A¹   Punishment: The man's painful labour in order to provide bread for his family (3.17-19).

In light of this pattern, Genesis 3.16-19 is not concerned with headship/submission or a hierarchic ranking of man and woman, but with the survival of humankind and the practicalities of life in an existence that has turned painful and hard. Nowhere in the Bible as a whole is Genesis 3.16 explicitly referred to as involving male supremacy. To the contrary, however, Paul alludes to the caring and nurturing role of the husband in his description of the ideal Christian marriage in Ephesians 5.21-33.[86]

The sense of *mashal be* should be understood from this perspective. In at least three other instances in the book of Genesis (1.18; 24.2; 41.45), this verb has the *management* senses of 'be responsible for, be in charge of, take care of'. As in 3.16, (a) the object of the verb in these instances is 'in need to be served', and the wife in 3.16 is in such need after her punishment of painful labour in childbirth; (b) the function of the verb *mashal be* in 3.16d is to balance the infliction of painful labour in 3.16a-b by providing for the husband's care and response to the wife's positive desire in 3.16c; and (c) the action undertaken by the husband in 3.16d is *in the service of* God who in this very statement confides the childbearing wife into the responsible care of her husband.

---

[86] This is further explored in 9.5.3 below.

The Function of Genesis 3.16 in 2.4-3.24 as a Whole

The understanding of Genesis 3.16 that has been chiselled out above has implications for Genesis 1-3 as a whole. In 3.16, God demonstrates his faithfulness to his own words of blessing to man and woman who were made 'in his image' (1.28) and proves himself true to the ordinance of marriage that he has established (2.24). As a result, despite their crime and the necessity of punishment, he still cares about their intimate life together, their procreation (3.16c), and the protection of the childbearing woman (3.16d). By naming his wife 'Eve' in 3.20, the man calls attention to her role as 'mother of all the living', and this function of the woman is central to the continued mission of God, since it is through the continued life of the humans that 'the seed of the woman' will eventually come to fulfil God's plan of salvation (3.15).

A particular structural relationship arises in the text from this reading between Genesis 3.16 and 2.18-24. The cooperative interdependence in marriage, which we noted earlier in our exegesis of Genesis 2, continues after the Fall, but *under different conditions*. Thus, the passage in Genesis 2.24 makes it plain that even *after the Fall* 'a man clings to his wife and they become one flesh'. However, this interdependence is now based on (a) the woman's *longing desire* (*teshuqah*) for him, which balances the threat of her painful labour in childbearing and (b) his support and care for her, based on his painful toil of the ground that yields the sustenance of life.

This new situation *contrasts* sharply with the setting in Genesis 2, where the cooperative interdependence is described with reference to the woman as being a 'support' (*'ezer*) to the husband (2.18), while the husband abandons father and mother and 'clings to' (*dabaq*) his wife (2.24). The contrast pattern is as follows:

The wife *supports* her husband and the husband *clings to* his wife (Genesis 2.18, 24).

The wife *longs for* her husband and the husband *cares for* his wife (Genesis 3.16).

This pattern would give another argument in favour of the understanding of *mashal be* as 'be responsible for, support, look after, take care of'.

This understanding of the text means that, while God pronounces his sentence on the woman for her disobedience in 3.16a-b, acting as a righteous judge concerned with justice, he *also* pronounces his care for the survival of the humans in the dangerous situation they have created for themselves. Nothing can change their righteous punishment, but God, who has a mission of redemption, provides a solution that will accomplish the best that can be done under the circumstances.

It is in God's character to care about the humans although they have disobeyed the divine rules of order in creation. And by doing so, God provides an important condition for the story that is to be told in Genesis 4-11, where the author gives us an introduction to the story of Abraham and the election of Israel beginning in 11.27-32, namely the reproduction and multiplication of human beings, their genealogies and generations, and the spreading of humans across the earth, creating a world of nations.

It is from the central role of the 'seed of the woman' in Genesis 4-11 that God's promises about 'Abraham's seed' become significant. And the 'woman's seed' in 3.15, with its promise of victory over and salvation from evil, depends on God's provision for the *continued fruitfulness* of human beings and the *continued birth* of new human lives.

From this perspective, God's provision for the woman in 3.16 and her name in 3.20 forms one of the climactic points in the story of human beings, which is then picked up in 4.1 and developed in Genesis 4-11. Thus, the blessing in Genesis 1.28 is implicitly confirmed in 3.16c-d and 3.20, and forms an important bridge in the flow of the narrative in the Pentateuch as a whole. We will see later on that the understanding of Genesis 3.16 that is presented here explains some peculiar marital laws in the Old Testament and Paul's exposition of the Christian marriage in Ephesians 5.[87]

God as Judge and Provider

It seems that readers of Genesis 3.16 have too narrowly seen the passage in terms *only* of judgment and punishment. However, from the perspective of the mission of God, the God we encounter in Genesis 1-3, and in the Bible as a whole, also acts as a provider, like a father, for the humans he has created in his image – the same observation can be made regarding God's acts in the Flood story (Genesis 6-9). After their fall, God provides man and woman with clothing, which may have a deeper meaning than merely covering their nakedness (3.21); he seeks to limit the damage of human disobedience by preventing man from eating of the tree of life (3.22-24); he involves himself with Cain's anger when his offering is not accepted and provides him with a way out (4.6-7), and, as Cain complains that his punishment is more than he can bear, God protects Cain after he has killed his brother and ensures that he forms a family with descendants (4.13-24).

Thus, it is in keeping with God's character and actions in Genesis that he acts as a provider also towards the woman and arranges her new existence in order to protect her and the continued reproduction of human life. Thus, while the curses and punishments and their later consequences throughout human history (3.14-24) do indeed upset the order God instituted in 1.28 and 2.21-25, God is still on man's side. Recognising this, Davidson says: 'The divine judgment/blessing in Genesis 3:16 is to facilitate the achievement of the original divine design within the context of a sinful world, and it is thus appropriate

---

[87] This is further developed in 7.4.2 and 9.5.3 below.

for marriage partners to seek to return as much as possible to total egalitarianism in the marriage relationship.'[88]

Genesis 3:16 Concerns the Relationship between Husband and Wife

The changes resulting from the Fall affect the relationship between husband and wife in marriage, but not the relationship between men and women in the institutions of the covenant community or the church. Davidson concludes: 'Any attempt to extend this prescription beyond the husband-wife relationship is not warranted by the text.'[89]

Consequently, there is no *ontological* hierarchical ordering of the status of man and woman in Genesis 3.16. The relationship defined there concerns the practical roles of husband and wife within the marriage relationship, not the genders. The dependence of the wife on her husband, as well as that of the husband upon the cursed ground, is a *consequence* of the Fall that is *described*, not *prescribed*.

The egalitarian view of man and woman – as governors of the world (1.26-28) and in the marriage relationship in the Garden of Eden (Genesis 2) – continues as far as God is concerned. In all the Old Testament, there is no indication that Genesis 3.16 was understood and applied as a divine injunction that man was to 'rule over' woman or as a divine prohibition against a woman being the 'head of men' in public or communal life. The examples of women in leadership roles in the Old Testament are recorded without any criticism or disapproval whatsoever.

6.5.2 Atonement and Priests

Signs in the creation passages in Genesis 1-2 indicate that the humans have an implied role of *mediating* the relationship between God and his created world and that they are caretakers of the

---

[88] R. M. Davidson, 'Headship, Submission, and Equality in Scripture', 1998, p. 269.
[89] Ibid.

sanctuary symbolised by the Garden of Eden where God dwells.[90] After the Fall, God's act of clothing the man and the woman in tunics of skin (Genesis 3.21) continues this thread in the story, preparing the readers for the first sacrifices offered by humans which are presented rather abruptly in 4.1-7.

A deep study of Genesis 3.21 in its full biblical context indicates that the clothing of man and woman in tunics of skin concerns the human *guilt* before God (cf. 3.7-8) and the function of the humans as *mediators* between God and the world to which they had been commissioned (1.26-28). The text subtly hints at this in 3.21 by associative meanings that are retroactively explained in the episode of Noah's sacrifice after the Flood (9.4-7) and in the story of the institution of priests and Israel's sanctuary service in Exodus-Numbers.

The Association of 'Skin Tunics' with Priestly Atonement

God's act in 3.21 stands out as rather odd in its immediate context. Why would *God* 'clothe' the man and his wife at this point – *after* his justiciary proceedings and *before* the expulsion from Eden? In particular, why would God *make* 'tunics' or 'garments' and use the material of 'skin', which implies the death and shedding of the blood of animals? The expression 'tunics of skin' is found only here in the entire Bible, and God's act of '*making* tunics of skin and *clothing* somebody with them' is equally unique in the Bible.

These questions receive meaningful answers by the recognition that the *combined* use of 'clothe' (*hilbish*) and 'tunic' (*ketonet*) occurs only when these terms function as technical terms for the clothing of the priests in connection with their consecration for the priestly office (Exodus 28.41; 29.5-9; 40.12-15; Leviticus 8.7, 13; Numbers 20.25-26). Indeed, the peculiar circumstance that 'the priest who offers anyone's burnt-offering shall keep the *skin* of the burnt-offering that he has offered' (Leviticus 7.8) suggests a particular link between

---

[90] See 6.3 and 6.4 above.

the priestly office and the skin of a sacrificial animal[91] – a priestly privilege that seems to have been more widely used in the ancient Near East, judging from a Syro-Phoenician inscription.[92]

The *reason* for priestly clothing is given in Exodus 28.42-43: '*Make ('asah) for them* linen undergarments to *cover their naked flesh*; they shall reach from the hips to the thighs. Aaron and his sons shall wear them when they go into the tent of meeting, or when they come near the altar to minister in the holy place, *so that they will not carry guilt and die.*' We note that the use of 'make', *'asah*, is the same verb used of God 'making' the tunics of skin in Genesis 3.21.

Protection against Human Guilt

According to a priestly explanation of 'making tunics' and 'clothing with a tunic', God's act in 3.21 means that, since the man and the woman disobeyed his instructions and will die as a consequence (2.17), he *protects* them against their guilt which has sentenced them to death. This is part of a series of protective actions against guilt, struggle with evil, pain in childbearing and providing food, and inevitable death (3.7-15, 17-19). God deals with these threats by his promised salvation through the woman's seed (3.15), by safeguarding procreation and the mutual bonds and duties in marriage (3.16), by the woman's life-giving power (3.20), and by God's covering man and woman with tunics of skin (3.21).

---

[91] This is argued by J. Doukhan who concludes that 'the Genesis story implicitly recognises Eve as priest alongside Adam' ('Women Priests in Israel: A Case for their Absence', 1998, pp. 36-37); he is followed by R. M. Davidson ('Should Women Be Ordained as Pastors?', pp. 32-33). Doukhan's argument is rejected by P. G. Damsteegt ('Eve, a Priest in Eden?', 2000, pp. 123-128); for the weaknesses in Damsteegt's arguments, see TED-TOSCR, 2013, section 3.1.1.3.

[92] A fragmentary inscription found in Carthage, dating from the third or second century BC, offers a tariff of how the different parts of 'whole offerings or substitute offerings' in the temple are to be distributed. Consistently, the priests are to have 'the skins', except when the offering is brought by someone 'poor in cattle', when the priests shall have 'nothing whatever' (J. B. Pritchard [ed.], *Ancient Near Eastern Texts relating to the Old* Testament, 1969, p. 637).

Confirmation of the Commissioning of Man and Woman in Genesis 1.26-28

The priestly understanding of Genesis 3.21 means that God is *confirming* his commissioning of man and woman in 1.26-28. Being created 'in God's image' means that humans still *represent* God and still retain their *mediating* role between him and the world, albeit fraught with much failure. By their 'priestly investiture' in 3.21, man and woman are confirmed as priestly representatives and mediators, as long as their own nakedness and 'shame' is covered and atoned for (cf. Exodus 28.42-43). This is done by God through the tunics of skin from slaughtered animals. It is a special outward sign of the new reality that their priestly duty of mediation – given by being created in the image of God – now also includes mediation *for themselves* and that *their presence with God* requires the restitution of sacrificed blood (i.e. life) of offering animals that will vicariously substitute their own blood (i.e. life).

A Bridge to the First Human Sacrificial Offerings in Genesis 4:1-5

The act takes place while the humans are in the presence of God in the Garden of Eden, which is a most holy place and requires atonement. The need for atonement and the duty to bring it about is consequently instituted in Eden and brought from there into the world when the humans are expelled. Actually, God's act in 3.21 functions as a bridge in the Genesis story, for it prepares for Cain's and Abel's offerings in 4.1-5, the atonement by the blood of sacrificial animals in 9.4-7 (Noah), the practice of the patriarchs building altars and making sacrifices to God (Genesis 12-38), and the peculiar link between the skins of the sacrificial animals and the priests in Israel's sanctuary (e.g. Leviticus 7.8).

Association with Sacrificial Animals as Substitutes for Human Lives

Genesis 3.21 implies the divine declaration in Genesis 9.4-7 that 'for your own lifeblood I will surely require a reckoning: from every animal I will require it' which is connected with the idea that, being created in the image of God, human beings must not have their blood shed and lose their life by the hand of another human being (9.6). Since humans have transgressed God's law and deserve death (2.17) – although the life of humans must not be taken because they are created in the image of God (9.6) – the blood of animals shall be shed as a 'demand' (*darash*) for man's transgression (9.5), thus fulfilling the law that man will die as a consequence of sin (2.17).

Atonement and the Ordination of the Priests

The expression in Genesis 3.21 fits the ordination of the priests. Aaron and his sons shall 'cover their naked flesh' so that they may 'serve God as priests', in order not to incur 'guilt on themselves and die' (Exodus 28.40-43).

In order to continue living, the humans need help to deal with their guilt and the fact that they are under a death sentence. God's confirmation of their role as priestly mediators in 3.21 is part of a dual investiture, namely the clothing with leaves (by themselves, in order to cover their shame and fear) and the clothing with tunics of skin (by God, in order to mediate and atone for their guilt). The nakedness of fallen man is, by God's *corrective* action, covered by a substitutionary death.

In a very subtle manner, man's clothing with leaves and God's clothing with skins indicate a connection with Cain's sacrifice (*minkhah*) of *fruit* as opposed to Abel's sacrifice of the *first born of his flock*. That the author of Genesis intentionally links chapter 3 with chapter 4 is already clear from the striking verbal parallels between 3.16c-d and 4.7.

The theological significance of God clothing man and woman with skins would then be that he covers their nakedness, shame, disobedience and guilt with skins that derive from the shedding of blood and of the life of a (sacrificial) animal, thus anticipating the manner in which sinful man after the Fall will need to worship God (confirmed by the episode of Cain and Abel), and alluding to the covenants with Noah, Abraham, Isaac, and Jacob, and the people of Israel, and the final, perfect covenant with all believers in Jesus Christ.

Association with Israel and the Church as 'a Kingdom of Priests'

This line of thought suggests a connection between the hints regarding man and woman as priestly mediators in Eden and God's later declaration that the whole nation of Israel – upon being freed from slavery in Egypt – is to be 'a kingdom of priests' and a 'holy people' (Exodus 19.6; Leviticus 11.44-45; Numbers 15.40-41; Isaiah 61.6). This priesthood involves all Israel, men and women, and functions as God's way of dealing with the fallen created world. It is later on fulfilled and improved in the priesthood of all believers in new Israel which has Christ as High Priest.

The joint priesthood of man and woman established at Creation (Genesis 1-2) and confirmed in Eden after the Fall (3.21) is fulfilled according to the book of Revelation: (a) in the service to God by the church on earth (Revelation 1.6); (b) in the ministry of Christ (Revelation 5.9-10); and (c) in the new heaven and earth (Revelation 5.10; 20.6).[93] The passages in Revelation 5.10 and 20.6 explicitly resume the theme of man and woman as *priests* and *rulers* of the earth in Genesis 1-3. They do so, on the one hand, in the context of an emphatic reference to the sacrifice and blood of Christ which fulfils God's promise of salvation by 'the seed of the woman' (Genesis 3.15), and, on the other hand, in the context of the priestly mediation instituted in Eden for men and women which continues in humanity through Cain and Abel, and later on by Noah (Genesis 3.20; 4.1-7; 8.20-9.17), and by Israel and the church (Revelation 5.9-10; 20.6).

Summary

Superficially, Genesis 3.21 expresses God's protection of the man and the woman against the consequences of their sin. At a deeper level of meaning, in view of the Old Testament priestly terminology, the

---

[93] Cf. B. Wiklander, 'The Mission of God and the Faithfulness of His People', 2009, pp. 284-285.

content of the Pentateuch as a whole, the immediate context in Genesis 1.1-4.7, and the wider biblical context of the mission of God, the act of clothing with tunics of skin may have a wide variety of meanings:

It alludes to a *priestly investiture* of man and woman (cf. Exodus 28-29; Leviticus 7.9), which is then *followed* by Cain's and Abel's sacrifices showing that human sin can only be managed by a substitutionary death of an animal (Genesis 4.1-7). It is *confirmed* by Noah on behalf of all humanity after the Flood (Genesis 9.1-7). It *prefigures* the mediating ministry of the male priests in the Israelite sanctuary (e.g. Exodus 28-29; Leviticus 8-9) and *explains* the basis for God's election of all men and women in Israel as a kingdom of 'priests' (Exodus 19.5-6) and for Christ's calling his believers to be his 'priests' in God's great mission to save the world (I Peter 2.4-10; Revelation 1.5-6; 5.9-10; 20.6).

God's clothing of man and woman in garments of skin serves as a special outward sign of the new reality after the Fall that their priestly duty of mediation (cf. 'the image of God') now also includes mediation *for themselves* and that their presence with God requires the sacrificed blood of offering animals that will vicariously die in their place. This is however expressed in very terse language, and the fuller meaning emerges only when the passage is related to other significant parts of Genesis, the Pentateuch, and the Bible as a whole.

6.5.3 Patriarchy

In the biblical story line, following the expulsion of the humans from the Garden of Eden, patriarchy makes its appearance as a form of family organisation. Humans of the male gender take charge in family life, which has consequences in the tribal organisation of public life, in villages and cities. This characterises the life of the nations. It impacts the social setting also of ancient Israel and continues in the Jewish and Graeco-Roman milieu of Jesus and early Christianity.

However, the relation of patriarchy to the people of God is not straightforward and the Bible witnesses to clear attempts to subdue its influence, especially by returning to God's own ideal of male and female equality in the Garden of Eden.

In the present section, we will consider the phenomenon of patriarchy as it first emerges in the biblical setting. Later on, we will see how it influences the institutions of ancient Israel[94] and the view of man and woman in the New Testament.[95]

Genesis: Patriarchy Corrupts God's Ideal of Human Equality

According to the Bible, patriarchy arises in the context of human corruption. Genesis 4-11 records fallen mankind's futile attempts to serve God after the expulsion from Eden. The few who remain faithful, such as Abel, Seth, Enoch, and Noah, bring no lasting success to God's mission.

The humans multiply,[96] but their wickedness and pride continue even after the new beginning caused by the Flood (9.18-29). They act contrary to the Creator's charge to fill the earth by refusing to be (*horizontally*) 'scattered over the face of the whole earth' (11.4), and instead they build a tower that (*vertically*) reaches to the heavens, attempting again to transcend the border between human and divine that led to the Fall (Genesis 3) and the Flood (Genesis 6-9). In order to accomplish his mission, God interferes by confusing their language, which scatters them over the face of the earth (11.8-9). With this event, the history of the world of nations begins (10.32), and, at this point, God calls Abraham and promises to make a great *nation* of his seed (12.1-3), thus fulfilling the promise of salvation through 'the woman's seed' in 3.15.

The role of the woman changes drastically in the context of human corruption. In God's ideal world (Genesis 1-2), she shares with her

---

[94] See 7.3 and 7.4 below.
[95] See 9.5 below.
[96] Note the genealogies in Genesis 4.1-5.32; 9.18-10.32; 11.10-32.

husband a royal-priestly function in the service of God. Both are created in his image and God commissions and blesses them both. The creation of the woman is the climax in the expanded creation story in chapter 2. Her equality and unity with the man are underlined in many ways, as we have seen above, and she is his equal partner. Quite the opposite of a patriarchal family shines through in Genesis 2.24. In the *future* existence of the man (husband) and the woman (wife), the man 'leaves his father and mother and clings to his wife'. This has a 'matriarchal' ring about it, but serves to highlight that in Eden, with God, *there was no patriarchy, only equality*.

A similar lack of concern with ranking is evident even when Genesis turns to God's punishment of the man and the woman after the Fall. We have seen above (6.5.1) that Genesis 3.16-19 is not concerned with headship/submission or a hierarchic ranking of man and woman, but with the survival of the humans and with the practicalities of life in an existence that has turned painful and hard. God clothes both with animal skins, symbolising the need for atonement and their calling to serve as priests to God, offering sacrifices for themselves, their family and whatever wider social entity they are part of (see 6.5.2 above).

However, the primeval story of Genesis 4-11 is silent concerning Eve and the women following her, except for a few references in passing to wives and mothers. All actors and movers are males. This expresses a *patriarchal* perversion of God's original plan. Two examples may illustrate this.

Firstly, in the genealogy of Adam (Genesis 5.1b-5), the repeated phrase 'and he died' occurs in each refrain. This repeated phrase underlines the gap between man's past existence in Eden and his present existence on the cursed ground ending with his death (cf. 5.29). The Creator's blessing is active in the procreation of man, but the 'likeness' of God in which God had created man and woman (the 'image' is not mentioned in 5.1) is now merely Adam's 'likeness' and 'image' in his son Seth (5.3). The representative *function* of man and woman together, i.e. God's delegated power to exercise dominion over the world, has become reduced to a genetical *status* of representing *the father*. Eve, the wife and mother, is left out, although she was also created in the image of God and was her husband's equal in Eden. This *patriarchal* corruption of God's ideal is then applied in the line of new generations.

Secondly, while Adam's genealogy mentions 'sons and daughters', not a single woman is *named* in Genesis 4-11. Eve was honoured in Eden by being named as 'the mother of all who live' (3.20), but now the generations are simply named after the father. The same feature characterises the genealogy in Genesis 10.1-32.

Thus, the ideal of equality and cooperative interdependence that applies to man and woman in Genesis 1-3 disappears in fallen man's history in chapters 4-11. This disappearance is not explained, and the patriarchal concept of the family structure is not directly commanded or instituted by God in the Bible.[97] The responsibility and duty of care for the wife that God had assigned to the husband (3.16) is turned into male self-seeking and abusive dominance (4.19-24; 6.1-4, 5, 11-12).

Only with the story of Terah and Abram in 12.27-32 do we encounter wives by name together with their husbands, which restores the focus on family relationships and descendants of men and women serving God.

Patriarchy in the Old Testament Tribal Organisation

As Terah's family appears on the scene in Genesis 11.27-32, they are semi-nomads becoming a settled people.[98] Based on what is known from the Old Testament and from the conditions of life among Arab Bedouins, the unit of society in the desert 'must be

---

[97] For some New Testament passages relating to the motif of headship, see section 9.5 below.
[98] R. de Vaux, *Ancient Israel*, 1973, p. 4.

compact enough to remain mobile, yet strong enough to ensure its own safety; this unit is the tribe'.[99] The tribal organisation originated in order for families to survive in a dangerous and arid environment. The tribe has an internal organisation which is founded on *blood-ties*. The *bet 'ab* is the 'family', which consisted of the father, his wife or wives and their unmarried children but also their married sons with their wives and children, and the servants.[100] Several families constituted a clan, the *mishpakhah*. Each clan was ruled by the heads of families, the *zekenim*, 'elders', and in time of war it provided a contingent commanded by a *sar*, 'chief'.

Both men and women could lead such a group of tribal contingents, as we see in the story of Deborah (Judges 4), where the Canaanite army commander Sisera is said to be 'handed over by the Lord to a woman' (4.9). The tribal system did not prevent women from taking leadership, which is a sign that the patriarchal model was not the only model followed by tribes (see below).

After the settlement in Canaan, the tribal organisation begins to give way to the clans led by 'elders' as the central element.[101] The village now stands for the clan, but the 'elders' retain their leadership role by virtue of the institution of the patriarchal concept that assigns to the firstborn son the right to represent the father and carry his authority.

The authority and sanctity of *the firstborn male* is a heritage from Israel's early, nomadic or semi-nomadic existence and is widely attested in the Old Testament and the ancient Near East.[102] The ideas associated with the firstborn have been summarised as follows:

> The emphasis on ancestry, family and inheritance among the Hebrews gave a special distinction to the firstborn son. As the first strength of the father, he

---
[99] Ibid.
[100] Ibid., pp. 7-8.
[101] R. de Vaux, *Ancient Israel*, 1973, pp. 12-13
[102] See V. H. Kooy, 'First-Born', *IDB*, vol. 2, pp. 270-271.

> became the next head of the family (or clan or tribe), and embodied the soul and character of the social group, becoming responsible for its continuance and welfare. As such he acted with a certain authority, felt a greater responsibility [...] and received a preferential treatment.[103]

Thus the socially accepted leadership system in ancient Israel was based on the patriarchal blood-ties within the family and the concept of the firstborn male. The firstborn became an 'elder' representing the clan and was confirmed in his rights by the father's laying on of hands (Genesis 27.1-4, 35-37; 48). Thus a form of 'ordination' was included, but the ordinand was determined not by choice but inheritance.

The patriarchal model of leadership in ancient Israel is not a model to be followed today in the Christian church. It belongs to Israel's historical setting and is no longer binding. However, it influenced the patterns of leadership in ancient Israel (see 7.3 below).

Patriarchy the Dominant but Not the Only Family Pattern

Humans in the ancient Near East developed different kinds of family patterns, although patriarchy seems to have become more predominant during the Israelite monarchy, judging from the texts of the Old Testament.

The Bible gives evidence of other models of family organisation. One is *fratriarchy*, where the eldest brother is the head. This is also found among the Hittites, Hurrites, Assyrians, and Elamites.[104] One biblical example of this family pattern is the 'levirate' marriage.[105]

Another model is *matriarchy*, where the lineage is traced through the mother and the rights of inheritance are passed on through her line. The mother serves as the head. This form of family structure

---

[103] Ibid., p. 271.
[104] R. de Vaux, *Ancient Israel*, 1973, p. 19.
[105] See Deuteronomy 25.5-10; cf. Genesis 38; Ruth 2-4. Cf. the survey in ibid., pp. 37-38.

remains in the world today. In the Bible we have only a few hints at matriarchy, although it should be noted that there are scholars who attribute a larger influence to it.[106]

Patriarchy is the dominant family pattern in the Old Testament writings.[107] The father is the head and descent follows his line. He is the family authority who blesses his firstborn son by the imposition of hands and appoints him to succeed him. It has been suggested that the generally accepted understanding of patriarchy in ancient Mediterranean and Near Eastern culture has to do with a certain view of the male 'seed'. This view has been summarised as follows:

> We might characterise the patriarchal period as symbolled by kinship ties, a sacred or holy kinship group chosen by God and consisting of the patriarch and 'his seed'. The first-century author Seneca tells us what the ancients believed 'the seed' to be: 'In the semen there is contained the entire record of the man to be, and the not-yet born infant has the laws governing a beard and grey hair. The features of the entire body and its successive phases are there, in a tiny and hidden form.'[108] In antiquity, 'seed', which only males have, is much like the Russian nesting dolls or Chinese boxes, each containing the whole of forthcoming posterity. The patriarch heads his family, with worship centred in the kin group and with norms governing social interaction deriving from family custom.[109]

This detailed concept of the 'seed' is not explicitly referred to in the Old Testament, but, assuming that some such idea existed in ancient

---

[106] See Genesis 2.25; 24.67; 28.2-5; Ruth 1.8; Judges 14; Song of Solomon 3.4. Cf. ibid., pp. 19-20.

[107] C. L. Meyers has questioned the use of 'patriarchy' for Israel in the Iron Age (c. 1200-550 BC), considering it to be an anachronism. Instead, as a more accurate term, she uses 'heterarchy' which allows for multiple but different ranking systems in any given society: id., *Rediscovering Eve: Ancient Israelite Women in Context*, 2013; id., '"Eves" of Everyday Ancient Israel', 2014, pp. 50-54, 66-68.

[108] Seneca, *Natural Questions*, vol. 1, book 3, 1971, 29:3.

[109] B. J. Malina, *The New Testament World*, 2001, p. 147.

Israel's social setting, it would explain the use of biblical language when 'Abraham's seed' is seen as the carrier of a future people along the patrilineal descent by God's covenant with Abraham.[110]

In the Bible, patriarchy was normal in a pastoral society where the family kept flocks of animals and was mobile like nomads or semi-nomads. This is reflected in the stories about Terah, Abraham, Isaac, and Jacob/Israel (Genesis 12-50). Later on, Israel would take up a more settled life and this created tensions with the old customs. The family was no longer self-sufficient. The standards of material welfare became more important and the production units more central. The authority of the family head became more limited. Women took responsibility for specific production units in the agricultural society and exercised independence (see e.g. Proverbs 31.10-31). Legal decisions were taken by the elders in the village community, with appeals to the king being permitted. Thus, individualism gradually impacted not only the family patterns and the authority of the head of the family but also religion (Deuteronomy 24.16; II Kings 14.6; Jeremiah 31.29-30; Ezekiel 14.12-20; 18.10-20).[111]

God's Tolerance of Patriarchy

The Old Testament gives the impression that the patriarchal concept of the family structure in ancient Israel was tolerated by God. When God called Abraham, confirmed his promises to Isaac and Jacob/Israel, delivered Israel from slavery in Egypt and brought them to Canaan, he called people who were already living as families and tribes who eventually constituted the people of Israel. The patriarchal structure helped Israel to exist as a people in their setting and was a form of organisation that was widely accepted in the ancient Near East.

Thus, a conclusion that is near at hand is that, at the time of ancient Israel, patriarchy was not a hindrance but practically useful to God's mission. God's plan was to fulfil his promise of salvation by

---
[110] See, for example, Genesis 12.7; 13.15-16; 15.13; 17.7; 21.12; 22.18; 28.13-14; cf. 5.3.
[111] R. de Vaux, *Ancient Israel*, 1973, pp. 22-23.

'the woman's seed' (Genesis 3.15) through his promise to Abraham that his descendants would be multiplied and that 'in his seed' all nations would be blessed (12.1-3). The focus in God's mission at this stage is obviously on preserving a *seed line* leading to the formation of a *people* in whom God would reveal his glory for the benefit of the fallen world. Thus, even in a patriarchal family setting, husband and wife could provide the 'seed' that would achieve the mission of God to the world through Israel (Genesis 3.15; 12.1-3).

Divine accommodations to human social conventions abound in the Old Testament legal texts as well as in their practical application in stories and prophecies, for example, in the areas of death penalty, slavery, covenant-making, polygamy, bride price, divorce, levirate marriages, and kingship. The difference between the New Testament and the Old Testament ethical principles in these areas tells us among other things that, since Christ reveals God's true will on these practices, their acceptance in the Old Testament was temporary and a sign of God's accommodation to Israel's culture.

Slavery was temporarily accepted, but in principle rejected (see 9.5.7 below). Christ and the early church accepted only the monogamous marriage, while the Old Testament had all sorts of marriage and divorce rules (Matthew 19.2-9; Deuteronomy 24.1-4; see 7.4.2 below). God even accepted that the twelve tribes came from Jacob's four wives, but the original ideal was one wife (Genesis 2; Matthew 19.2-9). In I Samuel 8.4-22 the people desire a king against the will of the Lord; but their desire is nevertheless granted and already in Deuteronomy 17.14-20 Moses instructed Israel about what to do when they instituted a king over them. Even when God makes a covenant with Israel, certain features in the culturally acknowledged ways of making an agreement by oath were used.[112]

---

[112] See G. E. Mendenhall, 'Covenant', *IDB*, vol. 1, pp. 714-723.

God's Will and Mission Overrule Patriarchy

Many examples exist of clear *moderations* of patriarchy in order to protect the rights of women. For example, in the Old Testament legislation for Israel, several laws intended to protect the rights of women against male abuse (see e.g. Exodus 21.7-11; Deuteronomy 15.12-15; 21.10-14; 22.13-19; 24.1-4).

It is also evident that the patterns of patriarchy were *not always followed* in the Bible. Thus, God asks Abraham to deviate from patriarchal rules by leaving his father's house and settling down in the Promised Land (Genesis 12.1). The blessing that belonged to the firstborn would at times be re-directed to the second born, either by deceit (Jacob and Esau; Genesis 27) or by the patriarch's personal preference (Manasseh and Ephraim; Genesis 48). Among the twelve tribes of Israel, the tribal ancestor Judah was not firstborn but the fact that, by God's will, he would become the ancestor of David and the Messiah gave him prominence over his brothers: his father Jacob blessed him with the words 'your father's sons will bow down to you' (Genesis 49.8). Similarly, Levi was not firstborn, but as ancestor of Moses and Aaron, his tribe received the favoured position of belonging to God *in the place of the firstborn* of each Israelite family. All these deviations from established customs are accepted by God as a means of carrying out his mission through Israel for humanity.

Another set of examples of great importance in the present study is where women would at times replace men in positions of leadership that patriarchy would reserve for males. *Gender would not bar women from leadership*, if their abilities and God's power was with them. We will come back to some striking examples below.

In his teaching, Jesus often referred to how things were at the beginning and instructs his disciples to live according to God's original plan, and not according to the way in which sinful humanity has distorted life (e.g. Matthew 19.3-9). Thus, in the new Israel, in Christ, the human institution of patriarchy is ideally *transcended* –

which we see by the way in which Christ relates to women[113] and passages such as Galatians 3:28. However, patriarchy still lingers in the New Testament church as a practical challenge for evangelism. The church needed internal order and the respect of outsiders as it began to share the gospel within societies where patriarchy was still predominant.[114] In all cultural contexts of mission – even in a patriarchal environment – wise decisions are required concerning what is appropriate, decent and honourable behaviour within the church family and in its relationship with the surrounding world.[115]

The fact that the Bible records many instances when the patriarchal rule was moderated, or put aside, or supplemented by other rules, or even transcended by returning to the ideal at the creation of man and woman, indicates that patriarchy is not commanded by God in the Bible and is no absolute rule for Christians. *God's will and mission overrules patriarchy.*

Women in Leadership despite Patriarchy

The existence of patriarchy does not rule out the possibility that in ancient Israel women may have had 'considerable agency' in household life and that women's groups and institutions had 'their own hierarchies'.[116] In the society of ancient Israel as a whole, there were other inequalities that barred even men from various kinds of leadership roles. 'Servants, slaves and people of other ethnicities held inferior positions in ancient Israel and men who were not of the priestly tribe were excluded from the national priesthood'.[117]

The life situation in which the Old Testament texts were formed and into which they spoke was not the same as a contemporary western-style society today. 'More than 90 percent of the ancient Israelite population was agrarian throughout the Iron Age down to

---

[113] See V. Norskov Olsen, *The New Relatedness for Man and Woman in Christ*, 1993, pp. 85-103.
[114] Ibid., pp. 63-82.
[115] Ibid., pp. 107-120.
[116] C. L. Meyers, '"Eves" of Everyday Ancient Israel', 2014, p. 66.
[117] Ibid.

the sixth century B.C. [i.e. ca. 1200-550 B.C.]. In other words, most Israelites were farmers, not the urban elites, royal servitors, military personnel, priestly establishment and other small groups that figure so prominently in the Hebrew Bible. Instead, they were "peasant farmers", small-scale independent agrarians who produced mainly for their own needs and not for sale or profit.'[118]

This meant that the household was managed by a sharing of duties between husbands and wives; women often formed social networks that had significant impact on community life; and religion was very much a household religion where women had prominent roles.[119] These and other circumstances suggest that we need to be cautious in literally applying to our times what the Bible says concerning the roles of men and women in ancient Israel.

In the Bible, women take leadership in situations (a) when Israel is in transition and the woman has blood-ties with a strong leader (Miriam); (b) where there is some small-scale cultivation and no strong central organisation (Deborah); and (c) where the spirit of God equips the woman with wisdom in a city setting where individualism has become acceptable (Huldah). The Bible shows that *God does not engineer human cultures, but he accepts them as part of the life out of which he calls individuals to take part in his mission.*

The Bible incorporates various cultural elements in its texts, elements that originated with man and undergo constant change. We must therefore be cautious when we apply literal readings of biblical texts to modern situations. The underlying principle needs to be identified, since many of our societies today are not at all patriarchal, and patriarchal preferences are not commissioned to the servants of Christ.

---

[118] Ibid., pp. 54, 66.
[119] Ibid.. p. 66.

CHAPTER 7
The Mission of Israel

The mission of God proceeds after Genesis 3 by 'seed line' characters who are followed from generation to generation in Genesis 4-11. It begins with Seth (second generation) followed by Enoch (seventh), Noah (tenth), and Abram (twentieth). When Abram appears on the scene, the mission theme returns to being focused and specific.[1]

7.1 *The Election of Israel*

The stories of the tower of Babel (Genesis 11.1-9) and Abram's calling (12.1-3) suggest that Abram's destiny 'will be to reverse the effects of God's judgment on Babel'.[2] The earth turned into a world of nations in Genesis 10-11, but the nations were dispersed, could not communicate, and were estranged from their Creator. Abram's descendants will now draw the nations together under the one true God. This theme is central in the Bible as a whole.[3]

The Calling of Abraham within the Mission of God

God's call of *Abram* ('high father'), his promises and change of Abram's name into *Abraham* ('father of many'), and the election of Israel is the second special focus of the theme of the mission of God in the Bible. At this stage, God's mission will be to extend to the world

---

[1] J. Barna, 'Towards a Biblical-Systematic Theology of Ordination', 2014, p. 102.
[2] L. Turner, *Genesis*, 2000, p. 63.
[3] This is convincingly demonstrated in C. J. H. Wright, *The Mission of God: Unlocking the Bible's Grand Narrative*, 2006.

the 'blessing' given to Abraham and Israel,[4] which is an echo of the creation ideal,[5] and is also reflected in the genealogies in Genesis 5 and 11.10-32, in the table of nations in Genesis 10, and in the blessing of Noah and his sons in Genesis 9.1.[6]

Israel's function is the same as that of Abraham and the first humans. It operates on a global scale as a nation that is to 'unmask the lies of the serpent about God, tell the true story of God, share God's presence and extend his good rule to other nations.'[7] Much later in the history of Israel, through the prophet Isaiah, God defines Israel as a nation set as 'a light to the nations' (Isaiah 42.6; 49.6). Through his prophet, he will call them 'priests of the Lord' and name them 'ministers of our God' (Isaiah 61.6). Even the nations will become 'priests and Levites' of the Lord and 'declare his glory among the nations' (Isaiah 66.18-21). This summarises the purpose of God's mission through Israel.

The Key Passage in God's Mission through Israel

In order to understand commissioning-ordination of servants-ministers in Israel, the passage in Exodus 19.1-6 is theologically significant. The people of Israel are to be 'a royal priesthood' and to function as 'royals' and 'priests', just as man and woman were commissioned at Creation.[8] No gender distinction is expressed in God's declaration of all Israel being 'a kingdom of priests'. If such a distinction would have had any significance, it would have been stated.

The story of the election of Israel in Genesis–Exodus ends with instructions for building a sanctuary where God will dwell and Israel will meet him.[9] The seven-fold account of the construction of the

---

[4] Genesis 12.1-3; 15; 17.
[5] Genesis. 1.28; 2.18, 23.
[6] Cf. D. J. A. Clines, *The Theme of the Pentateuch,* 1984, pp. 66-69.
[7] J. Barna, 'Towards a Biblical-Systematic Theology of Ordination', 2014, pp. 102-103.
[8] Ibid., p. 103.
[9] Ibid.

sanctuary in Exodus imitates the seven-fold creation account in 1.1-2.4a,[10] as if it intends to say that God is now making a new attempt to live with his people. Thus, Exodus 25.8 forms the climax of this thematic context: 'And let them make me a sanctuary; that I may dwell among them.' This is repeated for emphasis in Exodus 29.45-46, in connection with the commissioning and consecration of the Aaronic priests in the sanctuary:

> And I will dwell among the children of Israel, and will be their God. And they shall know that I am the Lord their God, that brought them forth out of the land of Egypt, that I may dwell among them: I am the Lord their God.

Israel can now know God at close range and they are to share his presence and good rule. This was God's mission goal in the creation and the blueprint of the Garden of Eden. Israel is now the centre from where God's grace and good rule will spread to the whole world.

Theologically, this context frames all that Israel will do, including the cultic commission of the priestly descendants of Aaron and the Levites.[11] As priests and servants, they will function within the context of all Israel being 'royals' and 'priests'.[12]

The special function of priests and Levites within Israel is to enable the people to carry out God's mission in the world *by ritually mediating God's holy presence among them*. However, the commissioning of priests

---

[10] For the analogy between creation and sanctuary, see 6.3 above; for the parallel hints showing that the arrangement of the Garden of Eden resembled the sanctuary in Israel, see 6.4 above.

[11] Exodus 28.1-29.46, Numbers 8.5-26; 27.12-23 and Deuteronomy 34.9. The duties of the Levitical priesthood included: the teaching of the Law (Leviticus 10.11); offering sacrifices (Leviticus 9); maintaining the Tabernacle and the Temple (Numbers 18.3); officiating in the Holy Place (Exodus 30.7-10); inspecting ceremonially unclean persons (Leviticus 13 and 14); they arbitrated in disputes (Deuteronomy 17.8-13); they functioned as tithe collectors (Numbers 18.21, 26; Hebrews 7:5).

[12] J. Barna, 'Towards a Biblical-Systematic Theology of Ordination', 2014, p.103.

and Levites is *limited* to the sanctuary context and is *subordinated* to the primary *divine* ordination of all Israel, men and women, as God's 'kingdom of priests' in the context of his world-wide mission.

It is in this context that all God's provisions for Israel – not just the cultic ones – need to be understood. Thus, the laws (moral, social and health), the formal organisation, the leadership structure, the sacrificial system, the priestly order and its functions, the religious festivals and the sanctuary functions are all meant to teach Israel to be God's 'royals' and 'priests' to keep them faithful to his mission. *God's mission is the higher aim and positions of leadership and commissioning for such office are fully subject to that.*

All that God provides for Israel is meant to equip them for their specific task of sharing God's presence and his good rule to the whole earth. None of the institutions of Israel, including the Levitical priesthood, have any purpose in themselves, but 'they must all be seen in the light of their larger purpose, as defined by Exodus 19'.[13] Thus, as a tool for God's mission, commissioning-ordination is introduced in Israel *in view of its practical efficiency in that mission and in a specific historical setting*. It is not carried out in one standardised way but shows *significant variations*, as we will see below. All this means that it is inherently open to adaptations to *the needs of God's mission to the world*.

God's Mission Supersedes Human Gender and Hierarchy

The Levitical and Aaronic priesthood is often singled out as the necessary context for priests in the Bible. From the perspective of God's mission, however, making God's presence and his good rule known was not primarily dependent on them, but on *all Israel*. God's call to carry out his mission is to a *people* that represents *a complete humanity* (men and women) *created* by him. The temporary role of Israel's priests and Levites is to enable the people as a whole to carry out God's mission as 'a holy nation'.[14]

---

[13] Ibid.
[14] Cf. ibid., p. 104.

The ceremonial purification and commissioning to the priesthood[15] did not make the priests and Levites more prominent than God's people as a 'royal priesthood'. The people were commissioned and ceremonially purified at Sinai as his 'royal priests' (Exodus 19). The purpose of this act was the mission of God in the world, for which God gave all Israel responsibility. God's direct appointment of Israel as his kingdom of priests *confirms them as his special servants-ministers for the purpose of the salvation of the nations and the eradication of evil.*[16]

In order for all Israel to become a priesthood in God's service, acknowledgment of God's call and descent from Abraham was sufficient. The divine declarations and events in Exodus 19 confirm that God is the God of the people he has chosen to save the world. *God's purpose in his mission to the world defines and gives ordination its significance.*

7.2 Ordination in the Old Testament

For the sake of convenience and clarity, the general concept of 'ordination' will be replaced here with the following terminological distinctions: *commissioning* is God's designation and call to an individual or a group to serve him; *consecration* is the specific ritual for the purification of the Aaronic priests and Levites serving in the sanctuary; *ordination* is an individual's or a group's laying on of hands as a recognition of God's designation; *appointment* is a king's or a leader's assignment of responsibility to a servant.

Commissioning by God happens all the time in the Old Testament, while *consecration* and *ordination* happen only in a few specific situations on God's instruction through Moses. Consecration, ordination, and appointment are always linked to an institutional setting where someone is installed in a position of trust.

---

[15] See 7.2.2 below.
[16] This was Ellen White's clear understanding of ministry and ordination (see chapter 4 above; for a more detailed exposition of this point, see TED-TOSCR, 2013, sections 4.6.2, especially 4.6.2.4).

Terminologically, the Old Testament uses a wide range of common words for commissioning, ordination and appointment. The general technical term is Hebrew *paqad* which is an international word rooted in royal administration but is used of God's commissioning (e.g. Jeremiah 1.10), royal appointments (e.g. Genesis 39.4-5; 41.34; II Kings 25.22) and consecrations to the priesthood (e.g. Numbers 1.50; 3.10).

The technical term for appointing or consecrating a priest is *mille' yad*, 'fill the hand of', which has an uncertain etymology and origin, but possibly refers to the giving of part of the sacrificial offerings to the priests themselves.

The rite of the imposition of hands is referred to by various expressions, primarily *samak yadim 'al*, which presupposes a leaning on with some pressure, and is also used for laying hands on the sacrificial animals or a blasphemer before he is executed. Other expressions are *sim, shit*, or *natan yadim 'al*, which are common terms for 'put' or 'give'.

Considering the usage of Hebrew *paqad*, 'appoint', the one who appoints is always a person of authority, a king, Moses, or even the Lord. The practice of ordaining somebody *by decision of an authoritative individual* was generally accepted in antiquity and is commonly termed *Designation*.[17] The designation may be *confirmed* by a congregation, but this is merely a formal, public act. Thus, the consecration, ordination or appointment in the Old Testament is very often built on the understanding that God has made his 'designation' of his servant, and the congregation merely confirms this divine decision.

---

[17] See E. Ferguson, 'Selection and Installation to Office in Roman, Greek, Jewish and Christian Antiquity', 1974, pp. 273-284, note especially pp. 274-275.

7.2.1 Assistants of Moses – Judges and Elders

As God leads Israel out of Egypt and forms a covenant community with them, institutions and offices are regularised. Moses appoints assistants, both judges and elders (Exodus 18; Numbers 11.16-17, 24-25). These are all male, based on the patriarchal custom of the firstborn male being the head of the clan or tribe. No ordination is mentioned here, but God alone performs the act of placing Moses' spirit on the seventy elders, which reflects a 'charismatic-prophetic' commissioning. However, Miriam takes part in the leadership of the people,[18] proving that female gender is not an obstacle to leadership or headship over men. Thus, blood ties within the Levitical-Mosaic family overruled female gender as a condition for leadership in Israel.

7.2.2 The Consecration of Priests and Levites

Priests and Levites were consecrated for the sanctuary service (Exodus 29; Leviticus 8; Numbers 8.5-22). The rituals remove impurity and consecrate men for service in the sacred area of the sanctuary. The exclusive male gender for this role is rooted in Israel's tradition of the firstborn male, and by the peculiar Israelite concept of the sacrificial blood with purifying power as opposed to the impure menstrual blood of women.[19]

Only the Levites received the imposition of hands of the people at their ordination. This is because, by ordination, the Levites were made the people's *representatives* as they replaced the firstborn among the people as God's special possession. They were chosen by God to replace the firstborn pledged to God at the exodus from Egypt (Exodus 13). The Lord later recognised the loyalty of the tribe of Levi during the incident of the golden calf at Sinai (Exodus 32.26) and therefore entrusted to them the services of the sanctuary, which originally were

---

[18] Exodus 15.20; Numbers 12.4-8; Micah 6.4.
[19] This is explored in connection with patriarchy in 6.5.3 above and, more specifically, in 7.3 below.

to be in the hands of the firstborn sons of Israel (Exodus 13.1, 11-16; Numbers 3.5-9, 11-13, 38-51; 8.14-20). God took the Levites from among the people of Israel to be his own special possession (Numbers 3.12-13, 41, 45; 8.14, 16; 18.6).

Thus, *the imposition of hands was not a standard feature in priestly ordination* but in the unique case of the Levites it was used in order to *duplicate* or make a *substitute* for somebody else. The ordination of the Levites is not repeated through history, but only the ritual cleansing before assuming office. The Levites did not ordain new Levites. The office was theirs by birth and inheritance, but a ceremony was needed to consecrate them for their special duty in the sanctuary. The high priests (successors of Moses and Aaron) would have ritually *purified* the Levites (see e.g. Numbers 8.6-7, 15, 21-22), thus separating them from the people (8.12-14, 21), but they did not ordain them.

As pointed out by Jacques Doukhan, 'no reason is given for the selection of Aaron as the founder of a hereditary priesthood, but the "house of Aaron" was identified as the only legitimate priestly line (I Chronicles 6.49-52; Ezra 7.1-3)'.[20] Later on, the Aaronic priesthood was connected to the tribe of Levi (Numbers 18.2, 4).

The purpose of consecrating Aaron and his sons as priests for ministry in the sanctuary had two aspects. Firstly, the *immediate* purpose was ritually to enable God to live among his people and for his people to meet him *in the sanctuary* (Exodus 29.44-46 – note how the wording is reflected in Revelation 21.1-5). Thus, God's original plan to rule the creation together with man by having communion with him is now implemented in Israel – note that God's purpose behind the exodus from Egypt was to meet and be worshipped by his people.[21] Since Israel was part of fallen humanity, however, atonement was necessary to enable such communion (Genesis 3.21).[22]

---

[20] J. Doukhan, 'Women Priests in Israel: A Case for their Absence', 1998, p. 30.
[21] Exodus 25.8; cf. 3.18; 7.16; 8.1, 20; 9.1, 13; 10.3, 24-26; 12.31.
[22] See also 6.5.2 above.

Secondly, having ritually enabled God to have communion with his people, the priestly ministry was *ultimately* to enable Israel to serve him *in the world* by making known that 'he is God'. God is now enthroned among his people as King of the world, and, as a nation and a people, they are his royal priesthood *in the world* (Exodus 19).

Thus, the priestly consecration in Israel was meant only indirectly to 'commission ministers' for working outside the sanctuary or for doing ministry in the world among believers and non-believers. The selection of candidates was based on *hereditary* criteria, i.e. being a descendant of the tribe of Levi and the family of Aaron, and the induction to office was characterised by the need to achieve *ritual purity* for the sanctuary service. Nowhere is the imposition of hands applied to the priests themselves in Exodus 29 and Leviticus 8, and the congregation does not make them priests.

The Function of Blood as a Means of Ritual Purification

The role of the blood of the offering animals in the consecration ritual in Exodus 29 and Leviticus 8 deserves attention. Three times, Aaron and his sons must lay their hands on the bull and each of the two rams, obviously *transferring* their own ritual impurities to the animals which are then slaughtered. The blood of the sacrificial animal is then used to ritually *purify* the horns of the altar (by touching), the base of the altar (by pouring), and around the altar (by sprinkling) (Exodus 29.12, 16, 20). The blood is also put on Aaron and his sons, 'on the tip of the right ear of Aaron and on the tip of the right ears of his sons, on the thumb of their right hand and on the big toe of their right foot' and some of the blood that is on the altar and some of the anointing oil is to be 'sprinkled on Aaron and on his vestments, on his sons and on the vestments of his sons with him'. Thus, he and his garments shall be 'consecrated' (29.20-21).

Consequently, the priestly function in the sanctuary was closely connected with the handling of blood at the altar for ritual purification. This may be relevant for understanding the absence of female priests in Israel, although there is no biblical text that states it. The woman's menstrual blood was considered impure and the danger of confusing it with the purifying blood of the sacrificial animal may explain why there were no female priests in Israel. However, there were also other important reasons for excluding women from conducting the ritual sanctuary service (see 7.3 below).

The facts gathered in this section provide clear evidence that using the priestly consecration or the ordination of the Levites in Israel as models for Christian ordination of ministers of the gospel leads into all sorts of contradictions and complications. These rites are bound to a specific function in historic Israel and do not apply to the mission and ministry of Christ. The priests and Levites were commissioned by God but the office was inherited and the selection was based on ancient traditions of the firstborn and certain concepts of the symbolic role of blood. There is no support in the New Testament for maintaining any of these offices in the Christian church, or the rituals accompanying them. Nowhere is a Christian leader given the title of 'priest' in the New Testament. Only Christ is the High Priest and his followers are (collectively) 'priests in his service'.

7.2.3 The Commissioning of Joshua

Moses inducts Joshua into the role of being his successor upon God's command and instructions, but this is a unique act for a unique office which is not repeated (Numbers 27.15-23; Deuteronomy 34.9). The imposition of hands is a key ingredient in the ceremony. By this act, Moses symbolically imparts to Joshua some of his 'authority, honour' (*hod*) or 'spirit of wisdom'.

It is not clearly stated in the text if (a) the imposition of the hand of Moses automatically conveys this 'honour/wisdom', or (b) if it is merely a symbolic act that demonstrates Joshua's endorsement by Moses, or (c) if the transfer of Moses' 'honour/wisdom' is God's work (since Moses acts in compliance with God's commands).

It is clear, however, that Joshua is selected by God, because he already has the 'spirit'. This is therefore a clear example of 'designation' as defined above. It is also clear that Moses is seen as a unique spiritual leader, because he is the only man who had talked to God face to face.[23] Thus, Joshua's ordination by Moses is non-repeatable, and it was not followed by any recorded acts of successive ordination.

Joshua already has 'the spirit' (*ruakh*, Numbers 27.18) – and that is why he is commissioned by God – which means that the imposition of hands *follows* the recognition of Joshua's qualification of having the spirit (27.18, 23). The 'spirit' is not defined in Numbers 27.15-23, but it is explained as a 'spirit of wisdom' in Deuteronomy 34.9, which is fully in harmony with the general usage of 'spirit' (*ruakh*), as we will see below.

Prayer is not mentioned as part of the act of ordination. This circumstance was noted by the Jewish scribes who did not include prayer in their ordination practice.[24] In the New Testament, however, it seems that prayer may have been an important part of inductions into tasks and offices (see Acts 6.1-6; cf. 13.3; 14.23).[25]

The Hebrew expression for 'laying on of hand' (27.18, 23) is *samak yad 'al* (note the singular form here). The verb *samak* is used in the Old Testament in the case of consecration and offering, but it is used here in Joshua's ordination, as well as when the people placed their hands on the Levites. However, there are other terms too: *sim* and *shit* are used with the sense 'place, put' in normal blessings and acts of healing (see 9.4.1 below). While the latter terms are characterised by a light touch, *samak* refers to a heavy touch as in 'lean upon'.

When *samak* is used, the person transfers 'something' (depending on the event) to another person or a sacrificial animal who or which then became his substitute or representative. Study is given to this in

---

[23] Numbers 12.6; Deuteronomy 18.5, 18; 34.10.
[24] See TED-TOSCR, 2013, section 3.4.
[25] E. Ferguson, 'Jewish and Christian Ordination: Some Observations', 1963, p. 15.

more detail in 9.4 below, but it should be noted that the ordination of Joshua clearly marks that he had the 'spirit' *before* the ceremony and that the imposition of Moses' hand serves primarily to convey Moses' authority. Deuteronomy 34.9 may describe the imposition of Moses' hands in a way that suggests a transfer of his 'spirit of wisdom', but the passage can be read in different ways and describes a unique event which is taking place on God's command and under his supervision and co-involvement.

Keeping in mind the symbolic meaning of 'hand' and its association with 'power, authority, honour, majesty' (see 9.4 below), God's instruction to Moses to 'give [Joshua] some of your authority (*hod*) so the whole Israelite community will obey him' (Numbers 27.20) is an act accomplished by the imposition of Moses' hand on Joshua. The purpose is to ensure that the people respect and obey Joshua (cf. Deuteronomy 34.9). In order for them to do so, some of Moses' 'authority' is visually and publicly conveyed to Joshua by Moses' hand being laid on him. It is tempting to consider this act as one that is rooted in the old patriarchal custom of the father conveying his authority and blessing to the firstborn son.

7.2.4 *The Concept of the Spirit in Leaders*

The 'spirit' (*ruakh*) is involved in God's commissioning of the seventy elders (Numbers 11.16-17, 24-25) and Moses' ordination of Joshua (Numbers 27.15-23; Deuteronomy 34.9). There is some fluidity in the referential meaning of *ruakh*: 'power, ability, knowledge, wisdom'.[26] It either comes explicitly and directly from God (prophetic and charismatic concept), or it is conveyed by God in connection with or following the ritual of the laying on of hands, but nothing is stated that leads us to understand it as a magical rite that controls or automatically conveys the 'spirit of God'.

---

[26] See the more detailed study in TED-TOSCR, 2013, section 3.2.2.

However, there is also the idea of the 'spirit' in or upon the outstanding and unique leader Moses. His leadership and authority is of such a nature that his role is non-repeatable in that he had talked to God face to face (Numbers 12.6; Deuteronomy 18.5, 18; 34.10). His spirit is somehow *transferred* to his assistants (elders) and his successor Joshua. The transferring act occurs in two ways:

1. In the story of the appointment of the seventy elders, God takes some of the 'spirit' of Moses and transfers it to the elders – Moses only deals with the selection of the individuals. This implies a charismatic-prophetic concept of commissioning and ordination. God acts himself without a confirming human ordination.

2. In Moses' appointment and induction of Joshua, reference is made to Moses' 'power, authority, ability' or 'spirit of wisdom' which is transferred by Moses to Joshua by the imposition of his hand. On this occasion, God does the selection and instructs Moses on how to proceed. Joshua already has the 'spirit' when he is selected for his task; the imposition of Moses' hand *confirms* the spirit in Joshua and visibly *symbolises* the granting of God's blessing and wisdom, which he had bestowed on Moses. Its purpose is to impress the witnessing community, so that they will respect Joshua as a leader with Moses' authority.

7.2.5 Conclusions

Strictly speaking, ordination in the Old Testament involves the commissioning of the seventy elders, the Levites, and Joshua's appointment as Moses' successor:

1. The *appointment* of the seventy elders expresses a *charismatic* rather than a ritualistic understanding of induction in leadership. God is the only agent and no imposition of hands is involved.

2. The *consecration* of the priests and the Levites applies a *ritualistic and sacramental* concept. No laying on of hands is mentioned in

connection with the priests. The Levitical *ordination* includes the idea that the leaning of the congregation's hands on the candidates (*samak yadim 'al*), without prayer, is a symbolic way of expressing the creation of a *substitute* – the Levites replaced the firstborn and represented the Israelites. Although the Levites may have had other duties, too, such as teaching and administration, the ordination focuses primarily on their ritual purity for serving in the sanctuary.

Attempts to exclude women as priests in the history of the Christian church have often been rooted in sacramental interests and attempts to strengthen the authority and status of leaders. Such attempts have drawn on the priestly and Levitical installations, which is evident in the patristic material (especially Irenaeus)[27] and in parts of the contemporary discussion.[28] Our review here shows, however, that the sacramental mode of ordaining the priests in Israel cannot be a reliable foundation for Christian ordination.

3. In Joshua's *ordination* by Moses, a *civil* and *priestly-political* concept is applied. Joshua is ordained by Moses, who is asked to transfer some of his 'authority and honour' to Joshua by the leaning of his hand on him (no prayer). This is based on Moses' unique role as the only man who had talked to God face to face. Joshua's duty is to be a civil, military and spiritual leader as Moses is taken away and the people are to enter Canaan. This ordination is therefore not repeated in the Old Testament. It is a unique event and is conditioned by Moses' special status and Israel's decisive challenge on the other side of the Jordan River.

Thus, *no consistent ceremony of ordination is found in the Old Testament*. With the imposition of hands it occurs only in the two *unique* cases of the Levites and Joshua. Since these two ordinations aim at creating a *substitute* (Levites replacing the firstborn Israelites

---

[27] See M. Warkentin, *Ordination*, 1982, p. 39. See also TED-TOSCR, 2013, section 4.1.4.

[28] E.g. T. B. Dozeman, *Holiness and Ministry: A Biblical Theology of Ordination*, 2008, pp. 35-103.

and Joshua as a substitute for Moses), no prayer is involved. The creation of a substitute is a conferral of personal qualities or some authority by a personal decision and is not a spiritual event which requires blessing. However, in the few examples of ordination in the New Testament that exist, prayer is included (Acts 6.1-6; 13.1-3). Besides the fact that no Old Testament ordinations are explicitly mentioned in the New Testament, these observations give grounds for concluding that Old Testament ordination is not applicable in the Christian church. This was also the view of James and Ellen White (see chapter 2 above).

7.3 *The Absence of Female Priests*

The present section is included because it is argued by opponents to women's ordination that 'The office within Israel most illustrative for our understanding of ordination is that of the priesthood [...] the priest represents the closest parallel to the leadership offices of the New Testament church'.[29]

At the outset, however, we should bear in mind that the priestly office was hereditary and permitted exclusively for male descendants of Aaron and the Levites.[30] This hereditary institution is *replaced* in the New Testament by Christ as High Priest in the heavenly sanctuary – instead, priesthood becomes a Christian ministry based on God's commission and his spiritual gifts. The Old Testament priesthood also *disappeared* with the destruction of the Jerusalem Temple in 70 AD. Therefore, the issue of whether or not women served as priests in Israel is indeed *irrelevant* in the discussion of women's ordination in the Christian church. Nevertheless, the case for women's ordination in the church will benefit from a review of the plausible reasons for women being excluded from the ceremonial priesthood in Israel, which seems to be a unique feature among the peoples in the ancient Near East.

---

[29] As expressed by position #1 in GC-TOSCR, 2014, pp. 44-45.
[30] See 7.2.2 above.

The Priestly Duties

There were three kinds of 'priestly' duties in Israel (Deuteronomy 33.8-10).[31] In each of them the priest functioned as a *mediator* (cf. Hebrews 5.1).[32] He mediated God's *will*, God's *word*, and sacrificial and ritual *atonement* for sins:

1. Didactic and administrative functions were carried out by priests and Levites in daily civil life. They participated in the courts as judges (Deuteronomy 17.9; 21.5; cf. 19.17) and functioned as teachers of the law (Deuteronomy 33.10; cf. Malachi 2.6-7; Jeremiah 18.18).

2. Prophetic functions gave knowledge of God's will, the future, and wise counsel. The mediums included the Urim and Thummim (Numbers 27.21; Deuteronomy 33.8), dreams, and various prophetic revelations (Deuteronomy 18.15-22; 33.8-10; I Samuel 28.6). Moses was a prophet (Deuteronomy 18.15) and some prophets were linked to priestly families (e.g. Jeremiah 1.1), or received their call in the temple (Isaiah 6), or were deeply involved with the sanctuary (Ezekiel 40-48). After David's reign, the Urim and Thummim disappear and the kings seek counsel from prophets, including the prophetess Huldah (II Kings 22.14; Jeremiah 21.1-2).

3. Cultic functions included ministering in the sanctuary, dealing with ritual impurity, illnesses, and atonement for sin. Central in this function was the performance of sacrificial offerings and various rites connected with them (Leviticus 1-16).

Women were allowed to perform the first two of the above-mentioned functions of the priest, namely administration and prophecy, as we see by the examples of Miriam, Deborah, and Huldah. Israel allowed women to hold offices of leadership such as judge (Judges 4.4-5.31) or queen (I Kings 11.3), and female sages

---

[31] J. Doukhan, 'Women Priests in Israel', 1998, p. 32; J. Pedersen, *Israel: Its Life and Culture*, Parts 3-4, 1963, pp. 157-164; R. de Vaux, *Ancient Israel*, 1973, pp. 349-356.

[32] Cf. R. de Vaux, *Ancient Israel*, 1973, p. 357. Cf. TED-TOSCR, 2013, section 3.2.5.

forming a special social class.[33] In a divine revelation the prophet Joel does not hesitate to speak of women 'prophesying' (Joel 2.28), which is the same outcome as when God ordained the seventy elders in Numbers 11.16-17, 24-25. Women were explicitly allowed to serve as Nazirites based on a vow and with full consecration to the Lord (Numbers 6.2) and there were rules suggesting an accommodation of the Nazirite to the priesthood.[34]

Women could perform some ritual functions. They participated in the sacrificial meals (Numbers 18.8-19; Deuteronomy 12.12; 14.22-29: 15.19-23; 16.9-15; I Samuel 1.4), religious gatherings (Nehemiah 8.2, 13; 12.43) and were physically present at the ceremony of sacrifice (I Samuel 2.19). They also ministered at the entrance to the tabernacle (Exodus 38.8; I Samuel 2.22) and served as singers in the temple (Nehemiah 7.67; Ezra 2.65; Psalm 68.24-25).[35]

Women's Absence from Ritual Functions in the Sanctuary
However, the ritual acts of slaughtering the sacrificial animals and serving at the altar by administering the blood of the victims were *not performed by women*, and 'it was perhaps the only religious domain that was denied to women, a prohibition which seems to have been peculiar to Israel'.[36]

No explicit reason is given for this circumstance in the Bible, but various possibilities have been considered, for example, (a) women's ritual impurity due to the blood flow connected with the menstrual cycle and childbirths made it inappropriate for them to handle the use of blood (cf. our observation on this in 7.2.2 above), but it should be noted that men could also be excluded from the sanctuary services, because of 'impure' discharges; (b) the need to avert pagan influences from priestesses who were involved in sacred marriage and temple prostitution among the surrounding peoples; (c) the old patriarchal

---

[33] See TED-TOSCR, 2013, section 3.1.2.3.
[34] Ibid.
[35] J. Doukhan, 'Women Priests in Israel', 1998, p. 33.
[36] Ibid.

tradition of the firstborn male of the family and clan, being the elder and having a priestly role which was transferred to the priesthood of the sanctuary; and (d) reverence for the woman's role of giving life, which did not lend itself to the function of slaughtering animals and handling offerings. These and similar circumstances have been analysed in depth elsewhere.[37] Here, I wish to highlight one of them in particular.

Going back to the origins of Israel, the concept of the 'seed' is essential (Genesis 3.15; 12.1-3). Belonging by blood-ties to Abraham's descendants was a condition for being part of Israel. This puts the focus on how the *people* of Israel were organised as Abraham's offspring. Through Jacob-Israel's 'seed', twelve *tribes* emerge and develop into sets of *clans* and *families*. In the patriarchal form of family,[38] the father is the head and descent follows his line. He is the family authority who blesses his firstborn son by the imposition of his hands and appoints him to succeed him. This act is a confirmation of a hereditary right, but was at times changed by the preference of the patriarch.[39]

We noted above that the emphasis on ancestry, family and inheritance among the Hebrews gave a special authority and sanctity to the firstborn son.[40] 'As the first strength of the father, he became the next head of the family (or clan or tribe), and embodied the soul and character of the social group, becoming responsible for its continuance and welfare.'[41] Thus, public acts of worship on behalf of the family or clan, especially sacrifice, were performed by the male head of the family who was a firstborn male (Genesis 22; 31.54; 46).[42] This

---

[37] TED-TOSCR 2013, section 3.2.5.
[38] See 6.5.3 above.
[39] As in the cases of Isaac (Genesis 17.19-21), Ephraim (Genesis 48.13-18), and Solomon (I Kings 1.32-37). However, the law prohibited this (Deuteronomy 21.15-17).
[40] Ibid.
[41] V. H. Kooy, 'First-Born', *IDB*, vol. 2, p. 271.
[42] R. de Vaux, *Ancient Ilsrael*, 1973, p. 345.

custom had roots in Israel's nomadic or semi-nomadic origins. It was not originally commanded by God, but rather taken for granted,[43] and was regulated in the covenant laws.[44] After the Passover at the exodus from Egypt, every firstborn male was consecrated to God[45] and was to be redeemed by a ransom payment.[46] This was later modified by the dedication of the tribe of Levi to special service for God in place of the firstborn male.[47]

Thus, the decision to commission a family (that turned into a clan) within the tribe of Levi (i.e. Aaron and his sons) to function as priests meant that *males* automatically assumed the role as priests. The same consequence would follow the decision to commission the Levites for service as subordinate servants in the sanctuary. They were commissioned by God as his priestly servants and *replaced* the first male offspring of every Israelite woman (Numbers 3.12-13; cf. 3.14-39). Thus, the Levites in particular, by replacing the firstborn, had to be males, and the gender of a woman from within the tribe of Levi would bar her from the Levitical role of replacing a firstborn male.

Belonging to the tribe of Levi, however, Miriam illustrates the ability of women to perform administrative and leadership tasks, as well as leading through prophecy and wisdom (see 7.4 below).

Levi was the priestly tribe which did not receive an allotment of the land of Canaan. The priests and Levites therefore lived spread out in all the lands of the other tribes, which made their living dependent on the right to own their land by a deed of purchase, not by the original 'covenantal' distribution of land under Joshua which was then kept according to laws of heredity. However, the patriarchal laws at the time prevented women from making deeds and owning land. With the exception of Zelophehad's daughters' request for land (applicable

---

[43] See e.g. Genesis 10.15; 22.21; 27.1-3, 35-37; 43.33; 49.3; Exodus 6.14.
[44] Deuteronomy 21.15-17.
[45] Exodus 13.2, 12; Numbers 3.13.
[46] Exodus 13.13, 15; Numbers 18.15-16.
[47] Numbers 3.12, 45; cf. 7.2.2 above.

when a father died without sons), only widows and divorced women in Israel were allowed to own land (Numbers 27.1-11; 36.1-12). However, widows and divorced women were considered as ritually 'defiled', which is indicated by the rule that a priest could not marry any of them since he was sanctified by his office and they were not (Leviticus 21.7, 13-14; Ezra 44.22). This, too, barred women from the ritual and cultic functions of the priesthood in the sanctuary.

Thus, a complex system of patriarchal rules current at the time and rooted in ancient Near Eastern culture made it practically impossible for a woman to serve in the office of a ceremonial priest with cultic functions in Israel. However, women could perform many other tasks handled by the Israelite priests, as is demonstrated in 7.4 below.

Conclusion

The absence of female priests in Israel is irrelevant as an argument against women's ordination for the Christian gospel ministry today. The requirements for the ordination of priests and Levites would not be fulfilled even by male ministers in the Seventh-day Adventist Church today. The absence of female priests is linked to the election of Israel as a people in a specific historical and cultural setting. The office of priest no longer exists today in the faith community of Israel and is absent in the New Testament, where the Old Testament priesthood is abolished in Christ and has been replaced by a 'better' ministry.

7.4 *Women as Servants of God*

The mission of God implies that God is the sovereign Creator and Ruler of the universe. The Bible as a whole presents him as one who appoints and commissions whom he wants, man or woman, as his 'servant' or *minister* (Latin for 'servant').

In Israel, God's *direct calling* of his servants has priority as the mode of appointment. There is a *charismatic-prophetic* current in the leadership appointments throughout Israel's history. This continues even when God adapts to Israel's culture and channels his calling through an institutional system, be it the sanctuary or the kingdom. Although the institutions involve certain rites of commissioning-ordination performed by humans, it is always implied that they act on God's command.

The divine pattern for man-woman relationships in Eden remains a consistent thread throughout the Old Testament.[48] Even if wives submitted to the expected social patterns of patriarchy in the home – patterns that were reflected in the wording of the laws that regulated public life – this 'does not bar women from positions of influence, leadership, and authority over men in the covenant community'.[49]

7.4.1 Women in the Priestly Kingdom and Holy Nation

After the miraculous exodus from Egypt, it is through his servant-people that God's mission will be carried out. Not only is Moses called 'God's servant',[50] but Israel as a nation receives the epithet of 'God's servant'.[51]

We have seen in 7.1 above that the calling of Israel as God's servant receives particular attention in Exodus 19.4-6. God declares that Israel is to be 'for me a kingdom of priests [*mamleket kohanim*] and a holy nation'. The emphatic *for me* implies service to God, to whom the whole earth belongs.

This service means two things: (a) on behalf of God, functioning as his servants in the world, Israel as a whole, men and women, are to *mediate* God's rule ('kingdom') and presence ('holiness') as 'priests

---
[48] As pointed out in R. M. Davidson, 'Headship, Submission, and Equality in Scripture', 1998, p. 270.
[49] Ibid.
[50] The designation of Moses as 'God's servant' is very common ; see, for example, Exodus 4.10; 14.31; Numbers 11.11; 12.7-8; Deuteronomy 3.24; 34.5; Joshua 1.1-2, 7, 13, 15; 8.33. Also Caleb (Numbers 14.24) and Joshua (Joshua 5.14) are designated as God's servants or ministers.
[51] Leviticus 25.42, 55.

for God' in the world of nations; and (b) in God's eyes, Israel as a whole, men and women, will be his 'treasured possession out of all the peoples' provided that they 'obey his voice and keep his covenant'. Thus, given the formal condition of belonging by blood ties to the people of Israel, *obedience to the word of God and the covenant rather than gender* is the explicit condition for being a priest in God's service.

Consequently, God's commissioning of Israel in Exodus 19-20 makes no difference between men and women. They are all priests and servants of God in a holy nation. This principle is confirmed by the prophet Isaiah who described the restored Israel by saying 'you shall be called priests of the Lord, you shall be named servants of our God' (Isaiah 61.6).

In the description of the Sinai event in Exodus 19 reference is made to a special class of 'priests' (Exodus 19.22, 24). We have seen in 7.3 above why women were not included in the body of priests serving in the sanctuary. The point in Exodus 19, however, is that *before God* these men who handled the blood of Israel's sacrifices have the same status as the people. *Gender matters in the human culture, not before God.*

We noted in 7.1 above, that God's definition of all men and women in Israel as priests is rooted in *a dual concept of priesthood*. Both are *mediating* ministries. The primary one, denoted by 'a kingdom of priests', is related to God's *witnessing* mission to the world. As priests, men and women of Israel are to proclaim God's glory to neighbours, immigrants, and the nations. They do so primarily in their worship of him (privately and in the temple), by teaching and prophecy, by living according to his will and by the organisation of the whole society (revealed in his word), thus *mediating* God's glory in Israel to the world.

The secondary one, 'a holy nation', concerned the *ritual-sacramental* life of Israel near the holiness of God in the sanctuary. It required a ritual concept of priesthood, namely a priesthood that *mediated* God's personal presence by managing the distance between the people's ritual impurity and God's holiness.

Both men and women are included in the *witnessing* priesthood of proclaiming God's royal glory to other people and to the nations, while only men were involved in the *ritual-sacramental* priesthood that maintained ritual purity and atonement for sin.

In view of this important distinction, we understand why the general priesthood in the New Testament church – i.e. the role of testifying to the nations of the glory of God – is *the only priesthood that remains* in Christ and the mission of the church. The Old Testament ritual-sacramental priesthood has disappeared with the sacrifice of Christ, his resurrection, and his role as high priest of the new Israel. In Christ, God has become present with his people in a new way that does not require ritual mediation but only a faith that expresses itself through love. And this new way opens the door for women as priestly servants to God in the church.

This is what Peter is talking about in I Peter 2.9 as he addresses men and women in the church: 'You are a chosen race, a royal priesthood, a holy nation, God's own people, *in order that you may proclaim the mighty acts of him who called you out of darkness into his marvellous light*'. The old ritual priesthood, which did not allow women to serve in the covenant with Israel, is now gone. In the new priesthood women and men *continue* to proclaim the glory of God, as they had done already in ancient Israel. But they now perform their witnessing and leadership as servants of Christ.

7.4.2 Husband-Wife Relationships

Husband and wife are servants of God in the marriage relationship according to the Creator's instructions.[52] The ideal remains from Eden, of complementarity, partnership, equality, and mutual love and

---

[52] See Genesis 2.4-25; 3.16; cf. 6.4 and 6.5.1 above.

respect. Even after the Fall, the wife is attracted to her husband and he is her provider of food, clothing, and love.

However, in the world of fallen human beings, God's marriage ideal is overtaken by various family patterns invented by humans. In the ancient Near East, patriarchy is the dominant social model. We noted above that patriarchy is not instituted by God but arises in the course of the corruption of fallen humanity.[53]

The patriarchal view of marriage was shared among the peoples of the ancient Near East. For example, in the stories of Abraham and Sarah, and of Isaac and Rebekah, as they relate to Pharaoh in Egypt and King Abimelech of Gerar,[54] the marriage values are not peculiar to Abraham's clan but shared with other nations. The crime of taking already-married Sarah as wife consists in the foreign king violating Abraham's right of possession of his wife Sarah, which poses a threat to the pure blood-line and name of Abraham's offspring. This patriarchal view of marriage aims at the protection of the pure kinship by blood ties, preserving the priority of the seed of the father. For the same reason, portions of the Mosaic law included severe punishments for violations of women who had been betrothed or married to another man.[55]

However, in Israel, the abuse of male headship in marriage became limited because it was contrary to God's will. It would not befit a people that was 'a kingdom of priests and a holy nation'. The spirit of several laws is to protect the woman in line with God's words of assurance in Genesis 3.16c-d. For example, the prohibition in Deuteronomy 24.1-4 against a certain kind of remarriage shows how the rights of the woman were protected from male desire for selfish financial gain.[56]

---

[53] See 6.5.3 above.
[54] Genesis 12.10-20; 20; 26.1-11.
[55] Numbers 5.11-31; 30.3-16; Deuteronomy 22.22-30.
[56] See TED-TOSCR, 2013, section 3.1.2.2.

Male headship in marriage was not an absolute rule. It could be dispensed with if a principle of higher dignity became involved. Exodus 21.2-6 shows that the headship of a slave in marriage was subordinated to the headship of the owner of the wife of the slave. If a slave was 'lord of a woman', i.e. married, when he came to serve his master, she will go with him after six years when he is free. However, if the slave's master gives him a wife and she bears him sons and daughters, the woman and her children shall belong to her 'master' and only the male slave goes free. If the slave then says that he loves his master, his wife and children, agreeing to give up his freedom, he can do so but remains a slave for life. *Thus, the headship of a married man over his wife was overruled by a law of ownership.*

In Exodus 21.7-11, another law regulating marriage stipulates that if a man buys a woman and takes her as wife, and if she then 'does not please her master who designated her for himself', he is to let her be redeemed and has no right to sell her to foreigners. If he then marries another woman, he must not deprive the first one of her 'food, clothing and marital rights'. If he does not provide her with these things she is to go free without any payment of money. This law stipulates a responsibility for the husband of caring for the wife by providing food, clothing and marital rights, which is a condition for his role as husband (cf. Ephesians 5.28-29). This is implied in God's words to the woman in Genesis 3.16d, that her husband will 'be responsible for her', 'be in charge of her', and 'care for her'. Thus, a husband had primarily an *obligation* to care for his wife, and this duty overruled his legal property rights.

In Exodus 21.22-25, a law stipulates that if someone inflicts an injury on a pregnant wife so that she gives birth prematurely, her husband determines the price for the damage done. Headship involves here both possession of the mother and her child and the legal right to require restitution. This role also includes protection of the rights and well-being of the wife.

The male headship in marriage within Israel has been summarised as follows: 'There is little question that in ancient Israel (and throughout the ancient Near East) a patriarchal structuring of society was the norm, and the husband/father was the titular head of the ancient family. In marital/familiar situations, the husband/father assumed legal responsibility for the household. His leadership and legal headship are evidenced in such concerns as genealogy, family inheritance and ownership of property, contracting marriages for the children, initiating divorce, and overall responsibility in speaking for his family.'[57]

However, this headship principle does not override the basic equality between the marriage partners, nor does it condone a husband's oppression, domination, or authoritative control over the wife. If such things are mentioned in the Bible, it is never with approval. The divine egalitarian ideal from the Garden of Eden is still attainable and praised. In a major work on the institutions of ancient Israel it is stated:

> The law condemned the faults of children against their mother as much as offences against their father (Ex. 21:17; Lev. 20:9; Deut. 21:18-21. 27:16), and the Decalogue (Ex. 20:12) commanded equal honour to be given to father and mother (cf. Lev. 19:3). The Wisdom books insist on the respect due to one's mother (Prov. 19:26; 20:20; 23:22; 30:17). And those rare passages which give us a glimpse into the intimacy of family life show that an Israelite wife was loved and listened to by her husband, and treated by him as an equal: Samuel's mother, for example (1 Sam. 1:4-8, 22-23), and the woman of Shunem (2 Kings 4:8-24). [...] And there is no doubt that this was the normal picture. It was a faithful reflection of the teaching enshrined in Genesis, where God is said to have created woman as

---

[57] R. M. Davidson, 'Headship, Submission, and Equality in Scripture', 1998, p. 270.

a helpmate for man, to whom he was to cling (Gen. 2:18, 24); and the last chapter of Proverbs sings the praises of a good housewife, blessed by her children, and the pride of her husband (Prov. 31:10-31).[58]

The considerable independence and initiative by Hannah, the mother of Samuel, will be considered in 7.4.6 below. Her vow and offering to perform her vow 'is without parallel in the Bible',[59] and her song is recorded as part of the word of God in the Bible (I Samuel 2.1-10). Deborah is another married woman who has co-authored the Bible (see 7.4.3 below).

Richard Davidson presents an impressive view of the wife in Song of Songs, which he rightly defines as 'the most extensive and penetrating Old Testament presentation of the divine ideal for husband-wife relationships in the post-Fall setting'.[60] He draws attention to the keynote of 'the egalitarianism of mutual love' in Song of Songs 2.16, namely: 'My beloved is mine and I am his.' The life of man and woman in mutual harmony after the Fall follows the divine norm of the husband as the protective provider given in Genesis 3.16c-d (see Song of Songs 2.3).[61] The divine ideal in Genesis 3.16c-d is balanced in Song of Songs 7.10: God promises the woman that 'your desire (*teshuqah*) shall be for your husband', and now, in Song of Songs, the woman says: 'I am my lover's and for me is his desire (*teshuqah*)'. Even after the Fall, the husband continues to 'cling to' his wife (Genesis 2.25).

---

[58] R. de Vaux, *Ancient Israel*, 1973, pp. 39-40.
[59] T. Dennis, *Sarah Laughed: Women's Voices in the Old Testament*, 1994, p. 132.
[60] R. M. Davidson, 'Headship, Submission, and Equality in Scripture', 1998, pp. 271-272.
[61] Davidson (ibid.) quotes the comment by Francis Landy who noted that the powerful erotic metaphor of the apple-tree 'provides nourishment and shelter, traditional male roles – the protective lover, man the provider' ('The Song of Songs and the Garden of Eden', *Journal of Biblical Literature* 98, 1979, p. 526).

Thus, the Old Testament teaches a mutuality of love in marriage based on God's words in Genesis 2:4-25 and 3.16c-d. The wife desires her husband (personally, socially, and sexually) while the husband cares for her (as the provider of bread, working the ground) and protects her. The practice of dominant headship on the part of the husband is connected with later practices of male rights of ownership of the wife, which is generated by corrupt patriarchal customs that are not implied in God's provisions for marriage after the Fall.

7.4.3 *The Judges – Men and Women*

The selection of the judges as leaders seems to have been a decision of the Lord, who raised them by his power and inspiration, i.e. we have here a type of charismatic leadership (cf. Judges 3.10). No formal ordination is involved either for men or women as judges.

Deborah was a 'prophetess' and the wife of Lappidoth, and 'was leading Israel as a judge at that time' (Judges 4.4). The term for 'lead' is *shapat*, 'act as judge'. She holds a triple role of leadership in that she is a prophetess with charismatic gifts (4.4), acts as judge and holds court so that 'the Israelites came to her to have their disputes decided' (4.5), and she leads the people in military conquest (4.6-23). In addition, she has authored the hymn of praise to God in Judges 5, which means that she had scribal education.

Deborah is important for many reasons; she demonstrates that (a) if God gave his Spirit to a woman, she was accepted for leadership, and (b) there was no reservation among Israelites at this time against having a woman as their head – obviously, like the writer of this book, they did not see Genesis 1-3 as instituting male headship and female submission.

7.4.4 *The Nazirites – Men and Women*

The law of the Nazirite in Numbers 6 opened up the opportunity for *both men and women* to take the vow 'to separate themselves to the Lord' (Numbers 6.2). Some Nazirites were significant leaders in Israel, for example, Samson and Samuel. Only a few of them are mentioned by name in the Bible.

The vow made the Nazirite bound by three provisions that became marks of his/her sanctity: (a) avoiding wine, strong drink, even grape juice and grapes, and all 'that is produced by the grapevine' (Numbers 6.3-4); (b) for the duration of the separation the hair is not to be cut (Numbers 6.5); and (c) the presence of the dead, even if they were close family, must be avoided (Numbers 6.6-7). These rules, particularly the last, placed the Nazirite 'in the same sphere of sanctity as the high priest (Leviticus 21.11), ahead of the other priests (Leviticus 21.1-10)' and suggest an accommodation of the Nazirite to the priesthood.[62]

God called both men and women to consecrate themselves as Nazirites (Numbers 6.2), and he gave them his Spirit. They are juxtaposed with 'the prophets' and have a high-priestly level of sanctity. The example of Samuel shows that a Nazirite could minister in the sanctuary doing priestly service and later function as leader, judge, and prophet in Israel. Although we have no record in the Bible of a woman fulfilling such ministry, the fact that the office was in principle open and available to women by God's command is significant.

7.4.5 *Women Proclaiming God's Word*

It is difficult to explain why Psalm 68.11 (68.12 in the Hebrew text) has been ignored in major treatments of women in the Old Testament. The passage expresses a powerful affirmation of women as proclaimers of the word of the Lord: 'The Lord gave the word; great was the company of the women who proclaimed the good news'. The participle form of Hebrew *basar*, 'proclaim good news', is in the feminine plural, which means that the translations 'company of the

---

[62] J. C. Rylaarsdam, 'Nazirite', *IDB*, vol. 3, 1962, pp. 526-527.

women' (NRSV, alternative reading) and 'the women who proclaim the good tidings' (NASB) are to be preferred.

From the context of the psalm, the content of 'God's word' is anything from praising his great power (68.1-10, 17-35) to thankfulness for his salvation (68.20, 24-26) and inviting the kingdoms of the earth to praise him as they listen to 'his mighty voice' (68.32-35). Literally, God's word is both his promise of salvation (68.22-23) and his mighty voice in the heavens (68.33). 'Here is a portrait of women preacher-evangelists – a great host of them! And there is no hint of them being in their 'proper subordinate position' under the leadership of men.'[63] This is a good example of the external proclamation of God's glory by the female priests of Israel to the world.

7.4.6 *Prophetesses and Leaders*

The Old Testament is clearly open to women being given the gift of prophecy and leadership. A few examples will be given here.

The story of the prophet Samuel builds on the extended account of his mother Hannah.[64] Her prayer and vow in I Samuel 1.10-11 introduces her leading role as a speaker and servant of God in the story. Although daughters or married women could not make legally binding vows without the consent of their father or husband (Numbers 30), in her initial prayer Hannah vows to dedicate the promised son as a Nazirite 'for all the days of his life' without apparent consultation with or dependence on her husband Elkanah. Her plan to dedicate Samuel is presented as something that she has already decided upon and she is simply informing Elkanah of this

---

[63] R. M. Davidson, 'Should Women Be Ordained as Pastors? Old Testament Considerations', 2013, p. 56.
[64] See the summary of Hannah's pivotal role in Israel's history in T. Dennis, *Sarah Laughed: Women's Voices in the Old Testament*, 1994, pp. 115-116. The relevant passages are quoted in J. A. Davidson, 'Women in Scripture', 1998, pp. 169-170.

decision (I Samuel 1.22).[65] Elkanah's permission is not requested; he merely gives his blessing (1.23). Thus Hannah takes all the initiatives in the dedication of Samuel as priest and prophet to the Lord. This is significant, since Hannah's activities 'are generally thought of as belonging to the male'.[66]

Moreover, Elkanah was a son of Levi (I Chronicles 6.25-27, 33-38) living in Ephraim (I Samuel 1.1), the country given to one of the sons of Joseph and therefore being associated with Joseph who was designed as the 'Nazirite of his brothers' in Jacob's blessing of the twelve tribes in Genesis 49.26. When Hannah eventually travelled to the house of the Lord in Shiloh with bulls, flour, and wine, she went 'expressly to perform her own vow' and 'it is she who has come with such fine offerings for sacrifice, and, remarkably, with her own child to dedicate to the service of God'.[67]

Hannah's leading role is all the more remarkable since God endorses her dedication of Samuel for 'ministry before the Lord' and the author of I Samuel accepts her action although she is a woman. The appointment and induction of Samuel as a servant of God, a priest and a prophet, has significance also in view of the law of the Nazirite in Numbers 6. Accordingly, Hannah's act was one of 'separating', 'setting apart', 'dedicating', or 'consecrating' her son to the Lord – these are meanings included in the root *nzr*.[68] Thus, in a sense, Hannah 'dedicated' or 'ordained'[69] Samuel as a Nazirite to the Lord 'for the whole of his life' (I Samuel 1.28) and committed him to 'serve before the Lord' in the temple of Shiloh under the priest Eli (2.11).

---

[65] As noted by T. Dennis (*Sarah Laughed: Women's Voices in the Old Testament*, 1994, p. 130); see also J. A. Davidson, 'Women in Scripture', 1998, p. 169.
[66] J. A. Davidson, 'Women in Scripture', 1998, p. 170.
[67] T. Dennis, *Sarah Laughed: Women's Voices in the Old Testament*, 1994, p. 132.
[68] *The SDA Bible Commentary*, vol. 1, 1978, p. 845.
[69] Thus W. L. Holladay, *A Concise Hebrew and Aramaic Lexicon of the Old Testament*, 1976, pp. 232-233.

Not only is Hannah 'the *only* woman in the Bible to utter a formal, spoken prayer, and have her prayer quoted in the text for us to read',[70] her vow and her offering to perform her own vow is without parallel in the Bible.[71] After leaving her son with the priest Eli, Hannah's song is recorded as part of the word of God in the Bible (I Samuel 2.1-10). Miriam, Deborah and Hannah have all written parts of Scripture.

We noted earlier that Deborah was a prophetess and a judge (Judges 4.4-5). There were other prophetesses in Israel. The primary example is Huldah in Jerusalem (II Kings 22.14; II Chronicles 34.22). As the law book is found in the temple in King Josiah's time c. 622 BC, the king sent some officials to 'go and inquire of the Lord for me and for the people and for all Judah about what is written in this book that has been found' (II Kings 22.11-13). They 'went to speak to the prophetess Huldah, who was the wife of Shallum, the keeper of the wardrobe' (22.14). Huldah then gives the king detailed instructions of the will of the Lord which led to a significant religious reform (22.15-20). Here is a woman 'chosen to authenticate that the scroll found in the temple was authoritative Scripture'.[72] According to II Kings 22.14, Huldah lived in Jerusalem in the *mishneh*, which most versions translate as the 'Second Quarter', but the NJPS (Jewish translation) transliterates as 'Mishneh' and the KJV translates as 'college'. 'This latter translation may actually represent the best one, inasmuch as some scholars have suggested that this term has reference to an academy perhaps even headed up by Huldah.'[73]

The practice of female prophets is not a temporary or odd feature in Israel's history. Moses' and Aaron's sister Miriam 'the prophetess' (Exodus 15.20) led the people in crafting and singing hymns of praise

---

[70] T. Dennis, *Sarah Laughed: Women's Voices in the Old Testament*, 1994, p. 124.
[71] Ibid., p. 132.
[72] R. M. Davidson, 'Should Women Be Ordained as Pastors? Old Testament Considerations', 2013, p. 58.
[73] Ibid.

after the miracle at the Red Sea. The three joint leaders of the people, Moses, Aaron and Miriam, are addressed by God personally when he rebukes Aaron and Miriam, while giving them instructions regarding the institution of prophets in Israel (Numbers 12.4-8). In the book of Micah, God speaks to his people and, referring to the exodus from Egypt and the redemption from the land of slavery, he says: 'I sent before you Moses, Aaron, and Miriam' (Micah 6.4). Miriam is even recorded among the sons of Amram (I Chronicles 6.3), which confirms her prominence as a leader.

Thus, the Old Testament indicates that a woman could 'go before' the people (i.e. Miriam), function as Israel's judge and military commander (i.e. Deborah), receive, speak and write the words of God (Miriam, Deborah and Hannah), and have the highly respected office of a prophetess by the power of the holy Spirit who would instruct even the king of Judah on what to do with a highly significant religious issue (Huldah).

Important evidence from the Elephantine papyri and Ezra-Nehemiah indicates that, after the Babylonian exile and the dissolution of the monarchy, there was a trend back towards gender parity and women in leadership on the part of the postexilic Jews.[74] Richard Davidson points out that 'Ezra-Nehemiah provides hints of such a trend of gender parity and women of prominence in the contemporaneous community of Jerusalem: the probable mention of a female scribe (Ezra 2.55; Nehemiah 7.57), a clan which appropriated the mother's and not the father's family name (Ezra 2.61; Nehemiah 7.63), female as well as male singers (Ezra 2.65; Nehemiah 7.67), descendants of a possible famed princess Shelomith (Ezra 8.10; I Chronicles 3.19),

---

[74] T. C. Eskenazi, 'Out from the Shadows: Biblical Women in the Postexilic Era', 1992, pp. 25–43. Cf. J. E. Cook, 'Women in Ezra and Nehemiah', 1999, pp. 212–216, who also points out 'egalitarian roles' (p. 216) of the women mentioned in Ezra-Nehemiah.

women as well as men who repaired the walls of the city (Nehemiah 3.12), and a woman prophetess Noadiah (Nehemiah 6.14)'.[75]

7.4.7 *The Sages – Men and Women*

Genuine wisdom is a gift of the Spirit of God to those who fear God.[76] The fundamental leadership quality is 'the Spirit of wisdom' (Genesis 41.38-39: Deuteronomy 34.9; Job 28.12-28; Isaiah 11.2).[77] The provision of wisdom from God was the special function of the sages in Israel,[78] who could even form a separate social class of leaders.[79] Besides male sages, it is obvious in the Old Testament that women also received the Spirit of wisdom from God which qualified them for leadership functions.

We read in Proverbs 14.1 that 'the wise woman builds her house, but the foolish tears it down with her own hands'. What a wise woman might be like as she builds her house is developed in the well-known praise of the woman of noble character in Proverbs 31.10-31. Among the many virtues listed here, we note her involvement in buying property and trading (31.16, 19); her activities to assist the poor and needy, which is a social responsibility (31.20); her being clothed in 'strength and dignity' (31.25); and the feature that 'she opens her mouth with wisdom' while 'the teaching of kindness is on her tongue' (31.26). This suggests that a woman's capacity to deal with social life outside the home was clearly recognised.

In the biblical texts we also notice the existence of 'wise women' who form a special class in society and who 'by their sagacity and their counsel exerted an active influence on the course of events'.[80] Striking

---

[75] R. M. Davidson, 'Should Women Be Ordained as Pastors? Old Testament Considerations', 2013, p. 59-60.
[76] See G. von Rad, *Weisheit in Israel*, 1970, pp. 75-101.
[77] S. H. Blank, 'Wisdom', *IDB*, vol. 4, p. 860.
[78] Ibid., pp. 852-861.
[79] Jeremiah 8.18; cf. 8.8-9; 10.7; 50.35-36.
[80] J. Doukhan, 'Women Priests in Israel', 1998, p. 32.

examples are found in the 'wise woman' from Tekoa (II Samuel 14.1-22) and the 'wise woman' in the city of Sheba (II Samuel 20.15-22).

During the monarchy the 'great/notable' woman of Shunem (II Kings 4.8-37; 8.1-6) is presented as a woman of wealth and self-reliance. One notices her verbal skills and competence, her initiative and self-reliance (in contrast to her husband) – 'a self-sufficiency and an authority independent of motherhood'.[81] Several interpreters have argued that in the perspective of the narrator, this great woman in some respects even overshadows the prophet Elisha with whom she interacts.[82]

7.4.8 Conclusions

In the Old Testament, there are eight major different positions of leadership according to God's ideal: priests, prophets, elders, judges, military leaders, sages, musicians/worship leaders, and preachers/proclaimers of the Word. The position related to monarchy/kingship may be omitted here – although there were queens (see 7.5 below) – inasmuch as this was not God's original plan and he warned of the dire results of choosing a king (see Deuteronomy 17.14-20; I Samuel 8-9).[83]

All eight of these positions of leadership were open to, and filled by women during some period of Old Testament history. Women were (a) priests (Eve, and all Israelite women according to God's original plan in Exodus 19), (b) prophets (Miriam, Deborah, Huldah, Noadiah), (c) elders (Deborah, and possibly some of the seventy elders), (d) judges (Deborah), (e) military leader (Deborah), (f) sages (the wise woman of Tekoa, and of Abel, and Abigail), (g) musicians

---

[81] C. V. Camp, '1 and 2 Kings', 1992, p. 107; note pp.106-108.
[82] See the multiple references to the scholarly literature in R. M. Davidson, 'Should Women Be Ordained as Pastors? Old Testament Considerations', 2013, p. 58, footnote 304.
[83] Ibid., p. 60.

(Miriam and the musicians in the time of Ezra-Nehemiah), and (h) preachers (the great host of preachers in Psalm 68.11).

7.5 The Davidic Line

After Israel's settlement in Canaan and the establishment of the kingdom of Israel, the story of King David's dynasty becomes the central focus of God's mission. When this dynasty disappears at the Babylonian exile in 587 BC, God's promises of a coming King of Davidic descent – a *Messiah* or 'Anointed One' – keeps Israel looking to the future with hope. The Davidic king constitutes a third focal point in the biblical mission of God.[84] He adds a mission through the Davidic king to his original plan with Israel.

God Adapts his Mission to Human Culture and Needs

The royal line of David and his descendants will now be the servants of the mission of God. This plan was initially not God's preference, but he acceded to the will of the people. Thus, in the same way as God accepted the human institution of patriarchy (see 6.5.3 above), he accepted the carrying out of his mission through Israel by the institution of kingship. This is not God's ideal and the prophet Samuel is strongly opposed to it, but in the end God accepts it, although he recognises that the people have 'rejected him from being king over them' (I Samuel 8.4-9). God then finds a way to turn this challenge into an advantage by calling and making a covenant with King David. This suggests again that, in pursuing his mission, *God accepts human and cultural concepts as long as they work as means of advancing his mission.*

A King of the Tribe of Judah

Although not the firstborn of the twelve sons of Jacob, the tribe of Judah has prophetically been designated in Genesis 49.9-12 for royal rule. The prophecy will be activated much later. The massive promise

---

[84] See J. Barna, 'Towards a Biblical-Systematic Theology of Ordination', 2014, pp. 104-105.

David received in II Samuel 7.3-16 changes the direction and language of God's mission theme.[85] From this time God's mission is verbalised by concepts such as 'kingdom', 'king', 'servant', 'son-father'.[86]

The Rule of King David

The theological perspective of the biblical writers from the first book of Samuel is directed towards the royal commissioning of David. 'Out of his descendants will come the decisive divine-human answer both to the particular (Gen. 3) and the general (Gen. 1) tasks of the mission of God.'[87] The coming king will be like David. In the logic of the biblical story, David's identity as king and how he rules his kingdom 'becomes the sign by which Israel will recognise the promised king, the Messiah'.[88]

It is a striking feature that God's ideal for the king is not that of a power figure. 'His kingdom champions social justice and knowledge of the Lord – but not power. The poor, the needy and the oppressed are not forgotten in his kingdom.'[89] The ultimate Davidic king must present these kingdom signs in order to verify his legitimacy.[90] And all along, through his prophets, God reminds Israel and its kings of their divine role of being 'a light to the nations' (Isaiah 42.6; 49.6).

The Descendants of David

However, the story of Davidic descendants is the story of their people being led astray. The Old Testament prophets often condemn the kings for lack of justice and righteousness (e.g. Zechariah 7.9-10). Nevertheless, 'the specific Davidic commission will not be forgotten and the Old Testament prophets will also cast a vision of a time when what was promised to David will indeed be fulfilled.' This fulfilment

---

[85] Ibid., p. 104.
[86] Ibid.
[87] Ibid.
[88] Ibid.
[89] Ibid.; see, for example Psalm 72.1-4, 12-14, Psalm 2.7-8, 12 and Psalm 89.36-7.
[90] Ibid.

171

is a concomitant fulfilment of God's plan through David, Israel and also Adam and Eve (Zechariah 6.12-13 and Jeremiah 23.5-6).[91]

The Anointed – Messiah

The king carried the title 'anointed' (Hebr. *mashiakh*, Gr. *christos*), which involved the symbol of oil for honour, blessing, and even the power of the Holy Spirit.[92] Anointing with oil was used both in civil and religious contexts in Israel, but it was a custom well attested across the ancient Near East. Both objects and persons were consecrated to cultic service by the rite of anointment.[93] Israel anointed the priests (Exodus 28.41; 29.7; Leviticus 6.13; 8.12; Numbers 3.3), the high priest (Leviticus 21.10), prophets (I Kings 19.16; Isaiah 61.1), the patriarchs referred to as 'anointed prophets' (Psalm 105.15; I Chronicles 16.22), and the king (e.g. Judges 9.15; I Samuel 10.16). The anointment of kings in Syro-Palestine is attested as early as in the Amarna Letters during the fourteenth century BC.[94]

The anointments of Saul (I Samuel 10.1), David (I Samuel 16.3), Solomon (I Kings 1.39), Jehu (II Kings 9.6), and Joash of Judah (II Kings 11.12) are reported in considerable detail, while the anointments of Absalom (II Samuel 19.10) and Jehoahaz (II Kings 23.30) are casually mentioned. Obviously, anointing belonged to the ritual of installation into the king's office, in accordance with the culturally conditioned customs in the ancient Near East. Concerning the significance of anointing, the following observation has been made:

> The anointment of the king was not merely a part of the ceremonial of enthronement; it was of decisive importance, for it conveyed the power for the exercise of royal authority. By strength of anointment, the king

---

[91] Ibid., p. 105.
[92] See Zechariah 4.1-14; Luke 4.18; Acts 10.38.
[93] For a survey, see S. Szikszai, 'Anoint', *IDB*, vol. 1, pp. 138-139.
[94] Ibid., p. 139.

became a theocratic vassal of the Lord, as texts like 1 Samuel 9:16 and 16:3 indicate.[95]

The theocratic character of the royal anointment is also exemplified by the fact that the king was the Lord's anointed (I Samuel 24.6, 10 [Hebrew 24.7, 11]; 26.16) and a vassal of God who reigned as a servant of God over his people (I Samuel 10.1; II Samuel 6.21).[96] The rite of royal anointment in ancient Israel was originally executed by a prophet (I Samuel 10.1; I Kings 1.45; 19.16; II Kings 9.6), but later on it became the exclusive privilege of the priests (I Kings 1.39; II Kings 11.12).

The kings were anointed as part of the enthronement ceremony (Judges 9.8, 15; I Samuel 9.16; 10.1; 15.1, 17). The rite symbolised the bestowal of authority which was associated with the gift of the Spirit of the Lord (I Samuel 16.13). Anointing equipped the king for the future. From the time of his anointment, he would be in need of special power and strength, and the anointment confirmed the promises of God and conveyed the king to the hands of the Lord. However, the laying on of hands was never part of the induction of a king.

Anointment with Oil as a Symbol of Receiving Power from the Holy Spirit

All through biblical times, oil was a necessity for life and considered a special gift of God. The cosmetic anointing with oil for festive occasions, joyous celebrations, and everyday cosmetics linked the practice with gladness (Deuteronomy 28.40; Ruth 3.3; Psalm 45.7 [Hebrew 45.8]). It was also used for medical treatment and healing (Isaiah 1.6; Ezekiel 16.9; Mark 6.13; Revelation 3.18), as a way of showing honour (Psalm 23.5; Amos 6.6; Luke 7.46), and as part of the sacrificial service in the sanctuary (e.g. Leviticus 2.4; see also 3.2.4). Thus, it became associated with power and with God's good will. Therefore, the metaphor of 'oil' could symbolise prosperity and

---
[95] Ibid.
[96] Ibid.

God's blessing (Job 29.6; Joel 2.24). In I Samuel 16.13 anointing with oil is associated with empowerment by the Spirit of the Lord.[97] Thus, anointing with oil is another example of how God used culturally conditioned customs to achieve his mission, but they are always local and temporal and can be changed.

Reviewing the Old Testament concept of the royal anointing with oil, its function may be understood by a comparison with Genesis 1.26-28. Both the king and the first humans were commissioned to 'rule'. Both received the authority of God (through anointing with oil or being created in the image of God). Both were 'blessed' (either through the symbol of the oil or by God's spoken words). Both were to function as servants or vassals of God to carry out his mission. Here, the royal anointing corresponds with God's blessing which includes the bestowal of power and prosperity.[98] This symbolism seems to survive as an end-time expectation after the demise of the Davidic line in the sixth century and is applied by the early Christians to Jesus Messiah.

The ritual of royal anointment confirms a special empowerment by the Spirit which is symbolically associated with oil. The coming of a royal Messiah is therefore connected with 'the Spirit of the Lord' (Isaiah 11.1-2) and, in Messianic prophecies, the concept of a 'kingdom of priests' (Exodus 19.5-6) is associated with the power of the Spirit through anointment (Isaiah 61.1-6).

We will see in connection with 'the Mission and Ministry of the Church' (chap. 9 below) how the inauguration of Jesus Christ as King is linked to being anointed in terms of the power of the Holy Spirit.

The Leadership of Queens

The kings were male, but the ancient rule of the priority of the firstborn was not always followed. However, queens and queen mothers also had significant authority in Israel and Judah, by marrying

---

[97] J. A. Thompson, 'Ointment', *IDB*, vol. 3, p. 595.
[98] C. A. Keller, '*barak*, segnen', section I-III, *THAT*, vol. 1, col. 355.

the king and being linked by blood-ties through sons and daughters or by being the king's mother.[99]

Thus the mother of King Solomon, Bathsheba, had a throne on the right hand of the king's throne (I Kings 2.19). Similarly, King Asa 'deposed' the queen mother 'from her position', because of her idolatry, but before that she had a position of authority (I Kings 14.12). The significance of these practices is that *the female gender of the queens is no hindrance from holding authority over men*. The queen's marital ties with the king *overrule any alleged impediment caused by her female gender*. Female gender does not remove a person from leadership and authority in the Old Testament.

An example of a queen who 'ruled the land' is Athaliah, the mother of Ahaziah, who ruled for six years in Judah (I Kings 11.3). She was the granddaughter of Omri king of Israel (II Kings 8.26). While she was not faithful to the Lord (like most of her male colleagues in office), she held the office as ruling queen and exercised authority, and the fact that she did so while being a woman is not negatively judged by the author of II Kings.

Other named queens in Israel are: Michal, Abigail, Maacah, Rizpah, Jezebel, Athaliah, and Nehushta.[100] It is therefore clear that the Davidic line of kings included queens. Female headship was accepted, although it was less common than a male ruler.

Although the Queen of Sheba came from a foreign land, she makes a very appropriate assessment of King Solomon's government and the blessings the people have received from the Lord through him. Her statement to Solomon has been recorded and is part of the Bible. When she praises the Lord, she acknowledges him as God and uses words that suggest inspiration by the Holy Spirit (I Kings 10.9).

---

[99] Note the concept of the 'Great Lady' in Israel: R. de Vaux, *Ancient Israel*, 1973, pp. 117-118.

[100] See the surveys in H. Lockyer, *All the Kings and Queens of the Bible*, 1961, pp. 222-246.

While Esther was queen in Persia, she belonged to God's people and her authority is nowhere disputed in the book that carries her name. She had the authority to make 'appointments' (8.2), and wrote 'with full authority to confirm the second letter concerning the Purim' (9.29). She makes 'decrees' that confirm the regulations about the Purim (9.31-32), and her actions benefit especially the people of God. Consequently, she was a woman with headship authority over many Jews in Persia. The positive view of Queen Esther and the fact that the book was included in the Old Testament canon indicates that her authority as a ruler of male individuals is not in question.

7.6 Summary

God called Abraham in order to form the people of Israel. The mission assigned to Israel is to draw the nations together under the one true God, which will extend to the world the blessing given to Abraham and Israel. Being 'a light to the nations', Israel is called to fulfil the original purpose of the creation of man and woman.

This plan is confirmed when God leads Israel out of Egypt. God will now dwell in his sanctuary and meet his people at close range. By obeying God's word and keeping the covenant with him, they will be 'a kingdom of priests and a holy nation' (Exodus 19.1-6). No gender requirement is mentioned. Israel's commissioning as God's appointed nation of royal priests confirms that men and women are servants-ministers of God for the purpose of the salvation of the nations.

This includes a dual ministry of mediation for Israel as a whole. The primary one, 'a kingdom of *priests*', is related to God's *witnessing* mission to Israelite neighbours and the nations of the world. As priests, men and women of Israel are to proclaim God's glory through their worship of him and through their life, thus *mediating* God's glory to the world. This priestly role is gender-inclusive and continues in the Christian church.

The secondary one, 'a *holy* nation', concerns the *ritual-sacramental* relationship of Israel to the holiness of God in the sanctuary. It requires a ritual concept of priesthood, namely a priesthood that *mediated* God's personal presence in Israel by ritually managing the distance between human frailties and God's holiness. This priestly role ceases to exist in Christ.

As Christ replaces the ritual priesthood, only the general priesthood remains in the New Testament – i.e. the role of testifying to the nations of the glory of God (as confirmed in I Peter 2.9). The ritual priesthood, which did not allow women to serve in the sanctuary, is now gone, but in the new priesthood in Christ women and men continue to proclaim the glory of God, as they had done already in ancient Israel.

There is no ordination of priests by the laying on of hands in Israel. The priests were merely consecrated or ritually purified for their service in the sanctuary. Only the Levites received the laying on of hands of the high priest and the people, but this was a unique ceremony conveying to the Levites the status of the firstborn among the people. The ordination of Joshua is a sacral-civil act by which Moses transfers some of his authority and gifts to Joshua by the imposition of his hand.

None of the examples of ordination in the Old Testament provide a model for the Christian church. They are all different and serve specific needs that no longer exist in the New Testament. Thus, as we will see later on, the New Testament provides no clear practice of ordination.

Women were not included in the ritual service of the priesthood. Ideas peculiar to ancient Israel made it inappropriate for women to handle the purifying nature of the sacrificial blood (since women were impure by their menstrual blood) and they could not assume the role of the firstborn male, who traditionally was the respected and sacred leader of families and clans. However, women could minister in many other priestly duties: teaching, administration, prophecy, and some ritual functions that did not involve the handling of sacrificial blood.

All eight of the positions of leadership in Israel were open to and filled by women during some period of Old Testament history: priests, prophets, elders, judges, military leaders, sages, musicians, and preachers. Some queens had power equal to the kings, and queens were regarded with great respect.

In the history of Israel, God incorporates a special role in his mission to the world through the Davidic royal line. This yields promises of a coming Messiah, a king, who will accomplish the will of God and re-establish his kingdom on earth.

As 'the anointed one', Messiah will fulfil the mission given to humanity in creation. The royal anointment confirms a special empowerment by the Spirit which is symbolically associated with oil. The coming of a royal Messiah is therefore connected with 'the Spirit of the Lord' (Isaiah 11.1-2) and, in Messianic prophecies, the concept of a 'kingdom of priests' (Exodus 19.5-6) is associated with the power of the Spirit through anointment (Isaiah 61.1-6).

This becomes significant as we turn our attention to the inauguration of Jesus Christ as King through the power of the Holy Spirit.

CHAPTER 8
The Mission of Christ

Jesus Christ brings victory to the mission of God. He is therefore the foundation of ministry and commissioning-ordination in the Christian church.

The New Testament divides the work of Christ into three phases: (a) his life, death, and the resurrection which puts him in charge of God's kingdom on earth; (b) his assumption to heaven where he ministers and maintains the benefits of his work before God, *mediating* between God and the world as High Priest; and (c) his return in glory which inaugurates the ultimate defeat of evil and death followed by the creation of a new heaven and a new earth where God will eternally dwell with humans and have communion with them.[1] The people of Christ, therefore, are a royal priesthood proclaiming the glory of God,[2] while they put all their hope on 'the grace that Jesus Christ will bring you when he is revealed' (I Peter 1.13). Christian ordination must be based on this biblical teaching.

8.1 Christ and the Kingdom of God

The New Testament presents Christ as the Son of God,[3] as one with God,[4] and revealing the fullness of God.[5] These are attributes

---
[1] Revelation 21.1-5.
[2] I Peter 2.9; Revelation 1.5-6; 5.9-10; 20.6.
[3] Matthew 3.17; 11.27.
[4] John 5.19-47; 10.30.
[5] Ephesians 3.19; Colossians 1.19; 2.9.

implied in man and woman created in the image of God, although Christ is 'more excellent' than any human being.[6] His humility and submissive faithfulness fulfil what God expects of his servants,[7] of the first human beings,[8] of Israel,[9] and of the promised Messiah of David's line.[10] Through his *atoning death*, God has reconciled man to himself,[11] and, as the embodiment of humanity, in him, humanity is brought back to God's ideal.[12] Through his *resurrection*, Christ has done away with the curse of death that came through the first humans and now 'all will be made alive in Christ'.[13]

Commissioning-Ordination Based on Christ as King and Lord

In Christ, men and women are 'a new creation'.[14] God now dwells with his people through a *person* (Christ), not in a place (Jerusalem), or a nation (Israel), or a royal line (David). God has endorsed him as his faithful servant and exalted him to be Lord of the world by raising him from the dead,[15] assuming him to his right side in heaven.[16] This means that God has assigned his kingdom on earth to Jesus Christ who serves God as the King and Lord of heaven and earth.[17] *On this basis*, he commissions his servants-ministers to carry out his mission to the world.[18] This is how Christian commissioning-ordination needs to be fundamentally understood.

---

[6] See Psalm 8.5; Hebrews 1.1-4.
[7] Genesis 15.6; Isaiah 57.15; Philippians 2.5-11.
[8] Genesis 1-3; Romans 5.12-21; I Corinthians 15.20-23, 45-49.
[9] Exodus 19.5-6.
[10] Isaiah 11.1-5.
[11] II Corinthians 5.17-19.
[12] Genesis 1-2.
[13] I Corinthians 15.20-23.
[14] II Corinthians 5.17.
[15] Philippians 2.9-11.
[16] Romans 8.34.
[17] Matthew 28.18; Luke 22.29; Acts 2.36; 10.36; I Corinthians 15.27; Philippians 2.10-11; Colossians 1.13; Hebrews 1.8; II Peter 1.11; Revelation 1.5; 11.15; 12.10. The title 'King' is less frequent in the New Testament for Jesus than the royal title 'the Anointed', i.e. 'Messiah' or 'Christ'.
[18] Matthew 28.18-20.

Ministry in the Church in Principle Gender-Inclusive

Christ restores the kingdom of God on earth as it was meant to be at the creation of the world. He assumes the royal-priestly function of man and woman who were created 'in the image of God', which we explored in 6.3 above. His *royal* function is initially expressed by the title 'Messiah' ('King') and his proclamation that 'the kingdom of God is near'. The *priestly* function is expressed by the title 'High Priest' and his installation of a new priesthood serving God. Since Christ restores the kingdom that man and woman were commissioned to rule as God's royal-priestly vice-kings at Creation, the church must permit the same gender-inclusive service-ministry for which God first appointed them (see 6.3 and 6.4 above). *According to the Bible, therefore, ministry in the church is in principle gender-inclusive.*

Christian Commissioning-Ordination Based on the Gifts of the Spirit

The royal title of 'Christ' ('Messiah' or 'Anointed') is rooted in the Old Testament. The title for Israel's king, 'the Lord's anointed',[19] was abbreviated to 'the anointed', i.e. 'the Messiah' (Hebrew) or 'Christ' (Greek), and then applied to Jesus of Nazareth (Matthew 16.16). According to the early Christian proclamation, God 'anointed Jesus of Nazareth with the Holy Spirit and with power' (Acts 10.38). His kingdom is a spiritual one among his followers (Luke 17.21), and his role as King and 'Lord' (*kyrios*) is by God's appointment. He calls his servants-ministers through the Holy Spirit,[20] and their mission is a work in the power of the Holy Spirit. Consequently, *Christian commissioning-ordination cannot be understood apart from the gifts of Spirit.*

---

[19] See e.g. I Samuel 12.3, 5; 16.6; 24.6, 10; 26.9, 11, 16, 23; II Samuel 22.51.

[20] Note Acts 20.28, where the appointment as 'overseer' (*episkopos*) in Ephesus is described as an appointment 'by the Holy Spirit'. Cf. Acts 13.1-3.

The Kingdom and its King in the Gospels

From the beginning, the theme of the kingdom and its king is emphasised in the Gospels.[21] Jesus is a descendant of David and his birth is surrounded with royal terminology (Matthew 1-2). He is described by the magi as 'the king of the Jews' (Matthew 2.2). He announces the kingdom as he begins his public ministry: 'The time is fulfilled and the kingdom of God *has drawn near*; repent and believe in the good news' (Mark 1.15) – the expression 'has drawn near' implies a significant link between 'coming' and 'being close' and actually 'being present', which is confirmed again by Jesus in John 4.23 and 5.25: 'the hour is coming and is now'.[22] The kingdom of God has come and is present in Jesus. He invites men and women to become part of it. When they do, it dwells inside them and its fruit is expressed in their life.

Israel's expectation that God is fulfilling his promises of a royal Messiah is central.[23] Nathaniel calls Jesus 'king of Israel'.[24] After the multiplication miracle the crowd wanted 'to take him and make him king'.[25] On his entry to Jerusalem he was called 'your king [who] comes to you'.[26] Before Pilate, when he was accused of being a king of the Jews, Jesus admits 'I am a king'.[27] When they crucified him they wrote above his head: 'King of the Jews'.[28] To his disciples he said that he will appear as a glorious king at his coming.[29]

---

[21] For biblical examples, see J. Barna, 'Towards a Biblical-Systematic Theology of Ordination', 2014, pp. 105-106. Barna points out that, statistically speaking, the expression 'kingdom of God' and its parallels appear almost 160 times in the New Testament, of which over 120 are found in the Gospels. In Matthew alone it appears fifty times.
[22] Ibid.
[23] Luke 1-2.
[24] John 1.49.
[25] John 6.15.
[26] Matthew 21.5, Luke 19.38, John 12.32, cf. Zechariah 9.9.
[27] John 18.37.
[28] Matthew 27.37; Mark 15.26; Luke 23.38; John 19.19-22.
[29] Matthew 25.31.

Thus, the Gospels describe Jesus as God's royal Servant who brings the promised kingdom to Israel. Reaching Israel first is vital, because Israel was called to be God's servant in the world and to Israel the promises were given. But Christ's mission goes beyond Israel – it is aiming at the whole world, according to the mission of God. This is in keeping with God's plan for the world and Israel.[30]

Christ's Servants-Ministers Reveal His Kingdom Characteristics

The men and women whom Christ calls to be his servants-ministers are expected to reveal the kingdom characteristics embodied in Christ and his teaching. Thus, 'there is a specific kingdom Christology in the Gospels, which will form the basis for the New Testament theology of the church, ministry and its ecclesiastical functions'.[31] *No ecclesiastical commissioning-ordination has any significance without it.*[32]

8.2 The Call to Become Part of the Kingdom Mission

Jesus brought the theme of God's mission to its climax. Those who hear his story according to the Gospels – within its antecedent Old Testament theme – receive a radical call to become part of his kingdom mission. This is at first a mission to Israel,[33] but already in the Gospels Jesus is moving the mission of God to the Gentiles.[34] This is in keeping with God's original call to all Israel to be a kingdom of priests and a light to the nations.[35]

Israel's Dual Priesthood Reduced to One in Christ

The definition of all men and women in Israel as a 'kingdom of priests' involves *a dual concept of priesthood.*[36] The male and female

---

[30] See chap. 6 and 7.1 above.
[31] J. Barna, 'Towards a Biblical-Systematic Theology of Ordination', 2014, pp. 105-106.
[32] The way this applies to the church is presented in chap. 9 below.
[33] See e.g. Matthew 10.5-6.
[34] Matthew 8.5-13, 28-34; 12.15-21; 15.21-28; 21.33-46; 22.1-14; and parallels.
[35] See 7.1 and 7.4.1 above.
[36] See 7.4.1 above.

kingdom-priests are to proclaim God's glory to the nations – in worship and conduct – thus they *mediate* his glory to the world. This is the task of the priesthood in Christ. It remains when the ritual priesthood implied in Exodus 19.5-6 disappears because Christ makes it insignificant. The ritual priesthood *mediated* God's holiness by purifying and atoning for the people's ritual impurity so that God might dwell among them. In Christ, God has become present with his people in *a new way* that does not require ritual mediation but only a faith that expresses itself through love. Peter hits the nail on the head when he addresses men and women in the church: 'You are a chosen race, a royal priesthood, a holy nation, God's own people, *in order that you may proclaim the mighty acts of him who called you out of darkness into his marvellous light*' (I Peter 2.9). In this priesthood of all believers in Christ, women and men continue to proclaim the glory of God, as they had done already in ancient Israel.

Christ's Call to a Gender-Inclusive Service-Ministry: God Shows No Partiality

After his resurrection, as Lord of the world with all divine authority, Christ sends his disciples as disciple-makers, baptizers and teachers to all nations[37] – the male gender of those who receive this commission in Matthew and Luke *represent* both women and men, as is common in most languages when the masculine form is being used,[38] as indicated by Mark,[39] and as the Seventh-day Adventist Church has always understood the text.[40] Christ's role as God's Servant bringing the news of the kingdom to Israel is the role that the church will now assume towards the world.[41] The men and women of the church

---

[37] E.g. Matthew 28.16-20.
[38] See 9.2.8 below.
[39] Mark 16.1-8 (note that the last part of v. 8 includes the women as the servants through whom 'Jesus himself sent out, from east to west, the sacred and imperishable proclamation of eternal salvation').
[40] See *The SDA Bible Commentary*, vol. 5, p. 557. Ellen White understood Matthew 28.28-20 as referring to the commissioning of 'all the believers who could be called together' (*Desire of Ages*, 1898, p. 818).
[41] J. Barna, 'Towards a Biblical-Systematic Theology of Ordination', 2014, p. 106.

will be God's ministers to the world, bringing the good news of the kingdom of God. *There is no biblical place here for shutting out one gender and reserving this ministry for men only* (see 9.1 below), for when God calls men and women as his servants-ministers, he 'shows no partiality to any human being'.[42]

8.3 Christ as High Priest

The kingdom mission of Christ merges with his high-priestly mission in the New Testament. Priestly functions were as a rule assigned to the king in the ancient Near East and in the Bible. Sanctified by his anointing and being seen as adopted by God, the king was sacred and empowered to perform priestly functions.[43]

As the servanthood of mankind at the Creation covered priestly and governing functions, Christ is similarly Priest and King. He is 'a second Adam' (including man and woman), restoring humanity to what God intended (Romans 5; I Corinthians 15).

The theme of Jesus as High Priest is particularly developed in the Letter to the Hebrews – note especially 1.8; 2.17; 3.1-6; 4.14-10.18. The passage in Hebrews 1.2-2.17 contains a complete summary of the biblical theme of the mission of God through the perspective of the mission of Christ.

The consecration of the priests in Israel was to make them ritually pure for the sacrifices and rituals in the temple service, in order to keep Israel near God, while all Israel, as part of the mission of God, was engaged in proclaiming the glory of God to their neighbours and the nations. Replacing the ritual-sacramental priesthood in Israel, Christ was made High Priest through a series of actions culminating in his being seated at the right hand of God.[44] His high-priestly *mediation* between God and the church aims at enabling the whole

---

[42] Galatians 2.6; see 9.1 below.
[43] R. de Vaux, *Ancient Israel*, 1973, pp. 113-114.
[44] Ephesians 1.22; Hebrews 1.2; 3.2; 5.1-10; 6.19-20; 7.28-8.7.

church, men and women, to take part in the mission of God to the world, i.e. proclaiming his glory to the peoples and nations (I Peter 2.9; Revelation 14.6-7). Men and women in the church are 'priests' (i.e. servants-ministers) in Christ's service without gender distinction (Revelation 1.5-6; 5.9-10; 20.6). *Any commissioning-ordination to an office or assignment in the church must therefore start from the fundamental recognition that all members are servants-ministers of God and serve him in roles depending on his/her spiritual gifts.* We will return to this point in 9.1 below.

8.4 Humility and Submission as Christ's Kingdom Characteristics

The breach of the peace in God's kingdom brought by the human Fall was restored through Christ's mission. Christ reconciled humanity with God (II Corinthians 5.18-20). He re-established the kingdom of God on earth, building it afresh upon his victory over sin and death.

The church is God's agent under the *headship of Christ* to complete his mission of salvation to 'every nation, tribe, language and people' (Revelation 14.6). While keeping his faithful people close to God through his ministry of intercession, Christ *authorises his followers (men and women) to minister as 'priests'*. Regardless of gender, all of them *are* God's 'kingdom' and 'priests to our God' (Revelation 5.9-10; cf. 1.4-6; 20.6).

Being ordained for ministry under the headship of Christ must therefore be defined by Christ's kingdom characteristics *where human hierarchies have no place*. Christ is the Head of the church and in charge of its ministry. All ministers, regardless of gender, are *submitted* to him. The five biblical passages that refer to Christ as Head of the church[45] indicate that 'head', defined in its biblical context, does not mean what it means in the English language. In this context, 'head' is never given the meaning of authority, boss or leader. It

---

[45] See Ephesians 1.22-23; 4.15-16; 5.23; Colossians 1.18-19; 2.19.

rather describes the *servant function* of a provider of life, growth and development. This function is not one of top-down oversight but of bottom-up support and nurture. Thus, *commissioning-ordination in the church must be defined in view of Christ's self-sacrificing humility in complete obedience to God, unto death* (Philippians 2.1-11). This is the basis of appointments to leadership, not authority exercised within a human hierarchy. This is the essence of the church that 'keeps the faithfulness of Jesus'.[46]

Christian *submission* is rooted in Christ. Emptying himself of his divinity, he became like a human and was *submissive* in everything unto his death on the cross. Because of his submission to God, he was given all authority in heaven and on earth, to the glory of God (Philippians 2.5-11). Christ will eventually *subject* himself to him who put all things under him, that God may be everything to every one (I Corinthians 15.24-28).[47] God's mission will then be fully accomplished.

In this context, ordination for the gospel ministry is an act of human submission to God, which imitates Christ. However, *this is distorted and corrupted if hierarchy of genders is involved*. It removes from God the privilege of appointing *whom he wants without partiality* and reduces God's prerogative to the level of shifting human cultures and preferences. The Bible does not give the church authority to usurp God's right of calling and appointing whom he wants to serve him, be it a man or a woman.

The New Testament teaches that submission through servanthood is the fundamental element of any minister in the church, which is the emphatic instruction by Ellen White.[48] According to the Bible, the

---

[46] Revelation 14.12. The 'faithfulness of Jesus' includes his servant attitude of submission until death (see B. Wiklander, 'The Mission of God and the Faithfulness of His People', 2009).

[47] Cf. the summary on submission in W. L. Richards, 'How Does a Woman Prophesy and Keep Silence at the Same Time? (1 Corinthians 11 and 14)', 1998, pp. 324-326.

[48] See TED-TOSCR, 2013, section 4.6.2.4.

only vital submission in the church is the submission of all servants and ministers to God and his servant Jesus Christ. Appointed leaders are told 'not to lord it over those in their charge, but to be examples to the flock' (I Peter 5.3). However, *advocating a specific female duty of submission to men in the church distorts the direct submission of women to God and distorts biblical commissioning-ordination.*

God's call to service-ministry in the church comes through the calling of Christ. His call to men and women is to bring the gospel to the world (Matthew 28.18-20) and minister to all kinds of human needs (Romans 12.3-8; I Corinthians 12-13; Ephesians 4.1-16). He equips men and women for their ministry through spiritual gifts (I Corinthians 12-13). No biblical text says that Christ restricts a function or service to a particular class or gender of people in the church. The very few restrictions that are found come from the needs of the church to promote the gospel successfully among outsiders and to preserve order and spiritual unity internally, but this is conditioned by the shifting cultural settings of the church.

Nowhere does the word of God teach female submission to men within the sphere of a God-given ministry. Submission in the church is in principle mutual (Ephesians 5.21). The few times when women/wives are counselled to be in submission are when the author's concern is what was considered appropriate and decent according to the public opinion at the time, following the conventional order in marriage or in the public church services.[49] These concessions to culture are, as a rule, not only associated with the shame/honour code of conduct in the biblical environment, but vital for the promotion of the gospel among outsiders. Those counsels are practical, time-bound, and conditioned by local and temporal customs and conditions, and the church has the duty of applying them wisely.

---

[49] See 9.5 below.

CHAPTER 9
The Mission and Ministry of the Church

The early church understood that Jesus of Nazareth became the resurrected Lord, the Messiah or the Christ. As a result, the kingdom of God began to take hold in this world with its new foundations in the risen Christ. The church was sent to invite the world to accept the kingship of God through the lordship of Christ (Matthew 28.18-20). The mission of God and the mission of Christ now include the mission of the church.[1]

The mission of God was in operation before the church, but the functions, ministries and gifts of the church are *new* means of advancing it. The mission of God defines the mission of the church:

> Mission, then, in biblical terms, while it inescapably involves us in planning and action, is not *primarily* a matter of our activity or our initiative. Mission, from the point of view of our human endeavour, means the committed *participation* of God's people in the purposes of God for the redemption of the whole creation. The mission is God's. The marvel is that he invites us.[2]

This means that all servants-ministers in the church – men and women – are functioning because *God* wants them, *God* needs them,

---

[1] Cf. J. Barna, 'Towards a Biblical-Systematic Theology of Ordination', 2014, p. 107.
[2] C. J. H. Wright, *The Mission of God: Unlocking the Bible's Grand Narrative*, 2006, p. 67.

and *God* calls them. (This understanding is emphatically maintained by Ellen White.)[3] Therefore, when the church thinks it can *limit* God's will and power to ordain or commission women as his servants-ministers, it is not allowing God to be God and loses his blessing in its work.

The Spirit at Pentecost: Men and Women Made into Prophets

Christ's commissioning of his servants-ministers was confirmed by the outpouring of the Spirit on the Day of Pentecost. It empowered men and women in the church as witnesses of the kingdom to the world,[4] so they *prophesied* in various languages.

To devout Jewish believers (Acts 2.5), this confirmation was reminiscent of God's commissioning of the seventy elders in Numbers 11.16-25, when God took some of the Spirit on Moses and put it on the elders so that they *prophesied* (11.25). In this context, Moses expresses a wish: 'Would that all the Lord's people were prophets, and that the Lord would put his spirit on them!' (11.28). The Spirit at Pentecost is a gift of Christ who has received it from God (Acts 2.33). Moses' wish for Israel is now fulfilled as the prophecy of Joel 2.28-32 becomes reality (Acts 2.16-21): 'Even upon my servants, men and women, in those days I will pour out my Spirit; and they shall *prophesy*'.

The meaning of this is that the Holy Spirit is given to women who are thus equipped like the elders for the task of proclaiming God's glory and witnessing about his work through the risen Christ. All believers are inducted into a *prophetic office* serving the mission of Christ. *In a prophetic office, no ordination is needed, because receiving the gift of prophecy fulfils the function of an ordination.* This seems to be how the New Testament church initially understood ministry, based on the experience at Pentecost. It also seems to explain the poor evidence of ecclesiastical offices and formal ordination by the imposition of hands.

---

[3] See TED-TOSCR, 2013, section 4.6.2.
[4] Acts 1.8, 14; 2.1, 2-4, 15-21.

The Spirit at Pentecost: Christ's Anointment of His Royal Servants

The scenario in Acts 2 is reminiscent of the ritual of the royal enthronement in ancient Israel (cf. 7.5 above). The royal installation was confirmed by anointing which authorised the king and symbolically bestowed upon him the power of the Spirit.[5] In King Saul's case, the first of the kings in Israel, this resulted in prophesying followed by the acclamation of the people.[6]

At Pentecost, Christ has already *designated* and *commissioned* his disciples – the twelve represent the body of all disciples at all times.[7] He then *anoints* them, men and women, by the power of the Holy Spirit so that they *prophesy* (Acts 2.1-4, 11, 16-21). The *acclamation* of the people is paralleled by the response of many 'devout Jews from every nation under heaven' (2.5, 11) who join the kingdom (2.37-41) after Peter's proclamation of the kingship of Christ (2.32-36).

Thus, the birth of the church assumes the character of Christ's anointment of his royal servants, men and women, not literally by oil but symbolically by his Spirit, and its impact extends into the world of nations. No special ceremony of ordination is applied. Christ's call and the power of the Spirit are sufficient. The same understanding applies to inductions into spiritual leadership in the New Testament church.

The Spirit at Pentecost: The Enthronement of Christ as King

Attention has also been called to another intriguing explicit biblical-theological link.[8] The New Testament assigns a dual significance to the events at Pentecost. In Acts, the outpouring of the Spirit inaugurates the church and launches its mission (Acts 2.1-42)

---

[5] Cf. 'The anointment of the king [...] conveyed the power for the exercise of royal authority. By strength of anointment, the king became a theocratic vassal of the Lord, as texts like 1 Samuel 9:16 and 16:3 indicate.' (S. Szikszai, 'Anoint', *IDB*, vol. 1, p. 139).

[6] I Samuel 10-11 (Saul); cf. I Samuel 16.13; II Samuel 2.4 (David); I Kings 1.38-40 (Solomon).

[7] Matthew 28.18-20; Luke 24.44-49; Acts 1.8.

[8] J. Barna, 'Towards a Biblical-Systematic Theology of Ordination', 2014, p. 107.

and, in Revelation, it confirms the enthronement of Christ as King at the right hand of God (Revelation 5.5-14).

John's vision in Revelation 5 describes Christ, the victory of 'the Lion of the tribe of Judah, the Root of David' (5.5), the 'sending out' of the Holy Spirit into all the earth – a Spirit that belongs to Christ (5.6), 'the kingdom and priests serving our God' from all the world that he has saved by his blood (5.9-10), and heaven's acclamation of Christ as King (5.11-14). Thus, the reality of Christ's royal inauguration at his resurrection – with women as the primary and most efficient witnesses[9] – is publicly confirmed by the outpouring of the Spirit at Pentecost which 'sends out' the power of the Holy Spirit to the world through the gospel of the kingdom and the enthronement of Jesus Christ.

Peter's words in Acts 2.33 refer to the royal installation of Christ as the justification of what is going on. Several times, the book of Acts confirms this vital link between Christ's kingship and the *sending* of the Spirit to his servants-ministers (Acts 5.31-32; 7.55-56). The perspective of Revelation 5 is that the *sending* of the Spirit to the world results in the church being made of 'saints from every tribe and language and people and nation' who are ransomed for God by the blood of Christ whom [Christ] has 'made to be a kingdom and priests serving our God' (Revelation 5.9-10). Christ makes men and women into the new Israel, 'a kingdom of priests' (cf. Exodus 19.5-6). They are royals and priests serving God within Christ's kingdom and as a result of his mission. The obvious links with Revelation 14.12 confirm that this applies particularly to the end-time church.

The Foundational Principles of Christ's Kingdom

The vision of Christ as King would 'mould the church into a community of kingdom-bringers'.[10] Christ's kingdom is founded on 'justice, true love, acceptance, forgiveness and healing, both spiritual

---

[9] Acts 2.32; cf. 9.2.2 below.
[10] Ibid., p. 108.

and physical, and all this springs from the true knowledge of God' that Christ has revealed.[11] In its ministry, the church 'will be promoting the same foundational kingdom values and message – and in this way it will be extending God's good rule and his presence in the world.'[12]

Thus, the church is engaged in God's mission to defeat evil, including long-lived prejudices that keep humans enslaved by cultural patterns. The fallen world is founded on human power, injustices and a false knowledge of God (cf. the symbol of Babylon in Revelation 14.8).[13] In opposition to this, 'the kingdom-oriented church ministry will model a different way of being a community and indeed humanity (Ephesians 2.15). It will actively advocate justice and equality – socially, economically, racially, and with regard to gender.'[14]

This means that the whole church, led by its servant-leaders, will *in everything* be in submission to Christ, the Head, as his faithful servants (see 8.4 above). It will confess in its faith, life, proclamation and church organisation (including ordination) that 'Jesus Christ is Lord' and that all his male and female servants are 'fellow citizens with God's people' and equal recipients of the spiritual gifts for ministry.

Men and Women in the Church as God's Sanctuary in Which God Dwells

In the context of the mission of the church, Ephesians 2.19-22 becomes a key passage:[15]

Consequently, you are no longer foreigners and strangers, but fellow citizens [language of kingdom] with God's people and also members of his household, built on the foundation of the apostles and prophets,

---

[11] Ibid.
[12] Ibid.
[13] See the exposition in B. Wiklander, 'The Mission of God and the Faithfulness of His People', 2009, pp. 286-288.
[14] J. Barna, Towards a Biblical-Systematic Theology of Ordination', 2014, p. 108.
[15] Ibid., p. 109.

with Christ [read: king] Jesus himself as the chief cornerstone [note the specific king/kingdom Christology being the foundation for the church]. In him the whole building is joined together and rises to become a holy temple in the Lord [a sanctuary]. And in him you [plural] too are being built together to become a dwelling in which God lives by his Spirit [echoes of Exodus 25:8].

The church is the new humanity in Christ. The individual members are 'God's sanctuary'. As the church grows, God's presence grows among his people. 'In this way the church is at the centre of God's original mission for the world – exactly what God wanted from the beginning for Adam and Eve to be and to do.'[16] The church's mission functions under God's mission theme set out in Genesis 1-2. The key that has made this possible is the installation of Jesus as King of the world,[17] based on his submission to God and his exaltation by the resurrection and his assumption to God's right hand side (Philippians 2.1-11). Ján Barna sums it up as follows:

> The church now spreads not just the *truth* about the kingdom, but the actual *presence* of the kingdom. The church is a different humanity where Gentiles and Jews are together, where slaves and masters are equal and where there is essential unity, not just doctrinal or policy unity. The citizenship is multi-dimensional, and importantly, it begins now, not in the future. Thus, the mission and ministry that the church is called to be part of must reflect this new reality.[18]

The Integrity of the Church Revealed in a Gender-Inclusive Leadership

The unity and equality in Christ is not restricted to the laity. If the church is to prove herself faithful to Christ, these characteristics must be seen in the leaders of the church. *The leaders will only poorly*

---
[16] Ibid., p. 109.
[17] Ibid.
[18] Ibid.

and deficiently represent the church as long as they include only men while discriminating against the majority of its members, the women. Consequently, men and women are to be equal in ordination and ministry to God. The world that God wants to save consists of men and women who are to be restored according to the Creator's original plan. If the world is shaped by egalitarian values, people will doubt the authenticity of a church that claims to represent a new humanity of unity and equality, but allows only men to lead them. Prohibiting women's ordination, therefore, is to undermine God's mission to the world.

9.1 Service-Ministry

Understanding the mission of the church as *part of* the mission of Christ has vital implications.

Implications for Ordination of Christ's Authority in the Church

Any authority in the church comes from Christ's authority as the Head of the church and Christ's authority comes from God. Any exercise of church authority, therefore, must be in accordance with the character of Jesus Christ. *Even ordination must be defined according to the character of Christ,[19] and it must be applied for the purpose of 'building up the church'[20] and promoting the mission of God in the world.[21]* There is not even a hint of hierarchy or gender distinction in this biblical context, because all that mattered in the ministry of Christ was self-giving service. Concerning leadership and offices, he declared to his disciples:

> *Mark 10.42-43* You know that among the Gentiles those whom they recognise as rulers lord it over them, and their great ones are tyrants over them. But it is not so among you; but whoever wishes to become great among you must be your servant, and whoever wishes

---
[19] See e.g. Philippians 2.1-11.
[20] See e.g. II Corinthians 10.8; 13.10; Ephesians 4.1-11.
[21] See e.g. Acts 26.15-18; I Timothy 2.1-7; II Timothy 1.8-12.

to become first among you must be slave of all, for the Son of Man came not to be served but to serve, and to give his life a ransom for many.

Jesus' theology of ministry builds on service, self-sacrifice, and humility, and not on power, rank, status, or gender. While some erroneously want to direct our attention to an alleged submission of women to men in ministry, God in his Word directs us to the submission of all members to each other (see 8.4 above and 9.5.7 below). 'Jesus was re-establishing in his church the divine principle of order that ruled over his cosmic kingdom before the origin of sin, namely divine love manifested in service to others.'[22]

In Christ's kingdom, which the church represents, positions of leadership are assigned on the basis of a life of service and not on the basis of which gender God prioritised at the creation.[23] There is no such prioritisation in Genesis 1-2.[24] 'Jesus does not qualify what he says on the basis of gender as if the service of females was always to be of an inferior nature to that of males. Leadership positions, he says, are assigned to *all* on the basis of service.'[25] One does not find in the New Testament a distinction between 'spiritual ministry (or clergy) and a secular laity'. Every follower of Christ is a servant-minister and is called to fulfil a ministry according to the will of the Holy Spirit.[26]

Christ as Servant and His Church as Servants

The concept of service or ministry is central in Jesus' teachings and the active verb to 'serve' is used to define the mission of Christ: 'the Son of Man came not to be served but to serve, and to give his life as a ransom for many'.[27] One of the epithets of Jesus is 'the servant of

---

[22] GC-TOSCR, 2014, p. 78.
[23] Ibid., pp. 78-79.
[24] See 7.1 and 7.2 above.
[25] GC-TOSCR, 2014, p. 79.
[26] Ibid.
[27] Matthew 10.45; cf. 23.11-12.

God',[28] which alludes to the use of this term in the Old Testament[29] and is rooted in kingdom terminology. But Christ's kingdom is 'not of this world' (John 18.16), and the finest example of Christ's servanthood is when he washed his disciples' feet, which was a task performed by *douloi*, 'slaves'.[30]

Clericalism is Unbiblical

All members of the church, men and women, are called and commissioned by Christ as his servants-ministers. To guide the church and equip it for its task, the power of the Holy Spirit was given to all members – men and women – at Pentecost (Acts 2). Christ continues to provide spiritual gifts to all (Romans 12.6-9; I Corinthians 12.6-11; Ephesians 4.7, 11-13). The New Testament indicates that the Holy Spirit conveys gifts to all believers regardless of race, gender, or social status (see 9.3.4 below). There cannot, therefore, be any essential difference between members and ministers in the church. 'Any form of clericalism (i.e. the idea that there is a class division in the church where some possess a higher spiritual status than others) is foreign to the thought of the New Testament (I Corinthians 12.22-25).'[31]

This principle remains especially when the church forms special offices and organises itself in order to preserve order and efficiency in mission. Turning to the issue of women's ordination, 'the fact that there is hardly any significant difference between gifts and offices (the gifts equip one for the office) indicates that considering gifts to be gender inclusive but not offices – thus excluding women from the offices – is not supported by the New Testament.'[32]

---

[28] Matthew 12.15-21; Philippians 2.1-11; cf. I Corinthians 15.24-28. This concept is implied in God's recognition of Jesus as 'Son' at his baptism (Matthew 3.17; Mark 1.11; Luke 3.22), since God's words seem to allude to Isaiah 42.1: 'Here is my servant, whom I uphold, my chosen, in whom my soul delights; I have put my Spirit upon him.' This passage is applied to Jesus in Matthew 12.15-21.

[29] See in particular Isaiah 41.8-9; 42.1, 19; 43.10; 44.1-2, 21, 26; 45.4; 48.20; 49.3, 5-7; 50.10; 52.13; 53.11; 54.17.

[30] K. H. Rengstorf, '*doulos*' etc., *ThDNT*, vol. 2, pp. 277-278.

[31] GC-TOSCR, 2014, p. 80.

[32] Ibid., p. 84.

Appointments and Ordination in the New Testament

There were certainly ways in which the New Testament church recognised Christ's call and commissioning as well as an individual's spiritual gifts for service. Generally speaking, the *fruit* of the ministry was vital – primarily seen in building up the church in love (Ephesians 4.11-16) and in the demonstration of the power of God (I Corinthians 2.1-5). The *faithfulness* to Christ in life and work would be equally important (I Timothy 4.6-10; 6.11-16).

It is striking, however, that the New Testament mentions no ordination or other ceremonial rite in inductions into leadership. The only clear examples of the laying on of hands in a congregational setting are specific, one-off events that do not reflect a repeated practice (Acts 6.1-6; 13.1-3). The New Testament lists some leadership functions in the church, but it is explicitly underlined that it is God (Christ) who appoints them, equips them, and makes them what they are (Romans 12.4-8; I Corinthians 12.27-31; Ephesians 4.7-13). The biblical texts are very restricted, almost silent on the role of the church in appointing and confirming such leaders. We will examine this further in regard to commissioning-ordination (9.3) and the laying on of hands (9.4).

9.2 Men and Women as Servants-Ministers of Christ

The New Testament indicates a rich variety of services provided by the church. While there are leaders, the functions are not organised hierarchically. And while a great diversity of nations, races and genders is involved, nobody is treated with partiality or discrimination. All the writings are filled with awe and joy at the marvellous acts of God and the commitment to carry out the mission of Christ.

As the church grows, however, issues arise that come from the Jewish and Graeco-Roman socio-cultural environment. In addressing this challenge, the church seeks to be true to the kingdom principles laid down by Christ (see 8.4 above) and at the same time ensure that unity and order prevails in the church, that God is revered, and that the respect of outsiders is maintained so that the gospel continues to incorporate men and women with the kingdom. This means that the instructions to the churches, especially by the apostle Paul, will deal with the issues of honour and shame attached to the relationship between men and women.

9.2.1 Disciples and Apostles

In the Gospels, the term 'disciples' designates the followers of Jesus, continuing even in Acts.[33] It is applied both to the general group of followers and the specific group of the twelve. While John 15.16 is directed to the twelve, the content is paradigmatic and applies to all followers of Jesus:

> *John 15.16* You did not choose me but I chose (*eklegomai*) you. And I appointed (*tithemi*) you to go and bear fruit, fruit that will last, so that the Father will give you whatever you ask him in my name.

The Greek verb *tithemi* means 'put (to some task or function)'. It is not connected with the modern concept of ordination but simply with appointment. Being *chosen* and *appointed* by Christ is the experience of all disciples, and this is the foundation of the biblical doctrine of the priesthood of all believers which is advocated in I Peter and Revelation based on Exodus 19.5-6. Peter defines it in this way:

> *I Peter 2.9* But you are a *chosen* (*eklektos*) race, a royal priesthood, a holy nation, God's own people, in order that you may *proclaim* (*exaggello*) the mighty acts of him who *called* (*kaleo*) you out of darkness into his marvellous light.

All believers bear witness to the kingdom of God as servants-ministers (I Peter 2.16).

---

[33] See, for example, Matthew 5.1-2; 10.1; 11.1; 16.21; 28.18-20; Acts 6.1-2, 7; 21.4-5, 16.

However, in a more narrow sense, in order to support his ministry, Jesus appointed twelve disciples from the wider group of followers, as did the contemporary Jewish torah-teachers. He 'made (*poieo*) twelve' (Mark 3.14) and 'designated them apostles' (Luke 6.13). However, *nowhere do the Greek Gospels state that Jesus ordained his disciples.* He may have blessed them, as he did in other circumstances,[34] but there is no biblical record of a formal ordination process involving the imposition of hands.[35] It is the *calling* and the *commission* by Jesus that matters – just as when Jesus called followers in general.

The task of the twelve is 'to be with him', 'to be sent out (*apostello*) to proclaim (*kerysso*) the message', and 'to have authority (*exousia*) to cast out demons'.[36] Significantly, Jesus grants them authority, not by an ordination procedure but *by his word*. Their authority concerns powers of the ministry of healing, not decision-making or leadership. Thus, as the twelve eventually lead the young church, their authority is based on two things only: Christ's commissioning and the outpouring of the Holy Spirit on the Day of Pentecost.

The Twelve Apostles as Leaders in the Church

In the book of Acts, Luke indicates the twelve apostles as the leading group when the church was born. Their leadership is based on being eyewitnesses of his ministry (Acts 1.21-22), a function for which he had appointed them. He entrusts to them various forms of authority and responsibilities.[37] However, they occupy a unique position in the church and are, together with the prophets, as Paul says, the foundation on which the church is built with Christ Jesus himself as the cornerstone (Ephesians 2:20). But their ministry is unique and not replicable in the church.

---

[34] See Luke 24.50-52; John 20.21-22; cf. the imposition of hands for blessings noted in 9.4 below.

[35] For Ellen White's homiletical version of Mark 3.14-15, see TED-TOSCR, 2013, section 4.6.2.5.

[36] Mark 3.14-15; cf. Matthew 10.1, 5-8.

[37] Matthew 16.19; 18.18; 28.18-20; Mark 3.13-14: 16.8-19; Acts 1.3, 8.

The term 'apostle' has a dual meaning. On the one hand, it may have a royal and authoritative character in that an apostle sent out to proclaim the kingdom of God is associated with the setting of a royal court where the king sends out his servants as heralds among his subjects, and they act on his command.[38]

On the other hand, the term was also rooted in contemporary Judaism, for 'the Hebrew equivalent of *apostolos* is *shaliakh*, a rabbinic term for the envoys used by the central authorities in Palestine to keep in touch with the diaspora'.[39] Luke's 'apostles' are in no way subordinate to the council of elders in Jerusalem, but, rather, Luke 'stresses repeatedly that the twelve (and Paul) received their commission directly from the Lord (Acts 1.2-8; 9.15)'.[40]

Thus, a direct link with the Lord, rather than ordination as we understand and apply it today, is the key to the function of an apostle. This understanding goes back to Jesus who in Matthew 10 gives the apostles a *charismatic* or *prophetic* role (10.20, 41). This is significant, because the induction into being a leader in the New Testament is primarily of a charismatic-prophetic nature, not one of ordination as we normally understand it, and women were clearly acknowledged in the Bible as a whole as recipients of the Spirit and prophetic servants.

The Appointment of Matthias

The appointment of Matthias as the twelfth apostle gives some insights into how a top leader was selected and installed before Pentecost. In a group of about one hundred and twenty believers – the same number that was required in the Babylonian Talmud (*Sanhedrin* 17b) as the minimum population of a city to qualify for a local Sanhedrin which elected an elder[41] – the apostles led out in the selection of Matthias by casting lots.

---

[38] See, for example, Matthew 9.38; 22.2-14.
[39] L. Alexander, 'Mapping Early Christianity: Acts and the Shape of Early Church History', 2003, pp. 167-168.
[40] Ibid.
[41] E. Ferguson, 'Jewish and Christian Ordination', 1963, p. 17.

Among the qualifications for nomination, it was important to have been with the group of disciples under the leadership of Jesus (1.21-22a). Peter also states that the candidate is to be a 'man' (*aner*), despite the fact that the first witnesses of Jesus' resurrection were women, who were explicitly called and sent by divine representatives to the disciples (see 9.2.2 and 9.2.3 below). Male gender overruled the women's role as the *de facto* primary witnesses of the resurrection. Peter does not explain why this is so but takes it for granted. The nearest we come to an explanation is that it was self-evident that the twelve patriarchs of Israel were men and that Jesus therefore appointed twelve male disciples. In the Jewish setting at the time, the twelve could not be anything but male (see 9.2.2 below).

As the twelve apostles died, they were not replaced, and there is no instruction from the Lord to replace them except for the reference to the work of the Holy Spirit. Thus, the twelve were designed for a special time, a one-off that is not a model for pastoral ministry and leadership today. Nowhere does the Bible commend this model as something to be followed by the church – it simply records what happened.

The position of apostle is called 'the position of this ministry and apostolate' (*topos tes diakonias tautes kai apostoles*) in Acts 1.25. The term 'ministry' (*diakonia*) is a general term for any function in the church (see 9.2.5 below). The position is also given a name in 1.20: *episcope* ('[role of] oversight') and in 1.25 the function of 'being an apostle' is formalised into a 'position of the apostolate' (*apostoles*). Thus, when Luke wrote about Matthias' appointment in Acts, the functions of 'overseer, bishop' (*episkopos*), 'servant' (*diakonos*) and 'apostle, emissary' (*apostolos*) were understood as one and the same thing.

Matthias' appointment is again a unique event that was not followed later. God makes the choice through the casting of lots. While there is prayer, there is no mentioning of the laying on of hands. Because of its uniqueness, because it takes place before Pentecost, and because the office of apostle gradually changed and disappeared when the twelve apostles passed away, it is difficult to see how this passage can give a pattern for ordination today. The fact, therefore, that Matthias is a male is irrelevant for a church policy on commissioning-ordination.

The Central Function of the Holy Spirit

As he 'made twelve' (Mark 3.14), Jesus indicated that he had in mind the preparation of a body that would represent God's exemplary people as a tool to reform Israel. That is however not what happens. Only the Holy Spirit at Pentecost equips the twelve and other disciples for ministry. Not even the formalisation and organisation of the church is stipulated by Jesus – it is left entirely to the continued leading of the Spirit.[42]

Thus, in order to build a modern pastoral ordination on the Bible, the *primary* place must be given to the calling and equipping of the Holy Spirit and the *secondary* place to the confirmation by the church, as Ellen White said (see chap. 4 above). If ordination is understood as an issuing of ecclesiastical authority in an organised system of the church, it becomes necessary to go outside of the Bible.

9.2.2 Female Disciples and Eyewitnesses to the Resurrection

The Gospels reveal that Jesus called women as well as men to discipleship.[43] There are rich narratives regarding women in all the four canonical Gospels.

---

[42] Cf. the reading of Acts in C. Vine, 'Listening to the Spirit: Lessons in Decision-Making from the Book of Acts', 2012, pp. 14-16.

[43] See, for example, H. Westphal Wilson, 'The Forgotten Disciples: The Empowering of Love vs. the Love of Power', 1995, pp. 179-195; J. A. Davidson, 'Women in Scripture', 1998, pp. 172-179; R. Bauckham, *Gospel Women*, 2002; E. W. Stegemann and W. Stegemann, *The Jesus Movement*, 1999, pp. 378-388.

Mary the Mother of Jesus

In the Gospel of Luke, *Mary the mother of Jesus* plays the central role in God's fulfilment of his promise of a 'woman's seed' that would 'crush the head of the serpent' (Genesis 3.15). Mary receives her assignment by a messenger sent by God (Luke 1.26-38) who tells her that 'the Holy Spirit will come upon you and the power of the Most High will overshadow you'. In her Song, which glorifies the power of God (1.46-55), she refers to herself as 'God's servant' (*doulos theou*, 1.47), which is the term generally used for apostles and leaders in the church (see 9.2.5 and 9.2.6 below).

In a comprehensive analysis of Mary's Song, Richard Bauckham has demonstrated persuasively that it stands in the great tradition initiated by Moses' Song (Exodus 15.1-18) and Miriam's Song (15.21), which was followed by the Old Testament and Jewish songs in Judges 5 (Deborah and Barak), I Samuel 2 (Hannah), II Samuel 22 (David), Isaiah 38.9-20 (Hezekiah), Judith 16 (Judith), Additions to Daniel (Shadrach, Meshach, and Abednego), Tobit 13 (Tobit), and Isaiah 12 (Israel at the new exodus).[44]

Thus, the salvation that Mary is celebrating has its ultimate precedent in the exodus from Egypt.[45] Bauckham also shows that the main theme of Mary's Song is the connection between Mary's lowly status as 'God's servant' (*diakonos autou*, Luke 1.48), for whom God 'has done great things' (1.49), and the lowly whom God 'has exalted' (1.52), as well as 'his servant Israel' (*paidos autou*) whom God has helped (1.54).[46] Thus, the central thought is the reversal of status for Israel, 'God's servant', and this is symbolically expressed in the reversal of status for Mary, 'God's servant'. As God's *lowly* servant, Mary is representative of his servant Israel and *precisely as a woman* she 'instantiates the weakness of the lowly before the oppressive power of the haughty'. However, Mary 'is not only aligned with the lowly,

---

[44] R. Bauckham, *Gospel Women*, 2002, p. 68.
[45] Ibid.
[46] Ibid., p. 69.

but herself is empowered by God to act as his agent in his exaltation of the lowly'.[47]

Thus, Luke opens his Gospel of Jesus Christ with the message that *female lowliness is and will be exalted by God through his Son Jesus*, as God now makes his move to bring his salvation to Israel and the world, restoring men and women to full participation in the presence of God that was lost as man and woman were expelled from the Garden of Eden. This presence of God is now revealed in the *person* of Jesus Christ, and, therefore, his relation to men and women will define their status in relationship to God and their role as witnesses, teachers and preachers of his mighty works. Men and women will take up these roles, and Mary is one of them. She and the brothers of Jesus are among the disciples who 'constantly devote themselves to prayer' before Pentecost (Acts 1.14), and she and her family exercised leadership in the church until the destruction of Jerusalem.

Anna Daughter of Phanuel

At the time of Christ's birth, Luke refers to the widow and prophetess *Anna daughter of Phanuel of the tribe of Asher* (Luke 2.36-38). As a prophetess (*profetis*), who worshipped in the temple and prayed and fasted daily, Anna was filled with the Holy Spirit and recognised Jesus as the promised Messiah.

In confirming Simeon's *spiritual* testimony that Jesus is 'God's salvation', 'a light for revelation to the Gentiles and for glory to your people Israel' (2.25-35), she fulfils the injunction of the Mosaic law that 'a matter must be established by the testimony of two or three witnesses' (Deuteronomy 19.15; Matthew 18.16) and, thus, she contributes *a female witness to establish the truth of Jesus' identity in God's plan of salvation*. Anna is also the first public preacher and teacher of Jesus as the promised Messiah: 'she spoke to all who were looking forward to the redemption of Jerusalem' (2.38).

---

[47] Ibid., pp. 69-76.

Bauckham has explored Luke's information that Anna was of the tribe of Asher, which is a remarkable circumstance, since Asher was part of the northern tribes (who inhabited the northern kingdom of Israel which was destroyed by the Assyrians in 721 BC) and not of the tribes usually represented in Jerusalem (Judah, Levi, Benjamin). Simeon and Anna 'form one of the pairs of man and woman of which Luke is fond'.[48] Simeon represents the 'hope of the centrifugal movement of salvation out from Jerusalem to the Gentiles',[49] while Anna, a returnee from the diaspora of the northern tribes, waiting for the redemption of Jerusalem (2.38), 'recognises the Messiah Jesus as the one who will fulfil Jerusalem's destiny to be the centre to which all the tribes of Israel are regathered', and therefore she represents 'the hope of the centripetal movement of salvation as the diaspora returns to Zion'.[50] Anna's spirit-filled witness and public preaching, and in particular her role as the *female* counterpart in a man-woman symbol of 'totality' for announcing hope for Israel and the world, sends a strong message to the church of women's spiritual gifts and ministry, and illustrates the egalitarian fullness of servanthood of God which is so clearly taught in Genesis 1-2.

Mary of Magdala

Among those who travelled with Jesus and his twelve disciples was *Mary of Magdala* (Luke 8.2). She is almost always mentioned first in a list of the female disciples of Jesus and may have been one of the leaders of that group who followed Jesus from the beginning of his ministry in Galilee to his death and afterwards.[51] The risen Jesus Christ appeared to her first and she was called by Christ to bring the first witness of his resurrection to the apostles (Mark 16.9; John 20.10-18) – at a time when women could not be legal witnesses

---

[48] Bauckham refers to T. K. Seim, *The Double Message: Patterns of Gender in Luke-Acts*, 1994, pp. 11-24.
[49] R. Bauckham, *Gospel Women*, 2002, p. 98.
[50] Ibid., p. 99.
[51] H. Westphal Wilson, 'The Forgotten Disciples', 1995, p. 181.

in public courts or attend popular assemblies,[52] although they had a central religious role outside Judaism in the home and in temple cults.[53]

Mary and Martha of Bethany
Mary and Martha of Bethany were two sisters who were disciples of Jesus. Martha gives one of the first confessions of faith in Christ in the New Testament. Martha's (John 11.27) and Peter's (Matthew 16.16) confessions of faith in Jesus as the Messiah/Christ are not only similar in wording but the first recorded instances of Christian faith in the New Testament. It has been noted that the Gospel of John tends to 'give to women roles normally associated with Peter in the other gospels'.[54]

Mary not only shared her faith in Jesus but is described as 'sitting at the Lord's feet listening to what he said', which is the classical position of a disciple (cf. Paul being 'thoroughly trained in the law of our fathers at the feet of Gamaliel', Acts 22.3). Jesus commends Mary for her choice of 'the one thing needed', which is 'the better thing', and 'it will not be taken away from her' (Luke 10.38-42). Jesus is referring to his teaching as that which will remain in Mary.

The Samaritan Woman
The story of the *Samaritan woman* in John 4 shows the encounter between Jesus and one of the lowliest beings in society becoming his disciple. By placing this story after the one where Jesus meets Nicodemus, John may want to contrast the weak faith of a prominent male Jewish religious leader with that of a Gentile woman.[55]

---

[52] For this general setting of women in New Testament times, see E. W. Stegemann and W. Stegemann, *The Jesus Movement*, 1999, pp. 364-377.
[53] L. H. Cohick, *Women in the World of the Earliest Christians*, 2009, pp. 195-224.
[54] F. Wheeler, 'Women in the Gospel of John', 1995, pp. 216-217; for this point of view, Wheeler makes reference to R. Brown, 'Role of Women in the Fourth Gospel', 1979, pp. 183-198.
[55] J. A. Davidson, 'Women in Scripture', 1998, p. 174.

The conversation Jesus has with the woman is 'the longest recorded discussion Jesus had with anyone – and she, a Gentile woman'.[56] Significantly, Ellen White described it as 'the most important discourse that Inspiration has given us'.[57] The woman is converted, brings others to Jesus, and through her testimony many of the Samaritans from her town believed in Jesus as the Saviour of the world (John 4.25, 28-30, 39-42). Ellen White says that she 'proved herself a more effective missionary than his own disciples'.[58] The woman is 'the first person recorded in Christ's public ministry whose witness brought a group of people into a believing relationship with the Messiah (4.39-42)'.[59]

A Disabled Woman

Luke has recorded the story of the healing of a *disabled woman* on Sabbath, in the synagogue, right in front of the synagogue ruler (Luke 13.10-17). Jesus puts his hands on her and heals her and she praises God. The protests of the synagogue ruler are met by Jesus with harsh words (13.15-16). By replacing the usual patriarchal phrase 'son of Abraham' with 'daughter of Abraham' (13.16), Jesus assigns as much value to her as to the male leaders of the synagogue, and creates a balance between man and woman in the kingdom of God, which we have seen was God's original intention (see 6.3 and 6.4 above). In the woman's praise of God (13.13), and in the people's delight with all the wonderful things he was doing (13.17), lies a reference to their belief in him. The woman leads people to faith by the work of the Holy Spirit.

Women the Real Witnesses and Preachers of the Resurrection

All four Gospels are structured with a view to the climax of the resurrection of Jesus. No doubt, the resurrection is the foundational and central doctrine of early Christian preaching (see I Corinthians 15). It is therefore a remarkable fact that *women have the determining*

---

[56] Ibid., p. 173.
[57] E. G. White, *Testimonies for the Church*, 1885-1909, vol. 3, p. 217.
[58] Id., *The Desire of Ages*, 1898, pp. 194-195.
[59] J. A. Davidson, 'Women in Scripture', 1998, p. 174.

role in establishing the empty tomb and the resurrection of Christ. Bauckham expresses it as follows:

> In the Gospel narratives the women disciples of Jesus are the first people to find the tomb of Jesus empty. Moreover, they are the only witnesses to the empty tomb who had seen Jesus buried and therefore could vouch for the fact that the empty tomb really was the tomb in which Jesus' body had been laid two days before. According to two of the Gospels, the women were also the first to meet the risen Lord.[60]

We might add that women, on divine instruction, were also the first to proclaim the resurrection of Christ, even to the eleven disciples/apostles themselves.

Bauckham has thoroughly investigated the issue of the credibility of women as witnesses, hence the credibility of the resurrection stories.[61] The following conclusion is worthy of our attention:

> If there is a problem in [the women's] Jewish context about the role of the women in the resurrection narratives, it may not be so much their supposed unreliability as witnesses or their susceptibility to delusion in religious matters, but something even dearer to patriarchal religious assumptions: *the priority of men in God's dealing with the world.* In these stories *women are given priority by God as recipients of revelation and thereby the role of mediators of that revelation to men.* Is this not part of the eschatological reversal of status, in which God makes the last first and the first last, so that no one might boast before God?[62]

Thus, in view of our review of the Old Testament material and the patriarchal dominance found there (see chap. 6 above), the role of the women disciples of Jesus in the resurrection stories of the Gospels

---

[60] R. Bauckham, *Gospel Women*, 2002, p. 257.
[61] Ibid., pp. 257-277
[62] Ibid., p. 275 (italics supplied); cf. B. Witherington III, *Women in the Earliest Churches*, 1988, p. 165.

reverses the roles of male and female and provides very strong evidence that the traditional 'priority of men in God's dealing with the world' is now *reverted* to women being 'given priority by God as recipients of revelation and thereby the role of mediators of that revelation to men'. One may well ask why God would do this, and Paul may have the answer, which ties in well with the Song of Mary in Luke 1.46-55: 'God chose the weak things of the world to shame the strong. He chose the lowly things of this world and the despised things – and the things that are not – to nullify the things that are, so that no one may boast before him. [...] Therefore, as it is written: "Let him who boasts boast in the Lord" [from Jeremiah 9.24].'

Regarding the resurrection, two traditions seem to be preserved in the Gospels – one says that Jesus 'appeared first to Mary Magdalene' (Mark 16.9; John 20.1-18), the other that a group of women were first commissioned by God to share the news of the resurrection with the disciples (Matthew 28.1-10; Mark 16.1-8; Luke 24.1-12).[63] According to the synoptic gospels this group of women included several individuals:

Matthew 28.1:	Mary Magdalene and the other Mary;
Mark 16.1:	Mary Magdalene, Mary the mother of James, and Salome;
Luke 24.10:	Mary Magdalene, Joanna, Mary the mother of James, 'and the others with them'.

The phrase 'and the others with them' in Luke suggests a larger group of women. In fact, Luke – who researched the historical events carefully (Luke 1.1) – knows of a group of women who 'followed Jesus [to Jerusalem] from Galilee' (Luke 23.49, 55) and witnessed all the

---

[63] For a reasoned attempt to explain these traditions, see R. Bauckham, *Gospel Women*, 2002, pp. 257-310; note especially his conclusion on pp. 303-304, where he states that the stories of the women of the empty tomb and the appearance of the Lord 'are substantially as the women themselves told them', and that, therefore, 'we must regard the differences between the stories as irreducible' and 'we cannot go behind them to a supposedly original version'.

decisive events including Jesus' suffering and crucifixion (23.27, 49), his death (23.49), his burial (23.55), his empty tomb (24.1-3), and who received the first commission to witness about his resurrection from the angel at the tomb (24.4-8). Luke even states that when the women heard the angel's explanation that what had happened was a fulfilment of Jesus' own prophetic words that he would be delivered and crucified, but then 'raised again on the third day' (24.6-7), 'they remembered [Jesus'] words' (24.8).

This is significant. The women were *disciples of Jesus*, received his teaching, and remembered it as a good disciple would be expected to do. This is quite different from the doubting and questioning reception the gospel received from the male disciples (24.11), who had to see Jesus in person, his hands and feet (24.38-39), and whose minds had to be opened 'so they could understand the Scriptures' when Jesus reminded them of his previous teachings to them about his suffering, death and resurrection (24.44-45). Male gender in the Gospels is therefore not at all a qualification for discipleship!

Probing backwards in the Gospel of Luke takes us down to the point where he introduces the women 'who had followed him from Galilee'. Luke states in 8.1 that, as Jesus travelled from one town and village to another in Galilee preaching the good news of the kingdom of God, 'the twelve were with him and also some women': Mary Magdalene, Joanna wife of Chuza, the manager of Herod's household, Susanna, and many others, and the comment is added that 'these women were helping to support [Jesus and the twelve] out of their own means' (8.1-3). These women are with the eleven after the resurrection and take part in the election of Matthias, the twelfth apostle, in Acts 1, and they are obviously included among the disciples who receive the Holy Spirit in Acts 2, when Peter applies to them the prophecy of Joel 2.28-32 and the outpouring of God's Spirit upon 'his servants, both men and women' (Acts 2.1, 17-18).

In view of this, one may well ask why one of these women would not be eligible for the office of apostle. They fulfilled all the explicit requirements mentioned by Peter in Acts 1.21-22: they had been with the twelve, as disciples of Jesus, 'the whole time that Jesus walked in and out among us' and they were 'witnesses of the resurrection'.

The answer is probably twofold. On the one hand, the twelve were to imitate the twelve patriarchs of old Israel, thus announcing that a new Israel had come based on the death and resurrection of Christ. On the other hand, as we have concluded with Bauckham above, there were dominant patriarchal customs protecting 'the priority of men in God's dealing with the world'. This, in turn, created a bias regarding how trustworthy the witness of a woman could be, and we see how this aspect plays out in Luke's description of the women's witness to the resurrection event, even though they are commissioned to witness by God's angel (Matthew 28.6-7; Mark 16.7; Luke 24.6-7) and Jesus himself (Matthew 28.8-10).

The disciples receive the gospel of the resurrection from the women with disbelief, and Luke adds in 24.11: 'for their words seemed to them like *nonsense*' (KJV: 'idle tales'). To put it plainly, there were socially accepted views of the role of women which make it understandable, even appropriate under the circumstances, to consider only a man as a member of the twelve. However, this concession to historical social customs that have changed and continue to change provides no biblical warrant for regarding this as a universal rule for all times.

9.2.3 The Women in the Johannine Writings

Many Bible scholars have noted that women disciples have a particular prominence in the Gospel of John. An example is the study by Sandra M. Schneiders[64] who partially relies on Raymond Brown's work.[65] Only a brief summary of her study can be presented here.

1. *All the women in the Fourth Gospel are presented positively and in intimate relation to Jesus.* No woman resists Jesus, failing to believe, deserting him, or betraying him. This is in sharp contrast to John's presentation of men who are frequently presented as vain (13.37), hypocritical (12.4-6), fickle (13.38; 16.31-32), obtuse, (3.10; 16.18), deliberately unbelieving (9.24-41; 20.24-25), or thoroughly evil (13.2, 27-30). Obviously, women are presented as positive exemplar figures, as characters for the reader to imitate, even male readers!

2. *John's positive presentation of women is neither one-dimensional nor stereotypical.* John's women appear as strikingly individual and original characters, especially in contrast to the shadowy male figures that frequently appear in close proximity to them. One may compare the stereotypical scribe, Nicodemus (3.1-12) with the Samaritan Woman (4.7-41) and the shadowy Lazarus with his sisters. The disciples in the resurrection narratives, with the exception of Thomas (20.2-8, 19-29), are not nearly as realistically drawn as is Mary Magdalene (20.12, 11-18). Thus, the author of the Fourth Gospel had a remarkably rich and nuanced understanding of feminine religious experience.[66]

3. *The women in John's Gospel play unconventional roles.* (a) The Samaritan woman with her complicated past, her uncommon theological knowledge and interests, and her spontaneous assumption of the role of public witness to Jesus; (b) Martha running the public aspects of funeral and mourning; (c) Mary of Bethany extravagantly anointing the feet of Jesus over the protests of the devious Judas; (e) Mary Magdalene roaming alone in a darkened cemetery, questioning

---

[64] S. M. Schneiders, 'Women in the Fourth Gospel and the Role of Women in the Contemporary Church', 1982, pp. 35-45. I am indebted to Schneiders' text in the present section even where this is not formally acknowledged.
[65] R. Brown, 'Role of Women in the Fourth Gospel', 1979, pp. 183-198.
[66] Cf. ibid., p. 183.

a strange man, and responsibly bearing apostolic witness to the assembled disciples – all these examples suggest that the Christian women of John's experience were not uneducated domestic recluses. Surprisingly, none of John's women, except the Mother of Jesus and Mary of Clopas, is presented as wife or mother or in any way essentially defined in relationship to men. On the contrary, Lazarus is identified through his relationship with Mary and Martha and named after them in relation to Jesus in John 11.5.[67] John's presentation makes it more than likely that these are real women, actually engaged in theological discussion, competently proclaiming the gospel, publicly confessing their faith, and serving at the table of the Lord.

The Fourth Gospel is also significant for what it says about the discipleship of Christian women. Firstly, women relate to Jesus directly and never through the mediation and/or by the permission of men. Secondly, there is no such thing as 'women' whose 'place' and 'role' are to be decided and assigned once and for all by some third (male) party. Their ministry to Jesus and to others in his name requires no approval or authorisation of anyone. Thirdly, unlike most of the male disciples, the women are remarkable for their initiative and decisive action. The Samaritan woman assumes on her own her mission of bearing witness to the people of her town; Martha and Mary immediately send for Jesus when Lazarus is ill; they host and prepare a supper six days before the Passover, and Mary performs the unusual anointing on her own initiative; Mary Magdalene is first at the tomb on the resurrection morning determined to find and remove the body of the Lord; she alerts the male disciples to Jesus' disappearance and she alone remains to continue the search while they hide for fear of the Jews. If leadership is a function of creative initiative and decisive action, the Johannine women qualify well for their role.

Women are the privileged recipients of three of Jesus' most important self-revelations: (a) his identity as the Messiah, (b) that he is

---

[67] Ibid., p. 192.

the resurrection and the life, and (c) that his glorification is complete and its salvific effects given to his disciples. Women are the two most important witnesses to him both during his public life and during his Hour. Thus, Schneiders' study demonstrates that women officially represent the community in the expression of its faith (Martha), its acceptance of salvation (Mary Magdalene), and its role as witness to the Gospel (Samaritan Woman, Mary Magdalene).

Together with John, the beloved disciple, two women in John's Gospel hold the place occupied by Peter in the synoptic gospels: Martha as confessor of faith and Mary Magdalene as recipient of the first resurrection appearance and the commission by the Lord as apostle being sent to the church and its leaders. Women were disciples in the strict sense of the word as students of the word of Jesus (Mary of Bethany). The women also played leading roles, along with the beloved disciple, in the Easter events: Mary's anointing and wiping of Jesus' feet (John 12.1-8), 'six days before the Passover', expresses the attitude of a true disciple and points to Jesus' foot washing in John 13. There are examples of male objections to the activity of women (the disciples in Samaria and Judas at Bethany), both of which were effectively suppressed by Jesus, and two examples of the acceptance and effectiveness of the witness of women (the Samaritans and the disciples after the glorification).

The openness and endorsement of women as disciples of Jesus and leaders in the church fellowship suggests that Jesus' involvement with the women in the Gospel was received without restrictions in the various audiences to whom John wrote his Gospel.

9.2.4 Elders

From early on, the twelve apostles became increasingly associated with the 'elders' (*presbyteroi*). This institution had roots in Judaism and ancient Israel and was patriarchal in the sense that it involved only the firstborn males in the seed-line of the people of God (see 6.5.3

above). Thus, the Greek term *presbyteros* refers predominantly in the New Testament to the elders associated with the Jewish Sanhedrin.

In the important decision recorded in Acts 15, the 'apostles and elders' in Jerusalem play a central role (Acts 11.30; 15.2, 4, 6, 22, 23; 16.4; 21.18). However, we hear of no ordination or laying on of hands for the office of elder in the body of the Jerusalem leadership. In his farewell speech to the 'overseers' (*episkopoi*) or 'elders' (*presbyteroi*) in Ephesus (Acts 20.17-35), Paul addresses them, saying that 'the Holy Spirit has made you overseers [over all the flock], to shepherd the church of God' (20.28). But he makes no reference to how this was done. Instead, he reinforces the inevitable conclusion that leadership office in the New Testament church is primarily a matter of a spiritual-prophetic calling.

The New Testament attests the existence of a Christian institution of elders in the local churches.[68] It is tempting to conclude that this emerged under the influence of the pattern of the Jewish synagogue. However, neither rabbinical sources nor the New Testament give evidence that ordination through the laying on of hands was used for elders before AD 70.[69] As it became common in Judaism after Jerusalem's destruction in AD 70, it may also have influenced the Christian church towards the latter part of the first century. Both Judaism and Christianity experienced a crisis after AD 70 which threatened their survival and ordination of elders may have been a way of strengthening their authority and bringing order. Following the death or dispersal of the early Christian leaders – particularly the family of Jesus and the apostles centred in Jerusalem – the institution of the elders gave stability in the difficult times after the destruction of Jerusalem in AD 70. 'Elder' (*presbyteros*) had by then become a title of honour, as was the case in Judaism.[70]

---

[68] Acts 20.17; I Timothy 4.14; 5.17; Titus 1.5.
[69] M. Warkentin, *Ordination*, 1982, pp. 18-21.
[70] Ibid., p. 19.

Paul and Barnabas 'appointed (*cheirotoneo*) elders' in each church and 'set them apart' (*paratithemi*) (Acts 14.23). The possibility cannot be excluded that this involved prayer and the imposition of hands, but *the Bible text does not state so* and there is no valid reason for assuming that the rite was so employed. Therefore, even a literal reading informs us that while elders existed who would be appointed by itinerant apostles such as Paul and Barnabas, there is no evidence at all that these elders were ordained by a ceremony that included the laying on of hands. The same pattern found in the Gospels continues.

The absence of explicit biblical evidence of Christian ordination of elders calls for careful thought. Reference is made in I Timothy 4.14 to the 'imposition of hands' by the 'presbytery'. The Greek noun *epithesis*, 'imposition', occurs only four times in the New Testament (Acts 8.18; I Timothy 4.14; II Timothy 1.6; Hebrews 6.2) and particularly in the formula 'through the imposition of the hand[s] of NN'. However, Acts 8.18 refers to the laying on of hands at baptism, and the meaning in II Timothy 1.6 and Hebrews 6.2 is uncertain (see 9.3.3.4 and 9.4.2 below). Likewise, in I Timothy 4.14, the meaning of the Greek text is unclear (see 9.4.2.4 below). The hands of the presbytery are either laid on young Timothy (although the purpose is not clear), or their act is performed on any member(s) of the congregation for blessing, healing, comfort, baptism or appointment for special tasks (the exact purpose cannot be determined). Timothy 5.22 is equally difficult to understand (see 9.4.2.3 below). We are simply left with conjecture and no clear 'Thus saith the Lord'.

9.2.5 Servants-Ministers

Men and women in various leadership roles are frequently called 'servants' in the New Testament. Via the Latin rendering of 'servant', *minister* has become an English term with various connotations.

Theologically, 'servant' and 'serving' had a rich background in the Old Testament. The epithet 'servant (of God)' is applied to Israel (cf.

Luke 1.54), Moses (cf. Hebrews 3.5), and David (cf. Luke 1.69). The same epithet is used about Jesus when the apostles address a Jewish audience (e.g. Acts 3.13). Jesus had laid the foundation for a theology of 'service' by his teaching, example and sacrificial death,[71] and had made 'service' the central concept in being a disciple and an apostle.

This conceptual context is fundamental to any leadership role in early Christianity. Thus, in his sermon on Pentecost, Peter announces the fulfilment of the prophecy in Joel 2.28-32. He describes God's authorisation of the Christian church as follows:

> *Acts 2.18* Even on my servants (*douloi*), both men and women, in those days I will pour out my Spirit, and they shall prophesy.

In this 'kingdom language', the submission to God implied by 'servants' (*douloi*) makes men and women equal before him who alone is King of the world.

The Old Testament Roots of 'Servant'

The Greek term for 'servant' (*doulos*) is rooted in kingdom terminology. In the Old Testament, being an *'ebed*, 'servant, slave', is the logical correspondence of man's relationship to God as Lord and King. The primary meaning of this word is not the subjection, but the belonging to and protection by the Lord.[72] Thus, the Hebrew word *'ebed*, 'servant', 'cannot be used without specifying to whom the service is rendered'.[73] The attitude of service to God is always connected with 'his unconditional majesty and absolute superiority to man'.[74]

---

[71] For example: Matthew 10.24-25; 12.18; 20.26; 23.11; 24.45-51; 25.14-30.
[72] C. Westermann, *'ebed'*, *THAT*, vol. 1, col. 191.
[73] K. H. Rengstorf, *'doulos'*, *ThDNT*, vol. 2, p. 267.
[74] Ibid., p. 268.

The Old Testament adopted *'ebed*, 'servant', into the *language of worship* to describe 'the relationship of dependence and service in which man stands to God'.[75]

By the use of the term *doulos*, 'servant', the young church recognised the absolute authority of God and his servant Jesus Christ who by his word and the Spirit authorises the service of any leader in his church. Nobody in the New Testament is ever 'made' a *doulos* by ordination, but *this is always the work of the Holy Spirit*, which means that *the commissioning and equipment with gifts by the Spirit is central in any induction into a leadership function.*

In a biblical understanding of ordination, therefore, the concept of 'servant-minister' always implies a unique and singular subordination to one King and Master, i.e. God or his Servant Jesus who is the Head of the church. In this context, therefore, it distorts the biblical teaching to build into our understanding of ordination a *secondary* subordination of women to men (which is a matter dealt with in completely different contexts and mainly referring to issues of order according to local social norms). *The New Testament nowhere compromises God's sovereign authority as he calls men and women to be his 'servants'.*

Various Greek Terms for 'Servant'

The New Testament church continued to call the apostles *douloi*, 'servants', but other terms were also used. Paul's appointment is by the Lord himself:

> *Acts 26.15-16* I am Jesus, whom you are persecuting. But get up and stand on your feet; for I have appeared to you for this purpose, to appoint (*procheirizomai*) you as a servant (*hyperetes*) and as a witness (*martys*) to the things in which you have seen me and to those in which I will appear to you.

---

[75] Ibid., p. 267.

The Greek *hyperetes*, 'servant', in Acts 26.16 is by far the most common Greek term for 'servant' and carries a certain nuance that is relevant in this passage. The special feature of *hyperetes* is that the servant 'willingly learns his task and goal from another who is over him in an organic order but without prejudice to his personal dignity and worth'.[76] The term *hyperetes* is vital in Christ's call of Paul in view of his address to King Agrippa in 26.19: 'So, then, I was not *disobedient* to the vision from heaven'.

The usage of servant-minister (*diakonos, doulos, hyperetes*) is found throughout the Greek New Testament for the apostles and leaders in the church, although with a dominance in the language of Paul and Luke. Thus, 'servant-minister' is used as a title for a spiritual leader, which we can see from its occurrences in the opening greetings in letters: note Peter and John (Acts 4.20 [*douloi*]); Paul (e.g. Romans 1.1 [*doulos*]; I Corinthians 4.1 [*hyperetes*]; II Corinthians 6.4 [*diakonos*]); Paul and his associates (Acts 16.17 [*douloi*]); Paul and Apollos (I Corinthians 3.5 [*diakonoi*]); Paul and Timothy (Philippians 1.1 [*douloi*]); James (1.1 [*doulos*]); Peter (II Peter 1.1 [*doulos*]) ; Jude (1.1 [*doulos*]). In II Timothy 2.24 'servant' (*doulos*) is used as a technical term for a church leader in the context of instructions concerning right behaviour. The young Tychicus is described in Colossians 4.7 as 'a dear brother, a faithful minister (*pistos diakonos*) and fellow servant (*syndoulos*) in the Lord'. It is noteworthy for the purposes of the present study that Phoebe, a woman, is designed 'servant, minister (*diakonos*) of the church in Cenchreae' (Romans 16.1); she is not a 'deacon' but a 'minister' (see 9.2.6 below).

While the Greek language had several terms for servant-minister, the Hebrew had only one term, namely *'ebed*, which means that behind the Greek distinctions we may assume the underlying Hebrew concept. The general 'servant' (*diakonos*) is not the same as the special church office of 'deacon' (*diakonos*), which represents another

---

[76] K. H. Rengstorf, '*hyperetes*', *ThDNT*, vol. 8, pp. 533-534, 542-543.

development in the New Testament church and is linked to the local church in tandem with the 'overseer' (*episkopos*) (I Timothy 3.1-13; see 9.2.8 below).

The apostles that emerged in addition to the twelve, particularly Paul and those working with him, began to call themselves 'servant[s] of the gospel, servant[s] of Christ, servant[s] of God' (Ephesians 3.7 [*diakonos*]; cf. II Corinthians 6.3 [*diakonia*]). This is where our modern term 'minister' originates.

9.2.6 Women as Servants-Ministers

We noted earlier that the story of Jesus' life and ministry is initiated by Mary, the mother of Jesus, who refers to herself as 'servant of God' (*doulos theou*) in Luke 1.47. The story of the early church is then initiated by Peter who describes the recipients of the outpouring of the Spirit by Joel's prophecy as being God's servants, 'both men and women', who will 'prophesy' (Acts 2.18). The early church viewed all members as servants-ministers who received the Holy Spirit and expressed themselves by prophetic (spirit-filled) speech. In this regard there was no distinction between men and women or clergy and laity. All are spirit-filled servants-ministers although *the tasks* may differ.

A similar inclusive language, which embraces both men and women, is found in I Peter 2.16, where the church is admonished to 'live as servants of God' (*douloi theou*). This is stated in the context of a series of household codes (2.13-3.7) following the passage on the church as 'a royal priesthood, a holy nation, a people belonging to God' (I Peter 2.4-12). Women are obviously included in these general references to servants, as we see from 3.1-7 which addresses wives. Later on in his letter, in 4.7-11, Peter makes an important appeal to men and women in the church, where 'service' (*diakonia*) is a general term for prayer (4.7), love (4.8), hospitality (4.9), and speech (4.11). Interspersed between these portions are two sections that define what it means to be a servant-minister:

> *1 Peter 4.10-11* Each one should serve others (*diakoneo*), according to the gift of grace (*charisma*) received, as good stewards of the grace (*charis*) of God in its various forms. [...] If anybody serves (*diakoneo*), it should be with the strength God provides, so that in all things God may be praised through Jesus Christ.

The service-ministry of men and women is based on God's gift of spiritual grace which provides the needed power and strength. The central issue is not the gender of the servant-minister but *the spiritual gift and the glory the service brings to God.*

Phoebe a Servant-Minister of Cenchreae

One of the servants-ministers in the church was 'our sister Phoebe', who is called *diakonos* of the church (*ekklesia*) in Cenchreae, the eastern port of Corinth on the Aegean Sea, and a *prostatis*, 'patron, benefactor', for many people (Romans 16.1-2).[77] The Greek terms for servant-minister varied and both for men and women the terms *doulos* and *diakonos* were used interchangeably. Phoebe's function as servant-minister has nothing to do with the modern deacon/deaconess but is an official office of the church and Paul commends her to the church in Rome which she is to visit as an emissary of the Lord.

A careful examination of the *diakonia* word group suggests a sense of representation or agency.[78] Thus, in calling Phoebe *diakonos*, 'Paul identified her as his agent or intermediary carrying his gospel message, or most specifically, his letter to the Romans'.[79] In view of the language in Romans 16.1, considering the letter as a whole and other instances in Paul's letters, it is a valid conclusion that Phoebe is acting in the same way as the male *diakonoi*, such as Tychicus (Ephesians 6.21; Colossians 4.7) and Timothy and Erastus (Acts 19.22), i.e. Phoebe acts as Paul's emissary, in Paul's name, and with

---

[77] See D. Jankiewicz, 'Phoebe: Was She an Early Church Leader?', 2013.
[78] See the references in: L. H. Cohick, *Women in the World of the Early Christians*, 2009, p. 304, footnote 64.
[79] Ibid.

his authority.[80] Thus, Paul emphasises Phoebe's role as a go-between for the Corinthian churches and the Roman congregation, as well as her specific duty to carry Paul's letter, with his authority.[81]

However, Phoebe is also called 'sister' and 'patron'. Thus, she is a member of the Christian family, and as patron she had obligations to care for them. The role of patron gave Phoebe status and authority in her home churches, but Paul is recommending her to the church in Rome so that they will reciprocate the favours and help she has given Paul and others elsewhere.[82] There are some other similar examples of servants-ministers who are women and who by their wealth and resources exerted a significant influence and had authority in the church: e.g. Lydia from Thyatira (Acts 16.14) and the prominent women from Thessalonica, Beroea, and Athens recorded by Luke in Acts 17.1-34.[83]

Tabitha in Joppa

Acts 9.36-43 describes Tabitha (Dorcas) in Joppa as 'a disciple who was always doing good things and helping the poor'. This is clearly a ministry, not only to help materially and practically, but to bring the gospel to people by acts of loving kindness and relieving people from poverty to open the doors for the gospel through the Spirit of God. Tabitha is surrounded by a congregation of female disciples who call for Peter when she passes away (9.36). As Tabitha is miraculously resurrected from death by Peter's prayer and spiritual powers, many people come to believe in the Lord and join the congregation.

---

[80] Ibid. p. 305.
[81] Ibid.; cf. J. N. Collins, *Diakonia: Re-interpreting the Ancient Sources*, 1990, p. 194.
[82] See the extensive study of this matter with the help of contemporary source material regarding the Roman woman Julia Theodora who had considerable political influence, in: L. H. Cohick, *Women in the World of the Early Christians*, 2009, pp. 301-307.
[83] See L. H. Cohick's detailed study (ibid., pp. 307-308).

Apphia Leader of a House Church

As an itinerant apostle, Paul connects with a large group of people. Among them we also note the presence of women. One of the recipients of the letter to Philemon is 'Apphia, our sister' (v. 2). She may be Philemon's wife, but it is noteworthy that she is held in high regard, being mentioned before other men in the household and even before 'the church that meets in your home'.

Mary, Tryphaena, Tryphosa and Persis

Paul's greetings to twenty-six people in Romans 16 include nine women. Obviously, women occupied a prominent place among Paul's associates. He thinks highly of them all and singles out four, Mary, Tryphaena, Tryphosa and Persis, who have 'worked hard' (*kopiao*), which in Greek implies strong exertion, and this is not stated about anyone else on the list.[84]

Priscilla a Fellow Worker in Christ

Besides Phoebe (considered above), Paul mentions also Priscilla and Junia. Junia will be examined in the next section (9.2.7). In Romans 16.3 and in three other New Testament instances (Acts 18.18, 26; II Timothy 4.19), Priscilla is named before her husband Aquila. Paul calls Priscilla 'my fellow worker (*synergos*) in Christ Jesus', and notes that she and her husband have risked their lives for Paul. Priscilla and Aquila have obviously worked in many churches and seem to be itinerant apostles or prophets and teachers like Barnabas and Paul (cf. Acts 13.1-3), because 'all the churches of the Gentiles are grateful to them'. In Acts 18.18-28, Luke records the event when Priscilla and Aquila in Ephesus explained 'the way of God more adequately' to Apollos, a learned Jew with 'a thorough knowledge of the Scriptures'. Thus, Priscilla was a co-worker with Paul, had an itinerant apostolic ministry, and was thoroughly educated in the Scriptures.

---

[84] J. Stott, *Romans: God's Good News for the World*, 1994, pp. 394-396.

Euodia and Syntyche Struggling with Paul in the Cause of the Gospel

The clear impression that Paul cooperated in ministry with many different women is further supported by a note in Philippians 4.2-3. Reference is made to Euodia and Syntyche who have a disagreement between themselves, but who 'have contended at my side in the cause of the gospel, along with Clement and the rest of my fellow workers (*meta loipon synergon mou*), whose names are in the book of life'. The Greek *synathleo*, 'struggle together with', is used in Philippians 1.27-30 in reference to standing firm to the point of suffering as one faces opposition to the faith of the gospel, which is the same struggle as that of the apostle Paul. The letter to the Philippians is addressed to 'all the saints in Christ Jesus at Philippi with the overseers (*episkopoi*) and servants (*diakonoi*)' and it is likely that the struggle for the gospel involved primarily the leaders. When Paul describes the two women as struggling with him 'for the gospel' together with his other fellow workers, he is referring to their active participation in 'the work of evangelisation'.[85]

Women with Prophetic Gifts

It is obvious that women served as teachers and speakers in early Christianity. Luke records from his and Paul's visit to Philip the evangelist (one of the seven) in Caesarea, that Philip had 'four unmarried daughters who had the gift of prophecy' (Acts 21.9). In Paul's dealings with the issues of church order in Corinth, he states that 'any woman who prays and prophesies with her head unveiled disgraces her head' (I Corinthians 11.5). Later on, he says: 'Pursue love and strive for the spiritual gifts, and especially that you may prophesy' (14.1). This exhortation follows the description of the church as a body where the Spirit has assigned various gifts to its members – utterance of wisdom and knowledge, faith, healing, miracles, prophecy, discernment of spirits, various kinds of tongues and interpretation of tongues (12.1-13) – and God has appointed in

---

[85] G. Friedrich, '*euangelion*', *ThDNT*, vol. 2, p. 729.

the church some to be apostles, prophets and teachers, then deeds of power, gifts of healing, forms of assistance, forms of leadership, various kinds of tongues (12.28-30).

The remarkable thing about I Corinthians 12 is that not by a single word does Paul make a gender distinction regarding who may *function* in these roles or *receive* the gifts of the Spirit. Rather, he states explicitly that 'it is God who activates all [gifts and activities] in everyone' and that 'all these are activities by one and the same Spirit [of God], who allots to each one individually just as the Spirit chooses' (12.6, 11). This teaching is directed to men and women in the church (12.1). Its openness to men and women as receivers of spiritual gifts and as appointees by God to carry various responsibilities in the church has only two caveats, which apply to both men and women, namely, the issue of church order (see e.g. 14.26-40) and the need to avoid bringing the gospel into disrepute among outsiders (see e.g. 14.23-25).

Conclusion

It is obvious that women took part in the work of the early church as servants-ministers, alongside the apostles. However, no man or woman is said to be formally ordained as a servant-minister by the laying on of hands in the New Testament.

9.2.7 *Women as Apostles*

Paul makes a remarkable statement in Romans 16.7:

> *Romans 16.7* Greet Andronicus and Junia, my relatives who were in prison with me; they are prominent among the apostles, and they were in Christ before I was.

This passage confirms that Junia, a woman, is seen by Paul as a prominent 'apostle' in some sense. Obviously, the passage has been much discussed.

That the name 'Junia' is the original text and that it refers to a woman is a well-founded conclusion.[86] This view has been adequately argued by scholars since the 1970s and is widely accepted.[87] The translation of *episemoi en tois apostolois* as 'prominent among the apostles' was supported by most of the apostolic fathers who express an opinion, and has been the most common view among modern commentators, endorsed by most modern translations.[88]

The information about Junia in Romans 16.7 is significant:

1. The name 'Junia' is well attested as a female Roman name, while, for example, the erroneous male name 'Junias' is unattested – this is a late insertion in the manuscripts by a copyist who did not accept a female name here. There is no other relevant evidence that has a bearing on this issue.[89]

2. Andronicus and Junia are described as Paul's 'relatives', which probably means that they were of Jewish descent.[90]

3. They are described as Paul's 'fellow prisoners'. The Greek term refers to 'captives taken in war'.[91] Junia and Andronicus are Paul's fellow prisoners in the sense that they too had suffered imprisonment for their allegiance to the gospel (cf. the expressions used of Euodia

---

[86] This has been demonstrated in detail by R. Bauckham, *Gospel Women*, 2002, pp. 165-186, 194-198; cf. N. Vyhmeister, 'Junia the Apostle', 2013, pp. 6-9.

[87] R. Bauckham, *Gospel Women*, 2002, p. 166; see also B. J. Brooten, 'Junia … Outstanding among the Apostles (Romans 16,7)', 1977, pp. 141-144; P. Lampe, 'Iunia/Iunias: Sklavenherkunft im Kreise der vorpaulinischen Apostel (Röm 16,7)', 1985, pp. 132-134; id., *Die Stadtrömischen Christen in den ersten beiden Jahrhundert*, 1987; R. S. Cervin, 'A Note regarding the Name "Junia(s)" in Romans 16,7', 1994, pp. 464-470; J. Thorley, 'Junia, a Woman Apostle', 1998, pp. 18-29.

[88] R. Bauckham, *Gospel Women*, 2002, p. 172; reference is made to the detailed survey in M. H. Burer and D. B. Wallace, 'Was Junia Really an Apostle?' A Re-examination of Rom 16:7', 2001, pp. 78-84. The challenge to the common view from Burer and Wallace (ibid.) has been effectively refuted by Bauckham (ibid., pp. 172-180).

[89] R. Bauckham, *Gospel Women*, 2002, pp. 167-169.

[90] Ibid., p. 170.

[91] Ibid., p. 170.

and Syntyche in Philippians 4.2-3; see 9.2.6 above). However, it is not possible to determine exactly what this is referring to. Three options exist: (a) at some time when Paul was in prison, they had come to share his confinement in order to encourage him and care for him; (b) they had been in prison, but not at the same time and place as Paul; (c) they were in prison in Rome when Paul wrote his letter.[92]

4. Together with Andronicus, Junia is 'prominent among (*en*) the apostles'. As mentioned already, there is convincing evidence that the Greek here does not mean 'well known to the apostles'.[93] Thus, Junia is not only an apostle but also 'prominent' or 'marked out, distinguished, outstanding'. What does 'apostle' mean here? Obviously she was not one of the twelve. However, there is a non-technical sense of the term 'apostle' that Paul uses twice (II Corinthians 8.23; Philippians 2.25) to designate official messengers of the churches. Bauckham appropriately points out, however, that 'this cannot be the meaning in Romans 16.7' and says: 'Such people are clearly designated "apostles of the churches" (2 Cor. 8.23) and "your [i.e. the Philippian Christians'] apostle" (Phil. 2.25)', and 'it is hard to see how they could form a known body of people among whom Andronicus and Junia could be said to be outstanding'.[94] Bauckham's well-founded conclusion is that 'the unqualified "apostles" of Romans 16.7 refers to the apostles of Christ, whom Paul generally refers to simply as "apostles".' Bauckham continues and points out the following:

> Paul's use of the term in this sense is broader than that of Matthew, Mark, and Luke, who restrict it to the twelve. For Paul the apostles of Christ included not only the twelve but also Barnabas (1 Cor. 9.6), the brothers of the Lord (Gal. 1.19; 1 Cor. 9:5), probably Silvanus/Silas (1 Thess. 2.7), and perhaps Apollos (1 Cor. 4.9), as well as Paul himself. Paul speaks of 'all the apostles' alongside the narrower

---

[92] Ibid., pp. 170-172.
[93] Ibid., pp. 172-180.
[94] Ibid., p. 180.

category of 'the twelve' (1 Cor. 15.5, 7). These are those who have been commissioned by the risen Christ himself in resurrection appearances, since it is in this sense that Paul can regard himself, the last to be so commissioned, as the least of the apostles (1 Cor. 15.9; cf. 9.1). It is important to consider that this category could have been considerably larger than the few names we know, and so there is no difficulty in supposing that Andronicus and Junia belonged to it, especially as Paul says specifically that they were Christians before him.[95]

Our previous presentation of the term 'apostle' concurs with the summary provided by Bauckham (see 9.2.1 above).

5. Andronicus and Junia 'were in Christ before Paul'. This suggests that they were Palestinian Jews or diaspora Jews converted while visiting Jerusalem, and probably members of the early Jerusalem church.[96] This may be the reason that they are 'prominent among the apostles'.

Bauckham presents a very interesting hypothesis regarding Junia in that he shows the possibility that she is identical with Joanna, the wife of Herod's manager Chuza, mentioned in Luke 8.3 and 24.10.[97] If this is correct, Junia/Joanna is an outstanding apostolic witness in that she witnessed the death and burial of Jesus as well as the empty tomb and is part of the group of women who are asked by the angel to bring the first gospel of Jesus' resurrection to the disciples (Luke 23.27-28, 49, 55-56; 24.1-12). We need not at this point go into the details of Bauckham's proposal regarding Joanna, but the established fact of the existence in Rome of Junia, a woman, as prominent among the apostles, is significant evidence of women being endorsed as servants, ministers and leaders in the Bible.

---

[95] Ibid.
[96] See the exposition in ibid., p. 181.
[97] Ibid., pp. 202.

We need to bear in mind, finally, that no apostle in the New Testament church – be it a man or a woman – was ordained by the laying on of hands for the position of the apostolate. The seven in Acts 6.1-6 did not become apostles – exactly what their leadership role was is not defined. In Acts 13.1-3, Barnabas and Paul were not ordained for an office but for an *ad hoc* missionary journey in Gentile territory (see 9.3.3.2 below).

9.2.8 The Offices of Elder, Overseer, and Deacon

Towards the end of the historical process unevenly reflected in the New Testament, rudimentary church offices emerge that would receive a firm shape in the second century, after the completion of the New Testament writings. The mission of Christ remains the central concern for the church, but factors such as the growth of the church, the need for order and unity under the threats of internal divisions, false teachings, and external pressure from Graeco-Roman society open the door for a greater emphasis on organisation. The development towards fixed offices with a professional body of leaders cannot be traced in detail, but the following points briefly summarise the trends evidenced by the New Testament:

The Twelve. See 9.2.1 above.

The Family of Jesus. Besides the twelve, from the beginning, the family of Jesus was also involved as leaders. Perhaps they were included in 'the apostles and elders' mentioned, for example, in Acts 15 where the role of elders could allude to Jesus' brothers James and Jude. As brothers of Jesus, their status was guaranteed by family relationships, regardless of any formal ceremony of induction.

Paul indicates in Galatians 1.11-2.10 that he visited Jerusalem twice and met the leading group there. Three years after his conversion, he met with Peter (Cephas) and James, the brother of Jesus, whom he calls 'apostles' (1.18-19). After another fourteen years, he met with 'the acknowledged leaders' (2.2, 6), i.e. literally 'those who were held in regard' (*dokountes*), and 'the acknowledged pillars' (*hoi dokountes styloi*) James, Cephas and John (2.9). It is perhaps significant that James the brother of Jesus is mentioned first, even before Peter. Paul does not seem to attach much importance to their position, however, because in referring to 'those who were supposed to be acknowledged leaders' he makes the comment that 'what they actually were makes no difference to me; God shows no partiality' (2.6). What matters for Paul is the calling that God has given him.

As evidenced by Eusebius,[98] the family of Jesus led the church up until the destruction of Jerusalem in AD 70. This may explain the curious fact that the New Testament does not describe the selection and induction of elders or apostolic leaders – it was generally not needed during the first generation of Christians, because the key forms of leadership were the family of Jesus (no ordination required), the twelve apostles (not ordained but appointed by Jesus), and the charismatic and prophetic apostles who (like Paul) had a direct appointment by Christ. The apostles and the family of Jesus eventually disappeared and were not replaced. The church now needed to be creative in finding new ways of passing on the leadership responsibility, which still allowed for a recognition of the divine call and the acknowledgment of the congregation.

The Seven. The apostles and elders in Jerusalem were *expanded* by the seven in Acts 6.1-6 in order to relieve the apostles from practical duties (cf. the judges and elders relieving Moses in Exodus 18 and Numbers 11), but this move did not lead to an institution of permanent new offices. The process involved both the decision of the apostles and of the congregation, but the ceremony does not result in a permanent order for leadership appointment. It is a unique and *ad hoc* event. The division of labour is significant, because it is stated that the apostles will do the ministry of the Word, while the seven will do

---

[98] *Historia Ecclesiastica*, Book 2, Chapter 23:1, 4; Book 3, Chapter11:1-2.

the ministry of tables. However, even the new group, at least Stephen and Philip, also taught the gospel in a powerful way (Acts 6.8-10; 8.5, 36-40; 21.8). See further 9.4.2.1 below.

Itinerant and Charismatic-Prophetic Apostles. The apostles and elders were also *expanded* by a widened concept of 'apostle' which was charismatically defined and may have applied the Jewish model of sending 'apostles' (*shelikhim*) to the diaspora synagogues (as exemplified by Barnabas and Paul in Acts 13.1-3).[99] This widening of the apostolate was driven by various needs:

(a) It occurred for practical mission purposes through the 'apostles of churches' (II Corinthians 8.23), i.e. leaders being appointed by the Holy Spirit and then confirmed, commissioned and sent out by the laying on of hands by the church (Acts 13.1-3). They functioned as itinerant preachers and teachers who founded and organised new congregations. Thus, both Barnabas and Paul, who were at first 'prophets and teachers' (Acts 13.1), are called 'apostles' (Acts 14.4, 14) as they appoint 'elders' in each church (Acts 14.23).

(b) The concept of 'apostle' received *prophetic-charismatic* significance. There was a personal sense of calling by God, as in the case of Paul (explicitly set out in Acts 26.15-18; I Corinthians 15.1-10; I Timothy 1.12; Titus 1.1). Paul argues that he, too, is an apostle (I Corinthians 9.1-2; Galatians 1.11-19) and introduces most of his letters by the claim that he is an apostle, even an 'apostle of Christ' (see 9.2.7 above). Thus, Paul understood 'apostles' as a wider group than the twelve.

In the local churches, for example in Ephesus, there would now be a variety of leaders set up by Christ for 'preparing God's people for works of service' and for 'building up the body of Christ', and 'apostles' is one of them, even the first of those mentioned (Ephesians 4.11-12; cf. I Corinthians 12.28). Consequently, some 'apostles' had

---

[99] See M. H. Shepherd, Jr, 'Apostle', *IDB*, vol. 1, p. 171.

a closer involvement in the life of churches that were expanding and growing far beyond Jerusalem and Judea.

Women were included among these charismatic appointees – note Junia as apostle (see 9.2.7 above) and Phoebe as a servant-minister of the church in Cenchreae (see 9.2.6 above). And spiritual leadership would also be given by men and women appointed directly by the Spirit, like Philip's daughters and Agabus (Acts 21.8-10).

The prophetic-charismatic expansion of the concept of 'apostle' was also eventually affected by the destruction of Jerusalem and the elimination of Jewish political independence. Power shifted away from the family of Jesus in Jerusalem to those 'chosen by the Spirit' in other cities, particularly in Antioch (cf. Acts 13.1-3; 14.23). Thus, Paul's emphasis on spiritual gifts (I Corinthians 12) anticipated the shift in authority that would be required as the apostles and elders died out.

The Beginning of Organised Church Offices. The Pastoral Epistles (the letters to Timothy, Titus, and Philemon) give some evidence of how the office of apostle was gradually transformed into organised offices in the local churches. While Timothy and Titus were itinerant assistants in Paul's ministry – although they could casually be included in a team of apostles (I Thessalonians 2.7) – Paul defines himself as 'a herald (*keryx*), apostle (*apostolos*) and teacher (*didaskalos*)' (I Timothy 2.7; II Timothy 1.11). Paul says he has been 'appointed' (*tithemi*) to these offices and introduces himself as 'Paul, an apostle of Christ Jesus *by the will of God*, according to the promise of life that is in Christ Jesus' (II Timothy 1.1). Thus, Christ has directly appointed him for his office:

> *I Timothy 1.12* I am grateful to Christ Jesus our Lord, who has strengthened me, because he judged me faithful and appointed (*tithemi*) me to his service (*diakonia*).

This is in harmony with Christ's direct calling of Paul recorded in Acts 26.15-18, which we considered earlier. In Titus 1.1, he introduces himself as 'a servant of God and an apostle of Jesus Christ'. He adds that God has 'revealed his word through the proclamation with which I have been entrusted by the command of God our Saviour' (1.3). God has commanded his appointment as apostle which includes teaching and preaching.

However, there is no mention of an ecclesiastical authority, or a hierarchy of offices, or a ceremony of ordination. Paul has a *charismatic* apostolate from God, and the decisive test of his ministry is its fruit and the gift of God's grace. Early in his ministry, he was endorsed by the 'pillars' in Jerusalem, but this is not a condition for his ministry which is given him by God (Acts 26.12-18; I Corinthians 15.8-11; Galatians 1.11-2:10). The leaders in Jerusalem recognised 'the grace' (*charis*) given to him (Galatians 2.9) and, to use Paul's own words, that 'God, who was at work in the ministry of Peter as an apostle to the Jews, was also at work in my ministry as an apostle to the Gentiles' (2.8).

In connection with the emergence of the elders (*presbyteroi*), we noted that Barnabas and Paul appointed elders in local churches (Acts 14.23; see 9.2.4 above). The sense of the Greek term *cheirotoneo* in Acts 14.23 is simply 'indicate by hand' or 'appoint', and the etymology of the word involves the raising of hands in a congregational vote. There is no explicit indication in the biblical texts that prayer and fasting became a fixed ritual in the churches under Paul's oversight (cf. Titus 1.5). This applies even more to the laying on of hands, which is a practice mentioned nowhere in connection with the appointments of elders. However, the fact that elders were appointed in the churches led to the establishment of regular offices in the local churches. We encounter the 'elder' (*presbyteros*) who may have been part of a collegial body called the 'presbytery' (I Timothy 4.14). The group of elders may have been led by an 'overseer, bishop' (*episkopos*), and some leadership tasks were evidently held by the 'servant, deacon' (*diakonos*), as we see in I Timothy 3.1-13.

Overseers and Elders. The relevant passages in I Timothy and Titus indicate that the terms 'elder' (*presbyteros*) and 'overseer' (*episkopos*) were occasionally applied interchangeably. In I Timothy 3.1-7, Paul first instructs Timothy regarding the moral qualifications of the overseer (*episkopos*) followed by similar instructions regarding the servant (*diakonos*) (3.8-13). However, in 5.17-21, he adds further instructions regarding 'the elders' (*presbyteroi*) who 'direct the affairs of the church and are worthy double honour, especially those whose work is teaching and preaching' (obviously, there were elders with different functions).

The relationship between overseer and elder is however not defined. Then, in Titus 1.5-9, Paul acknowledges that young Titus was left in Crete in order to 'appoint (*kathistemi*) elders (*presbyteroi*) in every town' according to Paul's instructions. Those instructions are summarised in 1.6-9, where Paul describes the *qualifications* of an elder/overseer – the terms 'elder' (*presbyteros*) and 'overseer' (*episkopos*) are used as if they refer to the same group (1.5, 7). These terms either refer to the same office, or they overlap in some way, but we cannot say how.

Also Paul's farewell speech to the elders/overseers in Ephesus (Acts 20.17-35) shows no real distinction between 'elder' (*presbyteros*) and 'overseer' (*episkopos*) (20.17, 28). Here, the task of the elder-overseer is defined as 'being overseers over all the flock' and 'shepherding the church of God'. This includes the central function of teaching the truth and protecting the church from 'savage wolves' coming even from within the group of the elders-overseers (20.29-30). One of the requirements of an elder-overseer in I Timothy 3.2 is that of being 'an apt teacher'.

The Deacon. Paul mentions another office in I Timothy 3.8-13, which is the 'servant, deacon' (*diakonos*). Again, all we have is a list of moral qualifications, but no information on the procedure of appointment or ordination or the laying on of hands. In Philippians 1.1, Paul addresses the readers as 'all the saints in Christ Jesus in Philippi, together with the overseers (*episkopoi*) and deacons (*diakonoi*)'. Both overseers and servants-deacons would be known as 'servants-ministers of God' or 'servants-ministers of Christ'. It has been assumed that the deacon was a 'servant' of the overseer, following the model of the judges (Exodus 18.22) and the seventy elders (Numbers 11.16-17, 24-25) who assisted Moses and the seven who assisted the apostles in Jerusalem (Acts 6.1-6). However, this is pure guesswork and may well imply a projection of later practices back into the Bible.

The Jewish Background. It is possible that the model of an overseer and deacon besides a presbytery was influenced by the practice in the Jewish synagogues, where two officers led the worship. One was called the 'head of the synagogue' (*archisynagogos*) and the other 'servant' (*hyperetes*).[100] The direction of the synagogue was in the hands of the presbytery or council of elders, an institution found in the church in Ephesus according to I Timothy 4.14. Early churches consisting essentially of Jewish converts would naturally follow the practice of the synagogue. With the passing of time and as the church continued to grow among the Gentiles, however, this Jewish influence may have diminished and various other models may have been used, thus producing a growing variety and flexibility.

Spiritual Gifts and Leadership Ministry. In the local church setting, however, as we see from Paul's letter to the church in Ephesus, a variety of 'services-ministries' were offered based on spiritual gifts or *charismata* which Jesus has apportioned to each one (Ephesians 4.7).

In Ephesians 4.11 we find various individuals called and equipped with spiritual gifts that allowed them to serve in more specialised forms of leadership: apostles, prophets, evangelists, pastors and teachers.

---

[100] H. W. Beyer, '*diakonos*', *ThDNT*, vol. 2, pp. 89-93.

In Romans 12.6-8 and I Corinthians 12.28-30, similar groups are mentioned and the function of 'leadership' is specifically mentioned. They were appointed by God to prepare God's people 'for the work of ministry, for building up the body of Christ, until all of us come to the unity of the faith and of the knowledge of the Son of God, to maturity, to the measure of the full stature of Christ' (Ephesians 4.12).

The Greek term for 'pastor' (*poimen*) occurs only in Ephesians 4.11 in the New Testament and is not defined, but it may originally have been connected with the concept of a leader as 'shepherd' of the flock.[101]

Deacons and Elders/Overseers. In view of the nature of the task given to the seven in Acts 6.1-6, it is probable that their function was gradually taken over by servants-deacons who were then appointed, besides the elders, in the local churches. This is what happens in Ephesus (I Timothy 3.1-13). If the procedure outlined in Acts 6.1-6 is characteristic of how appointive leaders were selected, we may also assume that local leaders were elected by the community and affirmed by the apostles or itinerant apostles like Paul and his associates Timothy and Titus. The church would begin by recognising the gift of leadership of candidates for deacons and elders/overseers and their being filled with the Spirit (Acts 6.3). Their task was spiritual oversight, protection of the community (i.e. shepherding), teaching and preaching (Acts 20.28; I Timothy 5.17). It needs to be added, however, that while a pattern of offices is being slowly established, the suggestions made here are based on reconstruction, since no explicit information is given. *Even if the texts are being read literally, there are no clear definitions of the tasks of leaders or how they were inducted into office.*

---

[101] See Numbers 27.17; Matthew 2.6; John 10.11; Acts 20.17, 28; Hebrews 13.20; I Peter 2.25; 5.1-4; Revelation 7.17.

As has been pointed out in one of the recent reports to the GC Theology of Ordination Study Committee,[102] gifts and offices in parts of the New Testament should not be radically distinguished, because elders/overseers were appointed to their office based on having received gifts that qualified them for their positions. For example, among the gifts of the Spirit we find the one for 'pastor' (Ephesians 4.11), which is included in the role of elder/overseer (I Peter 5.1-4; Acts 20.17, 28). The functions of elder and overseer are also interchangeable (Acts 20.17, 28; Titus 1.5, 7), and the gift of teaching is described as a responsibility of an elder/overseer (I Timothy 3.2; Titus 1.9). Thus, the roles of pastor/teacher and elder/overseer were not clearly distinguished.

In conclusion, the New Testament church is a body of believers, men and women, who are servants-ministers of Christ. Since they are many, since mission is challenging and requires training and organisation, the church has a *practical* need to *delegate* to gifted members certain specific tasks. This has over time developed to the establishment of special leadership positions or offices, in the Christian churches.

While the New Testament is explicit concerning the fundamental importance for leaders to be called by the Spirit and equipped by spiritual gifts (Acts 13.1-3; Romans 12; I Corinthians 12; Ephesians 4), it also supports *practical* reasons for the organisation of leadership offices (e.g. Acts 6.1-6). Thus, *the needs of the mission of the church* and the guidance of the Spirit and the teaching of the Scriptures shaped the nature of leadership offices and the individuals entrusted to fill them.

One such practical issue for the ministry of the church is the issue of the gender of the church leader (to be further considered in 9.2.9 below). Male gender was often preferred, not as a divine principle stated in Scripture, but because it was *practically* needed in settings

---

[102] GC-TOSCR, 2014, p. 82.

where the internal order and external cultural environment of the church made it appropriate.

9.2.9 *The Gender of Overseers and Deacons (I Timothy 3.1-13)*

In I Timothy 3.1-13, the apostle Paul outlines instructions to young Timothy regarding the qualifications of overseers (*episkopoi*) and servants (*diakonoi*) in the church in Ephesus. For both offices, most of the qualifications are the same as those expected of all Christians and are, therefore, not gender exclusive. Immediately following the lists of qualifications in 3.1-13, Paul explains why he conveys them:

> *I Timothy 3.14-15* I hope to come to you soon, but I am writing these instructions to you so that, if I am delayed, you may know how one ought to behave in the household of God, which is the church of the living God, the pillar and bulwark of the truth.

His purpose is not to deal with gender or even the tasks of overseers and deacons, but their *behaviour* in the household of the living God, in the foundation[103] of *the truth*. The two lists provide qualifications for leaders in order to build respect and acceptance of 'the truth' (2.3-4) within the church and among outsiders.

The office of the deacon or, literally, 'servant' carried important leadership responsibilities in the New Testament church. Although the qualifications for a servant-deacon are worded in a gender-specific form (masculine), they are not gender exclusive (I Timothy 3.8-10, 12, 13). *The New Testament church had female deacons.* Firstly, in Paul's instructions concerning deacons in 3.8-13, he provides a brief list of qualifications of 'women' who 'likewise must be serious, not slanderers, but temperate, faithful in all things' (3.11). Secondly, a

---

[103] For the central role of 3.14-16 in the letter as a whole and the translation of Greek *hedraioma* as 'foundation', see A. T. Hanson, *The Pastoral Epistles*, 1982, pp. 81-86.

female deacon is explicitly mentioned by Paul in Romans 16.1: 'I commend to you our sister Phoebe, a deacon (*diakonos* – masculine!) of the church at Cenchreae' (see 9.2.6 above). We may add here that Ellen White recommended that female 'deacons' be ordained with the laying on of hands, despite the fact that a deacon in I Timothy 3.12 must be 'the husband of one wife'![104] She apparently did not read the passage as do those who now wish to block women's ordination in the Seventh-day Adventist Church by referring to this literal phrase.

The passage about the overseer in I Timothy 3.1-7 resembles Titus 1.5-9, and the parallel passage for the deacon in 3.8-13 is also very similar, albeit somewhat shorter. Even the charge to Timothy in 5.11-16 covers essentially the same features. More or less the same elements are repeated for the widows (I Timothy 5.3-16) and women and men (Titus 2.3-13). The Christian behaviour that generates respect and good order is the same, regardless of gender.

The recurring concept in these passages is the requirement of being 'blameless' (*anepilemptos*, I Timothy 3.1; 6.14; *anegkletos*, I Timothy 3.10; Titus 1.6). In the following, therefore, we will focus our attention on 3.1-7 as a model passage. A fairly literal translation reads as follows:

> *I Timothy 3.1-7* If anyone aspires to the office of oversight (*episcope*) he desires a good work. Now an overseer (*episkopos*) ought to be blameless, the husband of one wife, sober, temperate, orderly, hospitable, with a gift of teaching, not over-fond of wine, not violent but considerate, not quarrelsome, and not a lover of money. He must supervise his own house well, keeping his children in submission in all dignity (for if somebody does not know how to supervise his own house, how will he look after the church of God?). He must not be a recent convert, so that he is not conceited and falls into the same condemnation as the devil. He must also have a good reputation among

---

[104] TED-TOSCR, 2013, section 4.6.2.3, point 11; GC-TOSCR, 2014, p. 85.

those outside, so that he will not fall into disgrace which is a snare of the devil.

This list of qualifications has been worded with a local church leader in mind, not an itinerant apostolic 'servant-minister'. The masculine gender in the text does not mean that, today, only males can be overseers and servants in the church. The language is gender specific (masculine) but also gender inclusive. This conclusion is based on the following observations:

1. Anyone: Paul says in 3.1: 'If *anyone* (*tis*, an indefinite pronoun referring to both male and female) aspires to the office of oversight […]' (cf. Titus 1.6). He continues in 3.2, saying, literally: 'Thus, it is appropriate for an overseer (*episkopos*) to be blameless'. In the same way that masculine forms of words in modern languages may refer to both men and women ('chairman', 'ombudsman'), the form *episkopos* is not in itself gender-exclusive. We have seen that the masculine *diakonos* may refer to a female deacon (Romans 16.1).

2. Masculine forms referring to male and female: The entire list of qualifications in 3.1-7 follows the same formal pattern. The verbs are in the third person singular, which may refer to male and female, but the nouns and the adjectives are in the masculine. In biblical Hebrew and Greek the masculine form is used for inclusive reference to male and female. As in many languages and societies today, gendered (usually male) word-forms are used any time one wishes to refer to both men and women together.

It is well-known that in the Hebrew Old Testament, the masculine gender is always inclusive of both male and female, unless the context would indicate that the reference is specifically male. The same applies to New Testament Greek. For example, in Exodus 20.17 the Israelites are told 'You shall not covet your neighbour's house […] wife […] or male or female slave […] or ox or donkey, or anything that belongs to your neighbour'. The masculine form of the acting person includes here both men and women. The fact that the commandment does not mention a woman's 'coveting of a husband' does not mean that the commandment allows a woman to covet her neighbour's husband.

3. Husband of one wife: Similarly, in I Timothy 3.2 (and Titus 1.6), ancient Greek had no word for the gender-neutral 'spouse', so Paul had to choose to say either 'husband [of one wife]' or 'wife [of one husband]'. If he chose the latter, it would exclude the men (which is actually the case in 5.9 where we find 'wife of one man'), but he chose the former because the expression is inclusive of both male and female. This is exemplified by the use of 'husband of one wife' about both overseer and deacon in 3.1, 12. Since a woman could hold the office of deacon (Phoebe in Romans 16.1), and *diakonos* in Greek is a masculine form applied to a woman, the phrase is gender-specific (masculine) but not gender exclusive (both male and female are indicated).

The phrase emphasises moral piety rather than gender (cf. I Timothy 5.9 and 5.12). This is supported by the fact that a faithful widow is a 'wife of one husband' or a 'one-man wife' according to 5.9. 'The husband of one wife' may on the one hand be understood as referring to the stance of avoiding a second marriage after the death of the spouse, which was held in high regard as an act of honour in Graeco-Roman society.[105] If, on the other hand, we understand it as an allusion to the high purity standards for the high priest in Israel, who could only marry a virgin and not a widow, a divorced woman, or a prostitute (see Leviticus 21.13-14), the act of having one spouse would generate honour and respect among Jewish people.

The concept behind the phrases 'husband of one wife' or 'wife of one husband' is a culturally accepted *cliché* that was applied to both men and women to underline their decency and honour. In Graeco-Roman society, 'the woman who had remained with one husband all

---

[105] See the four main interpretations of this expression in: A. T. Hanson, *The Pastoral Epistles*, 1982, pp. 77-78. Note especially the evidence provided for the high regard in Graeco-Roman society for avoiding a second marriage after the death of a spouse (p. 77).

her life, or who when widowed had not remarried, was honoured'.[106] The Latin epithet *unavira* ('married to one man only') is often found on epitaphs,[107] and Paul applies it to the widows in Ephesus in I Timothy 5.9, 12. The fact that Paul nevertheless urges remarriage for younger widows in 5.14 shows that he did not apply the set-phrase 'married to one man/woman' as a dictate for the Christian community, but that it had to do with decency, propriety, and respect in the specific local culture in Ephesus, and this is what he applies to the overseer in 3.2.

4. Managing his own household well: This phrase does not exclude women. The same qualification is required from deacons (3.12), and we have seen that a woman could function as a deacon. Women were indeed expected to manage their household well too (5.14), and a good example is Lydia in Acts 16.15. The point of the phrase is that overseers and deacons need good leadership ability so that their household does not bring reproach on them in society. We will see later on why the need to avoid reproach and be blameless is underlined in this passage.

These observations mean that the *wording* of the text in I Timothy 3.1-7 does not exclude women from being included as 'overseers' (or 'deacons' in 3.8-13).

In view of the interchangeability between 'overseer' (*episkopos*) and 'elder' (*presbyteros*) – see Acts 20. 17, 28; I Timothy 3.1-7; 4.14; 5:17-21; Titus 1.5-9 – it is not clear if this office is to be held by a local church elder within the presbytery, or a head of the local church. Elders or overseers could have different roles in the church (I Timothy 5.17).

The church in Ephesus may have followed the Jewish synagogue practice of having two officers leading the worship, one being called the 'head of the synagogue' (*archisynagogos*) and the other 'servant'

---

[106] Ibid., p. 77.
[107] See M. Lightman & W. Zeisel, 'Unavira: An Example of Continuity and Change in Roman Society', 1977, pp. 93-104.

(*hyperetes*).[108] The direction of judicial matters in the synagogue was in the hands of the presbytery or council of elders, and this institution existed also in the church in Ephesus (I Timothy 4.14). The uncertainty derives from the fact that our passage does not describe the tasks and responsibilities of the overseer, but only the personal and ethical qualifications.

There is no reference to how the appointment is made – no ordination is mentioned. And Paul indicates in Acts 20.28 that elders-overseers were 'made' by the Holy Spirit, just as Paul himself 'received' from the Lord Jesus his 'ministry to testify to the good news of God's grace' (20.23). It runs counter to common sense, therefore, to use I Timothy 3.1-7 as an argument against women's ordination for pastoral ministry when the office in question is another and no ordination is even included. The phrase 'husband of one wife' is gender-inclusive and deals with public decency, not gender.

Looking now at I Timothy 3:1-7 as a whole, the following features stand out:

1. The overseer's qualifications illustrate the spiritual Christian values according to Paul's teaching in Galatians 5.13-26, for they systematically refer to the 'desires of the flesh' that must be avoided (Galatians 5.19-21) and the 'fruit of the Spirit' that is to be displayed (Galatians 5.22-23). Thus, they describe the inner, spiritual qualifications of the candidate and express the ideal of *eusebeia*, 'godliness' or 'piety', which Paul places at the centre of his instructions in I Timothy 4.1-16 (note 4.7-10; cf. 6.11). These are qualifications that pertain to all Christians, men and women, but Paul makes the point in 3.1-7 that an overseer must be 'blameless' in this regard, i.e. there must not be any errors in an overseer's godliness or piety. The action to be taken in case of an erring elder is then addressed later on, in 5.20.

---

[108] H. W. Beyer, '*diakonos*', *ThDNT*, vol. 2, pp. 89-93.

The concept of *eusebeia* was one of the key virtues in the Graeco-Roman culture in Asia Minor, and we see how the apostle Paul builds on it, for example, in his speech to the Athenians in Acts 17.22-34, where it is used in 17.23 to establish a positive, common ground with his audience. Not least in the city of Ephesus, where the goddess Diana was fervently worshipped, *eusebeia*, 'godliness', and *sofrosyne*, 'self-discipline' would be conditions for the honour of a religious leader.[109]

Thus, Paul describes in our passage the qualifications of the ideal overseer who has *eusebeia*, that special virtue which commanded respect among the church members (especially various factions arguing about true and false teachings) but also among those outside, who valued *eusebeia* highly, albeit in worshipping pagan gods, but to whom the gospel could only be conveyed if they respected and honoured the leaders of the church.

2. A second point of interest in I Timothy 3.1-7 is that the qualifications include only one element relating to the actual performance of the overseer's tasks, namely 'having the gift of teaching' (*didaktikos*), while there is an overwhelming number of terms describing aspects of 'self-discipline' (*sofrosyne*): 'sober, temperate, orderly, not over-fond of wine, not violent but considerate, not quarrelsome, not a lover of money, not being conceited'. 'Self-discipline' is a repeated virtue in I Timothy 2.9, 16; 3.2; and Titus 1.8. In view of our first observation above, this points in the direction of a need to describe the overseer as a virtuous person, one with *eusebeia*, and *sofrosyne*, who would command the respect of church members and outsiders alike. This would be necessary for the overseer to be able to serve as a leader.

3. A third point of interest concerns the emphasis on being 'blameless', which, as noted previously, occurs in the parallel description

---

[109] W. Foerster, '*eusebeia*' etc., *ThDNT*, vol. 7, p. 178; note also the function of this concept in Hellenistic Judaism and the New Testament (ibid., pp. 179-181, 181-184).

of the overseer/elder in Titus 1.5-9, as well as in the description of the deacon in I Timothy 3.8-13 and the charge to Timothy in 6.11-16. This concept is connected with a series of references to actions that preserve the overseer's reputation and especially give him honour according to the customs widely accepted in the Graeco-Roman and Jewish-Hellenistic environment. A review of these customs points in the same direction, that is, a joint emphasis on honourable and pious behaviour:

(a) We have already outlined the honourable associations behind the phrase 'the husband of one wife' (I Timothy 3.2). Avoiding a second marriage after the death of the spouse was held in high regard as an act of honour in Graeco-Roman society.[110] In a Jewish setting also, such an act could be deemed honourable (see references above).

(b) The qualification of 'hospitality' is also an honourable virtue rooted in *eusebeia* in both Graeco-Roman and Jewish communities (besides the divine obligations in Exodus 22.20; 23.9; Leviticus 19.22, see also Romans 12.13; I Timothy 5.10; Titus 1.8; Hebrews 13.2; I Peter 4.9).[111]

(c) Being able to supervise one's own house and keeping one's children in submission 'with all dignity (*semnotes*)' was another highly regarded virtue at the time.[112]

---

[110] See the four main interpretations of this expression in: A. T. Hanson, *The Pastoral Epistles*, 1982, pp. 77-78. Note especially the evidence provided for the high regard in Graeco-Roman society for avoiding a second marriage after the death of a spouse (p. 77).

[111] V. H. Kooy says: '[Hospitality] was recognised as a sacred duty throughout the Mediterranean world, and more heartily and stringently kept than many a written law.' ('Hospitality', *IDB*, vol. 2, p. 654). The same author also outlines the examples in the Old and New Testaments (ibid.). For a careful review of biblical hospitality and its cultural context, especially its roots in *eusebeia*, 'godliness', see S. Thompson, 'The Boundaries of Christian Hospitality in a Postmodern Setting', 2009, pp. 327-331.

[112] Cf. B. J. Malina, *The New Testament World: Insights from Cultural Anthropology*, 2001, pp. 30-31.

(d) The emphasis on 'not being conceited' and thus avoiding *hybris* is yet another example. In Homer, *hybris* is 'to trespass beyond one's own sphere', and 'often the arrogant, wild and unrighteous are contrasted with the hospitable who are minded to fear God'.[113]

(e) The list in I Timothy 3 sums up these features finally by underlining the need to maintain a 'good reputation' among outsiders and avoid any 'disgrace' (*oneidismos*). Thus, the overseer's qualifications are meant to keep him/her blameless in the public eye, to preserve his/her good reputation and make him/her honourable to outsiders as a man/woman with true *eusebeia*, 'godliness'.

Paul urges that the worship in the church be characterised by 'supplications', prayers, intercessions, and thanksgivings for everyone, for kings and all who are in high positions, so that believers may lead a quiet and peaceable life in all godliness (*eusebeia*) and dignity (*semnotes*) (I Timothy 2.1-2; cf. 3.4). The reason is who God is and what he wants (2.3-6). It is for the gospel of God about Jesus Christ that Paul has been 'appointed a herald and an apostle [...] a teacher of the Gentiles in faith and truth' (2.7). Thus, *the qualifications of the overseer are motivated by the mission of God to the world and serve to build trust and acceptance of the gospel of Christ among outsiders.*

The passage in I Timothy 3.1-13, therefore, raises no hindrances for women to be overseers of a local church or being ordained for the gospel ministry. Its meaning is gender inclusive. If in New Testament times the office of the overseer was nevertheless held by a male, this was to safeguard the honour of the church, the glory of God, and the trustworthiness of the gospel in Graeco-Roman and Jewish settings (cf. Acts 20. 21) where women's involvement in public life could be considered inappropriate (see further in 9.5.1 below).

I Timothy 3.1-13 contains universal principles that the church should apply even today. The lists of qualifications for local church leaders are motivated by warnings against 'falling into disgrace' and

---

[113] G. Bertram, '*hybris*' etc., *ThDNT*, vol. 8, p. 296.

by exhortations to 'be well thought of by outsiders' and 'gain a good standing for themselves' (3.7, 13). The implied principle is that leaders *must be honourable and respected even among outsiders*. This is done differently in diverse cultures. In ancient Ephesus, women's access to a public office may have been restricted (see 9.5.1 below). In egalitarian modern societies, where it is a serious offence to violate egalitarian principles and prohibit a woman from leadership, the gospel will best be served by men and women serving as leaders – and that means being true to the teaching of the Bible!

9.2.10 Women behind the Expansion of Early Christianity

The second-century pagan intellectual and critic of Christian faith, Celsus, made some radical statements regarding women's central involvement in the evangelising strategies of the early Christians.[114] Starting from this point of view, Margaret MacDonald has examined the role of women in the expansion of early Christianity. Her conclusions, based on the available historical sources, may be summarised as follows:

1. Women were central in the evangelistic expansion of Christianity in the Roman Empire.

2. They were involved in diverse roles, such as patrons, heads of households, mothers, teachers, and various kinds of ambassadors of the new faith.

3. The unifying element was the household life. Women either met together in a house or home, seeking to build believing homes, or they struggled to preserve Christian allegiance in the home of a pagan householder.

4. Women did move in and out of houses and shops, taking risks and leading people – including children – to join the movement

---

[114] See Origen, *Contra Celsum* 3.44 and 3.50; quoted in M. Y. MacDonald, 'Was Celsus Right? The Role of Women in the Expansion of Early Christianity', 2003, pp. 157-158.

without permission from the 'proper' authorities. They did so, it seems, while conducting their daily business. No doubt they sometimes remained largely invisible, but in other cases they met with real resistance both inside and outside of church groups. They displayed a combination of boldness, challenge and concealment, which is a significant explanation of the rise of early Christianity.[115]

In her comprehensive study, MacDonald traces this major force in the growth of the Christian church to the New Testament with numerous references to women working as evangelists and heads of house churches, using their household as a basis. Reference is made to many of the instances we have noted above. Thus, the prominence of women in church work as house-church leaders, teachers and prophets is carefully reconstructed on the basis of the biblical evidence.[116]

Attention is also called to the evangelistic and ministerial *partnerships* created between the male and female gospel workers, sometimes between male and female, sometimes between male and male, and sometimes between female and female: Priscilla and Aquila (Romans 16.3-4; I Corinthians 16.19), Andronicus and Junia (Romans 16.7), Euodia and Syntyche (Philippians 4.2-3), Tryphaena and Tryphosa (Romans 16.12). The nature of these partnerships was not limited to husband and wife,[117] but it was formed for strategic and practical purposes and following the instruction of Jesus when he sent out the seventy-two apostles, two by two (Luke 10.1).

9.3 Commissioning-Ordination in the New Testament

The evidence of 'ordination' in the New Testament is very limited, and one hesitates even to use this term for the kinds of practices found. The book of Acts and the Pastoral Epistles contain the four

---

[115] M. Y. MacDonald, 'Was Celsus Right? The Role of Women in the Expansion of Early Christianity', 2003, p. 184; cf. pp. 157-184.
[116] Ibid., pp. 168-172.
[117] Ibid., pp. 162-168.

references that include the laying on of hands. Prayer and laying on of hands is used elsewhere in the New Testament, but not for ordination. Concerning prayer and the laying on of hands, it has been appropriately remarked that 'neither of these, nor yet the conjunction of the two, is peculiar to ordination'.[118]

What is the role of ordination in the mission of the church? In the following we will seek answers to this question in the New Testament, beginning with the Gospels.

9.3.1 *The Silent Gospels*

There is complete silence on the laying on of hands for the purpose of commissioning-ordination in the Gospels. This continues through the appointment of Matthias replacing Judas in Acts 1. Thus, while Jesus authorised the baptism of believers (John 3.22-30; 4.1-3; Matthew 28.19-20), appointed twelve apostles, and laid hands on the needy, he did not introduce a ceremony of ordination.[119]

---

[118] W. H. Frere, 'Early Forms of Ordination', 1918, p. 265.

[119] Many Adventist Bible readers might disagree with this conclusion in view of Ellen White's graphic portrayal of the scene of Jesus' appointment of his disciples (*Desire of Ages*, 1898, p. 296), which they take to be implied in the biblical text. However, considering her purpose, literary technique, and historical setting, it is a sound conclusion that Ellen White merely follows how ordination was commonly seen in her time and what she says can be understood as an illustrative instruction to the church in order to avoid formalism and ritualism. This understanding is argued in some detail in TED-TOSCR, 2013, section 4.6.2.5. Official documents by the Church state the position that Ellen White's writings 'were not intended to give new doctrine, but to direct minds to the truth already revealed in Scripture' (*Adventist Review* 157:41, 4 September 1980, p. 15). In this context, the following is underlined: 'We see the need for a careful exposition of the Ellen G. White writings. Not all her uses of Scripture were designed to provide a strict exposition of the Biblical text. At times she employs Scripture homiletically. At other times she looses [*sic*] passages from their Biblical context for special applications. Again, she may use Biblical language merely for literary style. Ellen G. White's total context and situation in life, with attention to time and place, must always be taken into consideration.' (Ibid.)

The Gospels tell us that Jesus was appointed directly by God through the Holy Spirit (Matthew 3.13-17; Mark 1.9-11; Luke 3.21-22). His divine commissioning emerged from a deep and intimate *relation* with God. The same *relational* emphasis is what he applied to his disciples. The twelve were chosen from a larger group of followers in order to be close to Jesus. They were to watch his example and receive his teaching, as disciples of scribes would do at the time.[120] What mattered primarily, however, was their intimate *relationship* with Jesus, their 'heart', and not a formal ordination rite. Jesus *chose, called, and commissioned* the twelve as he did any disciple (including women), but the precise task given may have differed. His choice, calling and commissioning for the gospel ministry according to Matthew 28.18-20 involved all disciples, men and women.[121]

As Christ empowers the church by the Holy Spirit at Pentecost, this includes the twelve, and it is from this time onwards that they lead out in the ministry of the Word (Acts 6.2; cf. their uncertainties and errors in Acts 1.1-8) and doing 'signs and wonders' (Acts 5.12-16; cf. their failure in Luke 9.1-2, 37-45). Their appointment by Christ is not valid for the church leadership until they receive the gift of the Holy Spirit at Pentecost. Their office then becomes a prophetic office in which men and women may share. The twelve later disappear and are not replaced by a formal office.

Thus, there is no biblical record that Jesus laid his hands on the twelve disciples when he appointed them (Matthew 9.35-10.42; Mark 3.13-19; Luke 6.12-16; John 1.35-51; 6.66-71). He did not call them to an office accompanied by a formally structured ordination procedure, but his appointment to ministry was based on a *spiritual* and *relational* understanding of their task, as noted in Mark 3.14 (the word 'ordained' in the KJV is a misleading translation which is replaced by 'appoint' in NKJV).[122]

---

[120] See J. Jeremias, *Jerusalem*, 1982, pp. 232-245; TED-TOSCR, 2013, section 3.4.
[121] Matthew 28.16-20; Mark 16.12-19; Luke 24.36-52; John 20.19-21.23; Acts 1.1-9. See also 8.2 and 9.2.1 above.
[122] See TED-TOSCR, 2013, section 4.5.4.

This understanding is confirmed by the terminology used for appointing the twelve. Only commonplace terms were used (see the list in 9.3.5 below). None of these Greek terms is a technical term for a formal ordination procedure that includes the imposition of hands.

What we do find in settings where Jesus commissioned his disciples is *blessing* and the *gift* of the Holy Spirit (Luke 24.50-52; John 20.21-22). If Jesus blessed his disciples as a father blessed his sons (cf. Jacob's blessing of his twelve sons in Genesis 49), the commissioning becomes an adoption or a bestowal of grace on loved ones, rather than functioning as a formal appointment to an office. This act conveys a personal endorsement and a commendation to the grace of God rather than an authorisation and installation into a defined office bestowing leadership power.

The striking absence of ordination by the laying on of hands continues immediately after Christ's ascension, when the disciples needed to select someone to replace Judas (Acts 1.15-25).[123]

There is no need to speculate about the reasons for the silence on ordination by the imposition of hands in the Gospels. But in some ways, it is to be expected in view of Jesus' teaching about the relationship between disciples. Jesus had told his disciples:

> *Matthew 10.24-25* A disciple is not above the teacher, nor a slave above the master; it is enough for the disciple to be like the teacher, and the slave like the master.
>
> *Matthew 23.8-12* But you are not to be called rabbi, for you have one teacher, and you are all students. And call no one your father on earth, for you have one Father – the one in heaven. Nor are you to be called instructors, for you have one instructor, the Messiah. The greatest among you will be your servant. All who exalt themselves will be humbled, and all who humble themselves will be exalted.

---

[123] See 9.2.1 above.

Mark 10.42-45 So Jesus called them and said to them, 'You know that among the Gentiles those whom they recognize as their rulers lord it over them, and their great ones are tyrants over them. But it is not so among you; but whoever wishes to become great among you must be your servant, and whoever wishes to be first among you must be slave of all. For the Son of Man came not to be served but to serve, and to give his life a ransom for many.'

Jesus taught servanthood, not hierarchy, and he explicitly criticised the titles and institutions associated with the scribes. It is therefore not surprising that in the writings of the New Testament and even a hundred years after the last of its books was completed, until around AD 200, the early Christian church used a very simple vocabulary for appointment to a leading church office.[124]

Some argue that, since Jesus chose twelve *male* disciples, the church today should have *male* pastors only. That conclusion completely ignores the point of the Gospels. In the plot of the Gospels the disciples start out well (note the stories of their calling) and then go from bad (note 'O, ye of little/no faith', 'Get behind me, Satan', etc.) to worse when they deny Jesus.[125] The disciples are a case study of how *not to be a follower of Jesus*, and the readers are not meant to imitate them. Instead, it is those characters that appear only once and exhibit only one characteristic – usually faith – whom the intended readers of the Gospels are to imitate. Thus, the point made by the Gospels is that we should not pattern ourselves after the twelve disciples – although Luke redeems them and portrays them as the vital initial leaders of the young church after Pentecost – but the reader should rather imitate the less prominent characters, including many women.[126]

---

[124] M. Warkentin, *Ordination*, 1982, p. 33.

[125] Cf. E. S. Malbon, *In the Company of Jesus: Characters in Mark's Gospel of Jesus*, 2000, p. 205.

[126] Examples in Mark include: the man healed of an unclean spirit (1.21-28); a female healed of a fever (1.29-31); a healed leper (1.40-45); the friends of the paralytic (2.2-5); the Gerasene demoniac (5.1-20); the woman with the haemorrhage (5.25-34); the Syrophoenician woman (7.24-30); the blind

This significant observation is in keeping with the lack of ordination of the twelve in the Gospels. They are not yet models to follow or ready-made leaders – they become ready after meeting the risen Christ and receiving the outpouring of the Holy Spirit. The male gender of the disciples is obviously not given as a model to follow – not in the Gospels and, consequently, not in the modern-time church context of the ordination of pastors.

9.3.2 The Origin of Christian Ordination

The first time the New Testament mentions an act of appointment with the imposition of hands is the appointment of the seven in Acts 6.1-6 (the passage is examined in further detail in 9.3.3.1 and 9.4.2.1 below). This was an *ad hoc* initiative – but with important strategic implications in the context of the mission of God.

Additional leaders were needed to relieve the twelve in Jerusalem of the growing burdens of work. Seven persons were appointed for this 'apostolic assistance', but no office is mentioned and the institution of the seven eventually disappears.

The practical need for assistant leaders has some similarity with Moses and the appointments of judges and elders to relieve him from pressure (Exodus 18; Numbers 11.16-25). An awareness of being God's new Israel, may have even have directed the attention towards models of appointments in the Old Testament Scriptures. The Levites, who assisted the Aaronic priests in the sanctuary, had been ordained by the congregation and the priests (Numbers 8.10-

---

man of Bethesda (8.22-26); the father of a boy with a spirit (9.17-24); blind Bartimaeus (10.46-52); and the anointing woman (14.3-9). In Matthew, positive exemplars include: a man healed of leprosy (8.1-4); a centurion whose faith leads to the healing of his servant (8.5-13); a paralysed man (9.2-8); the leader of the synagogue (9.18-26); two blind men (9.27-31); a mute demoniac (9.32-34); a Canaanite woman (15.21-28); the father of a demon-possessed boy (17.14-18); two blind men (20.3-34); and a woman who anoints Jesus (26.7-13). For significant studies of this feature in the Gospels, see E. S. Malbon, *In the Company of Jesus*, 2000. J. F. Williams, *Other Followers of Jesus: Minor Characters as Major Figures in Mark's Gospel*, 1994.

11). Moses bestowed his authority upon Joshua before the high priest and the congregation (Numbers 27.18-23), which is a variant of the case when God took some of the Spirit upon Moses and put it upon the seventy elders (Numbers 11.25).

The seven have Greek or Latin names (Stephanos, Philippos, Prochoros, Nicanor, Timon, Parmenas, Nikolaos)[127] and were probably 'Greek-Speaking Jewish Christians, normally resident overseas and temporarily living in Jerusalem, or, having been brought up overseas, now permanently settled in Jerusalem'.[128] Thus, extending apostolic leadership functions to seven Hellenistic Jews from *outside* Judea, meant that the leadership of the twelve – who were appointed by Jesus and up to then located in Jerusalem – was extended *outside* Jerusalem and Judea, i.e. *outside* the city of God and the Promised Land. This bold step challenged the traditional concept of the election of Israel and proof of its divine legitimacy was required, certainly in the eyes of the growing numbers of converted Jewish priests (Acts 6.7). This *internal* need in the church was addressed by showing that God was acting through his Spirit when the gospel moved to the Gentile world (this is a central theme in Acts). It was addressed publicly and in a culturally appropriate way according to Acts 6.1-6 by the establishment of a delegated authority according to how God had constituted Israel according to the Scriptures.

Consequently, a solution that appealed to Scripture and Jewish customs was required. This may have been achieved by using the number 'seven', which was associated with the Jewish institution of 'the Seven of a City' (see below), but it may simply have been achieved by resorting to prayer and blessing (a common Jewish practice used also by Jesus), and to the imposition of hands as an induction procedure that was reflected in the Scriptures and applied by the Jewish scribes, albeit without prayer.[129]

---

[127] Note 'Nikolaos from Antioch' (Acts 6.5) who is presented as 'a proselyte to Judaism'.
[128] W. Neil, *Acts*, 1981, p. 102.
[129] See TED-TOSCR, 2013, section 3.4.

The Great Sanhedrin in Jerusalem had seventy-one members,[130] but there were also smaller Sanhedrins with twenty-three or even seven members, the latter being named 'the Seven of a City'. Josephus, the Jewish historian (AD 37 – c. 100), refers to 'seven men to judge in every city'; if they were unable to make a decision on a matter, they would send the case to Jerusalem where the 'high priest and the prophet and the council of elders meet and pronounce as they think fit'.[131] The same information is found in the Talmud where seven men made up an administrative council in the local towns and as such they were also involved with the administration of the synagogue.[132] A local Jewish community of one hundred and twenty could choose seven to form the local judicial council named 'Sanhedrin'.[133]

The understanding of Acts 6.1-6 that emerges from these background facts has been well expressed by V. Norskov Olsen:

> The early primitive church lived as a Jewish Christian community within the framework of Jewish society. We see in the church-council of Jerusalem an analogy to the Jewish Council, and the council of the Seven also has its analogy in Judaism. The Christian councils have their own content and significance, but the analogy can help us locate their purpose in a historical setting. The administration and judicial aspects or work of the Seven resemble in principle that of the Seven of the city, which in turn was related to the major Council in Jerusalem. The Seven represented the interests of the Hellenistic Jews who had become Christians. The apostolate of the Twelve demonstrated that the ministry is one of service (*diakonia*) and involved missionary outreach; the same is the case with the Seven, who have accordingly been described

---

[130] E. Schürer, *The History of the Jewish People*, vol. 2, 1979, p. 226.
[131] Flavius Josephus, *Jewish Antiquities*, viii, 14 (pp. 578-581).
[132] This information is quoted in J. R. Lumby, *The Acts of the Apostles*, 1912, p. 383; V. Norskov Olsen, *Myth and Truth about Church, Priesthood and Ordination*, 1990, p. 84.
[133] T. F. Torrance, 'Consecration and Ordination', 1958, p. 237; *The Mishnah*, H. Danby (trans.), 1933, p. 383.

as the apostolate of the Seven. At the time when the apostolate of the Twelve ceased and the Council of Jerusalem came to an end, no doubt the council of the Seven likewise discontinued.[134]

There were also *external* reasons for the initiative in Acts 6.1-6. The seven are commissioned in the midst of a mounting conflict between the apostles and the Jerusalem Sanhedrin. (This conflict resulted in the great persecution recorded in Acts 8.1 that moved the gospel to the Gentile world.) This *external* conflict concerns the *authority* of teaching and preaching of the Christian leaders (Acts 4.1-31),[135] and the imposition of hands for ordination was, as we have seen in the Old Testament and as followed in contemporary Jewish practices, a formal procedure for bestowing a certain authority – cf. the symbol of the 'hand' (see 9.4.1 below). The young church needed to underline the *spiritual* and *prophetic* office of the apostles as something based directly on *the authority of God*. And, for this reason, the prayer and laying on of hands in Acts 6.6 was deemed an appropriate sign of *confirming* that the seven are called by God and have *already* received from him the Holy Spirit. This supersedes the priestly and scribal ordinations, because it is a *new act* of God which *directly* grants the same divine authority given to Moses, but without any human intermediaries or a long succession of acts of the imposition of hands beginning with Moses' ordination of Joshua.

We know of no instruction from Jesus regarding the rite of commissioning-ordination. However, three sources of the imposition of hands in Acts 6.1-6 may be considered. Firstly, the Scriptures – the ordinations of the seventy elders, Joshua and the Levites (see 9.3.3.1 below).

Secondly, the living tradition among contemporary Jewish scribes (some of whom served as judges in the sanhedrins), with which the

---

[134] V. Norskov Olsen, *Myth and Truth about Church, Priesthood and Ordination*, 1990, p. 84.
[135] For more details, see TED-TOSCR, 2013, section 3.5.2.

first Christians were closely familiar. The scribes advocated Moses as model and example.[136]

Thirdly, the apostles knew that Jesus laid his hands on various people in order to bless them, which included prayer. The fact that the earliest step towards ordination came to include prayer with the imposition of hands is therefore hardly a coincidence.[137] Prayer was neither included in the scriptural ordinations of the Levites or Joshua, nor in the Jewish scribal ordination.[138] Resorting to the simple blessing exemplified by the Master, which he never applied in a commissioning-ordination as far as we see in the Bible, would explain why the event in Acts 6.1-6 became a singular and temporary one.

The church did not simply copy the Scriptures or the Jewish practices. They invented a new practice based primarily on the simple prayer and blessing used by Jesus, which alluded both to the Scriptural ordinations and contemporary Jewish practices. In so doing, the church in Acts 6.1-6 made a powerful statement to all parties that the 'new Israel' *continues* God's mission of salvation. Preceded by Abraham, Isaac, Israel, Moses and the prophets, God's mission has now entered a new phase through the church of Christ.

Thus, the procedure taking place in Acts 6.1-6 intended to confirm publicly the *prophetic* and *spiritual* authority of the seven, as a witness to the Jerusalem congregation consisting mainly of Jews, as well as to the Sanhedrin and the many priests and scribes who were now joining the church. There was no need for it as a means to convey the power of the Holy Spirit, because the candidates were already 'full of faith and the Holy Spirit' (6.5).

However, the initiative was *temporary*. There is no record of a repetition or a defined practice of ordination by the imposition of hands in the New Testament.

---

[136] TED-TOSCR, 2013, section 3.4.
[137] See E. Ferguson, 'Jewish and Christian Ordination', 1963, pp. 14-16.
[138] Ibid., p. 16; A. Ehrhardt, 'Jewish and Christian Ordination', 1954, pp. 125.

9.3.3 The Proto-Ordination Texts

A study of the so-called ordination texts in the New Testament is presented in the following. A better term for these texts might be 'proto-ordination' texts, since none of these passages gives us a firm or commanded practice that is literally followed by the church today. For reasons given in 9.4.2.3 below, I Timothy 5.22 has been left out here.

The Seven (Acts 6.1-6)

The passage identifies the background issue: the Hellenistic converts complain against the Jewish converts because their widows were being overlooked in the daily distribution of food (Acts 6.1). The twelve call a church assembly and acknowledge that it would be inappropriate for them to neglect prayer and the ministry of the word of God 'in order to wait on tables' (6.2, 4). A process for dealing with the issue is outlined and followed (6.3, 5).

The elements of the process are: (a) *Proposal of procedure* by the twelve, probably through Peter (6.3-4); (b) *Approval of Procedure* by the congregation (6.5a); (c) *Nomination* of seven men by the congregation based on specific qualifications (6.5b); (d) *Presentation* to the apostles (6.6a); (e) *Prayer* by the apostles and/or the congregation (6.6b); and (f) *Imposition of Hands* by the apostles and/or the congregation (6.6c).

The nomination is followed by the appointment, expressed by the verb *kathistemi*, 'bring in, induct, make' – also used in Titus 1.5 for the appointment of elders in each town..[139] This is implemented by the public actions in 6.6, where the text literally reads: 'They put them before the apostles and praying they laid their hands on them'. Thus, the Greek text does not say who lays their hands on the seven – the congregation, or the apostles, or both.[140]

---

[139] W. Bauer, *Griechisch-Deutsches Wörterbuch zu den Schriften des Neuen Testaments und der übrigen urchristlichen Literatur*, 1963, col. 771.

[140] A later manuscript (Codex Bezae from the third century AD) reveals an attempt to sort this out by adding 'who' after 'the apostles', thus making it clear that they were the ones that performed the act, but this reflects the

Another important point is that the act of 'laying on [of hands]' is referred to by the Greek verb *epitithemi*, which simply means 'put or lay on' and is the common verb in the phrase 'lay on hands' in the New Testament: for blessing (Matthew 19.3, 5), healing (e.g. Matthew 9.18; Mark 16.18; Acts 9.17; Hebrews 6.2), for confirming the gift of the Spirit at baptism (Acts 8.17), for restoring a disciplined elder (I Timothy 5.22), and for all instances of commissioning-ordination in the New Testament (Acts 6.6; 13.3; I Timothy 4.14; II Timothy 1.6). In the Septuagint the same Greek verb is used as a translation of the Hebrew *samak yadim 'al*, 'lean hands on', whether for laying hands on the offering animals (Exodus 29.10; Leviticus 1.4; Numbers 8.12) or on the Levites (Numbers 8.10) or Joshua (Numbers 27.18, 23; Deuteronomy 34.9). It is therefore possible that the Greek *epitithemi* alludes to the Hebrew sense 'lean on' which carries with it the idea of making a substitute, a representative, or an extension of self (see further 9.4 below).

A close reading of the passage leads to the following major conclusions:

1. The significant *theological aspect* of the passage emerges from its larger context of Acts 4-7 (see 9.3.2 above). In the context of the mission of Christ, the event puts divine sanction on the extension of the kingdom of God to the Gentile world – that is why the mentioning of prayer, as in a benediction, is important. God's plan to become known in the world beyond Israel is moving forward. Two of the seven, Stephen and Philip, have a vital role in the continuing expansion of the kingdom beginning in Acts 6.

2. The *procedure* publicly underlines the given authority of the seven. It acknowledges their spiritual gifts and wisdom. It expresses the trust of the congregation and marks the receiving of representative authority by the congregation and/or the apostles.

---

ordination theology of the early Roman church, where only the bishop in apostolic succession could ordain (see V. Norskov Olsen, *Myth and Truth about Church, Priesthood and Ordination*, 1990, p. 142).

3. No explicit term is given for the *office* or precise function of the seven, which in itself is remarkable. Their function is presented as an *ad hoc* function. The young church did not yet have an organised structure of functions besides the spirit-led apostles and servants of God. The idea raised by the Church Father Irenaeus (c. 130-202)[141] that they were deacons in a technical sense of an office subordinated to the elders and overseers, which was widely accepted in the nineteenth century,[142] is now considered 'a very old error'.[143] The work of the seven went beyond the limited duties of a deacon as defined by the Seventh-day Adventist Church today, for at least two of the seven are subsequently involved in teaching and preaching: Stephen (6.10) and Philip (8.4-8; cf. 21.8).

4. Parts of the commissioning ritual may have been drawn from the following passages in the *Old Testament Scriptures*: Moses' delegation of tasks to judges (Exodus 18) and elders (Numbers 11.16-30), or his appointment of Joshua as his successor, (Numbers 27.12-23; Deuteronomy 34.9), or the Israelite congregation's imposition of hands upon the Levites as their representatives (Numbers 8.5-22).

It has been alleged that Luke is using *midrashic* principles of Jewish exegesis based on the analogy between Israel's exodus from Egypt and the law-giving at Sinai on the one hand, and, on the other hand, the Christian church, the new Israel, emerging in the power of the Lord after Pentecost.[144]

---

[141] As pointed out in H. Chadwick, *Early Church*, 1967, p. 48.
[142] See, for example, A. Barnes, *Notes on the Acts of the Apostles*, pp. 110-113.
[143] As pointed out by A. M. Farrer in *The Apostolic Ministry* and quoted in C. S. C. Williams, *A Commentary on the Acts of the Apostles*, 1957, p. 97, and V. Norskov Olsen, *Myth and Truth about Church, Priesthood and Ordination*, 1990, p. 84.
[144] This has been outlined in some detail with numerous examples in M. Warkentin, *Ordination*, 1982, pp. 120-130; see the summary in V. Norskov Olsen, *Myth and Truth about Church, Priesthood and Ordination*, 1990, pp. 81-85, 141-143.

Space does not allow for an outline of this suggestion in detail,[145] but the proposal deserves to be noticed. For example, if Luke was drawing on the appointment of the Levites in Numbers 8.5-22 as a 'filter' for reading Acts 6.1-6, the seven would *represent the congregation*. If, on the other hand, Luke is drawing on passages where some of the spirit and authority of Moses is conferred upon his successor Joshua, the apostles would be delegating authority to the seven who *represent the apostles*. The fact that the Greek text of Acts 6.1-6 does not clarify who is laying on their hands – the congregation, or the apostles, or both – means that Luke has left it open. In both cases, the hands symbolise the instrument that transfers authority and/or representation, as was the case with *samak yadim* in the Old Testament, i.e. the imposition of hands with some pressure (see 6.4.1 below).

5. The process in Acts 6.1-6 may also be understood in the light of *contemporary Jewish practices*. The seven in the church may have been introduced as a body of elders or an 'apostolate of the seven' based on the model of the 'Seven of a City' in first-century Judaism. In our study of the origin of Christian ordination (see 9.3.2 above), reference was made to the 'Seven of a City', who were elders acting as a body of judges that was distinct from but cooperated with the leaders and council of elders in each synagogue, acting in a subordinate role to the Great Sanhedrin in Jerusalem. Their role was to *judge* on matters of dispute, and this may be an essential function of the seven in Acts 6 where the issue is a conflict involving complaints regarding the distribution of alms. We see that the church in Antioch sent alms with Barnabas and Paul to the church in Jerusalem, 'to the elders' (*presbyteroi*, Acts 11.30).

However, at least two of the seven, Stephen and Philip, were spirit-filled persons being actively involved in evangelism and missionary work, and thus having the characteristics of an apostle-emissary or prophet and teacher. Possibly, the seven (a) functioned

---

[145] For details, see TED-TOSCR, 2013, section 3.5.3.1.

as elders-judges according to Jewish practice, (b) represented the spirit-filled congregation of believers where God's mighty hand was made visible, and (c) carried the leadership authority of the apostles in preaching, teaching, and working miracles. However, if based on these assumptions, we think of the seven as an 'apostolate of the seven' that functioned like a body of elders, it must be recognised that the biblical text does not state this.

6. Concerning the *qualifications* for the appointment, the apostles state that they need to be seven 'men' (*andres*) from among yourselves who are 'of good standing, full of the Spirit and of wisdom' (6.3; cf. 6.5).

Being 'full of the Spirit and of wisdom' (a) was the gift of Joshua from God via Moses (Deuteronomy 34.9; cf. Numbers 27.16,18) and of the seventy elders (Numbers 11.16-29); it (b) was of paramount importance for the Jewish ordination of the scribes;[146] and it (c) is a central theme in the events recorded after the ordination in Acts 6.6, both for Stephen (6.8; 7.55) and Philip (8.4-8, 25-40), but also in the spreading of the gospel outside Judea (7.54-8.4). Evidently, the role of leaders being filled with the Spirit underlines that the mission of Christ is moving forward by God's will.

Regarding the male gender of the seven, there would have been no other option in the Jewish cultural setting in Jerusalem at the time. Firstly, the function of the seven obviously included that of being judges, as mentioned above. Whether in Judea or in Graeco-Roman Asia Minor, the courts did not accept women as judges (see 9.5.1 below). Secondly, if we accept that the laying on of hands in Acts 6.6 involves 'leaning (*semikah*) with pressure of the hands', intended to create a substitution, a representative, or an extension of self, it is clear that the seven could not be women since the act of laying on of hands also *reproduced* the male gender (cf. the comments on II Timothy 1.6 in 9.3.3.4 below). Thus, the dominating patriarchal concept in the

---

[146] TED-TOSCR, 2013, section 3.4.

Old Testament setting of Israel that was continued in first-century Judaism would automatically eliminate female candidates.

However, as the biblical passage plainly reads, there is no prohibition against women being commissioned-ordained. The seven were not appointed to any regular church office. The procedure is not standardised and repeated in the New Testament, but it is a one-off event to deal with a specific challenge. Moreover, the concept of the Old Testament and Jewish 'leaning with pressure of the hands' is nowhere plainly spelt out in the Bible. Thus, the male gender in this passage is insignificant for a church policy on ordination today.

7. *The procedure* recorded in the text is straightforward with one interesting exception: it is not clear in the Greek text (6.3, 6) if the laying on of hands is performed by the congregation, or the apostles, or both.[147] Even if one applies a literal reading of the text, this uncertainty remains. If one goes beyond what the text says, arguments may support any of the three options.

However, the conclusion that both the congregation and the apostles conducted the prayer and the imposition of hands, possibly with the added assumption that the apostles represented the congregation,[148] has some advantages. It is what the Greek text says and it fits the literary context in Acts and the New Testament. It accounts for the allusions to the Old Testament model passages, if we merge the laying on of hands on the Levites (by the congregation) and on Joshua (by Moses). Thus, it has been proposed that the seven are 'elder-servants'[149] having the authority of the *congregation* (whom they serve by acting as judges and elders handling the relief for the

---

[147] This has been described in detail in TED-TOSCR, 2013, section 3.5.3.1.

[148] For this view, see, for example, T. F. Torrance, 'Consecration and Ordination', 1958, p. 235, 237; K. Mattingly, 'Laying on of Hands in Ordination', 1998, p. 68. Cf. the summary of Torrance's view in V. Norskov Olsen, *Myth and Truth about Church, Priesthood and Ordination*, 1990, pp. 142-143.

[149] T. F. Torrance, 'Consecration and Ordination', 1958, p. 237.

poor – Acts 11.30), the *apostles* (whom they serve by delegation), and *Christ* (whom they serve for his mission through the Holy Spirit).

8. *Prayer and the laying on of hands* are the key elements of the induction ceremony itself, but the significance of the ceremony is not explained. This is assumed to be known by the intended readers of Acts. The inclusion of prayer distances the rite from the Jewish scribal ordination (where prayer was excluded) and suggests a *spiritual* emphasis that involves God through the Holy Spirit, as in God's appointment of the seventy elders which led to prophesying (Numbers 11.16-29). It may also imply that the concept of blessing, as practised by Jesus (e.g. Matthew 19.13, 15), was essential.[150] Our understanding of the rite of the imposition of hands has been summarised in 9.4.2.1 below.

In conclusion, Acts 6.1-6 is the *first* New Testament instance of a ceremony with the imposition of hands for appointment to a responsibility in the church. It is the *only* instance in the New Testament where prayer and imposition of hands are explicitly used for some leadership *function*. And it is the *only* instance where a procedure of congregational nomination is followed by prayer and imposition of hands in an induction ritual.

However, there is no explanation of the origin or significance of the imposition of hands for the appointment. No office is mentioned. It is not clear who lays their hands on the candidates. In view of the New Testament context, it is an *ad hoc* procedure that is not repeated, and the other two or three proto-ordination passages do not reveal a *following* of the model in Acts 6. The reasons for nominating men only to belong to the seven are not stated in the text and there is no instruction that the male gender is a condition for leadership.

Being the clearest biblical passage dealing with commissioning-ordination in the church, even if one reads it literally, it is insufficient as a warrant for the current church policy on ordination. If we seek the

---

[150] E. Ferguson, 'Jewish and Christian Ordination', 1963, p. 15.

meaning of the procedure recorded, we must conclude that it is based on Old Testament rituals and Jewish contemporary customs that are not significant in the church today. The idea of leaning one's hands on somebody in order to produce a substitution or representative or extension of self is foreign to us.

The temporary and *ad hoc* nature of the procedure in Acts 6.1-6 is evidence that it was not meant to become a standard practice in the church. However, considering the post-biblical development, this passage (and others) as well as the Old Testament and the Jewish ordination became used later on to develop the full-fledged ordination format in Rome around 200 AD.[151]

Two Itinerant Prophets-Teachers (Acts 13.1-3)

Luke's report in Acts concerns a special work to which Barnabas and Paul are called by the Holy Spirit. It is a 'sending away' for a special and temporary mission, but does not involve a formal office. The prompting by the Spirit comes while the church and its prophets and teachers are worshipping and fasting.

1. *The Lord* takes the initiative through the Holy Spirit, which is the usual pattern in the book of Acts. The term *aphorizo*, which is translated as 'set apart' in NRSV, means 'separate, appoint'. When used in appointment contexts it refers to being set apart for 'the work' (Acts 13.2), 'the gospel of God' (Romans 1.1), and God's call to faith and service before being born (Galatians 1.15; cf. Jeremiah 1.5), but not for an office. *A spiritual call to a mission* has been given to Barnabas and Paul, and it is tempting to conclude that the laying on of hands symbolically 'sets them apart' or *confirms* the call of the Spirit. However, the text does not state that. What the text does say in 14.26 is that the act is a commendation to the grace of God for their mission, which defines it as an act of putting them under God's care (see point 7 below).

---

[151] See TED-TOSCR, 2013, sections 4.1 and 4.2.

2. No *office* is involved, but the call sends them to do 'the work to which the Spirit of God has called them'. Barnabas and Paul are among the 'prophets and teachers' and are sent as itinerant emissaries under God's care. While travelling, they preach and teach in the synagogues, and the church is growing also among the Gentiles (Acts 13.4-14.28). Paul is almost killed by stoning which illustrates the dangers of the journey. They appoint elders in each church (see 9.3.3.3 below).

3. No *authority* is explicitly conveyed, except the appointment by the Holy Spirit, the support of the congregation, and God's protective care.

4. The *selection* is made by the Holy Spirit but his human agents are not mentioned. There were 'prophets' in Antioch who may have conveyed the decision. Barnabas and Paul themselves, who are among the prophets and teachers, may simply have revealed their calling. The passage seems to have some connection with I Timothy 4.14 where Timothy is first *designated* by prophetic speech as a leader and given a *charisma*, and then the presbytery may lay their hands on him, if that is the sense of the Greek text (see the exegesis in 9.3.3.4 below).

5. The *qualifications* are not mentioned. Barnabas and Paul are both men. According to accepted norms at the time, which still exist in the Middle East, women did not travel alone. The tasks of Paul and Barnabas included the public proclamation of the word of God in Jewish synagogues (Acts 13.5, 13-44; 14.1) where women were not accepted as speakers (see 9.5.1 below). The appointment of elders was traditionally assigned to men (14.23). Thus, the fact that Barnabas and Paul were men is irrelevant for the issue of women's ordination to the gospel ministry in a modern egalitarian environment. They worked in a different cultural setting and might have jeopardised the success of the mission in Asia Minor if they had been women. Above all, this passage does not describe an ordination but a special commissioning for a temporary missionary task.

6. The act of commissioning happens in the church with the congregation present. Prayer and fasting is taking place. However, Acts 13.3 reflects the same ambiguity as 6.6 regarding whose hands are being laid upon the candidates. From the immediate context in 13.1-3, it may be the 'church in Antioch' or the specific group in that church called 'prophets and teachers' (five being named). Both parties are introduced in 13.1 and the Greek text uses only the personal pronoun 'they' in referring to the agents of the rite in 13.3.

Taking Acts 13.1-14.28 as a whole, however, it seems clear that the entire church in Antioch is involved both in the sending off of the two in 13.3 and in their return. Sailing back to Antioch, 'where they had been commended [*paradidomi*] to the grace of God for the work they had now completed', all the church gathers and a report of 'how God had opened the door of faith to the Gentiles' is given (14.26-27). Thus, we need to maintain the ambiguity found in Acts 6 in Acts 13 also. The laying on of hands is done by the congregation, or a group of 'prophets and teachers' as representatives of the congregation, or both. The biblical text does not make a clear distinction here, and what is done is decided by the clear command of the Holy Spirit.

7. In Acts 14.26 Luke defines the laying on of hands in 13.1-3 as being 'commended [*paradidomi*] to the grace of God [*charis tou theou*] for the work they had completed'. The act in 13.1-3 is a 'handing over' of Barnabas and Paul to God's care and protection and the commendation is limited to the specific mission that is now completed. This strict limitation is in harmony with the annual sending of Jewish rabbis from Judea to encourage the diaspora Jews (see below) – the authorisation was given for a limited term only. Above all, Luke's comment means that the act in 13.1-3 is not seen as an ordination but as a commitment of the apostles into God's protection during the journey.

8. The Old Testament and Jewish expression *samak yadim 'al*, 'lean hands on', implied that the ordinand *substituted* for the ordainer.[152] If this concept is included in the laying on of hands upon Barnabas and Paul, the church in Antioch would be making them into their *representatives*. The believers in Antioch are then symbolically 'extending themselves' to the Gentiles in Asia Minor.[153]

The idea of 'substitution' fits the consecration of the Levites who by the imposition of hands represented the people in their service for the Lord. As Barnabas and Paul are 'taken from' the group of prophets and teachers in Antioch (13.1), the Levites 'were taken from among the sons of Israel' (Numbers 8.6, 14). In Acts the instruction of the Holy Spirit was: 'Set apart for me Barnabas and Saul for the work to which I have called them' (Acts 13.2). The Levites were also 'set apart' for their work (Numbers 8.11, 15) to which God had called them. The laying on of hands in Acts 13.3 may not be immediately connected with the activity of prayer and fasting (in 13.2-3 they are worshipping and fasting already when the Holy Spirit directs them to set the two apart), and features in the text permit the association with the 'leaning of hands' in Numbers 8 where prayer is excluded. Thus, the language of Acts 13 'echoes that of the Old Testament in the chapter dealing with the consecration of the Levites'.[154]

However, the language also echoes Joshua's ordination in Numbers 27. The city of Antioch was fraught with considerable symbolic significance in first-century Judaism since it was thought to be the gateway between the Exile/Diaspora and the Promised Land.[155] As Barnabas and Paul leave the Promised Land and bring the gospel into Gentile territory where the church is consolidated, they reverse Israel's movement into Canaan under Joshua. Thus, the points of similarities

---

[152] As carefully established by D. Daube, *The New Testament and Rabbinic Judaism*, 2011, pp. 224-246.
[153] V. Norskov Olsen, *Myth and Truth about Church, Priesthood and Ordination*, 1990, p. 143.
[154] D. Daube, *The New Testament and Rabbinic Judaism*, 2011, p. 240.
[155] M. Bockmuehl, *Jewish Law in Gentile Churches*, 2000, pp. 61-70.

between Acts 13.1-3 and the ordination of Joshua concern (a) the divine designation, (b) the laying on of hands involving prophets and teachers (Moses was considered a prophet and teacher), and (c) the ordinand's roles of bringing Israel/the church of Christ into Gentile land where God will dwell through his people. This is not stated in the text, but is expressed by subtle allusions.

9. The sending of Paul and Barnabas from Antioch parallels the annual sending of rabbis from Judea to encourage the diaspora Jews and especially to 'collect the taxes for the support of the rabbinate'.[156] They were emissaries of the Jerusalem patriarchate called *shelukhim*, 'emissaries, apostles' and usually travelled in pairs. They sometimes preached or taught in the synagogues, but 'their commission ended with their return to Jerusalem and was not transferable to others'.[157] In the Old Testament, the term *shaliakh*, 'apostle', is used about Moses, Elijah, Elisha, and Ezekiel (all being prophets) in the sense of 'God's agent' by reason of power committed to them to perform miracles on God's behalf.[158] There are also examples of *shelukhim* being used in the Persian period as 'governmental agents sent on both civil and religious missions', but they had no institutional status or missionary responsibility. Their authority was precisely defined and given for a limited term.[159]

10. The key element is *the laying on of hands*. The distinction between praying in worship and praying in connection with the laying on of hands is not clearly marked in the text. Thus, while we have an almost complete description of the use of the laying on of hands in a church context, there is no information about *its meaning or origin*. It seems, rather, that it is a well-known, almost obvious formality in the context. The Holy Spirit is connected with the ceremony, and somehow it is accompanied by prayer and fasting, although we don't see exactly how.

---

[156] M. H. Shepherd, Jr, 'Apostle', *IDB*, vol. 1, p. 171.
[157] Ibid.
[158] Ibid.
[159] Ibid.

Acts 13.1-3 does not describe an ordination for a pastoral leadership office but a prophetic commissioning for a temporary missionary task that in many practical details follows a Jewish pattern.[160] The text states only one thing about its significance, namely, that the laying on of hands is a commendation into God's hands for a specific work. Most of the conclusions drawn from Acts 6.1-6 would apply here as well. There is no record in the New Testament of any apostle being inducted into the apostolate by the imposition of hands.[161] Paul was called directly as an apostle by Christ in a charismatic experience (Acts 26.12-18; cf. I Timothy 2.7).

The Local Church Elders (Acts 14.23; 20.28; Titus 1.5)

As Barnabas and Paul visited the churches and preached the gospel in Asia Minor, their purpose was to 'strengthen the disciples and encourage them to remain true to the faith' in the face of many hardships (Acts 14.21-22). Evidently, the appointment of elders served the purpose of strengthening the community. A literal translation of the passage is:

> *Acts 14.23* And appointing (*cheirotoneo*) elders for them in each church, praying with fasting, they entrusted (*paratithemi*) them to the Lord in whom they had come to believe.

The Greek term for 'appoint' (*cheirotoneo*) means 'raise the hand (in collective agreement)'. It is attested in classical Greek and is found in II Corinthians 8.19 in the sense of 'select (by the congregation)'.

However, in Acts 14.23, the sense of 'appoint' is not associated with the rite of the laying on of hands. The sense 'stretch out the hand' is found in the Septuagint version of Isaiah 58.9 in the noun form of *cheirotonia*, 'stretching out the hand' or 'pointing finger', but this is found only here in the Bible and without any connection with

---
[160] As pointed out by many Bible scholars: see, for example, A. Barnes, *Notes on the New Testament*, 1975 (1st edn 1834), p. 198.
[161] Ibid.

the imposition of hands.[162] This verb and the corresponding noun are used in Hippolytus's Apostolic Tradition (c. AD 217) as a Greek technical term for 'ordain' and 'ordination'.[163] However, there is no warrant for reading this usage back into the New Testament.

The fact that the appointment of elders is a systematic measure in each church suggests that it is already an accepted practice of some kind. When Paul wrote his letter to the Philippians, both overseers and deacons were leading the church (Philippians 1.1; cf. I Timothy 3.1-13). We have noted elsewhere that the Jewish synagogue was led by an overseer and a servant (see 9.2.9 above), and if this model was adopted by the Christian congregations, it was part of the conventional model of leadership and did not need an explanation. The fact that the synagogue overseer was not ordained but only appointed would fit Acts 14.23 – only the rabbis were ordained in first-century Judaism.

Following the procedure when Barnabas and Paul were set apart for their special task in the setting of prayer and fasting (Acts 13.1-3), the appointment of elders in Asia Minor may in some way have been accompanied by prayer and fasting. The expression 'entrust them to the Lord' relates primarily to 'the disciples' in 14.21-23 but includes the elders.

However, the laying on of hands is not mentioned. Thus, Acts 14.21-23 is consistent with the rest of the New Testament, which does not mention the laying on of hands in connection with appointments of elders. Further, there is no description of the tasks of an elder besides the implied general oversight. In Acts 20:28, the task is defined as 'keeping watch over all the flock' and 'shepherd the church of God', but, again, the appointment for this task is not linked to the laying on of hands, only to the work of the Holy Spirit.

---

[162] E. Lohse, '*cheir* etc.', ThDNT, vol. 9, p. 437.
[163] See TED-TOSCR, 2013, section 4.1.7.

The Spirit-Filled Son of Paul (I Timothy 4.14; II Timothy 1.6)

The two passages in Paul's letters to Timothy are often adduced as evidence of ordination in the New Testament church.[164] However, the Greek text reveals significant ambiguities and the limited information makes it hard to comprehend what kind of act is performed by the laying on of hands. Neither of these passages, therefore, reflects a biblical church practice of ordination as we understand it today, not even if one reads them literally.

Let us first consider II Timothy 1.6 where Paul mentions in passing that he has laid his hands on Timothy.

Paul's Prophetic-Charismatic Apostolate (II Timothy 1.6)

Paul writes from a senior position, and the foundation of his apostolic ministry is God's direct calling without ordination. The risen Lord (in vision) appointed him as an apostle to bring the gospel of the kingdom to the Gentiles (Acts 26.15-18), and this is what Paul says in II Timothy 1.8-14. Paul never refers to any congregational ceremony that authorised him for his office – the ceremony in Antioch according to Acts 13.1-3 is an *ad hoc* commissioning for a missionary journey (prompted by the Spirit) rather than an ordination as we define it today. When Paul mentions his contacts with the leading 'pillars' in Jerusalem and his agreement with them, he is adamant that his authority still comes from God (Galatians 1.10-2.13). Thus, Paul has a *prophetic-charismatic* apostolate instituted by God's grace in Christ (Romans 1.1-6). It is to this vision that he is obedient despite persecution and sufferings, and it is to this appointment he is referring when he calls himself 'a herald and an apostle and a teacher' (II Timothy 1.11). The only hierarchy involved is God and Christ who have called Paul as their authorised messenger of the gospel.

Paul's Authorisation of Timothy as His Apostolic Representative

However, the spreading of the gospel of the kingdom in Christ and Paul's growing itinerant ministry created the need for assistants. Thus,

---

[164] See A. T. Hanson, *The Pastoral Epistles*, 1982, pp. 31-38, 94-95, 120-121.

Timothy, Titus, and Onesimus are 'sons' (*tekna*) of Paul doing gospel work that he delegates to them (I Corinthians 4.17; Philippians 2.22; I Timothy 1.2, 18; II Timothy 1.2; 2.1; Titus 1.4; Philemon 10). The father-son relationship is 'in the faith' (I Timothy 1.2; Titus 1.4). This language is rooted in 'ancient ideas of adoption which are partly oriental, partly Jewish, and partly Greek', but which are re-orientated by the Christian context.[165] Thus, the term 'son' (*teknon*) refers to an 'adopted spiritual son' by the 'father' (i.e. the apostle-teacher).[166] Paul calls Timothy 'his son' to denote his role as Paul's *representative* in his apostolic ministry (I Corinthians 4.17; Philippians 2.19-22). As Paul's 'adopted spiritual son', Timothy is not only *replacing* Paul as a teacher but he also *imitates* Paul's life and character, while *working together* with Paul as a servant-minister of the gospel.

Thus, being Paul's 'son' means to function as his apostolic *representative* who carries his authority. For example, while Paul continues to Macedonia, he has charged Timothy to remain in Ephesus with the task of dealing with dangerous false teachers (I Timothy 1.3-11).

Timothy's Pauline *authority* is particularly vital in order to bring unity. He is overseeing the church order and the life of the Ephesian church and its members, the prayers and the worship, the reading of the Scriptures, the exhortation and doctrinal teaching (e.g. I Timothy 4.11-13). Similarly, Titus was left in Crete to 'straighten out what was left unfinished' and 'appoint elders in every town, *as I directed you*' (Titus 1.5). Paul gives him *all authority* in teaching and correcting the church (Titus 2.15).

This raises the question of how Paul authorised Timothy (or Titus) as his servant-disciple. It is possible that II Timothy 1.6 tells us how, namely by the laying on of Paul's hands. Although the explicit information in the text is insufficient to grant full certainty, a *valid*

---

[165] A. Oepke, '*pais/teknon*', *ThDNT*, vol. 5, p. 638.
[166] Ibid.

interpretation of II Timothy 1.6 is that Timothy received Paul's authority and was adopted as his 'son in the faith' by the laying on of Paul's hands. This is based on the following observations.

The Gift of God

Paul confirms Timothy's sincere faith (II Timothy 1.5; cf. 1.13), saying: 'Rekindle the gift [*charisma*] of God that is in you through the laying on of my hands'. The significance of the laying on of hands is not explained but presumed to be known. Considering the various functions of the laying on of hands in the New Testament (see 9.4.2 below), healing (e.g. Acts 9.17; 28.8) may be excluded since there is no reference to Timothy being ill. Blessing may also be excluded (Matthew 19.15; Mark 10.13) as well as commissioning (Acts 6.1-6; 13.1-3) since no prayer is included. This leaves us with the option of *a special spiritual empowerment* (cf. Hebrews 6.2) that was applied in certain situations relating to baptism (Acts 8.14-17; 19.1-7) and the restoration of an elder by forgiveness of sins (I Timothy 5.22; see 9.4.2.3 below).

The Making of a Substitute

A rite that conveyed a special spiritual empowerment would be known in the setting of first-century Jewish Christianity where the Jewish scribal ordination (*semikah*) was close at hand.[167] As the Jewish scribe laid his hands on his disciple, it was believed that he symbolically *reproduced* himself following the model of the imposition of Moses' hand on Joshua (Numbers 27.15-23; Deuteronomy 34.9; cf. the reproduction of Israel's firstborn sons in the Levites, Numbers 8.9-11).[168] No prayer was used in the Jewish *semikah*, because the gesture was meant to produce a substitute with judicial functions, and, similarly, no prayer is mentioned by Paul in II Timothy 1.6 (cf. however Acts 6.1-6; 13.1-3). The Greek noun *epithesis*, 'imposition, laying on', suggests an established practice and is perhaps a Greek translation of the Hebrew-Aramaic *semikah* (cf. I Timothy 4.14;

---

[167] See TED-TOSCR, 2013, section 3.4.
[168] See 7.4.1 above.

Hebrews 6.2) which derived from the Old Testament phrase *samak yadim 'al*, 'lean hands on'.[169]

Conceptual Similarities with Moses' Ordination of Joshua

The context in II Timothy 1.5-14 reveals some conceptual similarities with Moses and Joshua in Numbers 27.15-23 and Deuteronomy 34.9.

God made the appointment of Joshua and then commanded Moses to give Joshua some of his authority (*hod*), 'so that all the congregation of the Israelites may obey' (Numbers 27.20), and Joshua was afterwards 'full of the spirit of wisdom, because Moses had laid his hands on him; and the Israelites obeyed him, doing as the Lord had commanded Moses' (Deuteronomy 34.9).

There is no evidence that God instituted a rite that, whenever performed, would transfer one leader's spiritual gifts to another. God's purpose is the *effect* on the community in terms of respect and obedience towards Joshua's teaching of the word of God. This effect is enhanced by the public performance of the act (Numbers 27.18-23) and the public demonstration of being spirit-filled and having the wisdom of Moses in words and deeds (Deuteronomy 34.9).

Reading II Timothy 1.5-14 through the filter of Moses' ordination of Joshua, we see, firstly, that the laying on of Paul's hands does not transmit God's Holy Spirit – Joshua and Timothy already have the Spirit (cf. II Timothy 1.14) and only God gives the Spirit in ways that only he decides. The rekindling of the gift of God is to come through Timothy's 'sincere faith' (1.5-6). Secondly, Paul's hands transfer his own gift of being appointed for the gospel ministry by God, thus inviting Timothy to share this ministry in the power of God (II Timothy 1.7-14). Paul's act is therefore a personal *authorisation* of Timothy for taking part in Paul's own apostolic ministry and being his co-worker.

---

[169] See 7.2 above and 9.4.1 below.

Understanding the imposition of Paul's hands as *reproducing* Paul's divine gospel commission in Timothy fits the context well. Paul seeks to encourage Timothy in the face of hardship and sufferings. This purpose is stated in the conclusion of his exhortation in II Timothy 1.8-14. He begins with 'so, consequently' (Greek *oun*), and then places Timothy at the same level as himself under the power of God, Christ, and the Holy Spirit. He invites Timothy to share his apostolic ministry for the gospel, even at the price of suffering, and to imitate Paul and hold the standard of sound teaching 'that you have heard from me'. The 'good treasure entrusted to you' (1.14) includes the calling and power of God as well as Paul's authorisation of Timothy as his substitute by the laying on of his hands.

Paul makes the same emphasis in his charge to Timothy in II Timothy 3.10-4.8. Besides studying Paul's life and learning from him, Timothy has received from Paul the insight and example to carry out his leadership well (II Timothy 4.5). Since God has made Paul the servant he is, what Paul shares with Timothy by the imposition of his hands is a 'gift (*charisma*) of God' which Timothy must rekindle by his own faith.

Adaptation of a Jewish Practice
The laying on of Paul's hands on Timothy is not identical with the Jewish scribal ordination. While both practices may be modelled on Moses' ordination of Joshua in the Scriptures, Paul's authorisation of Timothy has developed further than the Jewish *semikah*. Paul's practical tools and concepts may derive from his scribal background (Acts 22.3-5; Philippians 3.4-6), but he is using them in a new context, not for the teaching of the Law of Moses within the mission of Israel, but for the spreading of the gospel of the kingdom of God through Jesus Christ to the world.

Conclusions on Laying on of Hands in II Timothy 1.6
In conclusion, the imposition of Paul's hands in II Timothy 1.6 functions as an authorisation of Timothy as Paul's servant and co-

worker – Paul even includes Timothy and Silvanus among 'the apostles of Christ' in I Thessalonians 2.7 (cf. 3.2). It is a known gesture in Paul's Jewish-Christian setting that makes Timothy a son and disciple of Paul, one who imitates his example, his life and faith. And it fits the individual reference to Paul's hands. Whether or not the act took place in a public setting (cf. I Timothy 4.14 below), we do not know.

Paul's own calling and his authorisation of Timothy are ultimately the work of God, 'who saved us and called us with a holy calling according to his own purpose and grace' (II Timothy 1.8). Paul says that this grace 'was given to us in Christ Jesus who abolished death and brought life and immortality to light through the gospel'. And this in turn defines his ministry: 'For this gospel I was appointed a herald and an apostle and a teacher, and for this reason I also suffer these things' (1.9-12). By the laying on of hands Paul has shared his calling and appointment, i.e. his 'gift of God', with Timothy, his 'son in the faith' who is now authorised to replace him in leadership. Paul can do this with confidence, because Timothy has been appointed by God through a prophetic revelation (I Timothy 1.18; 4.14).

If this is a correct understanding of II Timothy 1.6, we have here another *ad hoc* model of ordination which is leaning towards Jewish customs – besides Acts 6.1-6 and 13.1-3. However, it is not developed into a practice to follow in the New Testament. It characterises only the ministry of Paul and at a certain point in time. It explicitly involves only Paul and Timothy (the impact of Paul's authorisation of Timothy on the congregation may be implied, but this is not stated in the text). The imposition of hands does not include prayer. The significance of the rite is not explained in the text before us. It seems to be rooted in an Old Testament and partly Jewish concept of the imposition of hands.

If the suggested interpretation of II Timothy 1.6 is correct, it would also explain why this act of laying on of hands would not include women, for the central thought would have been to produce a substitute of a male apostle-teacher that was rooted in the patriarchy of ancient Israel (cf. the comments on Acts 6.1-6 and 13.1-3 in 9.3.3.1 and 9.3.3.2 above).

Timothy and the Laying on of the hands of the Presbytery (I Timothy 4.14)

The second passage relating to Timothy's alleged ordination is I Timothy 4.14. The presbytery or council of elders is involved in the laying on of hands which in some way is connected with Timothy.

However, the purpose of this act is not explained and the Greek text is ambiguous. The passage has been interpreted in many different ways by scholars without a consensus being reached.[170] It is therefore not a passage that clarifies ordination. Without an involved exegesis of the Greek text, this passage will give few clues to the significance of ordination in the Bible.

Beginning with the text itself, Paul's words may be literally translated as follows:

> *I Timothy 4.13-15* Until I come, give attention to public reading, exhortation and teaching. Do not neglect the spiritual gift (*charisma*) in you, which was given you by prophetic word (*dia profeteias*) when (*meta*) the imposition of the presbytery's hands took place. Put this into practice; be in these things, so that your progress will be evident to all.

The 'spiritual gift' (*charisma*) is the same Greek word that occurs in Romans 12.6 and I Corinthians 12.4, 9, 28, 30, 31 concerning various gifts of grace enabling men and women to minister in various functions in the church. In the New Testament context, the 'prophetic word' (*profeteia*) is an inspired message spoken by a charismatic preacher in the church.[171] The Greek preposition *meta* + genitive

---

[170] See, for example, the review in A. T. Hanson, *The Pastoral Epistles*, 1982, pp. 94-95.
[171] G. Friedrich and others, '*profetes* etc.', *ThDNT*, vol. 6, p. 848.

refers here to 'the attendant circumstances during which something takes place'.[172] The features in the text that lead to the conclusion below are as follows:

The Main Point in I Timothy 4.14

The main point in I Timothy 4.14 is not the imposition of the presbytery's hands but the spiritual gift conveyed to Timothy through the 'prophetic word' (*profeteia*). The content of the prophetic word and its functional relationship to the imposition of the presbytery's hands is therefore a key to understanding the passage.

Referring to I Timothy 1.18, it has been noted that the prophetic word 'seems to have preceded Timothy's calling and ordination'.[173] Paul addresses his 'son' Timothy in 1.18 and says: 'I entrust this command to you in keeping with the former prophetic words (*tas profeteias*) about you, so that in their strength you may fight the good fight'. The only occurrences of the word *profeteia* in Paul's letters to Timothy are in I Timothy 1.18 and 4.14. Both passages encourage Timothy to exercise his *authority*, obviously in the face of the widespread false teaching in Ephesus. Timothy's divine appointment for leadership has been revealed from early on by an inspired revelation from God to a prophet (perhaps to Paul himself). Timothy's case in Ephesus may therefore be an example of what is known in the Graeco-Roman culture as *Designation*. Since this concept may explain the difficulties in 4.14, we will return to it in more detail in the interpretation below.

The Vague Meaning of 'the Presbytery's Imposition of Hands'

The referential meaning of 'the presbytery's imposition of hands' is ambiguous. Elders performed the imposition of hands for various purposes, for example, blessings in connection with healing and forgiveness of sins (James 5.14-18; cf. I Timothy 5.22) and perhaps even at baptisms (Acts 2.38; 8.18-19; 19.6). Some have suggested

---

[172] W. Bauer, *Griechisch-Deutsches Wörterbuch zu den Schriften des Neuen Testaments und der übrigen urchristlichen Literatur*, 1963, cols. 1007-1008.

[173] M. Zerwick and M. Grosvenor, *A Grammatical Analysis of the Greek New Testament*, 1996, p. 633.

that the New Testament presbytery also ordained elders, but no biblical evidence sustains this assumption.

The Jewish practice of *semikat zeqenim* ('the leaning on of hands on persons in order to make elders')[174] did not refer to the ordination *by* elders but *of* elders[175] and was also performed for various purposes. Given the belief that Paul's letter to Timothy is genuine, it would have been written before Paul's death c. AD 67, but there is no evidence even in Jewish practice that elders in the synagogue were ordained by the imposition of hands before AD 70.[176] In any case, the passage in I Timothy 4.14 does not state that 'the imposition of the presbytery's hands' refers to an ordination.

The fact that Paul uses the noun form in *epithesis [ton cheiron tou presbyteriou]* ('the imposition [of the hands of the presbytery]') suggests that he refers to a well-known practice that belonged to the specific duties of the council of elders in the local church. (The same Greek construction occurs in Acts 8.18 and II Timothy 1.6, and in Hebrews 6.2 the imposition of hands is enumerated among the core doctrines of the church.)

Consequently, the 'imposition of the presbytery's hands' in I Timothy 4.14 may refer either to an *act* with a specific purpose, or it may be a set-phrase referring to an *occasion* when the council of elders exercised their authority and ministered by various kinds of the laying on of hands in the life of the Ephesian congregation, that is, on a significant occasion when the whole congregation was gathered under the leadership of the elders' council.

The Greek text (a) does not state that the presbytery's hands were placed on Timothy, and nowhere in Paul's letters is Timothy referred to as an 'elder' – he is rather a 'servant' or an 'apostle of Christ' related personally to Paul's itinerant ministry (see our exposition of

---

[174] See, for example, *The Babylonian Talmud, Tractate Sanhedrin* 13 b.
[175] D. Daube, *The New Testament and Rabbinic Judaism*, 2011, p. 244.
[176] See TED-TOSCR, 2013, section 3.4.

II Timothy 1.6 above). (b) The wording of the Greek text opens the possibility that the 'presbytery's imposition of hands' merely refers to *the attendant circumstances* when Timothy's spiritual gift was given *in the past* 'through a prophetic (inspired) word'; and (c) because of its ambiguous referential meaning, the 'imposition of hands' may have referred to other acts than ordination, for example, baptism, healing or forgiveness of sins. Even if one applies a literal reading, therefore, Timothy's alleged ordination by the council of elders is very uncertain.

The Meaning of 'the Spiritual Gift' by 'Prophetic Word'

What, then, does the 'spiritual gift' (*charisma*) in Timothy that was given him 'by prophetic word' refer to? No answer is given in the text, only a hint. The gift that should not be neglected is related to 'these things' in which Timothy is to be diligent (I Timothy 4.15) in order to counteract false teachings in the church (4.1-16).

Thus, his gift is to be used in his leadership by faith and godliness, commanding and teaching, being an example in speech, life, love, faith and purity, reading the scriptures, exhortation and teaching (4.6-16). The power (*dynamis*) to do this diligently, wholly and with perseverance is the spiritual gift (*charisma*) he has been given through 'prophetic speech'. However, the text says that this is brought to him by inspired words, not by the presbytery's imposition of their hands. What then is the relationship between these two acts?

The technical term *Designation* was used in ancient times for 'selection to an office made or announced by a person in authority', and 'Rome had a long history of the exercise of such authoritative designations to office'.[177] The election to office was reduced to a *confirmation* of what had been designated in advance by the person in authority, and this process was used by the Roman Emperors. Designation occurred also in the Greek world 'within the clubs and associations for the appointment of lesser functionaries by a higher

---

[177] E. Ferguson, 'Selection and Installation to Office in Roman, Greek, Jewish and Christian Antiquity', 1974, p. 274.

officer'.[178] Furthermore, the selection of rabbis among the Jews may appropriately be classified as Designation:

> At first each rabbi selected one of his students for ordination and raised him to a status equal to himself. Later this prerogative was centralised in the *Nasi* (or patriarch), and then a further modification requires the joint approval of both the *Nasi* and the *Beth Din* (council) for the ordination of a rabbi.[179]

Being raised and trained as a scribe, having spent years 'at the feet of Gamaliel' being 'educated strictly according to our ancestral law' (Acts 22.3; cf. Galatians 1.14), the apostle Paul would naturally be familiar with these practices from his Jewish roots. Everett Ferguson states with regard to Designation in the New Testament church:

> The New Testament era saw frequent manifestations of a type of Designation which is justly regarded as distinct from other expressions of this mode of selection – a choice made by a prophet as the inspired spokesman of the divine will (Acts 13:1-3; 1 Tim. 1:18; 4:14). Inspired Designations ceased with the cessation of an awareness of direct activity by the Holy Spirit in the church.[180]

The concept of Designation would link the commissioning of Barnabas and Paul in Acts 13.1-3 with Timothy in I Timothy 4.14. The same structure applies to both passages: the Holy Spirit speaks through a prophet and *appoints* the candidates, which is then *confirmed* by the imposition of hands. Designation simply means that a prophet or inspired person appoints Timothy as being filled with the spirit of prophecy and the formal confirmation would take place much later.

---

[178] Ibid.
[179] Ibid.
[180] Ibid.

Conclusions on Laying on of Hands in I Timothy 4.14

Bearing these considerations in mind, the passage in I Timothy 4.14 may be understood as follows.

From childhood, Timothy has excelled by his faith, knowledge of the Scriptures, spiritual power, and giftedness in teaching (I Timothy 6.12; II Timothy 3.14-15). Local charismatic teachers or prophets, or Paul himself, have from early on *designated* him as the man of God's choice (as was the case with Matthias in Acts 1 and Barnabas and Saul in Acts 13).

The *designation* is the Lord's appointment, but it has been received through a prophet or Paul himself and at some point in time it has then been publicly communicated to and acknowledged by the congregation in Ephesus. The public communication and confirmation of his designation would have been sufficient to authorise him as being appointed by God.

Thus, the point of the recorded event in 4.14 is not Timothy's ordination. There is no corroborating evidence of any ordination practice in the New Testament church. Moreover, in Timothy's case, it is not clear from the text when the ritual of the imposition of hands by the presbytery occurred. It may have occurred in connection with his baptism (which is not an ordination). It may have occurred on a later church occasion when the presbytery ministered to the church members in various ways (which would not necessarily have involved Timothy).

The point of 4.14 is the divine designation based on Timothy's vocation and spiritual gift, which is in some way publicly confirmed. The purpose of Timothy's public *authorisation* by prophetic words is to make him respected and obeyed. There is a direct similarity between Timothy's *charisma* as a means of having authority in the struggle with false teachers in Ephesus (I Timothy 4.14) and Joshua being full of the spirit of wisdom as a means of 'the Israelites obeying him and doing what the Lord had commanded Moses' (Deuteronomy

34.9). This biblical idea of a spiritual gift that is the basis of authority is essential in the letters to Timothy, because through and through they are dominated by a concern for *authorising* young Timothy for his work.[181]

However, the exact function of the imposition of hands in I Timothy 4.14 remains an enigma. Timothy is not mentioned in the text as a recipient of this ritual. His attested youth (4.12) means that it is doubtful if he could be ordained by the presbytery, for, if the rule later on attested in the *Talmud* and *Mishnah* applied in Timothy's case, he could not be ordained as an elder until he was forty years old.[182] Even the very practice of ordinations of elders is neither attested in the New Testament, nor in Judaism before AD 70. Timothy is never called an 'elder' in the New Testament, but he derived his authority from the prophetic designation (I Timothy 1.18; 4.14) and Paul's laying on of hands which authorised him as Paul's adopted son and assistant in the apostolic ministry (II Timothy 1.6).

The role of the imposition of the hands of the presbytery may therefore simply refer to an occasion when Timothy's divine *designation* was announced and acknowledged by the church. Another possibility is that, while the presbytery did not ordain Timothy as an elder, they *confirmed* the divine designation by 'commending him to the grace of God' (like Paul and Barnabas according to Acts 14.26) and bestowed upon him their blessing on behalf of the church.

9.3.4 *The Commissioning of Women and Spiritual Gifts*

Female servants-ministers in the New Testament (see 9.2.6 above) may well have been confirmed in their role by the local church, although we have no record of that. The record for commissioning-

---

[181] See E. Lohse, 'Die Ordination im Spätjudentum und im Neuen Testament', in: K. Kertelge (ed.), *Das kirchliche Amt im Neuen Testament*, Darmstadt, 1977, pp. 501-523; cf. A. T. Hanson, *The Pastoral Epistles*, 1982, p. 94.
[182] D. Daube, *The New Testament and Rabbinic* Judaism, 2011, p. 245 with references.

ordination of male servants-ministers is equally scant. As we have seen in 9.3 above, the New Testament contains no evidence of commissioning-ordination of apostles, servants-ministers, elders-overseers, or servants-deacons, whether these were male or female. The imposition of hands has a rare, specific, and *ad hoc* significance rooted in Jewish and Old Testament customs.

Recent research has confirmed, however, that in the early church women were ordained, and this practice – or its antecedents – would have had roots back into the first century when the New Testament was written.[183]

There is no instruction or even definition in the New Testament regarding commissioning-ordination that excludes women. In fact, neither is there any instruction in the New Testament to ordain male servants-ministers with or without the imposition of hands. The two clear instances of the imposition of hands in a congregational setting, in Acts 6.1-6 and 13.1-3, are not ordinations for any known office and both events are unique and *ad hoc* initiatives that are not repeated (see 9.3.3 above).

A Charismatic-Prophetic View of Commissioning-Ordination

A vital observation here is that commissioning-ordination in the New Testament is completely overshadowed by a *charismatic-prophetic* understanding of commissioning-ordination. It is seen as a spiritual event that comes from God, or Christ, or the Holy Spirit, or all of these. It took many decades for the New Testament church to develop institutions and organised church offices, and even when these occur – in Acts 14.23; I Timothy 3.1-13; Titus 1.5-9 – there is no mention of formal ordinations or the imposition of hands.

Therefore, *we cannot expect to find either men or women being 'ordained' in the New Testament*. Both men and women served as

---

[183] See G. Macy, *The Hidden History of Women's Ordination*, 2007, pp. 23-88; Macy opens his preface saying: 'The fact that women were ordained for the first twelve hundred years of Christianity will surprise many people' (p. vii).

'servants-ministers', some as 'apostles and prophets and teachers', but they were commissioned-ordained *spiritually*, by God, and that is sufficient in the New Testament. Even the apostle Paul strongly affirms this about himself (Acts 26.12-18; I Timothy 2.7; II Timothy 1.11). The process of the church's acceptance of such spiritual commissioning-ordination is not set out for us, but there are good grounds for concluding that it was based on the witness of a genuine Christian faith, visible spiritual gifts, and the fruit of the ministry – all serving to build up the church in Christ (Ephesians 4.7, 11-13). Thus, commissioning-ordination of men and women in the New Testament is *a spiritual work* of God, Christ, and the Holy Spirit. The visible signs – fruit, godliness, good deeds, abilities – were *witnessed and acknowledged by the church*.

Women Carried Out Ministerial Work

No distinction of gender is made at the imposition of hands in blessing (Matthew 19.15; Mark 10.13), healing (Mark 5.22-24, 35-43; Luke 15.10-13), or baptism (Acts 8.12, 17). Thus, female gender was not a hindrance for the imposition of hands *per se*. What matters is the *purpose* of the commissioning-ordination and the *function* a woman would then fulfil.

We have seen in some detail in 9.2 above that women had various important leadership *functions* in the New Testament church. The gospel writers pointedly included female exemplars or 'role-model' characters in their writings about Jesus – both female and male exemplars are introduced for the reader to imitate, but, in comparison, the twelve disciples come across as imperfect examples (see 9.2.2 and 9.2.3 above). Not only that, but we also have numerous named and described female servants-ministers in the New Testament who actually did ministerial work (see 9.2 above).

Thus, ministry and leadership were clearly open to women in the New Testament. Ordination did not exist and the only part of it that we find concerns the charismatic-prophetic calling by Christ who fills his servants-ministers with spiritual gifts that are by definition gender-inclusive. A closer look at the passages in I Corinthians 12 and Ephesians 4 will confirm this.

God Appoints His Servants-Ministers and Equips Them with Spiritual Gifts

Paul instructs the church in Corinth that the Spirit 'allots to each one individually just as the Spirit chooses' (I Corinthians 12.11). *Human beings or the church organisation are not involved here.* The Spirit shares himself with men and women for the good of the church: 'To each is given the manifestation of the Spirit for the common good.' (12.7; 8-11).

Thus, it is God who 'appointed in the church first apostles, second prophets, third teachers; then deeds of power, then gifts of healing, forms of assistance, forms of leadership, various kinds of tongues' (12.28). The gift of the Spirit *confirms* the appointment by God – nothing else is mentioned as relevant – and this divine confirmation is acknowledged by the fruit of an individual's service-ministry, be they a man or a woman.

The silence in the New Testament concerning the role of the church in evaluating and approving the divine confirmation of the gifts is understandable in the context of the mission of God – such a role would put the church above God, which would contradict the function of the church as the servant of God.

Thus, *the biblical kingdom theology reduces the role of the church in the appointment of leaders and enlarges the role of God, through Christ and the Holy Spirit.* The Seventh-day Adventist Church today must therefore be careful that it does not allow the institution of the Church, which is always wide open to human weakness, to marginalise the kingdom of God and the authority of Christ in its commissioning-ordination practice. That is precisely what a refusal to acknowledge Christ's gifts and appointments of women as his servants-ministers will accomplish.

Gender-Neutral Spiritual Gifts for Gender-Neutral Church Offices

When Paul instructs the church in Ephesus that '*each of us* was given grace according to the measure of Christ's gift' (Ephesians 4.7), he uses *inclusive* language, embracing men and women in the church. He then continues, saying that 'the gifts he gave were that some would be apostles, some prophets, some evangelists, some pastors and teachers' (4.11). The issue of gender is nowhere mentioned and is consequently irrelevant.

Instead, Paul defines the *purpose* of the gifts and the appointments for leadership: 'to equip the saints for *the work of ministry*, for *building up the body of Christ*, until all of us come to *the unity of the faith and of the knowledge of the Son of God*, to *maturity*, to *the measure of the full stature of Christ*' (4.12-13; emphasis supplied). This biblical definition of the purpose of commissioning-ordination is, again, expressed in *inclusive* language: the work is by all (4.7) and for all (4.13), but it is Christ who assigns the gifts (4.7) and the leadership functions (4.11).

A few verses further on in the same chapter, Christ is defined as 'the Head' – no other head in the church is mentioned – 'from whom the whole body, joined and knitted together by every ligament with which it is equipped, as each part is working properly, promotes the body's growth in building itself up in love' (4.15-16). 'The whole body' means men and women who have mutually submitted themselves to each other in fellowship and ministry and to Jesus Christ as servants-ministers in his kingdom mission.

According to the New Testament practices of appointments for ministry, therefore, the crucial *condition* is, for both men and women, if they have received spiritual gifts for leadership in some sense and a calling and appointment by Christ. A church that claims to follow the Bible as their only creed must build its theology of commissioning-ordination on these premises.

9.3.5 New Testament Ordination Terminology

The New Testament does not support the use of technical terms like 'ordain' or 'ordination'. Etymologically, these are terms with a Latin root that came into the Christian church from the pagan Roman Empire and the adaptation of the Roman Catholic Church to Roman customs and practices.[184]

The Greek terms used in the New Testament vary greatly and are common terms for 'put, place, make', which may sometimes be rendered 'appoint' in view of the context: *poieo*, 'make' (Mark 3.14); *eklegomai*, 'choose' (Luke 6.12; John 15.16); *ginomai*, 'become' (Acts 1.22); *cheirotoneo*, 'raise the hand (in a congregational agreement)', 'appoint' (II Corinthians 8.19; Acts 14.23); *tithemi*, 'place, set' (I Timothy 2.7); *kathistemi*, 'cause to be, appoint' (Acts 6.3; Titus 1.5); *epitithemi*, 'place, set' (Acts 6.6; 13.3; cf. the noun *epithesis* in I Timothy 4.14; II Timothy 1.6; Hebrews 6.2). None of these is a technical term for 'ordination' in the New Testament.

Much later, the verb *cheirotoneo* became the Greek technical term for 'ordain' in the post-biblical era[185] – and, incidentally, it is still used within the Seventh-day Adventist Church in Greek-speaking settings to denote 'ordination' – but its function in the New Testament is neither clear nor predominant. It occurs only twice and in slightly different contexts (Acts 14.23; II Corinthians 8.19). The very few instances where reference is made to an induction into a task by the imposition of hands are: Acts 6.6; 13.3; II Timothy 1.6 (for I Timothy 4.14, see 9.3.3.4 above). In none of these instances, however, is the induction made for a defined office in the church, but the functions are occasional and *ad hoc* initiatives that do not form an established church order. Moreover, the induction process varies and its significance is not explained (see 9.3.3 above).

---

[184] See TED-TOSCR, 2013, sections 4.1 and 4.2.
[185] See ibid., section 4.1.7.

9.3.6 Conclusions

The New Testament is clear on God's Mission to the world, the Church, the Ministry, and the divine call to Ministry. But it has very little to say about commissioning-ordination through the imposition of hands. What it does say is either difficult to understand with certainty or it refers to what might best be called 'proto-ordination'. The tasks and functions, if mentioned, do not correspond to the office of the gospel minister in modern Seventh-day Adventist terminology.

The Absence of Ordination Gives the Church Freedom of Choice

The New Testament makes two points about commissioning-ordination. Firstly, neither the twelve nor the apostle Paul were commissioned-ordained by the laying on of hands. They had a spiritual-prophetic office, being directly appointed by God.

Secondly, no commissioning-ordination of key office holders is mentioned in the New Testament. There was either no established practice for this in the New Testament church, or the biblical authors deemed it to be of no significance. (It did acquire significance later on, however, when the first generation of believers had gone, the centre of activity for the church had moved from Jerusalem, and disunity and false teachings became a real threat.)[186]

Thus, no biblical text commands or illustrates ordination as it is practised by the Seventh-day Adventist Church today, and this applies regardless of whether or not one reads the text literally. No *male* disciple, servant-minister, or apostle was ordained, and the imposition of hands for ordination was not conducted for any of the church offices existing in the church today, such as the gospel minister, the local church elder, or the deacon/deaconess. Certain principles may perhaps be deduced from the Bible, but these depend on a rather complex process of interpretation and are not easily identified – thus, consensus on those details will continue to be difficult to achieve.

---

[186] This post-biblical development is carefully explored in TED-TOSCR, 2013, chap. 4.

This means that, biblically, the church today has freedom to choose how it wishes to acknowledge the call, spiritual appointment, and spiritual gifts of a candidate for the gospel ministry. It has freedom to choose to ordain not only men but also women for the gospel ministry.

The Term 'Commissioning' More Biblical than 'Ordination'

Even our terminology is an open question. Based on the biblical terminology and what we know of the origin of the term 'ordination', a case can be made for 'commissioning' rather than 'ordination'. The New Testament has no technical term corresponding to our 'ordain' or 'ordination'. Etymologically, these are terms with a Latin root that came into the Christian church from the pagan Roman Empire through adaptations in the early church to Roman customs and practices. However, words that may be translated 'commission' or 'appoint' abound (e.g. Mark 3.14; Acts 14.23; NRSV).

It is perhaps significant that Ellen White, in her earliest reflection on the ordination of the first Sabbatarian Adventist ministers, 'does not use the word ordination but refers to setting apart and commission'.[187] Of equal interest is the fact that, much later on, she referred to her own calling as an 'ordination'. In 1909, as she looked back at her experiences in 1844, she said: 'In the city of Portland, *the Lord ordained me as His messenger.*'[188] Evidently, she applies here the biblical charismatic-prophetic concept of ordination to herself. The Seventh-day Adventist Church in her time issued to her an Ordained Minister's Credential, which she silently accepted, but without undergoing the ceremony of ordination.

---

[187] D. Fortin, 'Ellen White, Women in Ministry, and the Ordination of Women', 2013, p. 109.

[188] E. G. White, 'Letter 138, 1909', quoted in A. White, *The Ellen G. White Biography*, vol. 6, The Later Elmshaven Years, 1905-1915, 1986, p. 211 (emphasis supplied).

Silent Gospels and Various Proto-Ordination Passages

In the Gospels, the ministry of Jesus demonstrates an absence of ordination with the laying on of hands. This continues in Acts 1, where a twelfth apostle to replace Judas is appointed without any reference whatsoever to ordination or the imposition of hands. He is elected by God and that is all there is to say. In the rest of the New Testament we find only occasional and *ad hoc* commissioning events that may be referred to as proto-ordination acts.

Each of the passages involved gives us a different model of proto-ordination. None of them defines plainly the office or function for which the imposition of hands is used. The central point in all of them is the commissioning of God by the Holy Spirit.

The Strategic Function in God's Mission of Acts 6.1-6 and 13.1-3

In the context of the mission of God, the passages in Acts 6.1-6 and 13.1-3 mean much more than setting aside servants of God for an *ad hoc* specific task. They mark decisive strategic steps in God's mission through the church.

In Acts 6, the appointment of the seven means that the centre of governance of the church moves beyond the twelve apostles and the family of Jesus located in Jerusalem, which was seen as the throne and dwelling of God. Members of the diaspora with connections in the wider Graeco-Roman world are now invited in to serve as leaders in God's church (in fulfilment of Isaiah 66.21). The kingdom of God is moving out to the world through the church and its representatives.

Thus, the ordination of the seven is an important step in the mission of God and his salvation history, not just as a leadership appointment – and that seems to be why it is a *unique* action by the church in the New Testament which is not repeated or turned into a policy. It confirms that God's kingdom in Christ, *through the Holy Spirit*, is dwelling also in the seven, although they were not appointed by Jesus as were the twelve apostles, and that the borders of his kingdom are now being extended to the world.

In the same way, Acts 13.1-3 describes another crucial moment in God's mission, when two 'prophets and teachers', Barnabas and Paul, are authorised by the Holy Spirit and the gospel of the Kingdom is extended from the church body in Antioch into congregations in Asia Minor. They are to bring the kingdom of God to the Gentiles by preaching the Word and organising the work by establishing elders in each church (Acts 14.23). The city of Antioch was fraught with considerable symbolic significance in first-century Judaism since it was thought to be the gateway between the Exile/Diaspora and the Promised Land.[189] As Barnabas and Paul leave the Promised Land and bring the gospel into Gentile territory, they reverse Israel's movement into Canaan under Joshua. Thus, Acts 13.1-3 has points of similarities with the ordination of Joshua in Numbers 27, where God designates Joshua, where Moses, the prophet and teacher, lays his hand on Joshua, and where Joshua assumes the role of leading Israel into the Promised Land.

In these two central texts for biblical commissioning-ordination, what matters is God's mission through the ministry to which a person is called. Neither the individuals nor the ceremony itself are important. The act of laying on of hands signifies vital *changes* as God's mission is extended to the Gentiles. It is God who acts in the mission of the church.

Consequently, the apostle Paul, who plays a central role as Christ's agent of mission in the New Testament church, is called and commissioned directly by Christ, without a ceremony of ordination by the imposition of hands.[190] Thus, ordination in the New Testament is not a matter of authorising a church member to a special ministry in the church organisation, but it is *God's way of confirming a new development in his mission to save the world and have communion with his people.* The prayer and laying on of hands is a way of confirming that the growing flow of Gentiles into the church is in harmony with

---

[189] M. Bockmuehl, *Jewish Law in Gentile Churches*, 2000, pp. 61-70.
[190] See e.g. Acts 9; 26.12-18; Galatians 1-2.

God's will. In this context, the ceremony says that God's mission is to the world, not merely to Israel.

Women and Commissioning-Ordination

No example is found in the New Testament of the imposition of hands on a woman in order to confirm her function as a servant-minister of God. In fact, neither is there any instruction in the New Testament to ordain male servants-ministers with or without the imposition of hands. However, there is no instruction or even definition in the New Testament regarding commissioning-ordination that excludes women.

Ministry and leadership were clearly open to women in the New Testament. 'Ordination' in the sense we apply it today did not exist, and the only part of it that did exist was the charismatic-prophetic calling by Christ who fills his servants-ministers with spiritual gifts that are by definition gender-inclusive. A closer look at the passages in I Corinthians 12 and Ephesians 4 confirms this.

A Few Examples of Ritual Ordination Relate to Jewish Customs

There are a couple of examples of ceremonies including the laying on of hands for commissioning of some sort. Our study indicates that they are all performed for *different* purposes. They give the impression of being more or less connected with contemporary Jewish customs that are rooted in an Old Testament concept of 'leaning on of hands' in order to produce a substitute or representative. This is however not how Seventh-day Adventists understand the rite.

The Christian Tradition of Ordination

The mentioning of the laying on of hands in a few passages has been connected and converted by the Christian church into a practice – without recognition of its original meaning – and this has been adopted in the nearly two-thousand-year-old Christian tradition of ordination.

The KJV translation from 1611, where 'ordain' is a key word for many different common Greek words for 'appoint', created the possibility of making wide connections between passages that dealt with different things. It was also an ecclesiastical translation reflecting the position of the Anglican Church. Thus, King James gave the translators instructions designed to guarantee that the new translation would conform to the ecclesiology of the Church of England.[191] Certain Greek and Hebrew words were to be translated in a manner that reflected the traditional usage of the Anglican Church.[192] The new translation would reflect the episcopal structure of the Church of England and traditional beliefs about ordained clergy.[193] These influences on the concept of ordination in nineteenth century USA are not supported by the original texts of the Bible.

The Charismatic-Prophetic Concept of Commissioning

Commissioning-ordination in the New Testament is defined by a *charismatic-prophetic* concept. It is seen as a spiritual event that comes from God, or Christ, or the Holy Spirit, or all of these. Both men and women served as 'servants-ministers', some as 'apostles and prophets and teachers', but they were commissioned-ordained *spiritually*, by God, and that is sufficient in the New Testament.

Church Approval and the Crucial Condition for Service-Ministry

The silence in the New Testament concerning the role of the church in evaluating and approving the divine calling and confirming the presence of spiritual gifts is understandable in the context of the mission of God – such a role would put the church above God, which would contradict the function of the church as the servant of God. Thus, *the biblical kingdom theology reduces the role of the church in the appointment of leaders and enlarges the role of God, through Christ and the Holy Spirit.*

According to the New Testament practices of appointments for ministry, the crucial *condition* is, for both men and women, whether they have received spiritual gifts for leadership in some sense and a

---

[191] D. Daniell, *The Bible in* English, 2003, p. 439.
[192] Ibid.
[193] Ibid.

calling and appointment by Christ. As Head of the church, Christ decides who is worthy of serving him, and he *shows his decision by the spiritual gifts he provides to women and men*. The only role the church institution has is to acknowledge that those gifts are there. As the whole body 'clothes itself with Christ', 'there is no longer Jew or Greek, there is no longer slave or free, *there is no longer male and female*; for all of you are one in Christ Jesus' (Galatians 3.27-28; emphasis supplied).

9.4 The Laying On of Hands

The biblical practice of the laying on of hands is often regarded as a central element of ordination. However, the Bible neither commands ordination nor the use of the imposition of hands. Above all, there is no plain biblical explanation of what laying on of hands means. When churches use it today, it is based on a re-interpretation and adaptation of a few biblical passages to fit a very old Christian tradition that developed mainly in post-biblical times.[194] What the Bible says about laying on of hands will be briefly summarised in the following.

9.4.1 Old Testament Usage

The practice of the laying on of hands has various meanings and functions in the Bible.[195] It is clearly rooted in the Old Testament where it is used in blessing (e.g. Genesis 48.14, 17-18, 20; Hebr. *sim* or *shit*), sacrifice (e.g. Leviticus 4.4; 16.20-24; Hebr. *samak*), purging blasphemy (e.g. Leviticus 24.14, Hebr. *samak*), induction into an office (the Levites in Numbers 8.5-26, Hebr. *samak*), and commissioning-ordination for a special leadership task (Joshua in Numbers 27.23; Deuteronomy 34.9; Hebr. *samak*).[196]

---

[194] See TED-TOSCR, 2013, chapter 4.
[195] See the survey by M. H. Shepherd, 'Laying on of Hands', *IDB*, vol. 2, 1982, pp. 521-522.
[196] M. Warkentin, *Ordination*, 1982, p. 9.

Generally speaking, the laying on of hands almost always functions as a means of connecting two parties so that something that belongs to the agent is shared with the recipient. This may be a divine blessing, although God is then the primary agent. It may involve a transfer of sin and ritual impurity to an offering animal. It may also imply an extension of self or making a substitute or representative (Levites, Joshua). The act of the laying on of hands may be accompanied by words that define the nature of the act, i.e. a blessing, a confession, a commissioning or appointment, but most often the biblical text does not record any such words at all.

It is possible that the origin of the gesture of laying on of hands is to be found in the father's blessing of his firstborn son. On this occasion, the father confirmed the son as his representative and conveyed his authorisation of the firstborn as the next 'leader' of the family or tribe (for the custom of the firstborn in Israel, see 6.5.3 above). This may explain the application of the gesture in the case of the Levites and Joshua, where the making of representatives is central (see below).

The Symbol of the 'Hand'

The hand was a powerful symbol in the Old Testament and the ancient Near East. It is the part of the body that grasps and can be grasped, and the meaning 'strength' therefore belongs to the hand as the primary means of power.[197] It is also the body part that gives and receives, and may therefore represent the person in respect to his impact (as in Isaiah 1.12).[198] When the scapegoat is handed over to a man's care, it is said that it is given into 'his hand' (Leviticus 16.21).

Thus, the Hebrew word for 'hand', *yad*, may be associated with individuality, ability, possession, strength, power, authority, and creativity, but it is almost impossible to determine which of these are intended in the phrase 'laying on of hands'. Generally speaking, the act may imply a conveying of presence, strength, authority, sins and

---

[197] H. W. Wolff, *Anthropology of the Old Testament*, 1974, pp. 67-68.
[198] Ibid., p. 68.

defilement, and vicarious representation, but we are unable to make an informed choice in each passage.

Laying on of Hands as 'Leaning on of Hands'

While different verbs are used to express 'laying on [of hands]', the most important phrase is *samak [yadim] 'al*. It indicates a gesture by which a leaning pressure is applied to the recipient. It appears twenty-five times in a variety of contexts. Eighteen times hands are laid on animals in the context of sacrifice or on the scapegoat, five times on people, once on an inanimate object, and once expressing the Lord's support of one who stumbles.[199] When the laying on of hands is used in an act of blessing, *samak* is not used but various other verbs (*sim͎, shit*).

Thus, the phrase *samak yadim 'al*, 'lean hands on', is predominantly used when the agent is pressing himself on to the recipient, symbolically making a substitute or representative or an extension of himself. When hands are leaning on the offering animals, the guilty self is identified with the offering animal which then as a substitute pays the price of death for sin. The same is the case when those who have heard a blasphemer's words are to lean their hands on the blasphemer before he is put to death. It also applies to the two instances where a commissioning-ordination is performed:

Firstly, the people lay their hands on the Levites (Numbers 8.5-26) to express *substitution* in that the Levites *replaced* the firstborns belonging to the Lord and *represented* the congregation as a whole (see 7.2.2 above). The people symbolically *reproduce* their firstborns in the

 Levites by the leaning pressure of their hands and the Levites *represent* the firstborns and, by implication, Israel as a whole.

Secondly, Moses lays his hand on Joshua, his successor as a leader of Israel (Numbers 27.20, 23; Deuteronomy 34.9). The purpose is to *reproduce* 'some of Moses' authority' so that 'all the congregation

---

[199] For scriptural references, see TED-TOSCR, 2013, section 3.3.

of Israel may obey' (Numbers 27.20) and to *reproduce* symbolically Moses' 'spirit of wisdom' in Joshua (Deuteronomy 34.9), albeit with God's help. By the act of *samak yadim* Joshua becomes a *substitute* or *representative* who reflects Moses' leadership.

In both instances no prayer is included. This was also the case in the laying on of hands in the Jewish scribal ordination (*semikah*), for which Moses' ordination of Joshua was a model.[200] Prayer was not necessary here since the point of the ritual was to reproduce or substitute yourself or create an equal status by a leaning pressure of your hands.[201] However, in the New Testament, prayer is included in Acts 6.1-6 and possibly in 13.1-3, and the gesture is somehow linked to a spiritual gift (*charisma*) in I Timothy 4.14 and II Timothy 1.6.

Renderings in Hebrew and Greek

In the Septuagint the Greek verb *epitithemi* is used as a translation of the Hebrew *samak*, 'lean [one's hands] on', whether for laying hands on the offering animals (Exodus 29.10; Leviticus 1.4; Numbers 8.12) or on the Levites (Numbers 8.10) or Joshua (Numbers 27.18, 23; Deuteronomy 34.9). It is therefore possible that this Greek verb when used in the New Testament alludes to the Hebrew sense 'lean on' which carries with it the idea of making a substitute, a representative, or an extension of self. However, that must be determined based on its context.

9.4.2 New Testament Usage

The New Testament practice of the laying on of hands as part of commissioning-ordination is difficult to ascertain. From a total of twenty-one references, at best, the phrase 'lay hand(s) on' (Greek *epitithemi)* occurs only five times for someone being set apart or reinstated for a special function or ministry: Acts 6.6; 13.3; I Timothy

---

[200] TED-TOSCR, 2013, section 3.4.
[201] E. Ferguson, 'Jewish and Christian Ordination', 1963, pp. 15-16; TED-TOSCR, 2013, section 3.4.

4.14; 5.22; II Timothy 1.6. The significance of the gesture in these passages is uncertain because it is not plainly explained in the context. It was a known practice among the early Christians that needed no explanation. This is understandable in view of the Old Testament and Jewish roots of the practice and the predominantly Jewish environment of the first Christian communities.

The New Testament examples of the laying on of hands in general are equally mixed. The gesture is used for the purpose of blessing (Matthew 19.15; Mark 10.13), healing (Mark 5.23; 6.5; 16.18; Luke 4.40; 13.13; Acts 9.17; 28.8), gift of spiritual power at baptism (Acts 8.14-17; 19.1-7), forgiveness of sins (I Timothy 5.22), and commissioning for a task (Acts 6.1-6; 13.1-3).

Some of these occurrences stand in contexts lacking any information about its significance. This is the case in Hebrews 6.2. The immediate connection with repentance, faith in God, and baptism might suggest that the imposition of hands is part of an act of blessing or confirmation of the Spirit at baptism or forgiveness of sins rather than an appointment. The prominence of the act – being listed with the core beliefs of the church – suggests particular importance in the Graeco-Roman world where laying on of hands for healing was popular.[202]

The sense 'lay on [hands]' is referred to by the Greek verb *epitithemi*, 'put/lay on': for blessing (Matthew 19.13, 15), healing (e.g. Matthew 9.18; Mark 16.18; Acts 9.17; Hebrews 6.2), for confirming the gift of the Spirit at baptism (Acts 8.17), for restoring a disciplined elder (I Timothy 5.22), and for all instances of commissioning-ordination in the New Testament (Acts 6.6; 13.3; I Timothy 4.14; II Timothy 1.6). The use of this verb for the Hebrew *samak yadim 'al* in the Septuagint (noted above) means that the technical function of 'lean [hands] on', which is attached to this Hebrew expression, may be relevant in these instances.

---

[202] See C. Maurer, '*epitithemi*', *ThDNT*, vol.8, pp. 159-161.

The Seven in Acts 6.1-6

The commissioning-ordination of the seven in Acts 6.1-6 has been examined in some detail in 9.3.3.1 above (see also 9.3.2). The imposition of hands is introduced as a known practice in the Jerusalem congregation and to the intended readers. The gesture is accompanied by prayer, but the text does not state who is performing the act – the congregation, the apostles, or both.

An attractive interpretation is that the ceremony functions as an innovative blending of two concepts: (a) the blessing expressed through prayer that ensures the participation of the Spirit (following the example of Jesus who blessed his disciples), and (b) the Old Testament and Jewish concept of *samak yadim 'al*, 'lean hands on', which was understood as a symbolic sign of producing a substitute, i.e. making an authorised representative. Thus, by their appointment, the seven are authorised as representatives of both the congregation, the people of God, and the apostles who were appointed by Christ. This resembles a combination of the key elements in the ordination of the Levites in Numbers 8 and that of Joshua in Numbers 27. However, it must be added, these observations are only plausible deductions from a combination of various scriptural features. The usage of the laying on of hands in this passage is a temporary and *ad hoc* gesture that was known in the local setting but implied no established ritual.

Barnabas and Paul in Acts 13.1-3

There is no information here about the significance or origin of the laying on of hands. It was known to the 'prophets and teachers' in the church in Antioch (Acts 13.1), and Luke, the author of Acts, assumes it is known to the intended readers. He simply defines the act as a 'commendation' of the two to the grace of the Lord (Acts 14.26). It is not clear if the fasting and prayer belongs to the ritual, or if it was the setting in which the Spirit revealed his calling of Barnabas and Paul. However, in view of fasting and prayer being somehow linked to their appointment of elders in Acts 14.23, it is possibly also a feature in 13.3, but the text is not clear on this point.

The laying on of hands confirms the command of the Spirit. In view of the context (see 9.3.3.2 above), the gesture may be rooted in the *samak yadim 'al*, 'lean one's hands on', functioning as a symbolic sign of authorising representatives. One possible implication of the act, therefore, is that Barnabas and Paul are authorised as representatives of the believers in Antioch – a city fraught with considerable symbolic significance in first-century Judaism since it was thought to be the gateway between the Exile/Diaspora and the Promised Land[203] – as they are to bring the gospel into Gentile territory and consolidate the work.

If this interpretation is granted, the event would resemble the ordination of Joshua in Numbers 27, where God designates Joshua, where Moses, the prophet and teacher, leans his hand on Joshua, and where Joshua assumes the role of leading Israel into the Promised Land. Similarly, Paul and Barnabas are now consolidating the gospel work in the world.

As in Acts 6.1-6, the usage of the laying on of hands in this passage is not explained but has analogies in Jewish customs and the Old Testament. It is a temporary and *ad hoc* gesture that was known in the local setting, but was not repeated as part of a fixed ritual for setting someone apart for ministry.

The Elder in I Timothy 5.22

Two alternative views have been advanced about this passage, both connecting it with the preceding context that deals with elders:

1. *The passage concerns the commissioning-ordination of an elder.* According to this view, Timothy is advised to be circumspect about whom he ordains. If the appointee turns out later on to be a sinner, Timothy will be held responsible for his sins.[204]

This meaning of I Timothy 5.22 does not flow from the context in chapter 5. It does not explain the key phrase 'do not share in the

---

[203] M. Bockmuehl, *Jewish Law in Gentile Churches*, 2000, pp. 61-70.
[204] For references to scholars who support this view, and the arguments, see A. T. Hanson, *The Pastoral Epistles*, 1982, p. 103.

sins of others' but 'keep yourself pure'. Further, judging by 4.14, the laying on of hands was carried out by the presbytery, i.e. a *group* of elders. It is also unlikely that Timothy alone, who is nowhere referred to as 'overseer' (*episkopos*) or 'elder' (*presbyteros*) in the New Testament, would be in a position to ordain anyone in the Ephesian church, especially not hastily. Timothy worked for Paul as an itinerant apostolic servant and had his authorisation from him (see II Timothy 1.6 and 9.3.3.4 above). It is unlikely that Timothy, not being an elder himself, would ordain another elder. Further, the qualifications required of an overseer (3.1-7) ensured no haste in the laying on of hands for the induction into an office, if this were intended here. Finally, assuming that 5.22 refers to a commissioning-ordination, it would be the only New Testament instance of an elder being commissioned-ordained by the laying on of hands.

2. *The passage concerns the reconciliation of an elder under discipline.* This meaning picks up its theme from the instructions about how to deal with erring elders in 5.20-21. According to this view, Timothy is advised to avoid favouritism (5.21) in reinstating an erring elder to office by the laying on of hands.[205] The only argument against this reading is that the practice of laying hands on an erring elder who is reinstated after committing a sin is not plainly attested elsewhere in the New Testament. It is however strongly attested in the post-biblical practice of the early church, and it is therefore plausible that this instance gives biblical evidence of the early occurrence of this practice.

The arguments in favour of the second alternative are persuasive. It fits the context well. The statement that Timothy by hasty admission of a sinning elder will 'share in the sins of others' follows more naturally than if it were a warning against an ordination in haste that ignored the list of qualifications in 3.1-7. It also preserves the topic of the section, which is the discipline of elders.[206] In 5.19,

---

[205] For references to scholars who support this view, and the arguments, see ibid.
[206] Ibid.

we have the *accusation*; in 5.20, the *conviction* and *sentence*; in 5.22, the *restoration*.[207] A hasty reconciliation would give the offender the wrong message and threaten a full repentance, while making Timothy partaker of the offender's sin, thus making the final injunction to 'keep yourself pure' meaningful.

In conclusion, therefore, I Timothy 5.22 does not deal with the laying on of hands in a commissioning-ordination.[208] The passage may be closer to the case in Hebrews 6.2, where the laying on of hands may symbolise healing and the forgiveness of sins. The New Testament attests the belief that the gospel of Jesus Christ with its forgiveness of sins had the power of healing when combined with prayer by a person of strong faith (cf. James 5.14-18). Thus, the laying on of hands in I Timothy 5.22 gives implicit evidence of the sacred nature of an elder's appointment, for it is the laying on of hands that restores the elder to being a servant of God.

Timothy (I Timothy 4.14; II Timothy 1.6)

As we have seen in 9.3.3.4 above, it is possible that these passages refer to the laying on of hands in some kind of blessing linked to Timothy's task as a servant of the church and a servant of Paul. This may not have been a commissioning-ordination, however, for other alternative interpretations are possible.

From what the text says, it is not clear to what task or office Timothy would be appointed. It is not clear if the two passages refer to the same kind of authorisation. The passage in I Timothy 4.14 may not even refer to a laying on of hands involving Timothy, for it rather underlines the prophetic speech that announced him to be a man of God's choice, similar to the case with Barnabas and Paul in Acts 13.1-3.

---

[207] K. S. Wuest, *The Pastoral Epistles in the Greek New Testament*, 1953, pp. 87-88.

[208] This view is also supported by *The SDA Bible Commentary*, vol. 7, 1957, p. 314; A. T. Hanson, *The Pastoral Epistles*, 1982, p. 103; V. Norskov Olsen, *Myth and Truth about Church, Priesthood and Ordination*, 1990, p. 147.

By *Designation*, which was a common practice in the Graeco-Roman world, a senior official could designate a person for an office and much later the confirmation would take place. While carrying the verbal designation, however, the designee held the authorisation and the later imposition of hands was merely a formality. The references to the laying on of hands have a general character of authorising Timothy before the church.

In the same way as in Acts 6.1-6 and 13.1-3, the usage of the laying on of hands in these passages is not explained but has clear analogies in Jewish customs and the Old Testament. In II Timothy 1.6, it may be seen as a temporary and *ad hoc* gesture for Paul's 'adoption' of Timothy as his 'son' and servant. In I Timothy 4.14, the laying on of hands by the presbytery suggests a permanent practice, but it is not possible to say for what purpose it is mentioned here. In both cases, the gesture was known in the local setting. At the same time, we have seen that there are no traces in the New Testament of an established ritual.

Summary

The teaching of the Bible regarding the laying on of hands in commissioning-ordination is very limited. The few New Testament references are not clear in important ways. No church office is mentioned. The significance of laying on of hands is not explained, and there is no unambiguous reference to the body performing the act of the laying on of hands – whether the congregation, or a leading group, or both. *The significance of the laying on of hands in the New Testament cannot, therefore, be determined.*

The thought of some sort of *authorisation* for spiritual leadership can be discerned, and this is linked to a *confirmation* of God's prior designation of the appointee. When the act takes place in the presence of the congregation, or is performed by a group of leaders, the idea of making the appointment publicly known and endorsed by the congregation may perhaps be present, but whether or not this is an intentional feature is not explicitly stated in the biblical text.

In light of this, the laying on of hands in the New Testament church may simply have been an 'outward symbol of the prayer – a personal benediction on the candidate and a petition for divine blessing'.[209] But it may also have included some aspects of the Jewish understanding of *samak yadim 'al*, 'lean hands on', by which the candidate was symbolically authorised as a substitute or representative. This may have been achieved by relying on some Old Testament passages and would not need to be seen as a direct loan from Judaism, although the Jewish practices may certainly have functioned as a model as time went by. Most early Christian congregations functioned like the Jewish synagogues.

Theologically, there are no magical or sacramental biblical formulas for the induction into the ministry of the church. The laying on of hands has no power in itself. An ordination ceremony may symbolically *confirm* God's calling, *acknowledge* spiritual gifts, and *authorise* the appointee as a representative of the church, but there is no biblical passage that states this in plain words.

If the interpretation is correct, that the few New Testament proto-ordination texts that mention the imposition of hands for a leadership function are relying on the Old Testament and Jewish *semikah*, which was understood as producing a substitute, then it is understandable why women do not appear as recipients of the imposition of hands in the proto-ordination passages. The act producing a duplicate also reproduced the male gender. But more important than that is the fact that the casual and *ad hoc* nature of this act, which relied on customs in the Jewish setting of the earliest Christian churches, provides poor evidence against women's recognition and authorisation for the gospel ministry. Instead, *what matters is the charismatic-prophetic nature of ministry which dominates in the New Testament as a whole, and in this context women were frequent servant-ministers of God.*[210]

---

[209] E. Ferguson, 'Jewish and Christian Ordination', 1963, p. 15.
[210] See the introduction to chap. 9, and sections 9.1 and 9.2 above.

9.5 *The Meaning of Man as 'Head' and Woman in 'Submission'*

It is argued by some that the New Testament prohibits women from having positions of authority in the Seventh-day Adventist Church ('headship') and that they are commanded to be subordinate to men ('submission').[211] This view will be examined here in a study of the most prominent New Testament passages that include the Greek terms *hypotasso*, 'submit', or *hypotage*, 'submission'.

Studies have shown that 'there is a clear distinction in the New Testament between counsel regarding husband-wife relationships and general men-women relationships in the church'.[212] Addressing the issue of ordination, therefore, the Seventh-day Adventist Church must not carelessly apply biblical counsels intended for the husband-wife relationship to the ministry of the Church today. Firstly, not all women are *wives*. Secondly, not all marriages are built on *patriarchal* concepts. The *roles* in husband-wife relationships are created by the spouses based on personalities and needs, mutual love and care; the appropriateness of those roles is seen in their fruit, i.e. in a harmonious and happy marriage, and in the oneness of the two partners (Genesis 2.24). Thirdly, the *purpose* of the family is to live intimately together in love and common projects, while the *purpose* of the ministry of the church is to build up the church in many different ways. While the ethical principles are the same for church members and married couples, as we see, for example, in Ephesians 5.21-33, marriage is a constituent part of the fabric of the church. Nevertheless, in the Bible, the submission of wives to their husbands was not a hindrance for female leadership functions.[213]

---

[211] See, for example, the view of position #1 in GC-TOSCR, 2014, pp. 24-60. Contrary views are expressed, for example, by K. Haloviak ('Is *Headship* Theology Biblical?', 2013); by position #2 in GC-TOSCR, 2014 (pp. 62-97), and a statement of the Seventh-day Adventist Theological Seminary: 'On the Unique Headship of Christ in the Church' (http://news.adventist.org/all-news/news/go/2014-08-24/andrews-theologians-approve-statement-on-headship/).

[212] R. M. Davidson, 'Headship, Submission, and Equality in Scripture', 1998, p. 273.

[213] See, for example, Paul's reasoning in I Corinthians 7.332-35, 39-40.

We will see in the following, however, that the passages before us concern women in the specific setting of first-century Corinth and Ephesus. What Paul has to say to them concerns specific issues in the local and historical setting and he addresses these issues in view of conventional customs of patriarchy, shame/honour, and the need for the church to be internally united while making the gospel attractive to outsiders who shared the same cultural values at the time.

As we pursue the following study, it will become apparent that 'the language of headship is a cultural construct that we impose on the texts'.[214]

9.5.1 *The Socio-Cultural Environment of Women in Paul's Writings*

The four passages that we will examine here are found in Paul's letters to the churches in Corinth and Ephesus. These were flowering cities of prominence in the Graeco-Roman world. The generally accepted views of women and especially married women influenced the church members and caused conflicts and threats to church unity. As Paul addressed these issues, he consistently sought to preserve the honour of both husband and wife, order in the church, reverence for God in worship, and a good impression on outsiders who would judge the gospel from the honour of its proponents.

Two areas of particular importance need to be noted. Firstly, most of the young Christian churches in Asia Minor were formed from the Jewish synagogue and a large part of the members were Jews. Even the Gentiles who 'feared God' had a certain familiarity with Jewish tradition. Thus, the view of women in first-century Judaism would be an influential factor as Paul issued his instructions for the peace and well-being of the churches. The religious role of women was mostly limited to the home. Wives acting in subordination to their own husbands was part of the code of honour in ancient Mediterranean societies.

---

[214] K. Haloviak, 'Is *Headship* Theology Biblical?', 2013, p. 125.

A short passage by Philo of Alexandria (c. 20 BC-AD 50) illustrates the widespread Jewish and Graeco-Roman 'spatial' opposition of men and women and its public consequences:

> Marketplaces, council meetings, courts, social organisations, assemblies of large crowds of people, and interaction of word and deed in the open, in war and in peace, are suited only for men. The female sex, by contrast, is supposed to guard the house and stay at home; virgins are to remain in the back of the rooms and regard the connecting door as boundaries; married women, however, should regard the front door as the boundary. For there are two kinds of urban spheres, a larger and a smaller. The larger ones are called cities, the smaller ones households (*oikiai*). Of these two, on the basis of the division, the men are in charge of the larger one, which is called municipal administration (*politeia*); women, of the smaller one, which is called the household (*oikonomia*). Thus women are not supposed to concern themselves further with anything but the duties of the household.[215]

This is without doubt a prescription that shows only how things *should* be in Philo's opinion. In fact, 'women appeared in public in various connections, even before court, and they also belonged to social organisations. Yet direct participation in what Philo calls "municipal administration" (*politeia*) was the domain of men.'[216]

The Jewish rabbis were divided on the wisdom of teaching daughters the Torah.[217] In one rule preserved in the *Mishnah*, it is stated that 'a woman may not be a teacher of scribes' (Mishnah *Qiddushin* 4.13).[218] The patriarchal traditions we have noted in ancient Israel (see 6.5.3 above) were still strong in Paul's days.

---

[215] Philo, *De Specialibus Legibus*, 3.169-170; cf. 169-178; cf. E. W. Stegemann and W. Stegemann, *The Jesus Movement*, 1999, pp. 364-365.
[216] E. W. Stegemann and W. Stegemann, *The Jesus Movement*, 1999, p. 365.
[217] See N. Vyhmeister, '1 Timothy 2:8-15', 1998, p. 339.
[218] Ibid.

Secondly, the culturally conditioned *public* expectation of women in the Graeco-Roman setting has been described as follows:

> Thus one central aspect of the distinction of gender-specific spheres consists in the fact that women were generally excluded from holding public office as senators, equestrians, decurions, or judges, as well as subordinate positions.[219] They were not even allowed to belong to the most important political decision-making body of the *polis* (except for the magistrates), the popular assembly (*ekklesia*), in which women could neither vote nor speak.[220] Could they, nonetheless, at least be present as observers? We do not have an explicit testimony that Greek women, for example, were forbidden to participate in the popular assembly, but Just infers this prohibition from Aristophanes' comedy *Ekklesiazusae*.[221] Further indirect evidence is found in a dialogue in another of his comedies, *Lysistrata*, which clearly reveals that the wives interrogated their husbands when they came home from the popular assembly.[222]

For example, Paul's command in I Corinthians 14 that married women are to be silent in the *ekklesia* (14.34), and that they are to ask their husbands at home concerning teachings (14.35), is verbally reflected as *proper and decent conduct* in the Graeco-Roman environment (see 9.5.5 below). Paul's and the early Christians' strong concern to adapt their practices to what was considered 'appropriate' in the contemporary culture,[223] in order that the gospel would not be ridiculed but believed, gives a perfectly valid explanation for his

---

[219] This was later fixed in the Roman codes of law – see the Roman *Digests* (50.17.2) in the *Corpus Juris Civilis*, i.e. the body of civil law issued under Justinian I and later influencing the Code of Canon Law in the Roman Catholic Church; cf. W. Schuller, *Frauen in der römischen Geschichte*, 1992.

[220] R. Just, *Women in Athenian Law and Life*, 1991, p. 13.

[221] Ibid., p. 281.

[222] E. W. Stegemann and W. Stegemann, *The Jesus Movement*, 1999, p. 365 (the passage from *Lysistrata* is found on p. 400).

[223] See I Corinthians 7.12-16, 17-24; 9.19-23; 10.23-11.1; 14.24-25; Colossians 4.4-5; I Thessalonians 4.12; I Timothy 3.2, 7.

command in order to establish order in the church. A theological reason for order in the church, however, was the recognition that 'God is a God not of disorder but of peace' (I Corinthians 14.32).

The picture of women's status in the middle of the first century in the Roman Empire should be somewhat nuanced, however. Especially in Corinth, the Roman legislation had given women new rights, creating a certain fluidity in the expectations of women. For example, the system of guardianship (*tutela*) was liberalised, which meant that a woman could take legal action against a guardian who did not authorise her actions. 'This context raises nuances of meaning about the head in the sense of chief, in relation to mutuality and reciprocity.'[224]

The Greek term *hypotasso*, 'submit oneself', be subordinate', which we find in the four passages below, appears in an instruction on married life by Plutarch (c. AD 46-120), a Greek historian who received Roman citizenship. It is evidence that in the setting of both Ephesus and Corinth in the first century, the submission of the wife to her husband was deemed commendable and what it meant was that an honourable wife would avoid behaviour that could be understood as controlling (*krateo*) and governing (*archeo*):

> Rich men and princes by conferring honours on philosophers adorn both themselves and the philosophers; but, on the other hand, philosophers by paying court to the rich do not enhance the repute of the rich but lower their own. So it is with women also; if they subordinate themselves to their husbands, they are commended, but if they want to have control, they cut a sorrier figure than the subjects of their control. And control ought to be exercised by the man over the woman, not as the owner has control over a piece of property, but as the soul controls the body, by entering into her feelings and being knit to her through goodwill. As, therefore, it is possible to exercise care

---

[224] A. C. Thiselton, *The First Epistle to the* Corinthians, 2000, p. 802; note pp. 801-802.

over the body without being a slave to its pleasures and desires, so it is possible to govern a wife, and at the same time to delight and gratify her.[225]

Those who argue today that Paul's adaptations to 'common decency' in his first-century setting should be made a rule for the church's ordination practice are actually arguing that the patriarchy of the pagan Graeco-Roman culture, as described by Plutarch above, is followed by the church. However, we must not be blind to the new view of marriage that Paul teaches as a fruit of the gospel and how it changes patriarchy (see Ephesians 5.22-24).

The passage from Plutarch shows that the public display of a wife's subordination to her husband gave the husband honour and status in society, while any form of disrespect from the wife towards her husband would bring him dishonour and was by common consent considered disgraceful. In his instructions to the churches in Corinth and Ephesus, Paul teaches adaptation to the cultural conventions of the surrounding culture. As was the case with slavery (see 9.5.7 below), this does not mean that the commanded counsel was universally right, but it served at the time to preserve peace and ensure the spreading of the gospel. The adaptation to culture was a sacrifice made for the gospel in the same terms as when Paul said:

> I have made myself a slave to everyone, so that I might win more of them. To the Jews I became as a Jew, in order to win Jews. To those under the law I became as one under the law […] so that I might win those under the law. To those outside the law I became as one outside the law […] so that I might win those outside the law. To the weak I became weak, so that I might win the weak. I have become all things to all people so that I might by any means save some.' (I Corinthians 9.19-22).

---

[225] Plutarch, *Moralia*, 142E; Greek text and English translation in *Plutarch's Moralia*, vol. 2, trans. F. C. Babbin, Loeb Classical Library, London: Heinemann, 1962.

9.5.2 *The Word kephale in Ephesians 5.23 and I Corinthians 11.3*

The question of the lexical sense of the Greek word *kephale*, 'head', and its figurative reference in Ephesians 5.23 and I Corinthians 11.2-16 is a hotly-debated issue upon which there is no consensus.[226] Opponents to women's ordination tend to follow scholars who take *kephale* as referring to someone with 'authority over' another person, while proponents will follow scholars assigning other senses to *kephale*, such as 'source', or 'origin', or 'someone preeminent or a representative that deserves respect and honour'. Thus, being cautious and avoiding prejudice is important here.

Some General Points of Departure

For our study, the following acknowledgments provide reasonable points of departure:

1. The Greek noun *kephale* normally has the literal sense of the physiological 'head' of the human body but is also used in a variety of figurative senses.[227] The sense of *kephale* in Ephesians 5.23 and I Corinthians 11.3 is obviously figurative.

2. If *kephale* is conveniently translated by the English 'head', its sense is not equivalent to the English word. Thus, as a rendering of *kephale*, the English 'head' does not automatically signify one who has 'authority over' another person, which is a common figurative sense in English (cf. 'head' as 'boss', 'chief', 'leader', 'manager' etc.). Thus, 'head' is not a literal translation of the metaphorical meanings of *kephale*. The reference of the metaphor *kephale*, 'head', must be carefully ascertained in each context.

---

[226] For a valuable review of the research in 1954-2009, see A. F. Johnson, 'A Review of the Scholarly Debate on the Meaning of "Head" (*kephale*) in Paul's Writings', 2009.

[227] The standard classical lexicon for ancient Greek, *A Greek-English Lexicon* by Liddell, Scott & Jones, gives twenty-five different figurative meanings for *kephale*. Wayne Grudem found at least forty-nine metaphorical uses including the Septuagint and the New Testament (W. Grudem, 'Does *kephale* (Head) Mean "Source" or "Authority over" in Greek Literature? A Survey of 2,336 Examples', 1985, pp. 38-59).

3. As a metaphor, *kephale* 'can have different senses in different contexts and even different senses in the same context'.[228] Therefore it is a mistake first to establish one sense of *kephale* that would fit all or many of the eighteen instances in Paul's writings[229] and then force that sense onto the unique passages where *kephale* is used in contexts of husband-wife relationships, such as Ephesians 5.21-33 and I Corinthians 11.2-16.[230] Since metaphors are by nature very sensitive to their context,[231] the only safe criterion for determining the reference of *kephale* as metaphor is the context in which it is used.

4. It is well-known in the field of linguistics that 'the meaning of a "dead" metaphor (one having a common range of meanings) can be studied lexically and its meaning possibilities listed. "Live" metaphors on the other hand 'cannot be studied lexically since they are the creation of the author and get their meaning from some unexpected association with something else.'[232] Consequently, 'if Paul is using *kephale* as a *living* metaphor in any place (i.e. a rare or unique use), the precise sense of *kephale* may be ascertained only by the context, not by lexical studies of 'dead' metaphors (having acquired a standard sense).'[233] There are good reasons to assume that Paul uses *kephale*, 'head', in Ephesians 5.23 and I Corinthians 11.3 as a live metaphor.

---

[228] A. F. Johnson, 'A Review of the Scholarly Debate on the Meaning of "Head" (*kephale*) in Paul's Writings', 2009, p. 52; see also G. W. Dawes, *The Body in Question: Metaphor and Meaning in the Interpretation of Ephesians 5:21-33*, 1998, pp. 56-78.

[229] Romans 12.20; I Corinthians 11.3 (three times), 4 (twice), 5 (twice), 7, 10; 12.21; Ephesians 1.22; 4.15; 5.23 (twice); Colossians 1.18; 2.10, 19.

[230] Cf. J. M. Gundry-Volf ('Gender and Creation in 1 Corinthians 11:2-16: A Study in Paul's Theological Method', 1997, p. 159) and A. C. Perriman ('The Head of a Woman: The Meaning of *kephale* in 1 Corinthians 11:3', 1994, p. 613.

[231] See G. W. Dawes, *The Body in Question: Metaphor and Meaning in the Interpretation of Ephesians 5:21-33*, 1998, pp. 76-78.

[232] A. F. Johnson, 'A Review of the Scholarly Debate on the Meaning of "Head" (*kephale*) in Paul's Writings', 2009, p. 48 (referring to G. W. Dawes, *The Body in Question: Metaphor and Meaning in the Interpretation of Ephesians 5:21-33*, 1998, pp. 65-78).

[233] Ibid., p. 52; note especially Johnson's example of how a living metaphor requires a context to be meaningful (ibid., p. 48).

5. The way in which the physiological head of a person was perceived in the socio-cultural setting of Paul's letters may give clues to the kinds of concepts that would naturally fit *kephale* as a metaphor. Firstly, in general, 'the head is the preeminent part of the body, containing the organs of sight, hearing, taste, and smell; it is the locus of thought (albeit the heart also plays a role). From time immemorial it has been valued as the central place where the vital principle is crystallised. It is therefore surrounded by numerous rituals to preserve the requisites of life and seal fundamental human experiences.'[234]

Secondly, the head symbolised the person and played a prominent role in the context of the pivotal values of honour and shame.[235] 'Honour and dishonour are displayed when the head is crowned, anointed, touched, covered, uncovered, made bare by shaving, cut off, struck or slapped'.[236]

Thirdly, Graeco-Roman medical writers and thinkers believed that the body was *dependent* on the head, which was the *controlling* and most *prominent* part of the body, as well as the *source* that provided life, nourishment, and sustenance to the body.[237] Hippocrates of Cos (460-370 BC), Rufus of Ephesus (c. AD 100), and Galen of Pergamum (c. AD 130-200) held that 'the brain played a central role in the functioning of the human body'.[238] They understood the head to be the seat of the intellect and emotions and, we might add, therefore

---

[234] W. A. M. Beuken, '*rosh*' etc., *ThDOT*, vol. 13, p. 258.
[235] B. J. Malina, *The New Testament World*, 2001, pp. 38-39; cf. 27-57.
[236] Ibid., p. 39.
[237] See especially the material gathered by C. E. Arnold ('Jesus Christ: "Head" of the Church (Colossians and Ephesians)', 1994, pp. 346-366) and G. W. Dawes (*The Body in Question: Metaphor and Meaning in the Interpretation of Ephesians 5:21-33*, 1998, pp. 129-133).
[238] See the examples in C. E. Arnold, 'Jesus Christ: "Head" of the Church (Colossians and Ephesians)', 1994, pp. 350-355; G. W. Dawes, *The Body in Question: Metaphor and Meaning in the Interpretation of Ephesians 5:21-33*, 1998, pp. 129-133. Note, however, that these medical writers talk of the 'brain' (*enkephalos*), not the 'head' (*kephale*), and that they are not contemporary with the apostle Paul.

the source of life and governor of the thoughts, feelings, and actions of the body.[239] Hippocrates describes the head both as coordinating and controlling all the parts of the body (through the brain)[240] and as 'the source of supply for the members of the body. [...] From the head, the veins reach to every part of the body and give nourishment and provide what the body needs'.[241] Similar views were expressed by Rufus of Ephesus who taught anatomy and physiology in Asia Minor at the end of the first century AD, i.e. in an area that was famous in antiquity for its 'advanced medical science and excellent medical schools' (e.g. in Ephesus).[242]

That such views of the head might be used figuratively is illustrated by Seneca, who simultaneously with Paul's ministry (c. AD 55-56) writes to Emperor Nero: 'That kindness of your heart will be recounted, will be diffused little by little through the whole body of the empire, and all things will be moulded in your likeness. It is from the head that comes the health [of the body]; it is through it that all the parts are lively and alert or drooping according as their animating spirit has life or withers'.[243]

Within Judaism in the first century, Philo of Alexandria (c. 20 BC-AD 50) also reflects this common physiological understanding of the relationship of the head to the body.[244] He regarded the head of the physical body as 'the source of life to all the individual members' and stresses 'the prominence of the head by describing it as "the first"

---

[239] See the quotation from Galen's *On the Usefulness of the Parts of the Body* in G. W. Dawes, *The Body in Question: Metaphor and Meaning in the Interpretation of Ephesians 5:21-33*, 1998, p. 131.

[240] C. E. Arnold, 'Jesus Christ: "Head" of the Church (Colossians and Ephesians)', 1994, p. 351.

[241] *De Natura Hominis* 19.11; quoted in P. B. Payne, *Man and Woman, One in Christ*, 2009, p. 288.

[242] C. E. Arnold, 'Jesus Christ: "Head" of the Church (Colossians and Ephesians)', 1994, p. 355.

[243] Lucius Annaeus Seneca, *Moral Essays*, trans. by J. W. Basore, Loeb Classical Library, London: Heinemann, 1928, pp. 42-433.

[244] See C. E. Arnold, 'Jesus Christ: "Head" of the Church (Colossians and Ephesians)', 1994, pp. 355-358.

and "best" part'.[245] He also used this understanding in a commentary on Deuteronomy 28.13 to create a metaphorical image in which 'the virtuous one [...] will be the head of the human race and all the others like the limbs of a body which draw their life from the forces in the head and at the top'.[246] Philo's usage of the figurative meaning of *kephale*, 'head', shows that 'he may emphasise the *leadership* and *position of authority* that the head exercises and holds in relationship to the body, or he may stress the function of the head as the *source of provision* for the body, enabling it to function properly. On most occasions *both of these aspects are present in the same passage*.'[247]

In this setting, therefore, it is feasible that the apostle Paul was familiar with the physiological concepts of the 'head-body' and that he (like Seneca and Philo) developed an imagery that would powerfully describe Christ as preeminent, leader, and source of life for the church.[248] The circumstance that Paul's metaphor of the 'head' may not be listed in Greek dictionaries, which is an issue to some,[249] is irrelevant because if Paul introduces a 'live' metaphor, the usage is unique to that context and can only be understood by features in the context.

Three Possible Views of the Figurative Meaning of kephale ('Head')

Drawing on recent summaries and critiques of research,[250] three views commend themselves as possible figurative senses of the metaphor *kephale*, 'head':

---

[245] Ibid., p. 357.
[246] Ibid.
[247] Ibid., p. 358 (emphasis supplied).
[248] This is demonstrated in Ephesians and Colossians by C. E. Arnold (ibid. pp. 358-366).
[249] This is true especially of Wayne Grudem: see A. F. Johnson, 'A Review of the Scholarly Debate on the Meaning of "Head" (*kephale*) in Paul's Writings', 2009, pp. 41-42, 44-45, 49-50.
[250] A. C. Thiselton, *The First Epistle to the Corinthians*, 2000, pp. 812-823; D. E. Garland, *1 Corinthians*, 2003, pp. 514–516; A. F. Johnson, 'A Review of the Scholarly Debate on the Meaning of "Head" (*kephale*) in Paul's Writings', 2009, pp. 51-54.

Firstly, 'head' in the sense of 'authority', 'supremacy', 'leadership'.[251] There are instances in the New Testament where this metaphorical sense may work in view of the context (e.g. Ephesians 1.22; Colossians 1.18; 2.10). But it has many strong critics:

(a) This usage in Greek is predominantly found in the Septuagint, and very rarely so. In 6 out of 171 instances where the Hebrew *rosh*, 'head', may refer to 'leader', the Greek translators of the Old Testament used *kephale*.[252] And one commentator says: '"Head" does not (in the OT) denote sovereignty of one person over another, but over a community.'[253] Others have gone further, concluding that *kephale* 'does not seem to denote a relation of "subordination" or "authority over".'[254] The conclusion is that 'there is simply no basis for the assumption that a Hellenised Jew would instinctively give *kephale* the meaning "one having authority over someone".'[255]

(b) Andrew Perriman's study of the lexical texts cited by Wayne Grudem and Joseph Fitzmyer for 'authority' and 'leadership' reveals that in each case the metaphor *kephale* in these texts does *not* refer to 'ruler' or 'leader'. Rather, in each case the thought is 'representative', 'prominent', or 'illustrious'. Further, no text can be cited where

---

[251] This is the traditional understanding from the medieval period onwards. For a survey, see A. C. Thiselton, *The First Epistle to the Corinthians*, 2000, pp. 812-814, 820; A. F. Johnson, 'A Review of the Scholarly Debate on the Meaning of "Head" (*kephale*) in Paul's Writings', 2009. Advocates of this position are e.g. W. Grudem, 'Does *kephale* ("Head") Mean "Source" or "Authority over" in Greek Literature? A Survey of 2,336 Examples', 1985; id. 'The Meaning of *Kephale* ("Head"): A Response to Recent Studies', 1991; id. 'The Meaning of *Kephale* ("Head"): An Evaluation of New Evidence, Real or Alleged', 2001; J. A. Fitzmyer, 'Another Look at *Kephale* in 1 Corinthians 11.3', *New Testament Studies* 35, 1989, pp. 503-511; id. '*Kephale* in 1 Corinthians 11:3', *Interpretation* 47, 1993, pp. 52-59.
[252] P. B. Payne, *Man and Woman, One in Christ*, 2009, p. 119.
[253] H. Conzelmann, *1 Corinthians: A Commentary*, 1975, p. 183 n. 21 and n. 26.
[254] A. C. Thiselton, *The First Epistle to the Corinthians*, 2000, pp. 815–816.
[255] J. Murphy O'Connor, 'Sex and Logic in 1 Corinthians 11:2-16', 1980, p. 492; quoted by P. B. Payne (*Man and Woman, One in Christ*, 2009, p. 121).

kephale denotes the authority or sovereignty of one man or of men over others.[256]

(c) Similarly, Richard Cervin first offers a serious critique of Grudem's assumptions and method (meaning seems to be determined by lexicons not context!), stating that fourteen ancient Greek lexicons do *not* give 'authority over' as a possible meaning of *kephale*. Only one does and it indicates that 'leader' is a sense documented in the Byzantine period (fifth century AD).[257]

After setting aside the twelve Pauline references as evidence (since these are contested in the debate), Cervin examines in detail all the examples that Grudem gives for *kephale* meaning 'authority over'. He finds only four unambiguous cases where *kephale* could possibly mean 'ruler' or 'leader' (three from the Septuagint) and one case where 'source' would be better (from the *Shepherd of Hermas*). Otherwise in all the other examples that Grudem cites of *kephale* meaning 'authority over', Cervin finds that the meaning of *kephale* is better understood as 'preeminence'. In other words, the bulk of Grudem's examples turn out in Cervin's view to be non-examples.[258]

(d) It has been alleged that the Hebrew term *rosh*, 'head', is used in the Old Testament 180 times for a 'chief' or 'leader'. In 109 of these cases, *rosh* is translated by the Greek term *archon*, 'leader', 'chief', rather than *kephale*. *Kephale* is used only eight times (less than four percent) when *rosh* means 'leader', 'chief'. Thus, the use of *kephale* to translate *rosh* as 'leader' is rare and is not found in well-known

---

[256] A. C. Perriman, 'The Head of a Woman: The Meaning of *Kephale* in 1 Cor. 11:3', 1994, pp. 602-622.
[257] R. S. Cervin, 'Does *Kephale* Mean "Source" or "Authority Over" in Greek Literature? A Rebuttal', 1989, pp. 86-89. Cervin's finding is that, of Grudem's alleged forty-nine examples of *kephale* meaning 'authority over', 'two of his examples do not exist, and the vast majority of the rest are either ambiguous, false, or illegitimate on other grounds' (pp. 88-89).
[258] Ibid., pp. 85-118.

passages, thus limiting the knowledge of this sense to first-century readers/hearers.[259]

Secondly, 'origin' or 'source' in the sense of primary origin (in creation) or source of life.[260] This option would imply that Christ is the 'source' of man's existence as the agent of creation (cf. I Corinthians 8.6, 'through whom all things are') or as the archetypal man (I Corinthians 15.46-49). Man is the source of woman's existence, since woman was made from man (Genesis 2.18-23; cf. I Corinthians 11.12). God is the origin and final goal of all reality and is the source of Christ (I Corinthians 3.23; 8.6; 11.12; 15.28).

The metaphorical sense of 'source' would fit the non-biblical instances that draw on the medical and physiological understanding of the function of the head as 'controlling' and as 'source of life' and 'nourishment' for the body (see above). It would also fit instances in the New Testament where Christ is the Head of the church and where the church is described as nourished and made to grow by Christ (Ephesians 4.15-16; 5.23; Colossians 2.19).

The critique against this option is mainly the 'paucity of lexicographical evidence'[261] and that this connotation does not

---

[259] B. and A. Mickelsen, 'Does Male Dominance Tarnish Our Translations?', *Christianity Today*, 5 October, 1979, pp. 23-26; id., 'The Head of the Epistles', *Christianity Today*, 20 February, 1981, pp. 20-23; id., 'What Does *Kephale* Mean in the New Testament?', in: *Women, Authority and the Bible*, ed. A. Mickelsen, Grand Rapids, MI: Zondervan, 1986, pp. 97-132. The summary above is taken from A. F. Johnson, 'A review of the scholarly debate on the meaning of "head" (*kephale*) in Paul's writings', 2009, pp. 40-41.

[260] Besides the many names mentioned before 2009 in A. F. Johnson, 'A Review of the Scholarly Debate on the Meaning of "Head" (*kephale*) in Paul's Writings', 2009 (Bedale, Scroggs, Layman, B. and A. Mickelsen, Bruce, Fee, Schrage, Liefeld, Kroeger), this view is supported by e.g. J. Murphy-O'Connor, '1 Cor. 11:2-16 Once Again', 1988, pp. 265-274 (referring to his previous articles in 1976 and 1980); G. Bilezikian, *Beyond Sex Roles*, 2006, pp. 119-123; P. B. Payne, *Man and Woman, One in Christ*, 2009, pp. 109-215, 271-290 (Payne lists fifteen key reasons for interpreting *kephale* as 'source' on pp. 118-137.

[261] A. C. Thiselton, *The First Epistle to the Corinthians*, 2000, p. 820.

occur in the Septuagint.[262] Of course, both these objections could be rejected by reference to the fact that Paul may be using *kephale* as a live metaphor, and in various ways (see the points listed above). In his commentary on First Corinthians, A. C. Thiselton's hesitation to accept 'source' is mainly due to his insistence that there needs to be first-century evidence of how Paul's readers would be able to understand a metaphorical sense of *kephale* and that it is wise to stay as close as possible to a metaphorical meaning that interacts with the literal sense of the physiological head (which, he says, 'is far and away the most frequent, "normal" meaning').[263] These issues could be resolved, however, by considering the medical-physiological sense of the head as a 'controlling source of life' (see above).

Thirdly, there is a group of related senses stemming from the anatomical relation of the 'head' to the body as the part that is most 'preeminent', 'foremost', 'first', 'honourable' or 'representative' (using *kephale* as synecdoche, i.e. the part representing the whole).[264] R. S. Cervin proposes this meaning based on a close study of Grudem's and Fitzmyer's examples. His conclusions are:

> By way of concluding this paper, we may ask the following questions: Can *kephale* denote 'source'? The answer is *yes,* in Herodotus 4.91; *perhaps,* in the Orphic Fragment and elsewhere (in Artemidorus Daldianus, *T. Reuben* [no. 17], and in Philo [nos. 21-22]). Is the meaning 'source' common? Hardly! It is quite rare. Does *kephale* denote 'authority over' or 'leader'? No. The only clear and unambiguous examples of such a meaning stem from the Septuagint and The Shepherd of Hermas, and the metaphor may

---

[262] A. C. Perriman, 'The Head of a Woman: The Meaning of *kephale* in 1 Corinthians 11:3', 1994, pp. 612-614.

[263] A. C. Thiselton, *The First Epistle to the Corinthians*, 2000, p. 821.

[264] This is proposed by e.g. R. S. Cervin ('Does *Kephale* Mean "Source" or "Authority Over" in Greek Literature? A Rebuttal', 1989), A. C. Perriman ('The Head of a Woman: The Meaning of *kephale* in 1 Corinthians 11:3', 1994), and A. C. Thiselton (*The First Epistle to the Corinthians,* 2000, pp. 816-818).

very well have been influenced from Hebrew in the Septuagint. The metaphor 'leader' for *head* is alien to the Greek language until the Byzantine or Medieval period. In fact, the metaphor is quite restricted even in Modern Greek; one may speak of the *head* of a procession, the *head* of state, and, of course, Christ is the *head* of the church. But one cannot speak of the *head* of a department, or the *head* of a household in Modern Greek. What then does Paul mean by his use of *head* in his letters? He does not mean 'authority over', as the traditionalists assert, nor does he mean 'source' as the egalitarians assert. I think he is merely employing a head-body metaphor, and that his point is *preeminence*. This is fully in keeping with the normal and 'common' usage of the word.[265]

Thus, Cervin acknowledges that *kephale* may mean 'source' but that it is not a common meaning in Greek. He flatly denies that the word means 'authority over' or 'leader'. Looking for a more common meaning that would have been understood by Paul's readers, he suggests 'preeminence'. A. C. Perriman has done another careful investigation on the basis of which he draws the following conclusions:

> In the case of the texts cited in favour of the traditional view it has been shown either that the idea of 'ruler, chief' is quite out of place when the passage is properly understood, or that the more natural metaphorical sense of 'that which is prominent, foremost, first, representative' is at least as suitable. To be 'head' of a group of people simply means *to occupy the position at the top or front*. While the sort of prominence denoted by 'head' will in many instances also entail authority and leadership, it seems mistaken to include this as part of the common denotation of the term. That is, the metaphorical use of *kephale* cannot be thought to introduce in any *a priori* or necessary manner ideas of authority or sovereignty into the text. In very few, if any, of the passages considered does the argument

---

[265] R. S. Cervin, 'Does *Kephale* Mean "Source" or "Authority Over" in Greek Literature? A Rebuttal', 1989, p. 112.

depend on *kephale* having such a meaning. In none is the word directly linked with ideas of obedience or submission or authority.[266]

Perriman is aware of the possibility of different metaphorical meanings in *kephale* in Paul's writings and distinguishes its use in I Corinthians from the others: 'The problem is not just that the most interesting texts – those in Colossians and Ephesians – are later, but that they appear to draw, in a way that 1 Cor. 11:3 does not, on an established and determinative theological conception of Christ as 'Head'. It would not be surprising, under such special circumstances, if certain connotations had accrued to *kephale* that are not evident elsewhere.'[267]

Perhaps since these alternatives play a role in the contemporary church issue of women's ordination according to the Bible, there has been an underlying assumption that the first presumes patriarchy while the other two do not. However, it has been appropriately pointed out that '*all* these possible translations have patriarchal connotations'.[268]

Suggested Procedure in the Present Study

The following points form part of Alan Johnson's conclusion of his survey of scholarly contributions in the years 1956-2009:[269]

1. The actual *non-contested* evidence outside the Bible for *kephale* meaning 'source' or *kephale* meaning 'authority over' in first century Greek usage is shrinking (but not totally absent). Which option is 'weaker' remains debatable. Either option remains *rare* from a lexical standpoint.

---

[266] Ibid., pp. 616-617.
[267] Ibid., pp. 618-619.
[268] J. M. Gundry-Volf, 'Gender and Creation in 1 Corinthians 11:2-16: A Study in Paul's Theological Method', 1997, p. 159.
[269] A. F. Johnson, 'A Review of the Scholarly Debate on the Meaning of "Head" (*kephale*) in Paul's Writings', 2009, p. 51.

2. Almost all parties now agree that in certain contexts *kephale* may mean either 'authority over' or 'source'. Whether *both* senses are ever or always present is debatable.

3. A discernible trend may be noticed towards accepting the general background of the metaphorical sense of *kephale* as stemming from the anatomical relation of the head to the body as its most 'prominent', 'respected', 'preeminent', or 'illustrious' part.

Based on Johnson's conclusions, we will assign to *kephale* in Ephesians 5.23 (see 9.5.3) and I Corinthians 11.3 (see 9.5.4) the metaphorical meaning that is best fitted in the context. It should be acknowledged from the outset, however, that none of these metaphorical meanings is 'plain'. It is also clear from our previous survey that the uncertainty of the meaning of *kephale* rules out any firm conclusion on women's ordination based on this word.

9.5.3 Ephesians 5.21-33

The content of Ephesians 5.21-33 is not straightforward and presents several issues of interpretation. Thus, what Paul intends to say by his command that a married woman ought to 'be subject to' her husband (5.22-24) and that a husband, being the 'head' of his wife, ought to 'love' his wife (5.23-33) can only partially be understood in its present context. My purpose here is to show what a contextual reading of the passage really tells us about 'headship' and 'submission'.

The Setting

Features in the setting of the church in Ephesus made the relationship between husband and wife a serious issue of church unity that threatened the integrity of the gospel.

As explained in more detail in 9.5.6 below, under the influence of the cult of Artemis in Ephesus, sectarian Jewish and proto-gnostic[270] teachings were widespread concerning the superior role of the

---

[270] For this term, see 9.5.6 below.

woman in marriage and even ascetic abstention from marriage. This was mingled with a new emancipated role for women that emerged in first-century Roman society which threatened pivotal values of honour and shame, raising issues of marital decency and propriety. In particular, Paul was concerned about the 'darkened understanding' of people in the pagan city, 'alienated from the life of God because of their ignorance and hardness of heart', and about their 'licentiousness [as they were] greedy to practise every kind of impurity' (Ephesians 4.17-19; cf. 5.3-14).

The patriarchal conventions of the Graeco-Roman public setting and of the Jewish synagogue constituted another threat to the building up of the church in Christ (see 9.5.1 above). On the one hand, it contradicted the gospel of Christ (Galatians 3.25-28),[271] and on the other hand it was deeply rooted in the minds of all people and defined what was honourable and shameful in marriage, which is the smallest unit not only in society but also in the church fellowship.

The Literary Genre

Ephesians 5.21-33 is part of a series of 'household codes', which is a New Testament genre[272] that provides counsel for proper relationships between various members of domestic households: husbands and wives (5.22-23), parents and children (6.1-4), and masters and slaves (6.5-9). There is no doubt, therefore, that the passage has the husband-wife relationship in view and not men-women relationships in general.[273]

Paul's Purpose in 5.21-33

Paul accomplishes several objectives in Ephesians 5.21-33. Firstly, using the model of the relationship between Christ and the church,

---

[271] P. B. Payne, *Man and Woman, One in Christ*, 2009, pp. 79-104, 105-108, 273-290.

[272] See Colossians 1.8-4.1; I Timothy 2.18-15; 6.1-2; Titus 2.1-10; I Peter 2.18-3.7.

[273] R. M. Davidson, 'Headship, Submission, and Equality in Scripture', 1998, p. 274.

the passage as a whole advocates a Christian view of marriage based on mutual submission, love, and respect – sharply opposing the secular, Graeco-Roman view of marriage.

Secondly, in order to make the Christian witness credible, Paul also needs to preserve order and propriety. He therefore balances his radical, new teaching about marriage by also quoting the conventional social customs that required of an honourable husband to act as *pater familias* or master of the family and of a wife that she honoured her husband, herself, and the marriage by her submission to him (5.22-24). This would have been part of the traditional genre of the 'house code' and expressed a familiar and accepted way of regarding marriage among the readers of the letter.

The result is something like a 'contradiction' in what he says. The patriarchal section in 5.22-24 deviates from the main theme in 5.21-33 without plain explanation. Both 5.21 and 5.25-33 overrule the patriarchal, hierarchic roles of husband and wife and make their behaviour reciprocal and mutual in light of the essence of Christ.

What seems to be a 'contradiction' between 5.22-24 and 5.21-33 as a whole is however perfectly understandable in view of Paul's main purpose and the setting in Ephesus. He brings a radical Christian view of marriage that not only *challenges* long-held views of husband and wife, but he also *opposes* various pagan teachings that the woman was superior in marriage (see 9.5.1 and 'The Setting' above). He wants to teach how the gospel applies to marriage, but not going so far as to endanger order, propriety, and the credibility of the Christian witness. This is the same purpose that he states elsewhere: 'Encourage the young women to love their husbands [...] being submissive to their husbands, so that the word of God may not be discredited' (Titus 2.4-5).

Paul's guarded teaching of the love of Christ as the key in Christian marriage is part of his wider purpose for the Ephesians. In the context of 4.1-5.33, his emphatic intention is that the Christians in Ephesus 'must no longer live as the Gentiles live' (4.17). He tells them that 'you are to put away your former way of life, your old self, corrupt and deluded by its lusts, and to be renewed in the spirit of your minds, and to clothe yourselves with the new self, created according to the likeness of God in true righteousness and holiness' (4.22-24).

This had special significance when applied to Christian marriage, which in Paul's teaching differed significantly from the customary Graeco-Roman model. This becomes obvious when the biblical 'house codes' (especially Ephesians 5.21-33) are compared with secular house codes in the Graeco-Roman culture. As pointed out by Philip Payne,[274] the secular codes 'directly address only the duties of the party in authority (not the subordinate wife, children, or slaves) and serve only the interests of the patriarch'. Paul, however, includes all members of the church and aims at their nurture in order to live lives worthy of the gospel of Christ. 'Secular "house tables" focus on the patriarch controlling his wife, children, and slaves',[275] but Paul says nothing about husbands controlling their wives, parents their children, or masters their slaves. The secular goal was a well-ordered society, but Paul's goal is the 'new humanity' where 'all members of the body of Christ are filled with the Spirit and nurtured in Christ' (Ephesians 4.24; 5.18).[276]

The passage in Ephesians 5.21-33 fits well into Paul's general teaching about marriage. His teaching of the oneness of man and woman in Christ (Galatians 3.28) was coupled with the teaching of equal rights of man and woman in marriage. This is especially clear when he writes to the church in Corinth, which was more influenced by Roman than Greek culture, and Rome had through new laws in

---

[274] P. B. Payne, *Man and Woman: One in Christ*, 2009, p. 271.
[275] T. G. Gombis, 'A Radically New Humanity: The Function of the *Haustafel* in Ephesians', 2005, p. 323.
[276] P. B. Payne, *Man and Woman: One in Christ*, 2009, p. 271.

the first century given women significant authority in private and public life.[277]

For example, in I Corinthians 7.2, 3, 4, 5, 10-11, 12-13, 14, 15, 16, 28, 32/34a, and 33/34b, Paul specifies 'exactly the same conditions, opportunities, rights, and obligations for the woman as for the man regarding twelve distinct issues about marriage', and 'in each of these he addresses men and women as equals'.[278] He states, for example, that not only does the husband have 'authority' over his wife's body, but the wife has 'authority' over her husband's body (7.4). He acknowledges that a husband's interest is to 'please' his wife, while the wife's interest is to 'please' the husband (7.32-34). And he makes it very clear that any marital obligation between husband and wife ends when one of the spouses dies, which frees the surviving spouse to serve the Lord fully (see 7.39-40 in the light of 7.32-35). (Consequently, *a wife's submission to her husband is not a gender issue but a marital issue that concerns faithfulness to the temporary obligations of husband and wife.*)

Above all, as we see in Ephesians 5.21-33, Paul related man and woman to Christ and counselled them to take the attitude of *mutual submission* (5.21). However, being aware of the codes of honour and shame that influenced the public arena, he consistently counselled the members of the church to behave 'decently and properly', according to the social values at the time, in order to avoid behaviour that might bring the gospel into disrepute. In his ethical teaching, Paul was 'intelligently attuned to public social conventions, so as to cause no impediment to the gospel'.[279]

---

[277] This point is made by A. C. Thiselton and is supported by a wealth of historical data (id., *The First Epistle to the Corinthians*, 2000, pp. 5-6, 801-802).
[278] P. B. Payne, *Man and Woman: One in Christ*, 2009, pp. 105-108.
[279] M. Bockmuehl, *Jewish Law in Gentile Churches*, 2000, p. 135.

The Meaning of 'Submit' and 'Head'

This is the only New Testament passage where *kephale*, 'head', and *hypotasso*, 'submit', appear together. As the new life in Christ permeates the marriage relationships in the church, the traditional patriarchal marriage roles *change*. Instructing husbands and wives on how this change is to come about, Paul uses several imageries and analogies. One is the 'head-body' image in 5.22-24, but in 5.21-33 as a whole he distances himself from a simple hierarchical reading as we will see later on.

What sense does the Greek verb *hypotasso*, 'be subject to', 'submit to', bring *into* our passage? This verb occurs in some form thirty-nine times in the New Testament (of these twenty-three are in the Pauline epistles and six in I Peter). Seven occurrences of *hypotasso* – all in the middle voice – occur in the context of husband-wife relationships (I Corinthians 14.34; Ephesians 5.21-22, 24; Colossians 3.18; Titus 2.5; I Peter 3.1, 5). A standard explanation of its meaning in these instances is that it carries the concept 'of submission in the sense of voluntary yielding in love', alternatively 'defer to', 'acquiesce', 'surrender one's rights or will'.[280] However, the lexical sense of *hypotasso* does not automatically tell us what Paul is referring to when he uses this verb in Ephesians 5.21-33. Its referential meaning must be understood in view of how it is used in its context.

Many who oppose women's ordination in the church today argue from Ephesians 5.22-24 that the alleged hierarchical authority of the husband as 'head' of his wife is 'confirmed' by the command for wives to submit themselves to their husbands.[281] But does *hypotasso* always involve an act of submission to an authority? (We will come back to its referential meaning in Ephesians 5.21-33.) Philip Payne has collected a list of instances in the New Testament showing that

---

[280] W. Bauer, *A Greek-English Lexicon of the New Testament and Other Early Christian Literature*, 1979, s.v.; cf. P. B. Payne, *Man and Woman, One in Christ*, 2009, p. 281.

[281] This is alleged even by G. W. Dawes (*The Body in Question: Metaphor and Meaning in the Interpretation of Ephesians 5:21-33*, 1998, p. 134).

the act of *hypotasso* in the middle voice, i.e. '[voluntarily] submitting oneself', does not always take an object that signifies 'an authority',[282] for example:

1. 'For the creation was subjected [*hypotasso*, mid.-pass.] to futility [...] by the will of the one who subjected it' (Romans 8.20).

2. And the spirit of the prophets are subject to [*hypotasso*, mid.-pass.] the prophets' (I Corinthians 14.32).

3. First Corinthians 16.15-16 urges the 'brothers' in Corinth to submit (*hypotasso*, mid.-pass.) to the household of Stephanas, who devoted themselves to the service of their fellow Christians. It stands to reason that there were people in the church with higher authority than any member of the household of Stephanas.

4. The passage in I Peter 2.18-3.2 presents Jesus as an example of submission even to unjust treatment. He submitted himself to his disciples as he washed their feet (John 13.1-17) and by serving (Matthew 20.25-28; Luke 22.25-27). Any Christians, including husbands and wives, who imitate Jesus will submit to each other as equals (as stated in Ephesians 5.21 and implied in Philippians 2.1-11, where the example of Christ's submission is to be imitated in mutual submission).

Thus, the wife's submission in Ephesians 5.22-24 does not automatically mean that the husband's role as 'head' implies having 'authority over'. Christ's submission and his calling to mutual submission (5.21; cf. 8.4 and 9.5.7) stands in tension with a patriarchal hierarchy of husband and wife. We will come back to how Paul deals with this tension.

The Links of Ephesians 5.21-33 with Its Literary Context
Ephesians 5.21-33 is part of a lengthy section that deals with faithful and practical Christian living (4.1-6.20).

---

[282] P. B. Payne, *Man and Woman, One in Christ*, 2009, p. 282.

The passage in 5.21-33 is syntactically linked to 5.18-20. The finite verbs in 'do not get drunk with wine [...] but be filled with the Spirit' (5.18) govern five successive participles in 5.19-21: 'be filled with the Spirit [...] singing [psalms] [...] singing and playing [to the Lord] [...] giving thanks [to God the Father] [...] being subject to one another in reverence for Christ'. Thus, the command of *mutual submission* in the church (5.21) is the fruit of being filled with the Spirit and expresses itself in *common* praise to 'the Lord' and thanksgiving to 'God the Father at all times and for everything in the name of our Lord Jesus Christ' (5.18-20).

This concept of submission has nothing to do with human authorities – it concerns a submission to 'one another', which expresses a reciprocal relationship between equals, as repeatedly stated in 4.23, 25, 32 and elsewhere in Paul's teachings.[283] But it is made possible by the whole congregation's submission to their Lord Jesus Christ, which consists in acts of honouring God by praise and thanksgiving in the name of Jesus Christ who is 'the head of the church' (1.22-23; 4.15-16; 5.23).

However, 5.21 is also syntactically linked to 5.22, because there is no explicit verb in 5.22[284] (a fact that is hidden from readers of English translations), but the participle 'being subject to one another' in 5.21 has both the church and the wives as agents in 5.21-22. This means that *Paul has formally marked the submission of the wives to their husbands as being rooted in the general submission of all members to each other.*

The transitional function of 5.21 has important implications. It concludes 4.1-5.20 and introduces 5.22-33.

---

[283] See P. B. Payne, *Man and Woman, One in Christ*, 2009, pp. 279-283.

[284] The earliest manuscripts lack *hypotasso* in 5.22 and the later manuscripts restore it in various forms; for convincing arguments that the *lacuna* is the original reading, see P. B. Payne, *Man and Woman, One in Christ*, 2009, pp. 278-279.

The wife's submission to her husband in 5.22-24 is expressed in terse language. It is not defined and hardly explained, while the husband's love and provision for his wife is worked out in great detail in 5.25-33.

However, the mutual submission of all church members in 5.18-21 has already determined the nature of the wife's 'voluntary submission or yielding in love' to her husband in 5.22-24. This is the fruit of being 'filled with the Spirit' and goes along with a prior and consistent submission to Jesus Christ, the Head of the church. It follows that the wife's submission to her husband is a *spiritual* act, not a subjection to a hierarchical authority. It also means that the content of the wife's submission to her husband can be reconstructed from certain key statements in 4.1-5.20 (see 4.1-3, 11-16, 22-24; 4.31-5.2).

The voluntary submission in love that the members are to show each other according to 4.1-5.20, and which – by implication – the wife ought to show her husband, is very similar to the husband's love to his wife in 5.25-32. For example, (a) the phrase 'love as Christ loved us and gave himself up for us' is found in both places (5.2, 25); (b) nurturing and making the church/wife grow, as Christ does with the church, is also found in both passages (4.15-16; 5.29-30); and (c) the phrase that 'each member is clothed with the new self, according to the likeness of God in true righteousness and holiness' (4.24) corresponds with the husband's love as he imitates Christ who makes his body, the church, 'holy and without blemish' (5.25-30).

It appears, therefore, that Paul is using the household code for husbands and wives in 5.21-33 as an instruction on how the 'ligaments' and 'parts' of the church body in 4.16 are to be activated to 'promote the body's growth in building itself up in love'. *The purpose of our passage, therefore, is to ensure that husbands and wives in their relationships grow and build each other up in the love of Christ, the Head of the church.*

A Close Reading of Ephesians 5.21-33

The four parts of 5.21-33 may be displayed through this fairly literal translation:

Transitional exhortation to all church members including husbands and wives:

> 21 [...] while submitting [*hypotasso*] to one another in reverence [*phobos*] for Christ.

Exhortation to wives:

> 22 Wives, [submit] to your own husbands, as to the Lord. 23 For the husband is head [*kephale*] of the wife, as also Christ [is] head [*kephale*] of the church he [being] the Saviour of the body. 24 But as the church submits to [*hypotasso*] Christ, so also wives [ought to be] to husbands in everything.

Exhortation to husbands:

> 25 Husbands, love the wives just as also Christ loved the church and gave himself up for her, 26 in order to make her holy [by] cleansing her with a washing in water by word, 27 so as to present the church resplendent to himself, without a spot or wrinkle, or anything of the kind, but so that she is holy and without blemish. 28 In the same way, husbands should love their own wives as they do their own bodies. He who loves his own wife loves himself. 29 For no one ever hated his own body, but he nourishes and cares for it, just as also Christ does for the church, 30 because we are members of his body. 31 'For this reason a man will leave his father and mother and be joined to his wife, and the two will become one flesh.' 32 This is a great mystery; I am speaking about Christ and the church.

Summary of exhortations to husbands and wives:

> 33 But still, each of you should love his own wife as himself, and the wife should respect (*phobeomai*) the husband.

The passage has an admonitory function. The opening exhortation on mutual submission (5.21) is directed to all members including husbands and wives. The concluding one on love/respect (5.33) recapitulates the exhortations already given to husbands and wives.

These framing exhortations form an *inclusio* around 5.22-32. This is formally marked by the repetition of 'fear', 'reverence', 'respect' (*phobos, phobeomai*), but the framing exhortations also summarise the theme of the passage as a whole: *mutual submission and mutual love.*[285]

Wives are addressed in 5.22 and husbands in 5.25, which divides the text into two exhortations that form the core of the passage: 5.22-24 (wives) and 5.25-32 (husbands).

The passage in 5.22-24 contains two patterns of *inclusio*.[286] One concerns the admonition to wives and follows the pattern A (submission to husband) – B (reason) – A¹ (submission to husband). The repeated exhortation (A) expresses emphasis and is backed up by the reason (B). In a literal translation, this pattern works as follows:

A   wives to your own husbands, as to the Lord
    B   for the husband is head (*kephale*) of the wife, as also Christ [is] head (*kephale*) of the church, he [being] the Saviour of the body, but as the church submits to Christ,
A¹   so also wives to husbands in everything.

The other *inclusio* concerns the relationship between husband and wife and the analogy with the relationship between Christ and the church. It follows the pattern A (husband is head of wife) – B (Christ is Head of church) - B¹ (church submits to Christ) - A¹ (wife submits to husband):

---

[285] Cf. G. W. Dawes, *The Body in Question: Metaphor and Meaning in the Interpretation of Ephesians 5:21-33,* 1998, p. 82.
[286] Ibid., pp. 82-84.

> A wives to your own husbands, as to the Lord for the husband is head [kephale] of the wife
>
> B as also Christ [is] head [*kephale*] of the church, he [being] the Saviour of the body,
>
> B¹ but as the church submits to Christ,
>
> A¹ so also wives to husbands in everything.

Based on this description of the husband as head of the wife, as Christ is Head of the church, the wives are advised to submit themselves to their husbands, as the church submits to Christ.

However, one feature does not fit into these patterns and that is '[Christ] being the Saviour of the body' (5.23).[287] This phrase is in apposition to 'Christ [is] head of the church' and explains Christ's headship.[288] Taken as part of the analogy, it also explains the core element of the husband's headship. Moreover, 'Christ (as head) being the Saviour of the body' is the model for the husband's love in 5.25-32, which first describes *how* the husband is to love his wife, as Christ loves the church (5.25-28), and then *why* the husband is to love his wife, as Christ loves the church (5.29-32).

Notably, the 'head' metaphor is completely abandoned in 5.25-33. It is eclipsed by the theme of the husband's love for his wife, which expands the theme of 'Christ as the Saviour of the body' in response to the calling to all Christians to imitate Christ's love in the preceding context:

> *Ephesians 5.1-2* Therefore be imitators of God, as beloved children, and live in love, as Christ loved us and gave himself up for us […]

This general command directed to all members of the church is specifically directed to the husbands in 5.25-32, where the husband's love, provision and care for his wife is defined in the same terms:

---

[287] S. F. Miletic, *'One Flesh': Eph 5.22-24, 5.31. Marriage and the New Creation*, 1988, p. 44; cf. G. W. Dawes, *The Body in Question: Metaphor and Meaning in the Interpretation of Ephesians 5:21-33*, 1998, pp. 84-89.

[288] See P. B. Payne, *Man and Woman, One in Christ*, 2009, pp. 283-288.

> *Ephesians 5.25* Husbands, love the wives just as also Christ loved the church and gave himself up for her […]

Thus, in the following way, the text is structured as a chain of arguments in support of mutual submission and mutual love:

1. The command to wives to submit themselves to their husbands (5.22, 24) is defined by the general command of mutual submission in the church (5.21) but motivated by 'the husband is the head of the wife' (5.23a).

2. The husband's function as head is defined by 'Christ is the head of the church' (5.23b).

3. 'Christ is head of the church' is defined by 'Christ is the Saviour of the body', which stands out in the formally well-structured passage in 5.22-24.

4. The command to husbands to love their wives is motivated and defined by Christ's love for the church, which is defined by 'he gave himself up for her' (5.25).

5. The husband's love for the wife, which is first motivated and defined by Christ's love for the church, is then defined in 5.25-28 with regard to *how* a husband is to love his wife, namely by imitating Christ's love and 'giving himself up for her' ('making holy', 'making clean', 'present to oneself without a blemish' may not serve literally as a model for the husband's love but describes the specific work of Christ for the church).[289]

6. The command to husbands to love their wives in 5.28a resumes 5.25a, but with a different motivation and definition. The *manner* in which a husband's love is to be expressed alludes to the commandment to 'love your neighbour as yourself' (cf. Romans

---

[289] See M. Barth, *Ephesians*, 1974, p. 623; M. Gielen, *Tradition und Theologie neutestamentlicher Haustafelethik*, 1990, pp. 228, 265-266, 274-275, 278; G. W. Dawes, *The Body in Question: Metaphor and Meaning in the Interpretation of Ephesians 5:21-33*, 1998, pp. 93-96.

13.8-10), which introduces the literal concept of the husband's *soma*, 'body': 'husbands should love their wives as they do their own bodies'. This is repeated in 5.28b with a slight variation: 'as they do their own bodies' is replaced by 'himself' in 'he who loves his wife loves himself'. In other words, Paul is here *replacing* the head-body metaphor that 'separates' husband and wife (5.23) with the unifying image of husband and wife as being the same or one. The hint at the two being one body or one flesh is picked up in 5.29-31.

7. In 5.29-31, Paul explains *why* husbands are to love their wives. Drawing on 'he who loves his wife loves himself' (5.28b), he says that, since a wife is the husband's 'own flesh (*sarx*)', 'he nourishes and tenderly cares for it'. In so doing, he imitates what Christ does for the church, because 'we are members of his body'.

The reasons why a husband ought to love his wife are then stated as two: (a) they are one flesh (confirmed in 5.31 by a citation of Genesis 2.24), and (b) they are members of the body of Christ (i.e. since Christ loves each member of his body, they are to love each other as Christ loves them). Paul is here turning husband and wife into a reflection of the mutual love in the church that Christ has commanded (4.1-3, 15-16; 25-5.2). In 5.30, the words 'we are members of his body' (*mele esmen tou somatos autou*) echo 'we are members of one another' (*esmen allelon mele*) in 4.25, a phrase serving to motivate an ethical command in the church by referring to the unity of the body under one Head, Jesus Christ.

8. The brief comment in 5.32 returns the argument to the level of Christ and the church by applying the words of Genesis 2.24 also to that union.[290] The mystery concerning Christ and the church, then, refers to the closing words of 5.31, 'and the two will become one flesh', i.e. the fact that Christ and the church have become 'one flesh' or 'one body' of which the head is a prominent part.[291]

---

[290] G. W. Dawes, *The Body in Question: Metaphor and Meaning in the Interpretation of Ephesians 5:21-33*, 1998, p. 106; cf. pp. 178-191.
[291] Ibid., p. 183.

9. All of this is then wrapped in the framing exhortations concerning mutual submission and mutual love in 5.21 and 5.33. We will return to their interpretation below.

Thus, as we consider the relationship between 5.22-24 and 5.25-32, Paul seems to have started with the core elements of the traditional form of the house code, where the husband is 'head of the wife' and she 'submits herself to him' (5.22-24). This may have been what his intended readers would most easily identify with. This may even be how the Ephesian Christians were accustomed to view the relationship between husband and wife.

However, Paul has integrated with this old condition his new teaching of how husband and wife are to 'grow up in every way into him, who is the head [*kephale*], into Christ, from whom the whole body, joined and knitted together by every ligament with which it is equipped, as each part is working properly, promotes the body's growth in building itself up in love' (4.15-16). In order to expose husbands and wives to this new teaching, Paul has taken the husband's headship and the wife's submission from the genre of the house code (5.22-24) and (a) has expanded it by the analogy with Christ as Head (*kephale*) of the church (drawing on the image introduced in 4.15-16); he has then (b) defined 'Christ as head of the body' by the appositional 'he is the Saviour of the body' (5.23), and finally (c) added the extensive teaching in 5.25-32 of how and why husbands are to love their wives.

The Impact of the Metaphorical Patterns

In keeping with the function of all the New Testament household codes, 'the (overt) intention of Ephesians 5.21-33 is to make *different* instructions to wives and husbands'.[292] Wives are to 'submit themselves to' their husbands (5.22-24) and husbands are to 'love' their wives (5.25-32). However, a close reading reveals that Paul has a deeper intention which can be captured by understanding how he uses the key metaphors.

---

[292] Ibid., p. 201.

The two parts of Paul's argument in 5.22-24 and 5.25-32 correspond to two different uses of the metaphor *soma*, 'body'.[293] Firstly, in 5.22-24 (the instruction to the wives), Paul draws on the distinction of 'head' and 'body', which *separates* the role of the husband from that of his wife. The husband is 'head' of his wife just as Christ is 'Head' of the church. Thus, as the church is subordinate to Christ, so wives must be subordinate to their husbands. That this behaviour is asked *only* of the wives depends on the 'head' and 'body' metaphors. It is because the husband (like Christ) can be described as 'head' that wives (and not husbands) can be told to 'be subordinate'.

Secondly, in 5.25-32 the argument changes. Husbands are admonished to 'love' their wives 'as their own bodies' (5.28a): 'He who loves his wife loves himself, for no one ever hated his own body, but he nourishes and cares for it, just as also Christ does for the church, because we are members of his body' (5.28b-30). This explains what man's headship is all about.

The husband imitates 'Christ as Head of the church', which means that Christ is 'the Saviour of the body'. This phrase is defined in 5.25-27 with reference to the church and in 5.29 with reference to the wife ('nourishing and tenderly caring for her'). Paul now abandons the *distinction* between the head and the body, which he stated in 5.22-24 (*kephale*, 'head', is absent from 5.25-33). Instead he now relies on the *unifying* function of the term *soma*, 'body', which expresses the concept that wife and husband are 'one flesh' (*soma*, 'body' and *sarx*, 'flesh', are synonymous in 5.25-32). Since wife and husband are united in the 'one flesh' marriage (5.31 citing Genesis 2.24), the husband should love his wife.

The unifying of 'head' and 'body' in *soma/sarx*, i.e. the abolition of the distinction between 'head' and 'body', is expressed (a) in *soma*, 'body', taken in a literal sense about the husband's own body (5.28a), (b) in its metaphorical sense both about the wife as the husband's

---
[293] Ibid.

'body' (5.29), and (c) about the church as the 'body' of Christ: 'because we are members of his body' (5.30), and (d) in 'one flesh' (*sarx*), which is synonymous with *soma* here (5.31). Thus, husband and wife are *brought together as one* in 5.25-32, not only within the union of marriage (5.29, 31) but also within the metaphorical 'body of Christ' (5.30).[294] The content of 5.30, in fact, cuts through the scheme of equations – 'husband equals Christ equals authority' and 'wife equals church equals submission' – declaring that a husband stands alongside his wife in their common relation to Christ.[295] *They are one in Christ.*

The 'separation' of husband and wife brought by the ranking of patriarchy, and expressed in the traditional marriage house code (5.22-24), is first diluted by the analogy with Christ and his church, in which Christ is 'the Saviour of his body'. (This reverts to the love of Christ and the unity of Christ and the church, in 2.13-22; 3.14-19; 4.15-16; 5.1-2). Then, in 5.25-32, the husband's role as caring provider for his wife and the 'one flesh' unity of husband and wife completely take over as husband and wife are related to Christ as members of his body. Therefore, the concluding exhortation in 5.33 maintains that the husband ought to love his wife but changes the wording of the wife's obligation: she is not told to be subordinate to her husband but to 'respect' him, which in 5.21, through the same Greek root meaning of *phobos*, is associated with the 'reverence' for Christ that is the reason for mutual submission in the church. In this context, therefore, there is no room for the husband's headship in terms of ranking or authority.

The tension of metaphors in the passage is overcome when the marriage roles in 5.22-24 are subsumed in the unity of the members in the church. The argumentation in 5.25-32 *unifies* husband and wife

---

[294] Ibid., p. 202.
[295] M. Gielen, *Tradition und Theologie neutestamentlicher Haustafelethik*, 1990, p. 566; cf. G. W. Dawes, *The Body in Question: Metaphor and Meaning in the Interpretation of Ephesians 5:21-33*, 1998, p. 202.

into one which overrules their *separate* roles in 5.22-24 in the name of Christ, 'because we are members of his body' (5.30). The duty of the husband as head of his wife is to love his wife, as Christ loved the church and gave himself up for her. However, the argumentation in 5.25-32 demands that the command to love is not restricted to the husbands, because the context of 5.21-33 in Ephesians shows that this passage directs the same commands to married couples that are elsewhere directed to all Christians. Thus, the passage applies an ethic where there ought to be 'no longer male and female', for all Christians are one in Christ Jesus (Galatians 3.28).[296]

The unifying of members in the church is indicated already in 5.21, because the exhortation to the whole church to submit to one another overrules the restricted exhortation to the wives in 5.22-24. The common denominator for the use of both *kephale*, 'head', and *soma*, 'body', in Ephesians 5.21-33 is the concept of the 'body', i.e. the human body. When *soma* is used alone, it is associated with the body in its entirety, including the 'head'. But when *soma* is used in distinction from the 'head', it associates with a more narrow sense of 'body' because the 'body' is then opposed to the 'head'. The underlying thought in this argumentation seems to be the belief that 'the whole is prior to the part', which was a well-known principle in the Graeco-Roman culture.[297] Thus, the *unifying* concept of *soma* takes precedence over the *distinction* of roles in the patriarchal marriage. The *soma* metaphor points to the church with Christ as Head and the one-flesh marriage is integrated in it, which abolishes the separation of different roles for husband and wife. Thus, what husband and wife have in common is more important than what distinguishes them.[298]

---

[296] G. W. Dawes, *The Body in Question: Metaphor and Meaning in the Interpretation of Ephesians 5:21-33*, 1998, p. 232.

[297] Dawes calls attention to Aristotle's use of this principle in regard to the relationship between the state and the household and the interesting fact that he uses the human body as a metaphor to express this relationship (ibid., p. 204).

[298] Ibid., pp. 203-204.

The husbands are admonished to love their wives just as Christ loved the church and gave himself up for her (5.25). However, the inclusiveness of the term *soma*, 'body', in 5.25-32 implies that the argument directed to the husbands is *reversible*, for if the husband should love his wife because she is 'his own flesh' (5.28-31), the same may be said of wives.[299] The 'one flesh' union in marriage proves that both partners are bound to love one another as Christ loved the church and gave himself up for her. By the phrase 'Christ is the Saviour of the body' in 5.23, which is in apposition to and defines 'Christ is the head of the church', this *reciprocity* of love (as Christ has loved us) impacts the meaning of 'the husband is head of the wife'. For contextual reasons, therefore, Greek *kephale*, 'head', as applied to the husband, has a metaphorical reference that includes loving care and providing nourishment, rather than ranking or authority.

A similar case is the exhortation on mutual submission in 5.21. This command is the expression of a general Christian ethic, as we see from its syntactical integration with 5.18-5.20 and the thematic unity of 4.1-6.20.[300] It applies to all Christians including Christian couples who are members of the church. Our passage is therefore an example of how a command addressed (in 5.21) to all Christians is applied in the house code in 5.22-24 to only one of the partners in a Christian marriage.[301] Thus, the submission required of the wife in 5.22-24 is the same behaviour that all Christians should have towards one another, and it is therefore not necessary to motivate it by the husband's authority over the wife. If, however, *kephale*, 'head', is taken to mean 'source of life, provider, sustainer', and the wife's submission is a voluntary submission in love, then even 5.22-24 would come under the influence of the one flesh marriage ideal that is described in 5.25-32 and the section as a whole will then deal with mutual submission and mutual love, as indicated by 5.21 and 5.33.

---

[299] Ibid., p. 205.
[300] Ibid., p. 216.
[301] Ibid.

Both commands – to submit oneself (as directed to wives in 5.22-24) and to love (as directed to husbands in 5.25-32) – are expressions of a general Christian ethic. They can be strongly argued on the basis of Jesus Christ alone, as indicated by Ephesians as a whole. However, *both commands require the same behaviour*. Being subject to or giving up one's will in regard to the other is precisely what the husband's love of the wife implies in 5.25-32. And, based on the 'one flesh' unity in marriage, the love that is required from the husband should also be given to him by his wife.[302] *The passage deals with reciprocity and mutuality, not hierarchy or authority.*

The Metaphorical Meaning of kephale, 'head'

We established earlier that the lexical sense of *kephale*, 'head', is '[the physiological] head [of a person]'. This has then given rise to many different metaphorical references in Greek, but three of them have become particularly essential for the husband's 'headship' in marriage: (a) 'head' in the sense of 'authority over'; (b) 'origin' or 'source' in the sense of primary origin (in creation) or source of life; (c) a group of related senses stemming from the anatomical relation of the 'head' to the body as the part that is most 'preeminent', 'foremost', 'first', 'honourable', or 'representative' (the part representing the whole). All these are in theory possible references in Ephesians 5.23 (see 9.5.2 above).

However, judging from the context in Ephesians, the second option undoubtedly makes best sense. The head is the 'provider' and 'sustainer', as 'the source of life' that nourishes and cares for the wife (see 5.29).

This fits not only the common view of the medical-physiological head in Paul's time, which we considered above, but it also resumes the metaphor of Christ as Head of the church in the immediate context (4.15-16; cf. Colossians 2.18-19), where Christ as the *kephale*

---

[302] Ibid., pp. 232-233.

of the church promotes her growth in love through 'every ligament' and through 'every part working properly'.

It fits the analogy of Christ as Head of the church in 5.21-33, for, as 'the Saviour of the body', he has given up his life in order to give life to the church (2.5-6; 4.22-24), which is what *kephale* as 'source of life' is about. The husband's love for his wife is a form of submission that expresses itself in Christ's love for the church, especially when he gave himself up for her (5.25) and when he makes her grow (5.26-27). Since the husband's relationship to his wife is that he loves her as his own body (5.28), as himself (5.28-29, 33), and is one flesh with her according to Genesis 2.24 (5.31), then this passage is not talking of hierarchy or the authority of one over the other, but *it is subverting the patriarchal order by the presence of Christ and deals with husband and wife as one.*

As 'head' of the wife, a husband is encouraged to love, nourish, and cherish her, as Christ 'gave himself' for the church (5.25, 28). This matches the caring and supporting role of the husband according to God's words in Genesis 3.16 (see 6.5.1 above) and fits the initial point in Ephesians 5.21 that husband and wife are to 'be subject to one another out of reverence for Christ'.

There is not a word about the 'head' in the sense of 'authority over' the wife in Ephesians 5.21-33. For that sense to be assigned to 'head', one has to ignore the context and assume that the word *kephale* is intrinsically associated with 'authority', which would, firstly, violate the rules of language, for the lexical sense of a word is not automatically the sense it takes in its context, and, secondly, has not been proven correct in the intense recent research (see 9.5.2 above).

However, the mutual submission commanded in 5.21 and the 'one flesh', mutual love and care in 5.33 is associated with 'reverence' for Christ as Head and the wife's 'respect' for her husband (although even this would be reversible in a 'one flesh' oneness). This would fit the third of the plausible figurative meanings of Christ as the *kephale*,

'Head', of the church and the husband as the *kephale*, 'head', of the wife, namely the 'head' as 'preeminent', 'foremost', 'representative', and therefore 'worthy of honour, reverence and respect'. Although *kephale*, 'head', may have different senses in different contexts and even different senses in the same context,[303] the predominant referential meaning of the metaphor in Ephesians 5.21-33 is undoubtedly 'provider' and 'sustainer', as 'source of life'.

Conclusions

The main conclusions from our study of this passage are as follows:[304]

1. The context of Paul's counsel for husbands and wives in Ephesians 5.21-33 is one of *mutual submission*: 'submitting to one another in reverence for Christ' (5.21).

2. The word *hypotasso*, whether actually present in Ephesians 5.22 or implied in 5.21 (the manuscript evidence is divided), occurs in the middle voice, indicating that the wife's submission is a 'voluntary yielding in love',[305] not forced by the husband, but shared by the husband (5.21). No permission is given in the passage for the husband to demand that his wife submits to his headship.[306]

3. The wife's submission is not a blind yielding of her individuality; she is to submit only 'as to the Lord' (5.22).

4. The nature of the husband as 'head' is paralleled to that of Christ, who 'loved the church and gave himself up for it' (5.25). It is consequently a loving servant leadership, not an authoritarian rule. It consists of the husband loving his wife as his own body, nourishing

---

[303] Cf. the metaphorical meanings in I Corinthians 11.3; Ephesians 1.22; 4.15; 5.23 (twice); Colossians 1.18; 2.10, 14.

[304] Following R. M. Davidson, 'Headship, Submission, and Equality in Scripture', 1998, pp. 274-275.

[305] W. Bauer, *Griechisch-Deutsches Wörterbuch zu den Schriften des Neuen Testaments und der übrigen urchristlichen Literatur*, 1963, col. 1677.

[306] R. M. Davidson, 'Headship, Submission, and Equality in Scripture', 1998, p. 274.

and cherishing her, as Christ does the church (5.28-29) – being the 'head' of his wife may therefore mean to be her 'supporter, provider, source of life and nourishment'. This is the task God assigned to the husband after the Fall according to Genesis 3.16 (see 6.5.1 above).

5. While mutual submission is implied between husband and wife, this does not equal total interchangeability in the marriage relation. The term 'head' is used only of the husband within the marriage relationship, as was the public cultural convention in the Graeco-Roman and Jewish setting in first-century Ephesus. However, Paul re-defines what the man's headship means. It is not a role that gives 'authority' but a servant-role that, like Christ, serves the needy. By the reciprocity built into the passage, this service is also given by the wife to her husband. Mutual service and mutual love is the key concept.

6. The respective roles of husband and wife are not explicitly defined by the social setting or the qualifications of the partners, but from the model of Christ and his church.

7. The ultimate ideal of husband-wife relations is still the partnership of equals that is set forth from the beginning in Genesis 2.24: 'the two shall become one flesh', which is quoted in Ephesians 5.31.

This summary indicates that Paul qualifies and develops the idea of Christian marriage. This remarkable passage is a profound Christian argument against the aberrations in vogue in Ephesus at the time. The word *kephale*, 'head', is given a new content. Paul takes the patriarchal customs of his setting and explains that being the 'head' of one's wife does not involve rule, authority, or hierarchy, but servanthood characterised by sacrificial, self-giving, and saving love. Christ's submission by his self-giving on the cross and his spiritual empowering of the church (men and women) for ministry defines the husband's role as 'head'. 'Not one word is said in this passage about who makes the final decision on important matters. In Ephesians 5.21-33, Paul is seeking in his cultural setting to transform patriarchy – male authoritative leadership – not to endorse it. When first read it would have been the men in that church who felt threatened by the counter-cultural teaching Paul enunciates. In its original historical context, this was a liberating text. It should be read in this way today.'[307]

The important conclusion for the present study is that the statement in Ephesians 5.22-24 that wives ought to be subject to their husbands because the husband is the 'head' of the wife has nothing to do with women's ordination for the gospel ministry. It does not define the male gender as holding authority over the female gender as inferior. This conclusion is supported by the following points:

1. The passage addresses the husband-wife relationship and *not men-women relationships* in general. Some have argued that the church is a family and thus male headship in the family should be followed in the church. But the apostle does not equate *husband headship* in the home with *male headship* in the church. Instead, 'the only Husband/Head of the church is Christ, and all the church – including males – are his "bride", equally submissive to him'.[308]

2. A wife's submission to her husband is *not a gender issue* but a marital issue that concerns faithfulness to the specific obligations of husband and wife and may take different shapes due to the circumstances (see e.g. I Corinthians 7.39 where the authority between husband and wife is shared).

3. The wife's submission to her husband consists of *spiritual* acts – as defined by Ephesians 4.1-5.21 – not of subjection to a hierarchical authority.

4. No reference in Ephesians 5.21-33 *limits* women's ministry in response to God's calling. The roles of husband and wife in marriage are not intended to exclude either of them from serving God in the church and in the world, but to foster a harmonious and mutual

---

[307] These words by Kevin Giles are quoted in A. F. Johnson, 'A Review of the Scholarly Debate on the Meaning of "Head" (*kephale*) in Paul's Writings', 2009, pp. 53-54.
[308] GC-TOSCR, 2014, p. 74.

submission in a loving relationship within the sphere of the home, emulating the love and sacrifice of Christ and the nature of God.

5. A reading of 5.22-24 that completely ignores the context in 5.21-33, and regardless of what metaphorical sense one assigns to *kephale*, 'head', would suggest the presence of elements of patriarchy. These were commonly accepted in the original setting of the text. Paul may have used them to follow the house-code format and to incorporate beliefs that many converts had inherited from the Graeco-Roman or Jewish background. However, the whole point of Paul's teaching in 5.21-33 as a whole is to overrule patriarchy and place before the church the new order of the new creation in Jesus Christ.

9.5.4 I Corinthians 11.2-16

Besides Ephesians 5.23, I Corinthians 11.3 is the only other instance in the New Testament where the Greek noun *kephale*, head', is used in the context of man/husband-woman/wife relationships. Arguments in favour of male headship and female submission have been built on Paul's counsel in I Corinthians 11.2-16.

However, firstly, it is one of the most difficult passages in the Greek New Testament and, despite enormous efforts by scholars, there is little consensus – translations and commentaries give very diverse renderings of the text.[309] Thus, building a case against women's ordination on this passage makes it a weak case.

Secondly, Paul 'is not speaking here about church leadership and authority, nor about ordination', but 'the purpose of this passage is to instruct the Corinthians regarding the wearing or not wearing of head coverings when leading out in church gatherings, and giving his rationale for this instruction'.[310] And, we may add, these instructions are clearly given to both men and women, not just women (see 11.4-5,

---

[309] A. C. Thiselton's monumental commentary (1446 pages) demonstrates this in passage after passage (*The First Epistle to the Corinthians*, 2000).
[310] GC-TOSCR, 2014, p. 74.

7-9, 11-12, 14-15). The point is not subordination between the two genders, but respectability in their distinctiveness and relationship.

So, thirdly, as far as leadership in the church is concerned, the passage gives strong support for both men and women leading out in prayer and prophetic speech (teaching and preaching) in public worship (11.4-5). The following comments will substantiate these points.

The Setting. Paul's first letter to the church in Corinth addresses a series of specific issues, and he responds to them by placing them 'in the light of the cross, of divine grace, of the Lordship of Christ, and of respect for "the other" that builds the community in mutuality and love'.[311] In 11.2-14.40, he addresses proper conduct in Christian worship and in 11.2-16 the topic is the covering of the head during worship, which involves men and women.

The dress code during church services was made an issue by various influences. Firstly, Paul's letter is clearly opposing a divisive party promoting various false teachings. The leaders of this group displayed a struggle for speculative wisdom (I Corinthians 1.17-3.23); they insisted on 'knowledge' (*gnosis*) and the 'power/authority' (*exousia*) it gave them as 'spiritual' people in matters of personal conduct (6.12-20; 8.1-13) and in demonstrations of spiritual insights (10.1-14.40); they advocated asceticism (7.1-40) and denied the resurrection of the body (15.1-58).[312]

They illustrate the influence of Hellenistic philosophy which infiltrated Judaism and Christianity in the first century AD.[313] The essential 'knowledge' in these divisive circles was a knowledge of God consisting in a divine spark that was given by God and linked

---

[311] A. C. Thiselton, *The First Epistle to the Corinthians*, 2000, p. 34.
[312] R. Bultmann, '*ginosko, gnosis* etc.', *ThDNT*, vol. 1, p. 709.
[313] See, for example, O. A. Piper, 'Knowledge', *IDB*, vol. 3, pp. 42-48, particularly pp. 47-48; R. Bultmann, '*ginosko, gnosis* etc.', *ThDNT*, vol. 1, pp. 689-714; F. F. Bruce, *1 & 2 Corinthians*, 1980, pp. 20-23; B. D. Ehrman, *Lost Christianities*, 2005, pp. 116-120.

humans to their original being.³¹⁴ This became influenced by 'the Christian claims about Christ, as the one through whom salvation comes, the one who reveals the truth, the one who comes from God above to us below (see e.g. John 3:12-13; 6:41-42; 8:32)'.³¹⁵ Such ideas of 'knowledge' easily merged with Platonic dualism between spirit (good) and matter (evil). Thus, a follower of these beliefs was 'part of the divine, a person who was spiritual from all eternity', while 'everything connected with the material world (the opposite of the spiritual world) was considered evil'.³¹⁶ This resulted in beliefs that impacted the view of man and woman. For example, there was a tendency to ignore gender distinctions, because male and female belong to the world of 'fallenness', and the female was no different from the male, for 'both of them had the same divine spark'.³¹⁷

Secondly, another influence was the Roman fashion of dress or hair styles. Men and women leading out in prayers and prophetic speech adopted dress-codes and practices that deviated from the traditional customs of the churches and that were in fact considered 'disgraceful' in Roman, Greek and Jewish culture. Some Christian men adopted the cultural habit used by Gentile men who covered their heads as a status symbol, or who had long hair that was tied up as women used to do.³¹⁸ And some Christian women were leaving their hair uncovered, or loose-flowing. This blurred the distinction between the genders and brought dishonour on the gospel, the church, and Christ. Our passage makes good sense when read as an address against this behaviour and a call to use dress codes that express maleness and femaleness as a reminder of the order at creation established by God

---

[314] R. Bultmann, '*ginosko, gnosis* etc.', *ThDNT*, vol. 1, pp. 702-703 (referring to Philo of Alexandria).
[315] B. D. Ehrman, *Lost Christianities*, 2005, p. 120 (referring to Middle Platonism).
[316] W. L. Richards, '1 Corinthians 11 and 14', 1998, pp. 315.
[317] Ibid., p. 316.
[318] See the material gathered by A. C. Thiselton (*The First Epistle to the Corinthians*, 2000, pp. 801-802).

the Creator (11.7-9), while acknowledging that head coverings and hair styles are 'customs' (11.16).

Thirdly, reading 11.2-16 in the context of First Corinthians indicates that the arguments and themes in 8.1-11.1 *continue* in their application to issues in public worship in 11.2-14.40.[319] In 8.1-11.1, Paul offers an exposition of the themes of love and respect for 'the other', i.e. oneness, ordered differentiation, and respect and respectability. As pointed out by Anthony Thiselton, he does so in his teaching about (a) the unity and differentiation of the body, the church (12.12-31a); (b) the distribution of the gifts of the Holy Spirit (12.1-14.40); (c) love for 'the other' as the path to genuine maturity and end-time salvation (13.1-13); (d) the principle of 'building up' the other and ordered differentiation (14.1-40); (e) the everyday practical problems of relating to pagan cultural or cultic backgrounds (8.1-11.1), such as (i) whether or not socially privileged believers ('the strong') can continue with good conscience to accept social invitations to occasions and events held in the precincts of pagan temples (probably 8.4-13); (ii) the case of eating or not eating meat purchased through the city markets but probably coming from temple outlets (10.25-29); (iii) cases when 'strong' and 'weak' (weak or oversensitive) believers are invited to the same pagan household for a meal (10.27-33); and (iv) the handling of the incompatibility between the commitment to Christ pledged in the Lord's Supper and participating in more explicitly cultic sacrificial meals in pagan temples (10.1-10, 14-22), especially if put under pressure by colleagues, patrons, or civic duties (10.11-13).[320]

'In any and every one of these cases Paul rejects the maxim about "knowing my rights" in favour of following his personal example of "forgoing my rights" (9.1-27; 11.1).'[321] Thus, in 11.2-16, 'love

---

[319] A. C. Thiselton, *The First Epistle to the Corinthians*, 2000, pp. 607-612, 799.
[320] Ibid., p. 607.
[321] Ibid.

modifies "freedom" and "rights" if the good of the whole is thereby better served, and especially if the gospel is more effectively promoted (9.19-27)'.[322]

The passage in 11.2-16, therefore, deals with the issue of how believers are to remain faithful to the gospel in a pagan setting with patriarchy, dress codes for men and women, and a culture of honour and shame. The purpose is unity and order in the church and respectability among outsiders so that the gospel will be received.

The Main Topic. The topic of the passage is proper behaviour for men and women in public worship, specifically by the way in which the head or the hair was covered or bound up (I Corinthians 11.4-5).[323]

The background is that both men and women are leaders in worship by prayer and prophetic speech. 'Prophetic speech' may include 'applied theological teaching, encouragement, and exhortation to build the church'[324] (cf. I Corinthians 12.10, 28-29; 14.1-5, 24-39). 'The prophets' were repeatedly second in rank after the apostles in Paul's lists of church functions (I Corinthians 12.28-29; Ephesians 4.11). 'Such leadership is here described in exactly the same terms for male and female with no suggestion of disapproval or of differentiation between the two, either in the type or level of leadership in which they engaged'.[325]

Paul is, consequently, not addressing hierarchic relations between males and females that would impact their ministry in the church, and certainly not female ordination to the gospel ministry.

Cultural Practice. Among Hellenistic Greeks and Romans in the first century, the practices regarding head covering and hair were

---
[322] Ibid.
[323] Whether or not this involved a veil or a hood, or having flowing, loose hair, is debatable: see ibid., pp. 801, 828-833.
[324] Ibid., pp. 826, 956-965, 1016-1018, 1087-1094.
[325] GC-TOSCR, 2014, p. 74.

mixed. It is therefore difficult to pinpoint a specific practice in first-century Corinth against which Paul would react. What we see in I Corinthians 11.2-16, however, is that he deems it 'disgraceful' for a man to pray or prophesy 'with his head covered' or 'with long hair' (*kata kephales echon*, 11.4, 7-9, 14).[326] He also deems it 'disgraceful' for a woman while praying and prophesying not to 'cover her head' or to 'have her hair let down' (11.5-6, 15).

Evidence recently adduced by Philip Payne suggests that only the issue of the loose or fastened hair clarifies the distinction made between men and women. Paul's position of deeming the wrong male/female hair style 'disgraceful' reflects customs *in all three cultures* involved in Corinth: Greek, Roman and Jewish.[327] In public worship, a man should not have long hair, because it made him look like a woman (implying homosexual relations or drawing attention to himself suggesting pride and self-seeking). A woman with long hair – a married woman's long hair 'was a symbol in Roman society of a wife's relationship to her husband'[328] – would have it neatly and modestly tied up. A woman who discarded this practice was perceived as one who renounced modesty and refused to respect 'the other', i.e. her husband, father, other associates, family, church (in the context of patriarchy); in Rome, it would even be thought of as a signal that she was sexually available.[329]

---

[326] Note the debate regarding covering or loose hair recorded in A. C. Thiselton, *The First Epistle to the Corinthians*, 2000, pp. 823-826; P. B. Payne, *Man and Woman, One in Christ*, 2009, pp. 141-173.
[327] P. B. Payne, *Man and Woman, One in Christ*, 2009, pp., 165-169.
[328] Ibid., p. 160.
[329] P. B. Payne (ibid.) quotes D. W. J. Gill ('The Importance of Roman Portraiture for Head-Coverings in 1 Corinthians 11:2-16', 1993, pp. 251, 258), saying that 'Long hair [...] was a symbol in Roman society of a wife's relationship to her husband'. A. C. Thiselton cites Horace (65-8 BC), saying that 'certain male attire or hair-styles were deemed effeminate and overtly sexual, while appropriate head coverings for respectable Roman women served as a protection of their dignity and status as women not to be propositioned' (*The First Epistle to the Corinthians*, 2000, p. 801).

Thus, I Corinthians 11.2-16 concerns the values of honour and shame with specific reference to the distinction between the genders and as signalled in Paul's setting by male and female hair styles. There is nothing in the Greek text that prevents us from understanding it as referring to loose hair,[330] but this is not seen in the many Bible translations that have opted for a veil or a hood that covers the head. The significance of the appropriate 'head covering' as an honourable behaviour is the foundation for the apostle's whole argument in this paragraph.[331]

Paul's Arguments. Paul's arguments are divided into six steps, each of which 'is related to propriety in light of tradition, customs, respects, nature, and common sense'.[332] He does not address the 'head covering' or hair style as such, but rather the attitudes of self-seeking, lack of gender difference, and the dishonour caused to 'the other', which underlies the male and female behaviour. Paul's arguments are:

1. The importance of tradition (I Corinthians 11.2, 16). Paul begins and ends with an appeal to the traditional practice of all the churches. He praises the Corinthians for maintaining the *traditions* he has passed on to them (11.2). The gender distinction expressed by the hair style of those who prayed and prophesied in the public worship meetings is called a *custom* followed by the churches of God (11.16). 'The custom is the acceptance in the Christian churches of an equality of status in accordance with which woman may lead in public prayer or preaching side by side with a recognition that gender differences must not be blurred but appreciated, valued, and expressed in appropriate ways in response to God's unrevoked decree.'[333]

---

[330] Except the new word for 'covering, wrap, cloak, mantle' (*peribolaion*) in 11.15, but this is clearly a metaphor for the function of the woman's hair.
[331] C. Hodge, *An Exposition of the First Epistle to the Corinthians*, 1965, pp. 204-205.
[332] W. L. Richards, '1 Corinthians 11 and 14', 1998, p. 318.
[333] A. C. Thiselton, *The First Epistle to the Corinthians*, 2000, p. 847.

The male hair style of short hair and the female style of long hair that is tied up are acknowledged as a way of honouring the gender distinctions created by God and honouring all those individuals and groups (even the church of Christ) that are affected by disgraceful breaches of these customs. However, the implied principle is 'not seeking one's own advantage, but that of others' (10.24) and of 'doing everything for the glory of God' (11.31), i.e. 'giving no offence to Jews or to Greeks or to the church of God' (10.32). The aim is to seek the advantage of many, 'so that they may be saved' (10.33). All that Paul says in 11.2-16 is subject to this principle.

2. The use of the Greek term kephale, 'head' (I Corinthians 11.3, 7-9). The word *kephale* occurs in this passage nine times, which is unique in the New Testament. In 11.4-5, 7, 10, it is used for the literal, physiological head of a man's or a woman's body, but in 11.3 we have three occurrences of metaphorical meanings that then relate to a word-play on 'head' in 11.7-9.

The case of *kephale* has already been presented in 9.5.2 above and I shall build on that here. The literal sense of the word may be translated 'head' (with reference to the physiological head of the human body). This does not mean that *kephale*, 'head', is equivalent to the English word that is often associated with the metaphor of 'ruler, chief, leader'. As a metaphor, *kephale* can have different senses in different contexts and even different senses in the same context. Therefore, its meaning needs to be determined from its context and not be imported into the passage from other passages. If Paul is using *kephale* as a *living* metaphor in 11.3 (i.e. using it in a rare or unique sense created by him *ad hoc*), the sense of the word may be ascertained only by the context, not by lexical studies of 'dead' metaphors (i.e. metaphors that have been used so often that they have received a standard sense). However, the live metaphor needs to be used in such a way that there is reason to believe that the intended readers could understand it.

Scholars today consider three metaphorical senses of *kephale*, 'head' in 11.3: (a) 'head' in the sense of 'authority', 'supremacy', 'leadership' (see the proponents and the critique against this option in 9.5.2 above); (b) 'origin' or 'source' in the sense of primary origin (in creation) or source of life (see the proponents and the critique against this option in 9.5.2 above); (c) a group of related senses stemming from the anatomical relation of the 'head' to the body as the part that is most 'preeminent', 'foremost', 'first', 'representative', or 'honourable' (using *kephale* as synecdoche, i.e. the part representing the whole). It is my conclusion below that *kephale*, 'head', is used in 11.3 as a metaphor that leaves out the sense 'authority over', but mingles the senses 'origin, source of life' and 'first, worthy of honour and respect'. This is based on the function of 11.3 in 11.2-16 and 8.1-14.40.

Paul's point in I Corinthians 11.2-16 is expressed through a play on words: what believers do with their physical *kephale* impacts also their metaphorical *kephale*. His message is that the issue of the 'head covering (by hood or hair style)' is not merely about men's and women's freedom of choice but the 'honour' their behaviour causes others to give to Christ (and God) who is their 'Head'. A woman's choice regarding her head covering impacts not only her own honour, but also that of her male protector (husband, father, brother, guardian, etc.), of her family, of the church, and of God and the gospel.[334] Since the issue of 'head coverings' relates directly to those who pray, preach, and teach by inspired speech in public services – i.e. those who proclaim the gospel of Jesus Christ – their behaviour must be blameless in order to make the gospel attractive to outsiders (for this aspect being central to Paul, see e.g. 9.19-23; 14.25).

Paul's argumentation opens in 11.3 with a theological foundation for what he wants to say regarding the head coverings or hair styles of the leaders in the public worship services. This takes the form of a sequence of relationships: 'Christ is *kephale* of every man, and

---

[334] GC-TOSCR, 2014, p. 75.

the man/husband is *kephale* of a woman/wife, and God is *kephale* of Christ'. This is difficult to translate because of the ambiguity in the Greek text of *kephale*, *aner* ('man, husband'), and *gyne* ('woman, wife'). Such ambiguities are not unusual in the writings of Paul and are often intentional.[335] He often words his instructions by techniques learnt through his Jewish scribal education (cf. Galatians 1.13-14), and this may be what Peter refers to in II Peter 3.15-16. Among the rabbis, a word with two or more meanings was seen as an asset that provided a richness of meaning and a wider capacity of expressing the divine instruction.[336] Our only way to understand him is by a close reading of the context.

The passage in 11.3 is made of three carefully sequenced and related clauses:

The *kephale* of every *aner* ('man/humans') is Christ.

The *kephale* of the *gyne* ('woman/wife') is the *aner* ('man/husband').

The *kephale* of Christ is God.

Some interpreters have infused the word 'head' in this text in the sense of 'ruler' to obtain the following hierarchical order: God is Head over Christ – Christ is Head over man – man is head over woman. The top-down vertical chain of command then takes this form: God above Christ, Christ above man, and man above woman.[337] However, this interpretation is obtained by manipulating the biblical text. In order to make the text say what Scripture does not teach in this passage, its three clauses are taken out of their original sequence and rearranged. The apostle Paul knows exactly how to structure hierarchies in perfectly

---

[335] See, for example, B. Gerhardsson, *Memory and Manuscript: Oral Tradition and Written Transmission in Rabbinic Judaism and Early Christianity*, 1961, pp. 262-323.

[336] See, for example, D. Daube, *The New Testament and Rabbinic Judaism*, 2011, *passim*.

[337] This interpretation is very awkward for many reasons, but especially because it subordinates Christ under God in a way that challenges the Seventh-day Adventist doctrine of the Trinity.

descending order (see e.g. I Corinthians 12.28), but the context of I Corinthians 11.3 indicates that he is not structuring a hierarchy here. He is discussing the traditional significance of *origination* (i.e. source of life) or *preeminence* (i.e. who came first), because the sequence that links the three clauses is not hierarchy but *chronology*. As a whole, therefore, 11.3 should be understood as follows:

Initially, at creation, Christ was the *first* or *source of life* (*kephale*) of 'all' men/human beings (cf. 'through whom are all things and through whom we exist' in I Corinthians 8.6; 'in him all things were created', Colossians 1.16; cf. 1.15-20). Following that, man/husband was the *first* or *source of life* (*kephale*) of the woman/wife according to the Genesis creation story, for she was taken from him (11.8-9). Following that, God was the *first* or *source of life* of the Son (Messiah, Christ) who was incarnated as a human being and sent to save the human world. This reading of 11.3 means that 'all men (i.e. all men and women)' are to honour their 'Head', Jesus Christ, their origin, source of life, the first or preeminent. Then, women/wives (in a patriarchal social setting) are to honour their husband or any other man who is the 'head' of an unmarried woman (i.e. father, brother, guardian etc.). In the church, bringing honour to Christ and the patriarch in the family is ultimately bringing honour to God, who sent Jesus Christ as Saviour to the world and built the church for his mission.

The middle phrase 'the man is the *kephale* of woman' is framed by references to the role of Christ in creation and what God has achieved through Christ in his incarnation and work of salvation. The point underlined by this pattern is that the relationship of man and woman (including husband and wife) is to be seen 'in the light of two pivotal events, creation and redemption'.[338]

Paul expands on this in 11.7-9 (creation) and 11.11-12 (redemption). At the creation, 'woman was the reflection of man' in

---

[338] P. B. Payne, *Man and Woman, One in Christ*, 2009, p. 139 (quoting Murphy-O'Connor).

the sense that she 'was made from man and for the sake of man' (11.7-9), but 'in the Lord', that is, in the church, the fellowship of the saved, 'woman is not independent of man and man is not independent of woman, for just as woman came from man, so man comes through woman, but all things come from God' (11.11-12).

Thus, both man and woman come from God and are in that sense equals. The element of the oneness of man and woman in Christ's redemption in 11.11-12 is a necessary balance to Paul's exposition of creation in 11.7-9, because in the latter portion of the text he abbreviates the creation of man and woman and selects only the pieces from the creation story that he needs for his argument in 11.4-10. These are the pieces that speak of the *distinction* between the genders, which he can then apply to men, who should not cover their heads nor wear long hair that is tied up like women do, and to women, who should cover their heads and tie up their long hair 'because of the angels', i.e. in order to maintain the distinction between humans and angels in God's order of creation (see below).

When the biblical, chronological sequence of the three clauses is not tampered with, the consistent meaning of *kephale* in this verse is not that of an 'authority over', because this concept is nowhere referred to and plays no role whatsoever in the passage as a whole (apart from the fact that this metaphorical sense is seriously questioned on lexical grounds as applying to *kephale* in Greek – see 9.5.2 above).

Instead, Paul's play on metaphorical meanings involves those of a *servant function as originator and primary provider of life* and the function of being *first and preeminent, being worthy of honour*. This *double entendre* would be consistent with Paul's theology. Firstly, in the very context of 11.3, namely in 11.12, Paul says: woman 'comes from man' (*ek tou andros*) and man 'comes through woman' (*dia tes gynaikos*), using exactly the same terminology as in 8.6 about God and Christ:

> *I Corinthians 8.6* […] yet for us there is one God, the Father, from whom are all things (*ex hou ta panta*) and for whom we exist, and one Lord, Jesus Christ, through whom are all things (*dia hou ta panta*) and through whom we exist.

The underlying concept of 'originator and primary provider of life' runs not only through this passage (applied to God and Christ), but through the passages in 11.12 (applied to woman and man) and 11.3 (applied to Christ-man, man-woman, and God-Christ).

Secondly, Colossians 1.15-20 contains a 'midrash'[339] on Christ as *kephale*, 'Head', where several of the metaphorical senses of the word are applied to Christ:

> *Colossians 1.15-20* He is the image of the invisible God, the firstborn of all creation, 16 for in him all things […] were created […] 17 He himself is before all things, and in him all things hold together. 18 He is the head (*kephale*) of the body, the church; he is the beginning, the firstborn from the dead, so that he might come to have first place in everything. 19 For in him all the fullness of God was pleased to dwell, 20 and through him God was pleased to reconcile to himself all things […] by making peace through the blood of his cross.

Christ functions here as the first and the preeminent in the world – which is one of the metaphorical meanings of *kephale*. His role corresponds to I Corinthians 11.3 in that he is first the originator of all things and then it is through him that God has reconciled all things to himself and made peace. Here, Christ's work in creation and redemption is however framing Christ as Head (*kephale*) of the church, which differs from 11.3 where the focus is on the *distinctions* between man and woman in creation and their duty of honouring

---

[339] I.e. seeking (*darash*) the deeper meaning in a text by filling in gaps left in the biblical text that are only hinted at; see R. Longenecker, *Biblical Exegesis in the Apostolic Period*, 1975, pp. 97-98.

their 'head' (physical and metaphorical). These parallels indicate that we are clearly in the context of Paul's theology with the suggested metaphorical meanings of *kephale* in I Corinthians 11.3. This would therefore have been understood by the readers in Corinth.

Paul operates with dual meanings in 'man-husband' and 'woman-wife' in 11.3. It is clear that the main sense in the first phrase in 11.3 is 'man' and 'woman', because reference is made to creation and 'Christ is *kephale* of all men'. The middle phrase (literally) does have a meaningful ambiguity in 'man/husband is *kephale* of woman/wife', because it refers to the first human couple who were husband and wife, and this has some significance in 11.2-16, for a wife's behaviour relating to long hair and head coverings reflected either honour or shame on the husband (see above). The implied understanding of 'man/husband' as the *kephale* of his wife, i.e. as a servant of God who is the primary provider of life for her, is compatible both with God's words to the woman after the Fall in Genesis 3.16 (see 6.5.1 above), and the foundational text of the Christian marriage in Ephesians 5.21-33 (see 9.5.3 above).

As we focus attention on 11.7-9, certain correspondences emerge with 11.3. Thus, to Christ as the primary originator of man/humans (11.3) corresponds the fact that man is 'the image and glory' (*eikon kai doxa*) of God (11.7) – NRSV's translation 'reflection' for *doxa*, 'glory', is quite misleading here. To the position of man/husband as primary origin of the woman/wife corresponds the fact that she is 'the glory' (*doxa*) of her man/husband (11.7).[340]

There is a 'halakhic' abridgement and fusion here of the two creation accounts in Genesis 1-2,[341] for the story of the creation of

---

[340] H. Schlier, '*kefale*', *ThDNT*, vol. 3, p. 679.
[341] For this common 'halakhic' technique in Paul's scribal education, with examples in the New Testament and particularly I Corinthians, see, for example, B. Gerhardsson, *Memory and Manuscript: Oral Tradition and Written Transmission in Rabbinic Judaism and Early Christianity*, 1961, pp. 175, 312-323.

man and woman (as *humans* vis-à-vis God) states that they were *both* created in the image (and glory) of God (Genesis 1.27; Psalm 8), and the story of the creation of woman out of man (as *genders* and *husband/wife*) states that they were *both* reflecting each other as equals (Genesis 2.21-23). Thus, Paul is not literally quoting or explaining the meaning of the creation of man and woman, but he is using elements of the creation story to give a theological argument for women to cover their head or keep their hair tied up during the church services, as respectable women would do.

This means that, as Paul addresses women's behaviour (11.7-10), he draws on the *kephale* metaphor in 11.3 and explains it by elements from the creation story, proving that a woman should not *dishonour* her male patron (husband, father, brother, guardian, etc.) who is her origin, provider, source of life, first or preeminent, and worthy of honour.

Based on a 'halakhic' exegesis of the Genesis creation texts, he argues that the woman's head covering or long hair that is tied up honours her male counterpart who is the image and glory of God and who therefore does not need to have his head covered either by a hood or long hair (11.7).

However, the woman *completes* and *supplements* the man. She is therefore the 'glory' or 'sign of honour' (*doxa*) of her husband (11.7). This is explained in 11.8-9 by the point that woman was created *from* man and *for the sake of* man, not the opposite, which is 'the very foundation for gender differentiation'.[342] Thus, by his use of 'glory' (NRSV: 'reflection') in relation to 'image' and to the 'mutuality' in 11.11-12, Paul apparently means that 'the existence of the one brings honour and praise to the other'.[343] Gordon Fee develops this thought of his in a way that may be paraphrased as follows: By creating man in his own image God set his own glory in man. Yet man by himself is

---

[342] GC-TOSCR, 2014, p. 76.
[343] G. D. Fee, *The First Epistle to the Corinthians*, 1987, pp. 316-317.

not complete without a companion, one who is like him but different from him, one who is uniquely his own 'glory'. Thus, man 'glories' in her. Paul's point is that in the creation narrative this did not happen the other way around.

Thus, although Genesis 1-3 says more about the husband-wife relationship, Paul has selected some elements in the Genesis text to which he then assigns a deeper meaning. This argumentation technique regarding woman's *origin* then leads to his important conclusion in 11.10: 'For this reason, a woman ought to have a symbol of authority on her head, because of the angels'. We will return below to 'the symbol of authority'.

However, true to the equality of the genders in Genesis 2.21-23, he immediately adds: 'Nevertheless, in the Lord neither (is) woman (anything) apart from man, nor man from woman. For just as woman had her origin from man, so man comes through woman; but the source of everything is God.' (I Corinthians 11.11-12; my translation follows Thiselton's appropriate comments on the NRSV).[344] Paul admits here that, apart from the arguments for women covering their heads or keeping their long hair tied up, *men have their origin in women*. Any reader of this would be led to think that, if the gender that is the origin (*kephale*) of the other is to be, as some say, the 'ruler' over the opposite gender, then women should also be the 'ruler' of men!

Thus, the universal teaching of Paul to all Christians in this passage is that the sequence implied in the concept of 'x coming from y' is the following: God – the Lord (Christ) – man and woman. The passage underlines the equality and unity of man and woman 'in the Lord' and under God. The gender distinctions and behaviour of honour that Paul sifts out from Genesis 1-2 are geared to the specific issue of head coverings and hair styles in the Corinthian setting.

Thus, in 11.11-12, Paul abruptly turns and shows that he can also argue from the creation order now ('man comes through a woman')

---

[344] A. C. Thiselton, *The First Epistle to the Corinthians*, 2000, pp. 841-842.

and that in the new creation ('in the Lord') *woman* is now prior to man and 'all things are from God' including the woman, which is a view that *denies the exclusive privilege of man argued for in 11.7-9*. In a seminal study of 11.2-16, Judith Gundry-Volf says:

> Paul is not claiming here that man needs woman as his subordinate and woman needs man as her 'head', nor even simply that they are essential to each other according to God's design, but that since neither exists without the other, neither has exclusive priority over the other and therefore gender does not determine priority in their relationship 'in the Lord'. In 11:11-12, therefore, Paul undermines gender-based hierarchy in the *body of Christ*. [...] At the same time the difference between man and woman remains.[345]

3. The matter of honour (I Corinthians 11.4-6). Paul states that a woman who prays or prophesies (cf. Acts 2.18; 21.9) in public worship with her head uncovered (with short hair or no hood) *dishonours* her head to the point that it is seen as the same as having her head shaved (11.5). At the time, when a woman appeared in a public service with her head uncovered, she was sending a message that said at least one of three things: (a) she was a person of loose morals and sexual promiscuity; (b) she had been publicly disgraced because of some shameful act; or (c) she was openly flaunting her independence. Whichever of these were in Paul's mind – our information about the conditions in Corinth when Paul wrote his letter points to the last option[346] – the physiological head of the woman would be dishonouring her metaphorical 'head', i.e. Christ and her male protector.

4. 'Because of the angels' (I Corinthians 11.10). This phrase has been the object of intense discussion.[347] The best conclusion is that the angels are holy angels that veil their faces in the presence of God (cf.

---

[345] J. M. Gundry-Volf, 'Gender and Creation in 1 Corinthians 11:2-16: A Study in Paul's Theological Method', 1997, p. 163.

[346] A. C. Thiselton, *The First Epistle to the Corinthians*, 2000, pp. 319-320.

[347] Ibid., p. 320.

Isaiah 6.2). The Dead Sea Scrolls have revealed that the conservative Jewish Qumran community, which was contemporary with Paul's letter to Corinth, believed that holy angels attended their services and that respect for them was so vital that persons with a physical defect could not attend the sacred assembly.[348] This understanding of 11.10 would not exclude the possibility that this is a Jewish custom rooted in the disrespect for the order God had established in creation which distinguished between humans and angels (Genesis 6.1-4). Since gender distinction is a key argument in I Corinthians 11.2-16, the allusion to the sinful obliteration of the distinction between humans and angels may be relevant – even the human Fall came from man's abandonment of the distinction between God and man, which is part of the creation order (see Genesis 3.1-7, 22-24).

The meaning of 'the symbol of authority on her head' in 11.10 offers another exegetical difficulty. Literally, the Greek text states: 'Therefore, a woman ought to have authority on her head, because of the angels'. Clearly, the text does not speak of woman 'under authority'. The real issue is, however, how the woman has 'authority' on her head by the wearing of a head covering or by keeping her hair long. W. L. Richards' answer falls well into place in the specific context in I Corinthians:

> Elsewhere in 1 Corinthians, the Greek word for authority, *exousia*, means the right or freedom to act (see 7:37; 8:9; 9:4-6, 12, 18; see also Rom. 9:21; Rev. 22:14). This is, no doubt, the meaning of the word here. How does this usage affect this verse? The most natural meaning would be that the woman has 'authority', that is, the freedom to act or to worship, simply by following proper decorum and conventional practices. If she brazenly refuses to follow the accepted custom, which in itself shows disrespect for the angels, she forfeits the very authority she is attempting to claim for herself! *Paul's conclusion is that women did have authority to worship by having the proper head covering,*

---

[348] See H. N. Richardson, 'Some Notes on 1Qsa', 1957, p. 120.

and did not have authority by the maverick action of the Corinthian women of casting the custom aside.[349]

Thus, the head covering – whether a hood or bound up hair – is not degrading the woman, but as 'a symbol of authority' it *elevates and honours her*. It gives honour to her male patron or counterpart (in a patriarchal society) and is a sign of the man glorying in her. A woman who exercises the control that exemplifies respectability in Roman society, and retains the signs of her gender differentiation in public, with the head covering or bound hair, 'can go anywhere in security and profound respect'.[350]

5. Equality and mutuality of man and woman (I Corinthians 11.11-12). We have already commented on the meaning of these verses under step 2 above (11.3, 7-9). Paul says here in no uncertain terms that *man and woman are equal and mutually dependent*. The key elements in the statement are 'in the Lord' and 'all things come from God'. Regardless of cultural conventions, man and woman are one in the Lord and this unity comes from God. There is reference here both to the new creation of men and women in Christ (cf. Galatians 3.26-29), and to the ideal which God created in the Garden of Eden.

6. Appeal to common sense (I Corinthians 11.13-15). Paul's final appeal is to maintain appropriate gender distinctions on the basis of one's ordinary understanding of what is natural and in harmony with common sense. 'Judge for yourselves', Paul says, 'Is it proper?' This is a very time-bound part of the passage, for the answer would of course be very different depending on the readers' values in a certain socio-cultural setting.

---

[349] W. L. Richards, '1 Corinthians 11 and 14', 1998, pp. 320-321 (emphasis supplied).
[350] A. C. Thiselton, *The First Epistle to the Corinthians*, 2000, p. 839 (quoting the commentary by Robertson and Plummer ad loc.).

In conclusion, this passage does not teach that women as a gender are inferior to men in serving God as ordained ministers in the church. The following principles can be deduced from this passage:[351]

1. Men and women are equal human beings (11.11-12). Christian submission is mutual.

2. Men and women are distinct genders. The outward display of socio-cultural rules for respectability apply to both men and women.

3. The literal behaviour commanded by Paul, i.e. that women should honour their male protector (husband, father, brother, guardian, etc.) by wearing long hair ('given her for a covering', 11.15) that is covered or bound up, belongs to the local culture in Corinth in the first century and has no relevance for most Christians today. Given these time-bound, cultural norms for decency and propriety, such rules for women served to safeguard the internal unity in the church, and were needed to preserve respect and trust among outsiders for the sake of the gospel. Paul's principle in I Corinthians 11, therefore, is that 'violation of accepted social practices by a woman who wished to defy the distinctions of gender is unacceptable for a Christian'.[352]

4. The female honour expressed by wearing appropriate head covering or hair style during prayer and prophesying reflects a patriarchal heritage in terms of female behaviour and male honour which was common and 'decent' in Paul's time. It had become accepted as part of what was appropriate in the normal context of worship. Paul does not teach it based on Scripture or any special revelation, but based on tradition and common practice.

5. The appropriate covering of the head in I Corinthians 11.2-16 was a sign of the wife's honour, which honoured both her male protector and Christ. There is not a word here about women as a gender being submissive to male authority. The point is not authority but honour, and honour based on patriarchal customs and time-

---

[351] Cf. W. L. Richards, '1 Corinthians 11 and 14', 1998 p. 322.
[352] Ibid., p. 319.

bound social traditions. The underlying principle of order, decency and respect in public worship is universal and should apply everywhere in the churches and at all times, but the way in which this would be expressed may vary according to local social norms.

9.5.5 I Corinthians 14.33-40

Paul's instructions in I Corinthians 14.34-35 that women/wives are to 'be silent in the churches' and 'subordinate' should be understood from its context in I Corinthians and the cultural setting in Paul's days.

Context in I Corinthians

The central passage in 14.33b-35 functions within 14.1-40 as a whole, where Paul deals with the issues of prophetic speech and speaking in tongues at public worship services. This longer section, in turn, concludes 12.1-14.40 regarding 'spiritual gifts' and their use and function in the church (12.1), which is part of Paul's major treatise on order in public church services in 11.2-14.40. The theme of 14.33-40 is 'controlled speech' and 'order'.

Setting

The church in Corinth is divided into factions and the spirit of unity is replaced by 'quarrels' (1.10-11). Paul acknowledges that the believers are 'not lacking in any spiritual gift as you wait for the revealing of our Lord Jesus Christ' (1.4-9), underlining that 'in every way you have been enriched in him, in *speech and knowledge of every kind*' (1.5). But he knows that the abuse of these spiritual gifts is causing serious disorder in the public worship services.

Purpose

Paul's wider aim in 12.1-14.40 is to deal with a misunderstanding regarding a 'spiritual person' (*pneumatikos*). The fact that somebody has a spiritual gift does not raise him/her above others, does not condone internal divisions or rivalry in the church, does not excuse disorder, and does not do away with the need to maintain honour, decency and propriety. All spiritual gifts (12.8-10) are given by the *same* Spirit, the *same* Lord, and the *same* God (12.4-11), and the church is 'one body with many members' (12.12-26). In this church God has 'appointed' various functions in order to build up the church and strengthen its spiritual unity (12.27-30; note the background in 12.12-26).

Paul focuses particularly on *spiritual speech* as a 'manifestation of the Spirit for the common good' (12.7). All the gifts and related activities in 12.8-10 have to do with *speech* – even healing and miracles depended on utterances of spiritual words. The same connection with speech is implied in the list of services (12.28-30) and in the hymn about love (13.1-13); it is also the central aspect of the special focus on prophesying and speaking in tongues (14.1-40). Thus, our passage in 14.33-35 concerns how *public spiritual speech* in the church is to be ordered so that it builds up the church in faith and creates a reverential environment for outsiders which enables them to find God.

The public, spiritual speech in the church has several aspects: (a) prophesying (14.1, 3-5, 6, 22, 24, 29, 31-32, 37); (b) speaking in tongues (14.2, 4-6, 9, 13-14, 18-19, 21-23, 26-27, 39); (c) revelation (14.6, 26, 30); (d) sharing knowledge (14.6); (e) lesson of teaching (14.6, 26); (f) interpretation of tongues (14.13, 26-28); (g) prayer (14.15); (h) hymn of praise (14.15, 26); (i) blessing and thanksgiving (14.16-17). Women and men performed all these tasks and Paul deals with both genders.

Paul's principle is: 'Since you are eager for spiritual gifts, strive to excel in them for building up the church' (14.12). He gives detailed instructions regarding the *order* of those who speak in the church (14:27-33). Men and women may speak in a tongue, others may interpret the tongue; some prophesy, others weigh what is said; some have a revelation which is shared with a person sitting nearby. This scenario may easily get out of hand, but the practical rule is that one person speaks at a time and what is said is to be understandable, so that 'all may learn and be encouraged'. He does not even allow a prophet (man or woman) to use their spiritual gift as an excuse to speak when this disturbs the order, because 'the spirit of the prophets are subject to prophets' (14.32).

Thus, spiritual speech by men and women is needed in the church, but it has to be shared within an orderly procedure. Part of the order is that there are situations where men and women must 'keep silent'.

The Text

References to veneration of God, order and decency frame the passage in 14.33 and 14.40.

> *I Corinthians 14.33-40* For God is a God not of disorder but of peace. (As in all the Churches of the saints, 34 wives (*gynaikes*) should be silent in the churches. For they are not permitted to speak, but should be subordinate (*hypotasso*), as the law also says. 35 If there is anything they desire to know, let them ask their husbands at home. For it is shameful for a wife to speak in church. 36 Or did the word of God originate with you? Or are you the only ones it has reached?) 37 Anyone who claims to be a prophet, or to have spiritual powers, must acknowledge that what I am writing is a command of the Lord. 38 Anyone who does not recognise this is not to be recognised. 39 So, my friends, be eager to prophesy, and do not forbid speaking in tongues; 40 but all things should be done decently and in order.

The translation of 14.33 remains enigmatic. In Greek the phrase 'as in all the churches of the saints' may belong to the preceding or the following. Reading it with the preceding, as in NKJV, the text reads: 'For God is a God not of disorder but of peace, as in all the churches of the saints'. The NRSV translation above is based on reading it with what follows. *The SDA Bible Commentary* says: 'It is impossible to say with finality to which clause the phrase properly belongs'.[353] It

---
[353] *The SDA Bible Commentary*, vol. 6, 1957, p. 793.

could be argued, however, that there is a lack of stylistic elegance if the phrase is connected with the following as in NRSV, in that 'in the churches' is unnecessarily repeated twice: 'As in all the churches of the saints, women/wives should be silent in the churches.'[354] In any case, we leave the phrase aside in the present study, since it does not help us find certainty regarding Paul's instruction concerning women.

Paul has stated in I Corinthians 11.2-16 that women are permitted to speak in the church by praying and prophesying. Thus, the prohibition for them to speak in 14.34 may be based on the particular issue of order in the public services in Corinth where many different speakers would want to prophesy (leading to a weighing of the prophecy) or speak in tongues (leading to interpretations) or share a revelation with someone sitting nearby (possibly leading to a conversation).

The command for women to keep silence 'in the churches' in 14.34 is in fact the third in a sequence of three commands to keep silence (with the same Greek verb being used). Paul's purpose emerges clearly when we consider this sequence:

I Corinthians 14.28 'But if there is no one to interpret, let them *be silent* in church and speak to themselves and to God'. The speakers in tongues are to be silent for the sake of order, so that the church is being built up in the Spirit. Those who are commanded to be silent include males.

I Corinthians 14.30 'If a revelation is made to someone else sitting nearby, let the first person *be silent*'. The persons who are to be silent are the two to three speakers in tongues and their interpreters. Again, the persons commanded to be silent include males.

I Corinthians 14.33-34 'Women/wives (*gynaikes*) should be silent in the churches (*ekklesiai*). For they are not permitted to speak, but should be subordinate, as the law also says'. Like the men in 14.28 and 14.30, the women/wives also need to keep silent for the sake of order and building up the church, but it is noteworthy that the silence commanded

---

[354] See e.g. F. F. Bruce, *1 & 2 Corinthians*, 1980, p. 135.

for women/wives is not directly linked to a particular previous speaker in the church service; it rather has the character of a general command which provides a bottom line for 14.26-40 as a whole.

The commands in 14.33-34 can be understood by seeking answers to three questions: Which Women? What Kind of Silence? What Kind of Interrogation?[355]

1. Which Women? If we choose 'women' as one of two possible senses in the Greek word *gynaikes*, the command cannot prohibit the entire gender of women from speaking in acts of worship (praying, prophesying, and the like), partly because this would contradict Paul's instruction in I Corinthians 11.5, 13, where women lead out in prayer and inspired speech, and partly because women were clearly involved in the variety of spiritual speech being shared in the worship services in Corinth, in prophesying, speaking in tongues, interpreting, bringing a revelation, teaching, praying, blessing, and more – this is the tenor of 12.1-14.40 as a whole (note 'all of you' may speak in tongues and prophesy in 14.5), and no gender distinction is made until 14.34. If, nevertheless, Paul's recommendation also includes an address to women in general, this would be women bringing false teachings and/or disorderly women taking part in the speaking in tongues in a way that did not build up the church and brought the reproach of outsiders.

Taking *gynaikes* in its other sense of 'wives' is explicitly supported by 14.35: 'And if [wives] want to learn something, let them ask their own husbands at home'. This is in line with the point that wives are to 'be subordinate, as the law says' in 14.34. However, it is impossible to say which part of the law Paul is referring to here (Genesis 3.16 is never referred to in the Bible as a command regarding female submission; see my understanding of the text in 6.5.1 above). The issues of order that then open up in 14.26-33 would thus be as follows:

---

[355] A. C. Thiselton, *The First Epistle to the Corinthians*, 2000, p. 1150.

I Corinthians 14.26 'When you come together, each one has a hymn, a teaching lesson, a revelation, a tongue, or an interpretation'. This is inclusive language, and women, including married women, would want to share what the Spirit had given them.

I Corinthians 14.27 'If anyone speaks in a tongue, let there be only two or at most three, and each in turn; and let one interpret'. This could involve married women who would be speaking before or after their husbands, or speaking in tongues while their husbands interpreted, or interpreting what their husbands had spoken in tongues, and all this taking place in the name of the Spirit that activated their speech.

I Corinthians 14.29 'Let two or three prophets speak, and let the others weigh what is said'. This could mean that married women would prophesy (i.e. deliver spiritual speech), while their husbands would keep silent. That situation could in some cases raise the issue of his honour, since in a patriarchal culture the wife would normally not speak as a superior to her husband. It could also mean that after the delivery of a prophetic speech, wives would seek to weigh what was said, and in seeking understanding they might want to ask their husbands. If they were seated in separate sections – which was the common practice – this would certainly disturb the order. If they began talking between themselves, this, too, would disturb the order. Moreover, if the husband delivered a prophetic speech and the wife began sifting and weighing it in public, this would infringe strongly on the values of honour and shame linked to husband and wife. The counsel that wives should ask their husbands at home (14.35) makes sense in this setting as it brings order.

I Corinthians 14.30 'If a revelation is made to someone else sitting nearby, let the first person be silent'. If a married woman delivered the revelation, the same issue of decency would arise as when she prophesied or spoke in tongues. The wife spoke while the husband would have to keep silent. If the husband delivered a revelation and the wife was at the receiving end, 'sitting nearby', she may again have had questions as she was seeking understanding and this would, again, become an issue of order.

Clearly, the understanding of 'women' as 'married women' functions well in the passage as a whole. It is directly referred to in 14.35. Thus, the command to married women to be silent in the churches and the statement that it is disgraceful for a married woman to speak in the church is rooted in the conventional understanding of a woman's honour and shame. A disgraceful act by a woman in church would bring disgrace on her husband, on the church, on God, and on the gospel. This could not be permitted. On this point, E. Earle Ellis says:

> 1 Cor. 14:34-35 represents the application, in a particular cultural context, of an order of the present creation concerning the conduct of a wife vis-à-vis her husband. It reflects a situation in which the husband is participating in the prophetic ministries of a Christian meeting. In this context, the co-participation of his wife, which may involve her publicly 'testing' (*diakrinein*, 14:29) her husband's message, is considered to be a disgraceful disregard of him, of accepted priorities, and of her own wifely role. For these reasons it is prohibited.[356]

The categorical and generalising 'for it is shameful for a (married) woman to speak in church' (14.35) has the appearance of a proverbial or customary saying that was on everybody's lips in society. Its background is to be sought in the fundamental rule in the Graeco-Roman cities that women could not participate in city assemblies dealing with consultations and teaching dialogue. We will come back to this point in a moment.

2. What Kind of Silence? It has been noted that 14.34-35 takes up a large amount of significant vocabulary from the immediately

---

[356] E. Earle Ellis, 'The Silenced Wives of Corinth (1 Cor. 14:34-35)', 1981, p. 218.

preceding verses.[357] The four key terms are: *laleo,* 'speak' (repeatedly from 14.14-32), *sigao,* 'be silent, stop speaking, refrain from speaking' (14.28, 30, 34), *en ekklesia,* 'in the church' (14.28, 35; cf. 34), and *hypotasso,* 'submit oneself to' (14.32, 34). Thus, 14.34-35 addresses a situation that is part of 14.1-33a.

Depending on the context, the verb *sigao* means 'to stop speaking' (as in 14.30), or 'to hold one's tongue', or 'hold one's peace', or 'to refrain from using a particular kind of speech', or 'speech in a presupposed context'.[358] But the question is how this verb fits the passage in 14.29-33, which concerns 'prophetic speech', and 14.29b especially the 'weighing of prophetic speech'. A significant point is that, since 11.5 makes it clear that Paul approves of women using prophetic speech, their silence in 14.34-35 alludes either to 'stopping speaking' or more specifically to 'sitting in judgment over prophetic speech' which may come from their husbands, i.e. 'weighing' or 'sifting prophetic speech', or to a constant intervention of 'questions' (cf. 14.35) under the semblance of 'sifting' what has been said.[359]

The term *hypotasso,* 'subordinate oneself', is used in two ways. In 14.32 it denotes 'self-control', or 'controlled speech', and in 14.34 it is related to 'what the law says'. There is no single statement in the Pentateuch that would fit the concept of a wife subordinating herself by controlled speech. The common reference by interpreters to Genesis 3.16 in this connection is awkward, as demonstrated by F. F. Bruce[360] (see also 6.5.1 above).

The suggestion by Bruce that the phrase 'the law says' involves the creation narratives is developed by Anthony Thiselton who concludes that *the principle of order and differentiation is central in these narratives*: God has revealed his ordered ways through Scripture, and Paul makes

---

[357] See e.g. A. C. Thiselton, *The First Epistle to the Corinthians,* 2000, p. 1152.
[358] Ibid.
[359] Ibid., pp. 1152-1153.
[360] F. F. Bruce, *1 and 2 Corinthians,* 1980, p. 136.

frequent references to them in his writings.[361] Since the verb *hypotasso* is not used in 14.34 with an object indicating to whom the wife is to subordinate herself, it may well indicate her acceptance of the principle of God's order in creation (cf. 14.33, 40 in the context of 15.28). God's order for the wife is that she serves as *'ezer kenegdo* in relation to her husband, i.e. as 'benefactor' or 'helper' who is 'his counterpart' or 'his complement' (Genesis 2.18, 20; cf. 7.2 above). This is her proper place as wife, and this principle of unity is what she is in danger of breaking if she publicly interrupts or challenges her husband in interrogations.

3. What Kind of Interrogation? Another important verb is *laleo*, 'speak'. What does Paul mean by it in the context of the church practice in 14.34-35? Speaking cannot mean that women are not to speak in any way in church, because in 11:5 Paul has no reservation about women praying or using prophetic speech (in seeking adherence to his commands, he may imply that women are prophets in 14.37-38).

In view of the context in 14.26-40, the speaking that Paul refers to in 14.34-35 is best understood as 'failure to stop speaking' (as in 14.30), or more probably 'the disruptive sifting of prophetic speech (as in 14.29), which might involve (1) repetitive interruption with questioning; and (2) the possibility of wives cross-examining their husbands, especially if, as is developed in the *Didache*, issues of contextual lifestyle is part of the sifting'.[362] The women would in this case (a) 'be acting as judges over their husbands in public'; (b) 'risk turning worship into an extended discussion session with perhaps private interests'; (c) 'militate against the ethics of controlled and restrained speech in the context of which the congregation should be silently listening to God rather than eager to address one another';

---

[361] A. C. Thiselton, *The First Epistle to the Corinthians*, 2000, pp. 1154-1155 (referring to a study by A. C. Wire).

[362] Ibid., pp. 1156, 1158 (referring to a study by B. Witherington).

(d) 'disrupt the sense of respect for the orderliness of God's agency in creation and in the world'.[363]

The verbal expression *eperotatosan*, 'let them ask their own husbands' in 14.35 means more than simply 'asking'. Numerous examples can be given for the sense 'interrogate' which includes 'inquiry' and 'demand' with overtones of earnest intensity.[364] The embarrassing and humiliating cross-examination or interrogation of a prophet by a wife or a close relative who is a woman would have brought shame and dishonour to the husband, the marriage, and the church.[365]

Understanding 'speaking' as 'sifting or weighing prophetic speech' takes account of the context in 14.32-33, but it also prepares for what follows in 14.37. The phrase 'if anyone thinks that he or she is a prophet under the influence of the Spirit' means that the silence of wives has to do with how they handle their prophetic gift (14.31-32) with due respect for their marriage partner and the order God has instituted for marriage at creation (14.34-35).

Conclusion

The conclusion from this brief study of 14.33-40 is that Paul deals with a local issue of *order* in worship gatherings in the church of Corinth.

His command concerns *wives*, not women in general, and it reflects what was considered *appropriate* and *decent*, both in view of God's principles of order for marriage and the patriarchal contemporary society.

We noted previously that, in his ethical teaching, Paul was 'intelligently attuned to public social conventions, so as to cause no impediment to the gospel'.[366] Above all, however, his concern was with *order in public church worship services*. If his command also includes

---
[363] Ibid., p. 1158.
[364] Ibid., pp. 1159-1160.
[365] Ibid., p. 1160.
[366] M. Bockmuehl, *Jewish Law in Gentile Churches*, 2000, p. 135.

an address to women in general, this would be women bringing false teachings and/or disorderly women taking part in the speaking in tongues in a way that did not build up the church and brought the reproach of outsiders.

Our study shows that Paul's command cannot be taken literally, but requires a careful reading of the context. The content of 11.5 shows that he is not prohibiting women as a gender from speaking and leading out in the church. His command does not provide a universal rule for all times, but is clearly meant for *a local and culturally bound situation*. This is how the Seventh-day Adventist church has applied the passage in defence of Ellen White's ministry against those who sought to undermine it in view of her female gender.[367]

9.5.6 *I Timothy 2.8-15*

This important passage is best understood in the context of (a) the *purpose* of Paul's first letter to Timothy as a whole, (b) the specific *issues* he addresses in the church in Ephesus, and (c) the religious and cultural *conditions* in that particular city in Asia Minor.[368]

Paul's purpose in the letter is to instruct Timothy on how he is to maintain church unity by dealing with false teachings (see 1.3-7; 3.14-15). He wants Timothy to 'know how people ought to conduct themselves in God's household, which is the church of the living God, the pillar and foundation of the truth' (3.15).[369]

The false teachers in the church in Ephesus 'forbid marriage and enjoin abstinence from foods which God created to be received in thanksgiving' (I Timothy 4.3; cf. 6.3-5). Paul also says that Timothy

---

[367] D. Fortin, 'What Did Early Adventist Pioneers Think about Women in Ministry?', 2010; id., 'Ellen White, Women in Ministry, and Women's Ordination', 2013, pp. 98-101.

[368] I am indebted here to the study by Nancy Vyhmeister, even where this is not explicitly acknowledged: N. Vyhmeister, '1 Timothy 2:8-15', 1998, pp. 335-354; see also C. P. Cossaert, 'Paul, Women, and the Ephesian Church: An Examination of 1 Timothy 2:8-15', 2013.

[369] Cf. N. Vyhmeister, '1 Timothy 2:8-15', 1998, p. 336.

should 'avoid godless chatter and contradictions of what is falsely called knowledge (*gnosis*), for by professing it some have missed the mark as regards the faith' (6.20-21). The women in the church are not exempt from being influenced by these false teachers (4.7; 5.13; II Timothy 3.6-7). The false teaching has been summarised as follows:

> The teaching is godless, has to do with myths and genealogies, involves and promotes speculation, contains elements of asceticism (such as forbidding marriage), and has a negative effect on believers, causing useless discussion and ultimate departure from truth. Women are somehow especially vulnerable to these false teachings.[370]

These issues in the church setting are conditioned by the cultural and religious context in Ephesus, where four dominant influences may be detected: (a) the pagan worship of the mother goddess, in Ephesus called Artemis or Diana; (b) Judaism; (c) proto-Gnosticism;[371] and (d) the ideal of 'the new Roman woman'. Briefly, these influences may be described as follows:

1. The pagan worship of Artemis/Diana.[372] Luke records in Acts 19.23-41 the stir of the people of Ephesus in support of Artemis 'whom all Asia and the world worship'. Artemis of Ephesus was called a virgin, not because she was indeed a virgin, but because she had not submitted to a husband: 'No bonds tied Artemis to any male she would have to acknowledge as master'.[373] The cult of this goddess was connected with various myths, tales and fables. One of them, preserved in a hymn from the early second-century AD devoted to Isis

---

[370] Ibid., p. 338.
[371] Gnosticism flourished from the second century AD but it had roots in previous Hellenistic and Jewish philosophy – see e.g. L. W. Richards, 'How Does a Woman Prophesy and Keep Silence at the Same Time? (1 Corinthians 11 and 14)', 1998, p. 315.
[372] Ibid., pp. 338-339; C. P. Cossaert, 'Paul, Women, and the Ephesian Church', 2013, pp. 7-15.
[373] S. Hodgin Gritz, *Paul, Women Teachers, and the Mother Goddess at Ephesus*, 1991, p. 39; cf. N. Vyhmeister, '1 Timothy 2:8-15', 1998, p. 338.

who was often identified with Artemis, declares that the goddess vests women with power equal to that of men.[374] The whole city of Ephesus thrived on the Artemis cult. Few inhabitants remained unaffected by it. Women were especially attracted to her worship because she was perceived as 'chaste, beautiful, and intelligent', meeting the needs of the female worshippers.[375] The ultimate power in the cult was assumed by a high priestess.[376]

2. Judaism. In first-century Judaism, the religious role of women was mostly limited to the home (see the quotation from Philo in 9.5.1 above). Even the rabbis were divided on the wisdom of teaching daughters the Torah, and there were rules stating that 'a woman may not be a teacher of scribes' (see 9.5.1 above). The Jewish philosopher Philo of Alexandria also introduced Graeco-Roman notions into Judaism concerning Eve, who is associated with wisdom and life. He has female individuals like Sarah, Rebekah, and Zipporah bringing divine enlightenment to their husbands, with Eve directing 'massed light towards Adam's mind to disperse the mist'.[377] The *Apocalypse of Adam*, a pseudepigraphical work that contains proto-gnostic theology and may date from the first century AD, takes up this theme and affirms that Eve taught Adam 'a word of knowledge of the eternal God'.[378] Consequently, in some strands of first-century Judaism, a bridge was formed to proto-Gnosticism under the influence of Graeco-Roman philosophy.

---

[374] See 'Invocation of Isis', papyrus 1380, *Oxyrhynchus Papyri*, London: Egypt Exploration Fund, 1915, pp. 194-195; cf. N. Vyhmeister, '1 Timothy 2:8-15', 1998, p. 339.
[375] S. Hodgin Gritz, ibid., pp. 41-42; cf. N. Vyhmeister, '1 Timothy 2:8-15', 1998, p. 338.
[376] M. Barth, *Ephesians*, 1974, p. 661; S. M. Baugh, 'A Foreign World: Ephesus in the First Century', 1995, pp. 13-63; cf. N. Vyhmeister, '1 Timothy 2:8-15', 1998, p. 338.
[377] Philo, *On the Cherubim*, 9-14, 61; cf. N. Vyhmeister, '1 Timothy 2:8-15', 1998, p. 339.
[378] *Apocalypse of Adam*, 1:3; cf. N. Vyhmeister, '1 Timothy 2:8-15', 1998, p. 339.

3. *Proto-Gnosticism.* These ideas began to circulate as early as in the first century AD – although their peak was in the second to fifth century. Paul admonishes Timothy to 'avoid the godless chatter and contradictions of what is falsely called knowledge (*gnosis*)' (I Timothy 6.2). Assuming that the false teaching in Ephesus anticipates later Gnostic ideas, and bearing in mind the ideas of Philo noted above, two areas of proto-gnostic theology are relevant in Paul's letter to Timothy: Eve's part in the creation of Adam and the denigration of femaleness.[379]

Thus, there is a tendency in Gnostic traditions to exalt Eve, drawing on Genesis 2-3. For example, the Gnostics made Adam address Eve: 'You are the one who has given me life'[380] (cf. Genesis 3.20). Eve is said to have 'sent her breath into Adam, who had no soul'[381] (cf. Genesis 2.7). Eve is the one who teaches Adam 'about all the things which are in the eighth heaven'; she uncovers 'the veil which was upon his mind'[382] (cf. Genesis 3.5-6). Finally, Eve declares herself the 'mother of my father and the sister of my husband [...] to whom I gave birth'.[383]

Within the Gnostic tradition, another extreme idea of women was common. Some writings found in the so-called Nag Hammadi gnostic manuscripts (Egypt, fourth century but containing earlier texts) repeatedly show a negative view of females and their natural and God-given ability to bear children. Thus, the *Gospel of the Egyptians* (early second century) contains a passage where Jesus says: 'I came to destroy the works of the female'. He then points out that death will prevail as long as women bear children, to which Salome responds:

---

[379] N. Vyhmeister, '1 Timothy 2:8-15', 1998, p. 340.
[380] *Hypostasis of the Archons* 2.4.89.14-17; cf. N. Vyhmeister, '1 Timothy 2:8-15', 1998, p. 340.
[381] *On the Origin of the World*, 115; cf. N. Vyhmeister, '1 Timothy 2:8-15', 1998, p. 340.
[382] *On the Origin of the World*, 104; *Apocryphon of John*, 67-71; cf. N. Vyhmeister, '1 Timothy 2:8-15', 1998, p. 340.
[383] *Thunder, Perfect Mind*, 6.2.13.30-32; cf. N. Vyhmeister, '1 Timothy 2:8-15', 1998, p. 340.

'Then I have done well in bearing no children'.[384] According to the *Gospel of Thomas* (c. AD 140), Peter wanted to send Mary away, 'because women are not worthy of life'. Jesus in this Gospel then offered himself to make her into a male, 'because every woman who will make herself male shall enter into the kingdom of heaven'.[385] Being a female is seen as a defect, and salvation comes through masculinity, or even better, by an elimination of all sexuality.[386]

4. *The New Roman Woman*. A radical change took place in Roman society during the time of the Empire: 'legal, political, and social changes gave women an acceptable public persona'.[387] It has been noted that these changes resulted in a generation of women whose lifestyles and opportunities varied considerably from the traditional image of the modest Roman woman. Roman authors witness that this influence had spread around the Mediterranean, and, as the fourth largest city in the Empire, it should be no surprise that it reached Ephesus.[388] It resulted, among other things, in a weakening of the authority and status of the *pater familias* and women assuming an egalitarian status both in the home and in public life.[389]

These religious and social currents interacted and fed upon each other. As the gospel moved from the Jewish environment in Jerusalem and Judea and reached the Graeco-Roman Asia Minor, it was confronted with these challenging values.

---

[384] Clement of Alexandria, *Stromata* (Miscellanies), 3.45; cf. N. Vyhmeister, '1 Timothy 2:8-15', 1998, p. 340.

[385] *Gospel of Thomas*, 114; cf. N. Vyhmeister, '1 Timothy 2:8-15', 1998, p. 340.

[386] *Dialogue of the Saviour*, 90-95; *Gospel of Thomas*, 27; *Zostrianos*, 8.1.131; cf. N. Vyhmeister, '1 Timothy 2:8-15', 1998, p. 340.

[387] C. P. Cossaert, 'Paul, Women, and the Ephesian Church', 2013, p. 15; cf. pp. 15-21; reference is made to B. W. Winter, *Roman Wives, Roman Widows: The Appearance of New Roman Women in the Pauline Communities*, 2003. This change of women's status in Rome has long been known: see, for example, J. Carcopino, *Daily Life in Ancient Rome*, 1991, pp. 89-115 (first French edn 1939).

[388] C. P. Cossaert, 'Paul, Women, and the Ephesian Church', 2013, pp. 15-16.

[389] J. Carcopino, *Daily Life in Ancient Rome*, 1991, pp. 89-92, 104-108.

A very important circumstance for the interpretation of our passage is that many of these false teachings influenced especially the believing *women*.[390] Paul gives prominent attention to women in his discussions against false teachings. He is concerned with women's conduct in worship (2.10-15), with widows (5.5, 6, 10-11, 14), and with women who were going from house to house 'saying what they should not say' (5.13). This connects these women with those persons who were teaching a 'different doctrine' (1.3). The desire among young women not to marry and have children (5.11-16) was linked with false teachers advocating celibacy (4.1-3; 5.9-10).[391] We will see in 2.8-15 how Paul systematically addresses these issues.

Thus, Paul instructs Timothy how to deal with those women in the Ephesian congregation who lived in this mixed environment. Those from the background of the pagan Artemis cult, with its ascetic or sensual practices, held on to attitudes and teachings that were highly inappropriate for Christian women. Their promotion of female headship would ruin Christian marriage, unsettle the church, and call down the scorn of the unbelievers. Those who brought a Jewish-Hellenistic philosophy might teach contradictory rules that either silenced women in the Christian community or disseminated proto-gnostic ideas regarding female supremacy because women were seen to be in command of esoteric knowledge. Finally, the more pronounced proto-gnostic ideas, relating to asceticism and rejections of females, childbearing, and marriage, would need to be counteracted by a balanced view of God's command to man and his blessing at creation according to Genesis 1-2 and the mutual love and submission recommended for the pious Christian marriage.

Our passage is an instruction regarding worship for both men and women in the whole church. The main point is to behave in a

---

[390] P. B. Payne provides a list comparing Paul's descriptions of the false teachers and the women in I Timothy, which shows many striking similarities (*Man and Woman, One in Christ*, 2009, p. 300).
[391] GC-TOSCR, 2014, pp. 76-77.

way that reveres 'God our Saviour, who desires everyone to be saved and to come to the knowledge of the truth' (I Timothy 2.3-4). Paul then reminds Timothy of the gospel, that 'there is one God and one mediator between God and man, the man Jesus Christ, who gave himself as a ransom for all men' (2.5-6). This is a clear call to unity in the Ephesian church that was divided by false teachings.

Before beginning his argumentation in 2.8-15, Paul underlines his own calling as a herald and an apostle for the gospel to all men and underlines that he is 'a teacher of the true faith to the Gentiles' (2.7). This, too, is appropriate for the setting in Ephesus where false teachers are breaking down the unity of the church and clouding the truth of the gospel. This is the setting, then, when Paul opens our passage in 2.8.

I Timothy 2.8

Paul first addresses *the men*, asking them to apply the appropriate posture of prayer, namely the *Jewish* posture of lifting hands. The Christian church in Ephesus may have had a Jewish-Christian source of its worship practices (note Acts 19.1-20:1). The prayer must take place 'without anger or argument', which addresses the tensions caused by false teachers in the Ephesian church. Although the word translated by 'men' (*andres*) in 2.8 may refer both to single and married men, 'Paul's adaptation of the household code and the discussion of women in what follows suggest that he primarily has husbands in mind. This would certainly not have been a surprise since the vast majority of men at the time would have been married.'[392]

I Timothy 2.9-10

Paul turns to the *women/wives* in worship (publicly or at home) and brings advice on their clothing. 'The use of the word "likewise" that introduces the shift from men to women coupled with the issue of adornment suggests that Paul's comments in this section are best

---

[392] C. P. Cossaert, 'Paul, Women, and the Ephesian Church', 2013, p. 21, note 51.

understood in the context of a household code – i.e. societal rules that governed husband/wife, parent/child, and master/slave relationships. Further confirmation of this is seen in how this account parallels the contrast between outward and internal adornment in the household code in I Peter 3.3-5.'[393]

In order to 'proclaim' (*epaggellomai*) reverence for God appropriately (2.10), the women/wives who also pray at worship are to make themselves attractive inwardly, with becoming and honourable conduct, in modesty and good judgement. Outwardly they are to 'adorn' themselves with good works, rather than with extravagant hair styles, elegant clothing, gold, and pearls. As worshippers, then, the women/wives are to conduct themselves and dress in a way that 'is proper for women who proclaim reverence for God'. Propriety and decency in the cultural context of the church in Ephesus is the theme. This advice counteracts the influence from the new Roman woman, which, among other things, generated a more sensual and expensive dress.

I Timothy 2.11

'Let a woman/wife (*gynaika*) learn in silence (*hesychia*) with full submission (*hypotage*).' Paul shifts the attention from 'women' (*gynaikes*) in general to 'a woman' (*gyne*). This formal shift and the transition from outward appearance (2.9-10) to learning (2.11) suggests that Paul is now introducing instructions for a 'wife' – the Greek word *gyne* may refer to both 'woman' and 'wife'. In any case, in 2.11-15a it is clear that Paul is addressing wives. The meaning of 2.11 emerges from the context:

1. Paul has just described how Christian women are to 'appropriately *proclaim* the reverence for God' (2.10). He now points out how a woman/wife is to become such a Christian woman: 'Let her learn!' The Greek term used for 'learn' (*manthano*) means both

---

[393] Ibid. pp. 21-22.

formal instruction and practical learning and is of the same root as 'disciple' (*mathetes*).

2. The woman's/wife's learning is to take place in *hesychia*, 'peace, harmony, quietness'. This is the same word as in 2.2, where the governors and kings allow Christians to lead a 'peaceful life'. The term *hesychia* is a parallel to the men being admonished to pray 'without anger or argument' (2.8). Thus, 'the women are to be allowed to learn without being subjected to the dissensions and wrangling that exist among Ephesian Christians'.[394]

3. The woman/wife is to learn in 'full submission', but the passage does not say to whom they are to submit. This omission makes sense if we bear in mind that Paul sometimes addresses women and sometimes wives. On the one hand, women should submit to God in worship (2.3-5), to the gospel, to the teaching of Jesus, and to the true faith that Paul is teaching (2.5-7). On the other hand, besides submitting to all those things, wives are also to submit to their husbands (cf. Ephesians 5.22; Colossians 3.18). The same shift between a wife (singular) and women (plural) in general is found in 2.15.

4. As Paul urges that women should learn quietly, he is both following and deviating from Jewish tradition. To learn in silence was, according to Simon son of Rabban Gamaliel, the best way, since indulging in too many words brings about sin (*Mishnah Aboth* 17). Thus, Paul's counsel to 'let a woman/wife learn peacefully with full submission' is the way students or disciples learned from a teacher or rabbi in that day.[395] The phrase 'sitting at the feet' refers to the disciple's position before the teacher and is a sign of respect and submission.[396] On the other hand, the rabbis also denied religious instruction to women (*Mishnah Sotah* 3:4; *Qiddushin* 4:13), but Paul, who had himself been taught at the feet of Gamaliel, follows the example of gospel teaching given by his Master when teaching a female disciple

---

[394] N. Vyhmeister, '1 Timothy 2:8-15', 1998, p. 342.
[395] K. Haloviak, 'Is *Headship* Theology Biblical?', 2013, p. 124.
[396] Ibid.

(Luke 10.39-42). Paul's counsel endorses and encourages women to learn – against the prevailing contemporary customs.

5. The statement in 2.10 means, therefore, that instead of being taught by false teachers (some of whom would be women), they are to be taught in church by those who are well-versed in Christian doctrine. They are expected to learn in peace, harmony and silence, being submissive to the teacher and the Christian teachings.[397] This was how teaching was always done.

I Timothy 2.12

This is a very difficult Greek verse that has generated much discussion.[398] A literal translation reveals the complicated syntax: 'But to teach for a woman/wife I do not allow nor to *authentein* a man/husband, but to be at peace'. Three features are vital for the interpretation:

1. Paul spoke in 2.9-11 of women's appropriate behaviour *in worship* and how they are to *learn* the truth in submission. However, he now changes the topic in 2.12-15 and speaks about *women's* inappropriate way of *teaching* their (erroneous) views. Women are forbidden to teach because they have become influenced by the false teachings – many of them have changed their behaviour and promote the false teachings. '*The women in Ephesus were not fit to teach not because they were women, but because they had been or were deceived by the false teachers* – just as Eve had been deceived by the alluring words of the serpent (I Timothy 2.14; II Corinthians 11.3-4).'[399] Consequently, these women were not prepared to teach but first needed to learn the truth (2.11).

2. Nancy Vyhmeister has demonstrated – with scholarly rigour – that the very unusual Greek term *authenteo*, often translated 'to

---

[397] GC-TOSCR, 2014, p. 77.
[398] For a review of different proposals that should be discarded, see N. Vyhmeister, '1 Timothy 2:8-15', 1998, p. 343. For various possible interpretations, see K. Haloviak, 'Is *Headship* Theology Biblical?', p. 124.
[399] GC-TOSCR, 2014, p. 77.

have authority over' does not refer to official teaching authority. Her position has been corroborated by other careful examinations of the usage of this verb, which shows that 'there is no first-century warrant for translating *authenteo* as "to exercise authority"'.[400] Such authority is usually expressed through the verbal form of the common Greek word that Paul uses elsewhere to refer to authority, namely *exousia* (e.g. Romans 9.21; 13.3; II Corinthians 13.10; II Thessalonians 3.9). Instead he uses the very unusual verb *authenteo* – which is found *only here* in the entire New Testament. This verb has an adversative and negative sense such as 'taking independent action against, assuming responsibility over, actively wielding influence against, perpetrating a crime towards, or instigating violence against'.[401] It refers to 'a domineering and controlling form of behaviour.'[402] Thus, *authenteo* refers to an action that is in opposition to the peace and harmony and good judgement that Paul has called for in the passage as a whole. Perriman makes this pertinent observation regarding the meaning of *authenteo*:

> In v.12 Paul is thinking specifically of what Eve did to Adam; and Eve did not *have* authority, but *in her action became* responsible for – became the cause of – Adam's transgression. In the light of these associations the connotation of 'perpetrating a crime' is fully appropriate. In the overlapping of two contexts – that of a scriptural 'type' and that of the current circumstances at Ephesus – *authentein* refers both to what Eve once did and to what women now should not do.[403]

---

[400] L. L. Belleville, 'Teaching and Usurping Authority: 1 Timothy 2:11-15', 2004, p. 216; P. B. Payne, *Man and Woman, One in Christ*, 2009, pp. 361-397; Cf. GC-TOSCR, 2014, p. 77.

[401] Ibid., pp. 344-345. Another, similarly stringent approach that demonstrates a negative connotation in *authentein* is C. P. Cossaert, 'Paul, Women, and the Ephesians Church', 2013, pp. 28-34.

[402] GC-TOSCR, 2014, p. 77.

[403] A. C. Perriman, 'What Eve Did, What Women Shouldn't Do: The Meaning of *Authentein* in 1 Timothy 2:12', 1993, p. 148.

Thus, 2.12 states literally: 'But to teach for a woman/wife (*gyne*) I do not allow and not (*oude*) to offend a man/husband by domineering behaviour, but to be at peace (*hesychia*)'. The two verbs 'teach' and 'offend by domineering behaviour' have the same object, i.e. 'man/husband'. Both these verbal expressions, formally co-ordinated as one, are contrasted with the final clause 'but to be at peace'. This indicates that reference is made to one behaviour where 'teach' is the kind of activity and 'offend by domineering behaviour' is the manner in which they teach. A wealth of evidence indicates that the Greek particle *oude*, 'and not', which connects the two verbs 'to teach' (*didasko*) and 'to offend by domineering behaviour' (*authenteo*), functions as a *hendiadys*, i.e. it expresses one consistent action by two joined words, and this characterises especially Paul's writings.[404] The meaning, therefore, is in keeping with the issue Paul addresses in Ephesus, namely the domineering and controlling attitude women displayed when they were teaching or when they were instructed.

Paul's words in 2.12 cannot mean that he does not allow women (as a gender) to teach, because women did teach in the New Testament church and in other contexts Paul has no objection to that. For example, Priscilla was involved in setting forth the Way of God more accurately to a scribally trained Jew (Acts 18.26); women were teaching through prophetic speech (I Corinthians 11.5; Acts 21.9); Paul's command in Colossians 3.16 to 'let the word of Christ dwell in you richly' and to 'teach (*didasko*) and admonish one another in all wisdom' is clearly directed to women (note the inclusive recipients in 3.12-17 and the address to wives in 3.18); when Paul mentions that his co-workers Euodia and Syntyche have struggled with him 'in the gospel' (Philippians 4.2-3), he clearly implies that they have been teaching the gospel; and Paul openly declares that the older women are to 'teach what is good (*kalodidaskaloi*)' (Titus 2.3-4).

---

[404] See P. B. Payne, *Man and Woman, One in Christ*, 2009, pp. 337-359.

Moreover, the majority of the women addressed here would be married women. If they taught their husbands in an offensive manner that involved domineering behaviour, they brought dishonour on themselves, the church and the gospel in their cultural setting (cf. the comments on I Corinthians 14.33-40 in 9.5.5 above).

3. The term *hesychia* is usually understood as 'silence', which is not the primary sense of the word but may stem from the unwarranted assumption that this passage is to be read in the light of I Corinthians 14.33-35. However, applying a more appropriate *contextual* approach, it is easy to see that *hesychia* appears also in I Timothy 2.2 and 2.11, where its root meaning is 'quietness, peace' and where it is connected with 'godliness and holiness' and 'learning in submissiveness'.[405] This is its primary meaning which is used in the context. Concerning *hesychia*, 'quietness, peace', therefore, Vyhmeister is correct when she points out that 'there is no reason to choose a secondary meaning, not attested in the New Testament, when the primary meaning is logical'.[406] And it may be added, when the primary meaning is attested twice in the immediate context!

In view of these observations, what Paul says in 2.12 presupposes that there are women in Ephesus who teach and offend men by domineering behaviour – either as false teachers, being influenced by concepts associated with the pagan Artemis cult or proto-gnostic ideas, or as wives who inappropriately teach and influence their husbands. In his instruction, Paul seeks to put an end to this, because he wants these women to learn in modesty and submission the teaching of the gospel, in order to receive the truth (see 2.4, 7). These women should not emulate Eve – who in the Ephesian environment at the time might well have been used as a model of female superiority and particularly one who had been 'teaching' Adam with disastrous

---

[405] Cf. W. Bauer, *Griechisch-Deutsches Wörterbuch zu den Schriften des Neuen Testaments und der übrigen urchristlichen Literatur*, 1963, col. 690.

[406] N. Vyhmeister, '1 Timothy 2:8-15', 1998, p. 346.

consequences for humanity (cf. the false teachings noted previously in this section).

Thus, in I Timothy 2.12 Paul prohibits various forms of female teaching behaviour in Ephesus, and then he proceeds to explain the reason for this prohibition in 2.13. However, he says nothing at all about women in general being forbidden to teach. Just the very idea of the Bible saying this would be profoundly offensive to Seventh-day Adventists in view of the ministry of Ellen White.

I Timothy 2.13-14

Paul uses Adam and Eve in the creation story to substantiate his point that 'a woman/wife should *not teach and offend* a man/husband *by their domineering behaviour,* but to be at peace'. The passage is understood by some as if Paul were giving reasons for forbidding women to teach. Such an interpretation would agree with the Jewish tradition given in Sirach 25:24: 'Woman is the origin of sin, and it is through her that we all die'. The Jewish thinker Philo of Alexandria expressed similar sentiments.[407] However, such an interpretation disagrees with what Paul says elsewhere, and there is no reason for believing that he was inconsistent on this point. For example, in Romans 5.12-14, Adam is the one who sins and brings death to the human race.

A much better understanding of 2.13-14, therefore, is to read it as an example of what happens when *false teaching* is given (as was the case with the teaching of the serpent) and accepted (as it was by Eve). The Greek conjunction *gar,* 'for', which introduces 2.13, is often used to introduce an *example* of what has just been said.[408] Such a reading gives us a close parallel to II Corinthians 11.3:

---

[407] Ibid.
[408] A. T. Robertson, *A Grammar of the New Testament Greek in Light of Historical Research,* 1934, pp. 1189-1191.

> *II Corinthians 11.3* But I am afraid that as the serpent deceived Eve by its cunning, your thoughts will be led astray from a sincere and pure devotion to Christ.

This understanding makes 2.13-14 particularly fitting in the environment of false female teachers in Ephesus. Considering the specific issues with women in Ephesus noted earlier, Philip Payne concludes his interpretation, saying:

> Paul points to the example of Eve's deception which led to the fall as a warning to the church in Ephesus lest deception of women, there, too, lead to their fall.[409]

Paul, then, repeats in I Timothy 2.13-14 what the Bible clearly states, namely that Adam was created first (Genesis 2.7, 18, 21) and Eve was deceived by the serpent (Genesis 3.13).

In his arguments against the proto-gnostic women in Corinth (see I Corinthians 11.8; II Corinthians 11.8), Paul noted that woman was made from man. Similarly, if there had been no doubt in the church setting of I Timothy about whose creation came first, the point made in I Timothy 2.13, that 'Adam was formed first, then Eve', would not have been necessary, because it is obvious in Scripture. We noted earlier in our review of the setting of I Timothy in Ephesus, that the idea that Eve was somehow prior to Adam and responsible for his enlightenment was current by the mid-first century. Paul now seeks to address this erroneous teaching. Vyhmeister concludes: 'Eve was not created first, nor was she to be thanked for leading Adam into sin. Yet she was led completely astray. Ephesian women were in danger of the same fate.'[410]

The message of I Timothy 2.12-14, then, addresses a specific issue concerning the women in Ephesus: Paul permits no woman/wife in the church in Ephesus to teach or offend a man/husband by domineering behaviour, because (against the false teaching by women

---

[409] P. B. Payne, 'Libertarian Women in Ephesus: A Response to Douglas J. Moo's Article "1 Timothy 2:11-15: Meaning and Significance",' 1981, p. 177.
[410] N. Vyhmeister, '1 Timothy 2:8-15', 1998, p. 347.

in Ephesus) Adam was created before Eve and she was completely led astray (which will also be the result if the false teachers continue).

Thus, Paul is not providing an in-principle universal law about all female teachers at all times, but addresses a local issue in Ephesus. As he does so, he naturally applies the patriarchal language which was appropriate in his time. The underlying principle, however, is peace and harmony in the church as is proper for the worship of God, and this is a universal principle for the people of God.

I Timothy 2.15

Paul concludes by highlighting the positive way out for the women in Ephesus, who have gone astray or may be in danger of doing so under the influence of pagan and proto-gnostic teachings.

This verse presents very serious difficulties in vocabulary, syntax, and meaning, which have been examined carefully by Vyhmeister.[411] A literal translation (following NRSV) would be: 'Yet [woman] will be saved through childbearing, provided they continue in faith and love and holiness, with modesty.' If understood literally, however, this saying would mean that a childless woman would have no hope of salvation, which is incompatible with the teaching of the Bible as a whole. On the basis of a comprehensive review of suggested interpretations, Vyhmeister wisely takes the view that 2.15 responds to erroneous proto-gnostic teachings in Ephesus which implied that childbearing was an occasion for condemnation of Christian women.[412] David Kimberley summarises well the understanding that accounts for the literary and situational context of the passage:

The sense of the text is that women will be saved in childbearing, not condemned, as long as they continue in faith. Paul's intent is to restore this womanly vocation to its rightful place in contrast to the manner in which it was depreciated in Gnostic circles.[413]

---
[411] Ibid., pp. 348-349.
[412] Ibid., pp. 349-350.
[413] D. R. Kimberley, '1 Tim 2:15: A Possible Understanding of a Difficult Text', 1992, p. 486.

Conclusions

An important conclusion for the present study is that this passage does *not* say that a woman cannot hold an office of leadership in the church, or that a woman at all times must be submissive to men in general because of an alleged headship principle of husband over wife rooted in creation. The passage says instead that:

1. Christian women are to be modestly and decently dressed and are to display good deeds as they 'proclaim the reverence for God' (2.10).

2. Whether in public assemblies or at home, they are to learn in peace and submission (2.11) (against the aberrant women in Ephesus).

3. Whether in public assemblies or at home, they are not to wield domineering and controlling influence over a man or a husband in teaching, thus destroying the peace (2.12) (both for reasons of culturally accepted rules of female propriety and for the reasons generated by the Artemisian and proto-gnostic teachings regarding women's priority over men in Ephesus).

4. The women's false teaching in Ephesus regarding Adam and Eve (male and female) contradicts the truth that Adam was born first and that Eve, rather than giving him true knowledge, was initially deceived and misled Adam to transgression (2.13-14).

5. The false teaching regarding the woman's motherhood in creation, which was promoted by some women in Ephesus, contradicts the biblical truth that a married woman will be 'saved' by childbearing which is a gift of God (2.15a).

6. To the women who were influenced by false teachers, Paul says that a woman is to 'continue in faith, love and holiness with propriety' (2.15b).

The Pauline injunctions regarding women in 2.9-15 are tied to a specific local setting characterised by false teachings that appealed especially to women. We cannot apply them literally to our situation, just as we do not apply the injunction regarding men who should always be praying in the Jewish way with lifted hands (2.9). Our application of the Bible needs to be consistent, allowing for the recognition that the biblical text may have temporary and universal meanings and that it expresses its divine message in human language.[414]

9.5.7 Submission in the New Testament

How did early Christianity deal with the issue of *submission* in a society where the established system divided people into classes, or put them in relationships according to honour/shame values, and required submission from the inferior party?

In principle, the Christian view of submission was based on Christ's submission to God and to the human conditions he took upon himself as servant of God. (We have considered this New Testament teaching in 8.4 above under the heading 'Humility and Submission as Christ's Kingdom Characteristics'.)

Submission is the Appropriate Attitude of All Christians

Since submission is 'the correct thing to do for all Christians' and 'the Lord himself set an example for all Christians in submission to God',[415] it is not an attitude expected in the church from women only. It is for all believers and a sign of their following and serving Christ. It is implied in the concept of 'servant-minister', which applies to all believers and particularly to those who have been appointed as leaders. Paul's admonition to the Ephesians is the principal rule: 'Be subject to one another out of reverence for Christ' (Ephesians 5.21; cf. Colossians 3.18; Titus 2.5).

The fundamental biblical principle is not that women in the church are to submit to men, but that all are to submit to each other. This is a mutual submission in love:

---

[414] See TED-TOSCR, 2013, sections 2.4 and 2.5.
[415] W. L. Richards, '1 Corinthians 11 and 14', 1998, pp. 325-326.

Colossians 3.12-15 As God's chosen ones, holy and beloved, clothe yourselves with compassion, kindness, humility, meekness, and patience. Bear with each other and, if anyone has a complaint against another, forgive each other; just as the Lord has forgiven you, so you also must forgive. Above all, clothe yourselves with love, which binds everything together in perfect harmony. And let the peace of Christ rule in your hearts, to which indeed you were called in the one body.

The submission of the married woman to her husband (Ephesians 5.22-33; Colossians 3.18-19) is a compliance with social norms and values in an historical society that defined honourable and dishonourable behaviour (see 9.5.1 above). Thus, the Jewish and Graeco-Roman society *made* the requirement of a married woman's submission to her husband into a matter of *honour* (in marriage, as in Ephesians 5.22-33), or *order* (in the church, as in I Corinthians 14.33-40), or *respect* (in the society, as in Titus 2.5), or *reverence* (for God in worship, as in I Corinthians 11.2-16). This principle is a given for the apostle Paul as he teaches the high ideal of Christian marriage in Ephesians 5.21-33, but by inspiration he wraps the husband-wife relationship into the image of Christ and the church.

We have seen in 9.5.3 above that this means, in fact, that *mutual submission*, i.e. mutual love and respect, within the roles expected in the society is what Christian marriage is about. This is based on Genesis 1-3, where husband and wife are equally created in the image of God, being made of the same material, being suitable partners for each other, and being one in marriage (see 6.2 and 6.3 above). While the social customs could change, the mutual submission must remain – irrespective of the social system – if believers are to be faithful to the Christian view of marriage.

Analogy with Slavery

The meaning of 'submission' in Paul's thought may be explained by an analogy with slavery.[416]

Paul says, for example, in Titus 2.9: 'Tell slaves to be submissive to their masters and to give satisfaction in every respect; they are not to answer back' (cf. Ephesians 6.5-9). A wider concern than the injustice of slavery is hidden in this counsel concerning the submission of slaves, namely *attitude* as a testimony of Christ.

We all agree today that slavery is evil and, based on the Bible as a whole (not separate statements taken out of context), the Seventh-day Adventist Church has taken the stand that it must be abolished.[417] And yet, Paul does not state in Titus 2 or Ephesians 6 that this evil is to be abolished. He states, however, that in the given situation of the existence of slavery in a society, the recommended Christian attitude for slaves is to be submissive, because in that way Christ will be known and the gospel will enter the minds of more people (Romans 12.2; II Corinthians 5.17; Galatians 3.28).

Thus, in Paul's teaching, the wrong social norms may *temporarily* be left unaddressed, as in the case of slavery and the patriarchal submission of wives to husbands, in order to make room for the *permanent* principle that is mutual submission in imitation of Christ, which is the fruit of the gospel and characterises life in the kingdom of God. By focusing on the permanent kingdom principle, Paul's statements do not in any way make the wrong social norms valid or permanent in the church. As was once the case with slavery, which was one day thrown out of the window, the day has now come for the Seventh-day Adventist Church to acknowledge the equality of men and women as servants-ministers of God.

---

[416] Cf. ibid., pp. 325-326.
[417] For the biblical basis for this stand, see TED-TOSCR, 2013, section 2.5.

Submission in Jesus Christ as Head of the Church

The centrality and primacy of Christian submission is rooted in Jesus Christ. As he emptied himself of his divinity and became like one of us, he was submissive unto his death on the cross, and it is because of his attitude of submission to God, as a *servant-minister* of God, that he was given all authority to the glory of God (Philippians 2.5-11). Because Christ is the Head of the Church, submission to each other in Christ, even within the church leadership, is the appropriate way of all the church to acknowledge and confess that *Jesus Christ is Lord.*

Anyone, man or woman, who accepts the call to serve God in the gospel ministry is called to submission as a reflection of Christ. In this context, Richards makes this very pertinent remark:

> Submission should surely be something every Christian is willing to do for the benefit of others. To cite Paul's words as a support for insisting on the subjection of someone else in the family of God, be that woman, slave, or whoever, is to totally miss the message Paul wishes to convey in the verb *hypotasso*. The subjection demonstrated by heaven was completely unselfish: 'Christ emptied himself' (for our benefit, Phil. 2:6-7). 'Christ *subjected himself* (for our benefit, 1 Cor. 15:24-28). In both statements Paul is using heaven's example to counter self-promotion among the church members, male and female. The word clearly refers to an attitude regarding one's own submission, not to what one should be insisting on for the other person.[418]

The universal biblical principle is that all believers in the church, especially its leaders, submit to each other as Christ has submitted himself to God for our salvation. This principle overrules any societal norm, including the patriarchal model of relations between men and women.

---

[418] W. L. Richards, '1 Corinthians 11 and 14', 1998, p. 326.

9.5.8 Conclusions

The passages reviewed above have been adduced by some as evidence of an alleged biblical doctrine of male headship and female submission.[419] However, we have demonstrated here that there is no such doctrine in any of these passages.[420]

The passage in Ephesians 5.21-33 (see 9.5.3 above) *should not be applied to women as ministers or leaders in the church*, for there is no such instruction in the passage. It is about Christian marriage. Paul does not equate *husband headship* in the home with *male headship* in the church.

The passage in I Corinthians 11.2-16 (see 9.5.4 above) does not deal with women's leadership or authority but with the need for women to wear a veil in the church services in order to behave honourably. The gender subordination concerns that of wives to their husbands (11.9, 11-12), not of all women to all men.

In I Corinthians 14.33-40 (see 9.5.5 above), Paul deals with a local issue of *order* in worship. He quotes the common rule in Graeco-Roman society that married women are to be silent in the *ekklesia*, for they are not allowed to speak (14.34). They should be subordinate to their husbands and, if there is anything they desire to know, they are to ask their husbands – not in the church services – but at home (14.35). This is *proper and decent conduct* in the Jewish and Graeco-Roman environment (see 9.5.1 above). Paul's strong concern to adapt church practices to what was considered 'appropriate' in the contemporary culture,[421] in order that the gospel would not be ridiculed but believed, gives a perfectly valid explanation for his command to the church in Corinth.

---

[419] See the survey of opinions and the relevant literature in J. Barna, *Ordination of Women in Seventh-day Adventist Theology*, 2009, pp. 39-78.

[420] Cf. the same conclusion in GC-TOSCR, 2014, pp. 62-97, 121-122; M. Hanna and C. Tutsch (eds.), *Questions and Answers about Women's Ordination*, 2014, pp. 43-45, 56-59, 66-69.

[421] See I Corinthians 7.12-16, 17-24; 9.19-23; 10.23-11.1; 14.24-25; Colossians 4.4-5; I Thessalonians 4.12; I Timothy 3.2, 7.

The passage in I Timothy 2.8-15 (see 9.5.6 above) does *not* say that a woman cannot hold an office of leadership in the church, or that a woman at all times must be submissive to men in general. Instead, it says: (a) Christian women are to be modestly and decently dressed and are to display good deeds as they 'proclaim the reverence for God' (2.10); (b) whether in public assemblies or at home, they are to learn in peace and submission (2.11) (this is the standard rule for all teaching in the Jewish-Christian setting); (c) whether in public assemblies or at home (there were social rules for both settings), the women in Ephesus are not to teach in an offensive manner, thus destroying the peace by offending a man or the husband through domineering and controlling influence (2.12) (the reasons are both culturally accepted rules of female propriety and conditions generated by the Artemisian and proto-gnostic teachings regarding women's priority over men in Ephesus); (d) the women's false teaching in Ephesus regarding Adam and Eve (male and female) contradicts the truth that Adam was born first and that Eve, rather than giving him true knowledge, was initially deceived and misled Adam to transgression (2.13-14); (e) the false teaching regarding the woman's motherhood in creation, which was promoted by some women in Ephesus, contradicts the biblical truth that a married woman will be 'saved' by childbearing which is a gift of God (2.15a); (f) what matters for any woman (as for any man) is to 'continue in faith, love and holiness with propriety' (2.15b).

The fundamental biblical principle is not that women in the church are to submit to men, but that *all are to submit to each other.* The marital submission of the wife to her husband (Ephesians 5.22-33; see 9.5.3 above) is a compliance with social norms and values in an historical society that defined honourable and dishonourable behaviour according to patriarchy (see 9.5.1 above). Thus, the Jewish and Graeco-Roman society *made* the requirement of a woman's submission in marriage to her husband into a matter of *honour* (in marriage, as in Ephesians 5.22-33), or *order* (in the church, as in I

Corinthians 14.33-40), or *respect* (in the society, as in Titus 2.5), or *reverence* (for God in worship, as in I Corinthians 11.2-16).

As is the case with numerous culturally bound commands in the Bible as a whole, the patriarchal norms of the ancient Near Eastern society are not universal but temporal. Their rationale in biblical times was propriety and decency in the New Testament church, being a valid ground for ensuring the acceptance of the gospel among outsiders. In modern egalitarian societies, the effect that the patriarchal norms of behaviour were to bring will be just the opposite of what was intended. By barring women from pastoral leadership in the Seventh-day Adventist Church in egalitarian societies, the scorn of outsiders will dishonour the gospel and the God who has given it.

Part Three: The Biblical Vision for the Church
CHAPTER 10

Men and Women in Pastoral Ministry and Leadership

10.1 *'He Made Them to Be a Kingdom and Priests to Our God'*

The scene in John's vision recorded in Revelation 5.6-14 glorifies the ultimate victory of Jesus Christ in the mission of God. The 'new song' in 5.9-10 praises him for having ransomed for God saints from every tribe and language and people and nation (cf. 14.6) and for having made them 'to be a kingdom and priests to our God'; in the future 'they will reign on earth'. This is the church of Christ. He has made[1] men and women of all nations – without discrimination or hierarchy – into 'a kingdom and priests serving our God'.

This biblical vision of the church sets out from the mission of God in Genesis 1. In fulfilment of this mission, Christ has restored men and women in the church to be priests serving God, bringing them back to the very purpose for which man and woman were created. This provides sufficient biblical ground for the ordination of women in the church.

The components of the biblical vision of men and women as God's servants-ministers have been studied in some detail in chapters 6-9 above. In the following conclusion, this biblical vision is summarised.

---

[1] The aorist tense in *epoiesan*, 'he has made', underlines that the event is a fact that has taken place.

Creation

In the beginning God creates man and woman in his image. He commissions them as royal-priestly servants in his kingdom. They are to represent him, make his will known, and mediate his good rule to the world. He is close to them, dwells with them, relates to them in loving communion, and co-operates with them.

Together, they govern his kingdom and care for life on earth. He puts them as caretakers of his sanctuary in the Garden of Eden. He creates man and woman as equal partners who are suitable for each other and complement each other. He makes them husband and wife, and they depend on each other in a physical, mental and spiritual oneness. Neither of them is placed under the authority or superiority of the other.

Through their oneness, they multiply, fill the earth and rule over its creatures. God blesses them, and as royal priests they are to share this blessing with the earth and its life. This is the aim of God's mission in which man and woman serve as his ministers.[2]

The Fall

The failure of the humans destroys the peace of the kingdom of God and subjects them to death. But God's purpose does not change. His mission is now about the *restoration* of his kingdom where he will dwell with humankind.[3]

Neither man nor woman is now able to provide what was originally expected of them. To restore order and peace in his kingdom, God expels them from Eden, but he also takes measures to protect them from what is now a reality of toil and pain ending in death.

He promises salvation through the woman's seed – a descendant of humanity – who will restore the peace of God's kingdom. In order to protect the seed line, he safeguards the marriage, the wife's childbearing, the loving relationship, and the husband's responsibility

---

[2] See 6.3 and 6.4 above.
[3] Revelation 21.1-5.

and care for his wife.[4] The man is to work the ground and provide for her.

God brings atonement for their sin before they leave Eden and dresses them in animal skins as a sign of the new reality that their priestly duty of mediation now also includes mediation for themselves and that their presence with God requires the sacrificed blood of offering animals that will die vicariously in their place.[5]

In a world divorced from God, the humans (with few exceptions) fail to live good lives. The priestly mediation performed by the firstborn sons leads to murder. Even when God starts afresh with humanity after the Flood, the same hopeless situation continues. Humans multiply and spread across the world as nations.

The role of the woman now changes drastically. In God's kingdom man and woman shared their royal-priestly function in the service of God. Both were created in his image and God commissioned and blessed them both. The creation of the woman was the climax of God's creative work. Her equality and unity with the man, and her role as an equal partner, established order in the kingdom of God on earth. However, as the humans move away from the presence of God, men and women soon become related in a hierarchic way through patriarchy. God's seed line that would lead to salvation and blessing becomes perceived as carried by males, which is a patriarchal perversion of God's original plan. There is no command from God to make this happen, it simply arises in the sinful human world. God tolerates it, as a concession, because even in a patriarchal family setting man and woman may provide the 'seed' that will achieve his mission to the world. All through human history, God's will overrules patriarchy.[6]

---

[4] See 6.5.1 above.
[5] See 6.5.2 above.
[6] See section 6.5.3 above.

Israel

In the setting of the nations that are divided and spread across the earth, God initiates the election of Israel through Abraham. His intention is to fulfil the promise of salvation through the woman's seed and restore his blessing to the human world. He calls Abraham and his descendants to be his special people, saves them from slavery in Egypt, and declares at Sinai that Israel will be for him 'a kingdom of priests and a holy nation', provided that they obey his voice and keep his covenant.[7]

This defines the role of Israel in the world. Israel is to be a sanctuary in the world where God dwells with man. As 'a kingdom of priests', Israel represents God before the peoples of the world and the peoples of the world before God. Israel is the collective 'servant of the Lord' and 'a light to the nations'. In fulfilment of God's mission, the prophetic vision is that one day the nations will come and worship the God of Jacob on Mount Zion.[8]

God applies to Israel a dual concept of priesthood. The primary one is related to God's *witnessing* mission to neighbours, immigrants, and the nations of the world. As priests, men and women of Israel are to proclaim God's glory to the nations through their worship of him, their lives, culture, and social organisation, thus *mediating* God's glory to the world.

The secondary one concerns the life of Israel near the holiness of God in the sanctuary. It requires a ritual concept of priesthood, namely a priesthood that *mediates* God's personal presence by ritually managing the distance between the people's sinful and ritual impurity and the holiness of God.

Both men and women are included in the witnessing priesthood of proclaiming God's royal glory to the nations, while only men are

---

[7] Exodus 19.5-6.
[8] See chap. 7 above.

involved in the ritual-sacramental priesthood that maintained ritual purity and atonement for sin.

As a deviation from God's plan for his people, not only does a *sacramental* view of 'priests' become the common standard, but also a *patriarchal* view of 'people'. Thus, the elders represent the tribe and the families, and the priests and Levites come from one tribe and are either sons of Aaron or represent the firstborn in Israel.

Generally, 'priests' care for didactic and administrative functions, prophetic functions, and cultic functions in the sanctuary service. Women are excluded only from the last, mainly because of Israel's tribal organisation and its focus on the authority and sanctity of the firstborn male, which is a historical heritage from its early nomadic or semi-nomadic existence and is attested widely in its ancient Near Eastern environment. Blood-ties within the tribe of Levi and the family of Moses and Aaron would however elevate a woman (Miriam) to leadership over men. In Miriam's case, blood-ties overrule gender as a qualification for leadership.

Patriarchy does not bar women from positions of influence, leadership, and authority over men in the covenant community. By their wisdom and prophetic gifts, many women take part in leadership. There is a *charismatic-prophetic* current throughout Israel's history which continues into the Christian church. When the Spirit of God 'anoints' people, women are released as leaders, judges, prophets, Nazirites, heralds, writers, and wise counsellors.

God had declared all Israel to be 'a kingdom of priests', but for the institutions of the Israelite sanctuary and the kingdom, which shared many formal traits with Near Eastern culture, he adapts his plan to Israel's wish to 'be like other nations'.[9] In these institutions, women's leadership roles are more limited because of patriarchy and the ancient custom of the firstborn male as the representative of

---

[9] I Samuel 8; note especially verses 5, 19-20.

the people. However, both these institutions fail and disappear, the kingdom in 587 BC and the temple in AD 70.[10]

Formal ordination for serving God has a minor role in the life of Israel. Most leadership positions are hereditary – elders, priests, kings. The installations of Aaronic priests and Levites are either the setting apart of a tribe (Levi), or a family (Aaron's descendants), or Levites (representing the firstborns in Israel). These ordinations are not to be repeated, but they include elaborate ceremonies of consecration aiming at ritual purity that must be repeated each time the sanctuary is approached. The elders are not ordained either but their role is hereditary based on the authority and sanctity of the firstborn male.[11] This social custom is abolished by Jesus Christ, being replaced by the unity and oneness of his people.[12]

Only Joshua is 'commissioned-ordained' for civic and spiritual leadership. By the *leaning* of his hand on Joshua, Moses extends something of himself into Joshua, symbolically sharing some of his own authority and spirit of wisdom. The purpose of sharing his authority is to impress the people to obey Joshua and the word of God. This unique event is not repeated and does not form a model to be followed after Joshua.[13]

Although the kingdom was against God's will, he makes a covenant with David and promises the coming of a Messiah who will establish the kingdom of God. This kingdom champions social justice and knowledge of the Lord – but not domineering power. Messiah serves in humility, with responsibility for the poor and needy, and full submission to God.[14]

Rituals exist for the royal enthronement (usually involving anointment) that convey power for the exercise of royal authority.

---

[10] See 7.3 and 7.4 above.
[11] See 7.3 above.
[12] See Galatians 3.26-28.
[13] See 7.2.3 and 9.4.1 above.
[14] See 7.5, 8.4 and 9.5.7 above.

These rituals confirm a special empowerment by the Spirit which is symbolically associated with oil. The coming of a royal Messiah is connected with 'the Spirit of the Lord' (Isaiah 11.1-2) and, in Messianic prophecies, the concept of a 'kingdom of priests' (Exodus 19.5-6) is associated with the power of the Spirit through anointment (Isaiah 61.1-6).

Queens have significant power over the people of Israel, usually by being the spouse of the king but also as sole ruler. Queens in other nations are praised and respected.[15] Evidently, the female gender of the queens is no hindrance to holding authority over men.

As centuries pass and Israel and its kings fail to serve as God's agent of mission to the world, God takes initiatives for a restoration of Israel. According to Isaiah 61.6, which is linked to the promised Messiah (Isaiah 61.1-2; Luke 4.14-30), all God's people will again be called 'priests of the Lord' and 'ministers of our God' (Isaiah 61.6), and their ministry will continue for the sake of the nations. God is faithful and will make an everlasting covenant with his people, so that 'their descendants will be known among the nations and their offspring among the peoples', and 'all who see them will acknowledge that they are a people whom the Lord has blessed'.[16] In this future ministry, Israel will 'declare God's glory to the nations', all nations will be gathered to God, and God will 'also take some of them as priests and as Levites'.[17]

Jesus Christ

Jesus of Nazareth brings victory for the mission of God. He fulfils God's promises to Israel of a royal Messiah. He assumes the royal-priestly function implied in man being created 'in the image of God'.[18] By his submissive faithfulness he restores the kingdom of God to its origin at the creation. Until the end of time this spiritual kingdom

---

[15] See 7.5 above.
[16] Isaiah 61.8-9.
[17] Isaiah 66.18-21.
[18] See 6.3 above.

lives within his followers, is expressed in their church fellowship, and impacts the world by their ministry. God now dwells with his new Israel through the risen Christ, his word, and the Holy Spirit.

The mission of Christ is to make God known and establish his kingdom in the whole world. For this purpose, the men and women that are his servants-ministers must reveal the kingdom characteristics embodied in Christ and his teaching, i.e. love, acceptance, service, humility and submission. As the law of Christ, these characteristics form the basis for the New Testament theology of the church, ministry and its ecclesiastical functions. No ecclesiastical commissioning-ordination has any significance without them.[19]

Christ restores the kingdom of God that existed at the creation in which man and woman were commissioned as equals to rule as God's royal-priestly vice-kings. Thus, Christ calls the church to maintain the same equal ministry for which God first appointed man and woman.[20] *Ministry in the church is therefore in principle gender-inclusive.*

The church is to emulate a different leadership pattern than the hierarchic and authoritative system in the institutions of the world. Following Christ's life and teaching, the ministers in the church serve and give their life for the many and the greatest of them is the servant of the others.[21] Jesus teaches servanthood, not hierarchy, and he explicitly criticises the ranking and titles among the scribes, which were based on ordination. Jesus does not ordain anyone by the laying on of hands. He does not teach or command ordination. The New Testament church therefore uses a very simple vocabulary for appointment to a leading church office, because it is God's and not man's work.

---

[19] See 8.1 and 9.5.7 above.
[20] See 6.3 and 6.4 above. Cf. Exodus 19.5-6; 1 Peter 2.4-10; Revelation 1.5-6; 5.9-10; 20.6.
[21] Matthew 10.42-45; 23.8-12.

Jesus calls men and women as his disciples and servants. He appoints twelve men who are 'to be with him, be sent out to proclaim the message, and to have authority to cast out demons'.[22] Their task is unique in the church and not to be repeated. They are to represent the twelve patriarchs of Israel, who were all men according to Israel's patriarchal tradition, and they are to lead the church after Christ's ascension in a Jewish setting where only men were allowed to teach. The twelve eventually disappear, are not replaced, and no command exists to make their gender a pattern for the later leadership offices in the church. The leadership in the church is gradually given to servants-ministers with a charismatic-prophetic calling and women are among them.[23]

However, while calling twelve men for their unique and contextualised task, Jesus shows that *women are as important as men in maintaining his kingdom*, and sometimes they are even better at it than men, because of their lowliness and humility.[24] And the women that Jesus comes near respond well. Thus, women are the privileged recipients of three of Jesus' most important self-revelations: (a) his identity as the Messiah, (b) that he is the resurrection and the life, and (c) that his glorification is complete and its salvific effects given to his disciples.[25] Women officially represent the community in the expression of its faith (Martha), its acceptance of salvation (Mary Magdalene), and its role as witness to the gospel (Samaritan Woman, Mary Magdalene).[26]

Thus, Jesus makes a shocking break with the patriarchal ranking expected in the Jewish setting, because he sees men and women

---

[22] Mark 3.14-15.
[23] See 9.2.5 and 9.2.6 above.
[24] See 9.2.3 above. Cf. Ellen White who said that female gender is no obstacle for being used by God in soul-winning, but the Saviour will give self-sacrificing women 'a power that exceeds that of men'('Words to Lay Members', *R&H* 79:34, 26 August 1902, p. 7). See chap. 4 above.
[25] See 9.2.3 above.
[26] See 9.2.2 and 9.2.3 above.

from the perspective of what they may become when filled by the Holy Spirit. Women are his *primary* ministers at the resurrection, commissioned before any male disciple to bring the news of the resurrection.[27] Women have a deeper understanding of Christ's mission than any male disciple before the resurrection[28] and are better evangelists than the twelve in some situations.[29] The gospel writers pointedly include female exemplars or 'role-model' characters in their writings about Jesus – both female and male exemplars are introduced for the reader to imitate, but, in comparison, the twelve disciples come across as imperfect examples.[30]

Thus, according to the life and teachings of Christ, *ministry in the church is in principle gender-inclusive.* Gender in Christian ministry becomes an issue only when the Church develops a formal organisation that needs acceptance by Judaism or Graeco-Roman society. However, the ministry envisaged by Christ is not of this world but is based on the power of the Holy Spirit.

All the New Testament writers are aware that the church is founded on the witness of women and they are given priority by God as recipients of revelation and thereby the role of mediators of that revelation to men. Women are fundamental particularly as eyewitnesses of the death, burial and resurrection of Jesus, upon which the whole faith of the church is based.[31]

Thus, the female disciples of Jesus are the only disciples that do all of the following: they watch Jesus' death on the cross; they are the only witnesses to the empty tomb who had seen Jesus buried and therefore could vouch for the fact that the empty tomb really was the tomb in which Jesus' body had been laid two days before; they are the first people to find the tomb of Jesus empty; two of them were

---

[27] Luke 23.27, 49, 55; 24.1-11; see 9.2.2 above.
[28] John 12.1-8; see 9.2.3 above.
[29] John 4.7-41; see 9.2.2 above.
[30] See 9.2.2 and 9.2.3 above.
[31] I Corinthians 15.

the first to meet the risen Lord and, on divine instruction, they were the first to proclaim the resurrection of Christ, even to the eleven disciples/apostles themselves.[32]

However, the priority given by God to women as recipients of revelation and the role of mediators of that revelation to men shocks contemporary people in the Jewish setting. It is discreetly kept as evidence of the fact that the church is based on God's power because 'God chose what is low and despised in the world'.[33]

The Role of the Church and Its Ministry

Jesus Christ and all that he represents defines the church, its ministry, leadership, and the call and induction into ministry. Understanding the mission of the church as *part of* the mission of Christ has vital implications.

Any authority in the church comes from Christ's authority as the Head of the church and Christ's authority comes from God. Any exercise of church authority, therefore, must be in accordance with the character of Jesus Christ. Even ordination must be defined according to the character of Christ.[34] It must be applied for the purpose of 'building up the church'[35] and promoting the mission of God in the world.[36]

There is not even a hint of hierarchy or gender distinction in this biblical context, because all that mattered in the ministry of Christ was *self-giving service*. His theology of ministry builds on service, self-sacrifice, and humility, and not on power, rank, status, or gender distinction.

Christ makes the different church members one in him and before God. The apostle Paul says: 'For in Christ Jesus you are all children

---

[32] See 9.2.2 above.
[33] I Corinthians 1.28.
[34] See e.g. Philippians 2.1-11.
[35] See e.g. II Corinthians 10.8; 13.10; Ephesians 4.1-11.
[36] See e.g. Acts 26.15-18; I Timothy 2.1-7; II Timothy 1.8-12.

of God through faith. As many of you as were baptized into Christ have clothed yourselves with Christ. There is no longer Jew or Greek, there is no longer slave or free, there is no longer male and female; for all of you are one in Christ Jesus.'[37] This instruction confirms God's mission to *restore to man and woman their original calling at the creation*. Each of the terms 'Jew or Greek', 'slave or free', 'male and female' refers to the *reversal* of the consequences of the Fall, i.e. a return to the ideal of the Garden of Eden:

1. 'Jew or Greek' abolishes the separation of peoples and nations caused by sinful humans (Genesis 10-11), confirming the fulfilment of God's promise to Abraham (Genesis 12.1-3).

2. 'Slave or free' abolishes slavery introduced by sinful humans (Genesis 9.18-27), confirming the promises of God's past, present, and future delivery of Israel (Isaiah 40-66).

3. 'Male *and* female' (note that the Greek *kai*, 'and', is used only here) abolishes the patriarchal form of life caused by sinful humans (Genesis 4-11), confirming the fulfilment of God's original intentions for man and woman, as priests and rulers in his kingdom (Genesis 1-2).

Thus, the curse in Genesis 3 is reversed:

1. The enmity between 'the woman's seed' and 'the serpent's seed' (Genesis 3.15) is reversed by 'Jew and Greek' now being one in Christ.

2. The curse of the ground (Genesis 3.17-19), which caused painful toil and hard work to obtain the means of sustenance, and which caused the division into 'slave and free', is overcome in Christ.

3. The dependence of the wife upon her husband for sustenance and care, because of his dependence on the ground (Genesis 3.16-19), has been abolished as both of them are now as equals dependent on Christ who has restored them to how things were intended at the beginning ('man and woman').

---

[37] Galatians 3.26-28.

As a whole, this is a fulfilment of God's promise that 'the woman's seed' in Genesis 3.15 would bring salvation from the serpent's distortion of the creation. The *new inclusive order* for man and woman in Christ is the order of the kingdom of God at creation. It contains an inclusive ministry of men and women.

However, the church is situated in the sinful world and it may in some settings have to adapt its external, human order to the surrounding culture in which it operates. For example, in order to avoid a loss of respect for the gospel among outsiders, it may have to make concessions to patriarchal customs in the surrounding world. Such a concession is a sacrifice made for the sake of mission, but in essence it is not God's ideal. Thus, rather than labelling women's ordination as a concession to egalitarian ideas in the world, the church has to recognise that *preventing* women's ordination in the church is *a concession to patriarchal ideas in the sinful world*.

Ministry as Participation in the Mission of God

Since all Christian mission is ultimately rooted in the mission of God, all servants-ministers in the church – men and women – are functioning because *God* wants them, *God* needs them, and *God* calls them.[38] Therefore, when the church thinks it can *limit* God's will and power to commission-ordain women as his servants-ministers, it is not allowing God to be God and loses his blessing in its work.

Ministry as Being Called to Christ's 'Priesthood'

Christ calls men and women to join him and take up the ministry he assigns to them (cf. 'taking up your cross and following me').[39] His radical call to men and women to become part of his kingdom mission is at first directed to Israel,[40] but already in the Gospels Jesus

---

[38] This understanding is emphatically maintained by Ellen White: see TED-TOSCR, 2013, section 4.6.2.
[39] Matthew 10.38; 16.24; Mark 8.34.
[40] See Matthew 10.5-6.

is moving the mission of God to the Gentiles.[41] Christ here confirms God's original call to Israel's men and women to be a kingdom of priests and a light to the nations.[42]

The dual concept of priesthood in Israel's calling as 'a kingdom priests and a holy nation' is reduced to only *one* in the church.[43] The task of proclaiming and mediating God's glory to the nations remains, but the ritual priesthood disappears.

Peter captures this perfectly when he addresses men and women in the church as a royal priesthood and calls them to 'proclaim the mighty acts of him who called you out of darkness into his marvellous light'.[44] In this priesthood of all believers in Christ, women and men continue to proclaim the glory of God, as men and women had done in ancient Israel. The ritual priesthood is no longer needed. It mediated God's holiness by purifying and atoning for the people's ritual impurity so that God might dwell in Israel. But in Christ, God is present with his people in a new way that does not require ritual mediation but only 'faith that expresses itself through love'.[45]

Ministry as Being Called to Disciple-Making

After his resurrection, as Lord of the world with all authority from God, Christ sends his disciples as disciple-makers, baptizers and teachers to all nations.[46] He speaks to men and women[47] who from now on are God's ministers to the world, bringing the good news of the kingdom of God. Since the work of women disciple-makers is in response to Christ's commissioning, there is no biblical place for shutting out one gender and reserving this ministry for men only.

---

[41] See Matthew 8.5-13, 28-34; 12.15-21; 15.21-28; 21.33-46; 22.1-14; and parallels.
[42] See 7.1 above.
[43] Exodus 19.5-6; cf. 7.4.3.1 above.
[44] I Peter 2.9.
[45] Galatians 5.6.
[46] E.g. Matthew 28.18-20.
[47] See 8.1 above.

When God calls men and women as his servants-ministers, he 'shows no partiality to any human being'.[48]

The Abolishment of Patriarchy in Ministry

The old order of ministry is abandoned in the new and 'more excellent ministry' of Christ.[49] He abolishes not only the sacramental view of priests, but also *the patriarchal view of people.*

In the new covenant, God's laws are put in the minds and written on the hearts of all of his people. This is the foundation for the covenant relationship by which 'he will be their God, and they shall be his people'.[50] Thus, men and women in the church are made into teachers of the knowledge of God, for they shall all know him, 'from the least of them to the greatest'.[51]

In other words, men and women in God's new covenant are God's people on equal terms and their ministry is an inclusive ministry.[52] Diversity comes only from God's appointment of them and his distribution of spiritual gifts among them. This diversity is conditioned by the diverse demands of the task of mission. Thus, inductions into an office in the church start from this fundamental recognition: *all members are ministers of God and each serves him in roles depending on his/her spiritual gifts.*

Ministry as Submission

Being ordained for ministry under the headship of Christ is defined by Christ's kingdom characteristics. Regardless of gender, all ministers in the church are submitted to Christ, the Head of the church.

His headship is the servant function of a provider of life, growth and development. This function is not one of top-down oversight but of bottom-up support and nurture. Christ's self-sacrificing humility

---

[48] Galatians 2.6; see 9.1 above.
[49] Hebrews 8.6; cf. 8.1-10.39.
[50] Hebrews 8.10; Jeremiah 31.33.
[51] Hebrews 8.11: Jeremiah 31.33.
[52] See 8.3 above.

and his servanthood in complete obedience to God unto death is the basis of church offices and ordination, not authority exercised within a hierarchy.[53]

The mission of Christ is not to be served but to serve 'and to give his life as a ransom for many'. He is called 'the servant of God' which is a title rooted in Old Testament kingdom terminology. But his kingdom is 'not of this world' and the finest example of Christ's servanthood is when he washes his disciples' feet – a task normally performed by slaves.[54]

The essential kingdom characteristic of Christ is that he emptied himself of his divinity and became like one of us. Because of his attitude of submission to God, he was given all authority to the glory of God.[55] According to the Bible, therefore, authority in the church is based on a relationship to Christ that expresses itself in his humility and submission to God. It is not based on a hierarchic concept of organisation.

This means that ordination for the gospel ministry is *an act of human submission to God which is distorted and corrupted if hierarchy of genders is involved.* Gender discrimination and hierarchy removes from God the privilege of appointing whom he wants and reduces this divine responsibility to the level of human cultures and individual preferences. The church must not usurp God's right of calling and appointing whom he wants to serve him, be it man or woman.

The fallen world is founded on human power, injustices and a false knowledge of God (cf. the symbol of Babylon in Revelation 14.8).[56] In opposition to this, the kingdom-oriented church ministry will model a different way of being a community and indeed humanity, one that builds on the unity and equality that come from submission

---

[53] See 8.4 and 9.5 above.
[54] Ibid.
[55] Philippians 2.5-11.
[56] Cf. the exposition in B. Wiklander, 'The Mission of God and the Faithfulness of His People', 2009, pp. 286-288.

to Christ.[57] If the church is to prove herself faithful to Christ, this unity and equality must be seen not only in the laity but above all in the *leaders* of the church. Applied to the Seventh-day Adventist Church, this means that *the leaders will only poorly and deficiently represent the church as long as they include only men, discriminating against the majority of its members, the women.*

Consequently, men and women should not only be told that they *are* equal (in doctrine and policy) but they should be practically and visibly *treated as equals* in ordination and ministry to God.

The world that God wants to save consists of men and women created in the image of God who are to be restored according to the Creator's original plan. If these men and women are already shaped by an egalitarian culture before accepting the gospel, they will doubt the authenticity of a church that claims to represent a new humanity of unity and equality, but nevertheless allows only men to lead them. Prohibiting women from being ordained, therefore, is to *undermine God's mission to the world.*

Nowhere does the word of God teach female submission to men within the sphere of a God-given ministry. Submission to humans in the church is in principle mutual.[58] The few times women/wives are counselled to be submissive, it concerns honour and decency according to the conventional order in marriage or in the public church services.[59] This is associated with the shame/honour code of conduct in the biblical environment. Despite that, the New Testament teaches mutual submission, regardless of gender, i.e. Christ's attitude of servanthood. All members have equal status as 'God's helping hands'.[60]

---

[57] Galatians 3.26-28; Ephesians 2.15.
[58] Ephesians 5.21.
[59] See 9.5 above.
[60] See Ellen White's letter to the Brethren in 1901 (TED-TOSCR, 2013, section 4.6.2.4).

The Ministry Established at Pentecost

Christ commissioned his disciples to bring the kingdom of God to the world. He confirmed this by the outpouring of the Spirit at Pentecost, empowering all believers as witnesses of the kingdom in the whole world.

Christ gave the Spirit to men and women, so that they *prophesied* in various languages, i.e. so that they witnessed to the glory of God by spiritual and inspired speech.[61] Fulfilling the prophecy of Joel 2.28-32, Christ imitates the outpouring of the Spirit on the seventy elders who also *prophesied* as a result:[62] 'Even upon my servants, men and women, in those days I will pour out my Spirit; and they shall *prophesy*'.[63] The Holy Spirit is given also to women who are equipped with the Spirit like Israel's elders for the task of proclaiming God's glory and witnessing about his work through the risen Christ.

Thus, all believers are inducted into a *charismatic-prophetic office* serving the mission of Christ. For such an office, no ordination is needed, because *receiving* the gift of prophecy fulfils the function of an ordination. This seems to be how the New Testament church initially understood ministry, based on the experience at Pentecost. It also seems to explain the poor biblical evidence of ecclesiastical offices and ordination.

The outpouring of the Spirit at Pentecost is also an installation of men and women in the church as representatives of the kingdom of God.[64] This has the character of Christ's anointment by his Spirit of men and women as his royal servants, and it extends his kingdom into the world of nations. No ceremony of ordination is applied by the church. Christ's call and the power of the Spirit are sufficient.

---

[61] Christ is the agent according to Acts 2.33. For the presence of men and women, see Acts 1.14; 2.1, 4, 15-21; 2.2-4.
[62] See the introduction to chap. 9 above.
[63] Acts 2.16-21.
[64] See the introduction to chap. 9 above.

In these terms, members and leaders of the church, men and women, are called and commissioned by Christ as his servants-ministers.

Ministry of Spiritual Gifts: Given by God

The spiritual gifts, ministries and operations[65] receive their theological significance from the mission of God in the Bible. They fulfil the same function as the various institutions that God put in place to build up and edify Israel for its mission.

However, in the New Testament there is no formal organisation comparable to that of the Old Testament. There is no leadership structure or sacrificial system, no priestly order or functions, no religious festivals or tabernacle functions which provided edification for Israel. But there is the provision of gifts, ministries and operations to provide edification for God's new Israel. The gifts become *the means* that support the mission and ministry of the church.

Paul instructs the church in Corinth that the Spirit 'allots to each one individually just as the Spirit chooses'.[66] Human beings or the church organisation are not primary here. The Spirit shares himself with men and women for the good of the church: 'To each is given the manifestation of the Spirit for the common good.'[67]

Thus, it is God who appoints in the church 'first apostles, second prophets, third teachers; then deeds of power, then gifts of healing, forms of assistance, forms of leadership, various kinds of tongues'.[68] The gift of the Spirit *confirms* the appointment by God – nothing else is mentioned as relevant – and this divine confirmation can only be acknowledged by *the fruit* of an individual's service-ministry, be they a man or a woman.

---

[65] I Corinthians 12.4-13; cf. Romans 12.4-8; Ephesians 4.11-13.
[66] I Corinthians 12.11.
[67] I Corinthians 12.7; cf. vv. 8-11.
[68] I Corinthians 12.28.

The biblical silence concerning the role of the church in testing and approving the divine confirmation of the gifts is understandable in the context of the mission of God, for such a role would put the church above God, which would contradict the function of the church as servant of God. Thus, *the biblical kingdom theology reduces the role of the church in the appointment of leaders and enlarges the role of God, through Christ and the Holy Spirit.*

The Seventh-day Adventist Church today must therefore be careful that it does not allow the institution of the Church, which is always wide open to human weakness, to marginalise the kingdom of God and the authority of Christ in its commissioning-ordination practices. But that is precisely what a refusal to acknowledge Christ's gifts and appointments of women as his servants-ministers accomplishes.

Ministry of Spiritual Gifts: No Difference between Laity and Pastors/Officers

The New Testament indicates that the Holy Spirit conveys gifts to all believers regardless of race, gender, or social status.[69] There cannot, therefore, be any essential difference between ministers who are members and ministers-officers in the church. 'Any form of clericalism (i.e. the idea that there is a class division in the church where some possess a higher spiritual status than others) is foreign to the thought of the New Testament (1 Cor. 12:22-25)'.[70]

In order to preserve order and efficiency in mission, the church needs to form special offices and organise itself. However, any office in the church is in submission to Christ. Whether male or female, the office-holders have received spiritual gifts for the task that Christ has assigned to them. And, whether or not holding such office, each member remains under the obligation of 'being mutually subject to each other out of reverence for Jesus Christ'.[71] There is, therefore, no *ontological* difference in the church between ministers of laity

---

[69] See 9.3.4 above.
[70] GC-TOSCR, 2014, p. 80.
[71] Ephesians 5.21.

and ministers of elected officers – 'ontological' here means what they essentially *are* 'in Christ'. They are the same *before God*.

It is thus very important to acknowledge that the New Testament makes no significant difference between gifts and offices – the gifts equip an individual for the office. This means that the Bible does not support concepts where the *gifts* are gender inclusive while *offices* are gender exclusive. Such concepts are human devices in order to exclude women from ordination and leadership.[72]

Ministry of Spiritual Gifts: Gender-Inclusive

When Paul instructs the church in Ephesus that 'each of us was given grace according to the measure of Christ's gift',[73] this is *inclusive* language, embracing men and women in the church. He then continues, saying that 'the gifts he gave were that some would be apostles, some prophets, some evangelists, some pastors and teachers'.[74] The issue of gender is nowhere mentioned and is consequently irrelevant.

Instead, Paul defines the *purpose* of the gifts and the appointments for leadership: 'to equip the saints for the work of ministry, for building up the body of Christ, until all of us come to the unity of the faith and of the knowledge of the Son of God, to maturity, to the measure of the full stature of Christ.'[75] This biblical definition of the purpose of commissioning-ordination is, again, formulated in *inclusive* language emphasising *submission* only to Christ: the work is by all (Ephesians 4.7) and for all (4.13), but it is Christ who assigns both gifts (4.7) and leadership functions (4.11).

A few verses further on in Ephesians 4, Christ is defined as 'the Head' – no other head in the church is mentioned – 'from whom the whole body, joined and knitted together by every ligament with which it is equipped, as each part is working properly, promotes the body's

---

[72] Ibid., p. 84.
[73] Ephesians 4.7.
[74] Ephesians 4.11.
[75] Ephesians 4.12-13.

growth in building itself up in love'.[76] 'The whole body' means men and women who have mutually submitted themselves to each other in fellowship and ministry and to Jesus Christ as servants-ministers in his kingdom mission.[77]

According to the New Testament practices of appointments for ministry, therefore, the crucial *condition* is whether men and women have received spiritual gifts for leadership in some sense and a calling and appointment by Christ. There are sound biblical ways in which the church may ascertain and acknowledge this under the guidance of the Holy Spirit. But there is no biblical support for including gender as a criterion for spiritual gifts or appointments for ministry.

Ministry of Spiritual Gifts: Functions and Offices

The New Testament indicates a rich variety of services provided by the church. The spiritual leaders ('prophets') are in direct communication with God and their functions are not organised hierarchically. A great diversity of nations, races and genders is involved, but nobody is treated with intentional partiality or discrimination. All are filled with awe and joy at the marvellous acts of God and the commitment to carry out the mission of Christ.

In the local church setting, a variety of 'services-ministries' are offered based on spiritual gifts or *charismata* which Christ has apportioned to each one.[78] Individuals are called and equipped with spiritual gifts that allow them to serve as apostles, prophets, evangelists, pastors and teachers.[79] Similar groups are mentioned elsewhere and the function of 'leadership' is specifically included.[80] All these positions are filled by *God's appointments* to prepare God's people for 'the work of ministry'.[81] *The language is gender-inclusive.*

---

[76] Ephesians 4.15-16.
[77] Ephesians 5.21. See the exposition in 9.5.3 above.
[78] Ephesians 4.7.
[79] Ephesians 4.11.
[80] Romans 12.6-8; I Corinthians 12.28-30.
[81] See the definition of 'ministry' in Ephesians 4.11.

As the church grows, however, issues arise from the Jewish and Graeco-Roman socio-cultural environment. The church addresses these challenges by being true to the kingdom principles laid down by Christ while ensuring that unity and order prevails in the church. The central principle is that God is glorified and that respect towards outsiders is maintained, so that the gospel continues to incorporate men and women into his kingdom. To this end, the instructions to the churches, especially by the apostle Paul, maintain order by dealing with the social issues of honour and shame that were attached to men and women at the time.

Although the social customs of honour and shame disadvantaged many women in the New Testament era, women are still active in various functions and offices. Firstly, making disciples of Christ is the mission of the church, and both men and women were such disciples. They are also called 'servants-ministers', which is either a general term for the church members or a specific term for someone with a responsibility. Both men and women are 'servants-ministers' and some have responsibility.[82]

Secondly, leaders travelling from congregation to congregation are called 'apostles'. The twelve apostles are a special group appointed by Jesus, but their office does not survive. Other apostles are 'apostles of Christ' who like Paul are called directly by Christ, or 'apostles of the churches' who are appointed by local congregations.

The name of one woman survives in the New Testament writings as an apostle of Christ: Junia in Romans 16.7. She is not only an apostle, but is 'prominent among the apostles'. Regardless of attempts over nearly two thousand years to eliminate this fact from the Bible, the case for Junia remains solid and clear.[83] Junia was a Jewish woman and the fact that she is prominent among the apostles may indicate that she is among the women who witnessed the cross, the tomb and

---

[82] See 9.2 above.
[83] See 9.2.7 above.

the resurrection, but we do not know.[84] When Luke writes about Matthias' appointment in Acts, the functions of 'overseer, bishop' (*episkopos*), 'servant' (*diakonos*), and 'apostle, emissary' (*apostolos*) are understood as referring to one and the same thing.[85] In light of this, Junia's role as apostle may be juxtaposed with Phoebe's undisputed role as 'servant' (*diakonos*) appointed by a local church and including an itinerant ministry.[86]

There is no instruction or even definition in the New Testament regarding commissioning-ordination that excludes women as servants-ministers.[87] In fact, neither is there any instruction in the New Testament about ordaining male servants-ministers with or without the imposition of hands. The two clear instances of the imposition of hands in a congregational setting, in Acts 6.1-6 and 13.1-3, are not ordinations for any known office and both events are different in character, unique, and *ad hoc* initiatives that were not repeated according to the New Testament.[88] Instead, commissioning-ordination is defined in terms of a *charismatic-prophetic* concept. It is a spiritual act of God, or Christ, or the Holy Spirit, or all of these, in which men and women had an equal part.

It takes many decades for the New Testament church to develop institutions and organised church offices, and even when these occur, there is no mention of formal commissioning-ordination or the imposition of hands.[89] Therefore, since such formal practices are not yet developed in the biblical era, *we cannot expect to find either men or women being ordained in the New Testament*.

Ordination in the sense we apply it today does not exist in the New Testament. Instead, it testifies to a concept of commissioning-

---

[84] Cf. Richard Bauckham's hypothesis mentioned in 9.2.7 above.
[85] See 9.2.1 above.
[86] See 9.2.6 above.
[87] See the examples in 9.2.6 above.
[88] See 9.3.4 above.
[89] Acts 14.23; I Timothy 3.1-13; Titus 1.5-9.

ordination built on the charismatic-prophetic calling by Christ who fills his servants-ministers with spiritual gifts that are by definition gender-inclusive. Solid evidence of organised offices and ordination as we understand it today is found only after the New Testament, in the post-biblical setting of the Apostolic Fathers.[90]

The Offices of Overseer/Elder and Servant/Deacon

The New Testament understanding of the induction into a church office is very much determined by Paul's own experience. In keeping with the outpouring of the Spirit on Pentecost, he has a *charismatic* apostolate from God, and the decisive test of his ministry is its fruit and the gift of God's grace.

Paul does not experience Pentecost, but Christ calls him in a prophetic vision that leaves an indelible mark on him. Early in his ministry, he is endorsed by the 'pillars' in Jerusalem, but this is not a condition for his ministry which is given him by God (Acts 26.12-18; I Corinthians 15.8-11; Galatians 1.11-2.10). The leaders in Jerusalem recognise 'the grace' (*charis*) given to him (Galatians 2.9) and that God, who was at work in the ministry of Peter as an apostle to the Jews, is also at work in Paul's ministry as an apostle to the Gentiles (2.8). A similar view is what we find in the first indications of established church offices.

Barnabas and Paul appoint elders in local churches, and Titus is instructed to do the same in Crete, but there is no indication of a formal ceremony of ordination or what functions this office includes.[91] The 'elder' (*presbyteros*) may have been part of a collegial body called the 'presbytery'.[92] This group of elders may have been led by an 'overseer, bishop' (*episkopos*), and some leadership tasks are evidently held by the 'deacon' (*diakonos*).[93] Passages in I Timothy and

---

[90] See TED-TOSCR, 2013, section 4.1.
[91] Acts 14.23; Titus 1.5-9; see 9.2.4 above.
[92] I Timothy 4.14.
[93] I Timothy 3.1-13.

Titus indicate that the terms 'elder' and 'overseer' are occasionally applied interchangeably.

Paul instructs Timothy regarding the moral qualifications of the overseer followed by similar instructions regarding the deacon.[94] Further instructions are added regarding the elders who 'direct the affairs of the church and are worthy double honour, especially those whose work is teaching and preaching'[95] (obviously, there are elders with different functions).

It is possible that the model of an overseer and deacon besides a presbytery was influenced by the practice in the Jewish synagogues, where two officers led the worship. One was called the 'head of the synagogue' and the other 'servant'. The direction of the synagogue is in the hands of the presbytery or council of elders.[96] These Jewish officers were generally selected on the basis of patriarchal customs.

The lists of moral qualities of an overseer/elder and a deacon in I Timothy 3.1-13 and Titus 1.5-9 raise no hindrances for women to be overseers of a local church or being ordained for the gospel ministry. These lists are gender inclusive. If in New Testament times the office of the overseer is nevertheless held by a male, this is to safeguard the honour of the church, the glory of God, and the trustworthiness of the gospel *specifically* in the Graeco-Roman and Jewish setting, where women normally have little or no involvement in public affairs.[97]

The moral requirements of an overseer-elder in I Timothy 3.1-7[98] are today seen by some as a passage that bars women from leadership in the church. However, this is a complete misunderstanding of the passage, as demonstrated above.[99]

---

[94] Ibid.
[95] I Timothy 5.17-21.
[96] See 9.2.8 above.
[97] See 9.2.9 above.
[98] See also Titus 1.5-9 (elders); I Timothy 3.8-13 (deacons); I Timothy 5.3-16 (widows); Titus 2.3-13 (women and men).
[99] See the detailed examination of the passage in 9.2.9 above.

In the same way that masculine forms of words in the Bible and in modern languages may refer to both men and women (cf. the male gender in the Ten Commandments, 'chairman', 'ombudsman'), masculine forms in the passage are gender-specific but not gender-exclusive. For example, we see that the masculine *diakonos*, 'servant-minister' may refer to a woman (Romans 16.1).

The lists of qualifications for overseers and deacons conclude emphatically with references to their reputation among outsiders and warnings against 'falling into disgrace' and exhortations to 'gain a good standing for themselves'.[100] Thus, the principle underlying I Timothy 3.1-7 is that *the overseer must be in good standing among the outsiders.*

Being in good standing among outsiders may take different shapes and forms in diverse cultures. In Ephesus, women's right to hold office and participate in decision-making was severely restricted.[101] In egalitarian modern societies where it is a serious offence to violate egalitarian principles and prohibit a woman from leadership, the gospel will be best served by both men and women serving as overseers – and that means being true to the teaching of the Bible!

The Expression 'Husband of One Wife'
In the contemporary debate about women's ordination, much attention has been given to the expression 'husband of one wife'.[102] However, as demonstrated in some detail in this book,[103] this expression can under no circumstances be adduced as evidence against the ordination of women. The concept behind the phrases 'husband of one wife' or 'wife of one husband' is simply a culturally accepted *cliché* in Paul's time, being applied to both men and women to underline their decency and honour.

---

[100] I Timothy 3.7, 13.
[101] See 9.5.1 above.
[102] I Timothy 3.2 (overseers), 12 (deacons); 5.9 (widows); Titus 1.6 (elders).
[103] See 9.2.9 above.

The crucial argument against the popular but erroneous interpretation of 'husband of one wife' as binding the office of elder to males is the following. Ancient Greek had no word for the gender-neutral 'spouse', so Paul had to choose to say either 'husband [of one wife]' or 'wife [of one husband]' in his list of an elder's moral qualities. If he chose the latter, it would exclude the men (which is actually the case in I Timothy 5.9 where we find 'wife of one man'), but he chose the former because *the expression is inclusive of both male and female*. This is exemplified by the use of 'husband of one wife' about both overseer and deacon in 3.1, 12. Since a woman could hold the office of deacon (Phoebe in Romans 16.1), and *diakonos* in Greek is a masculine form applied to a woman, the phrase 'husband of one wife' is gender-specific (masculine) *but not gender exclusive*, for it refers to both male and female.

Alleged Male Headship and Female Submission

A few New Testament passages have been adduced as evidence of an alleged biblical doctrine of male headship and female submission. However, there is no such doctrine in any of these passages.[104] All of them address specific issues in the local settings of Corinth and Ephesus where conventional concepts of honour/shame are mingled with conventional customs of what women and wives could honourably do and not do. These customs have as little to do with Christian life today as has the counsel that women must wear a veil over their heads in the church services. But the implied principle of showing respect and honour for God in the worship service remains as a universal principle for Christians.

Laying on of Hands and Ordination

As an immediate context for ordination, the laying on of hands for some kind of induction into a task or an office appears in only four out of twenty-five New Testament passages where the phrase appears.[105] In these four passages, the candidate is known for fullness

---

[104] See 9.5 above.
[105] Acts 6.6; 13.3, I Timothy 4.14; II Timothy 1.6.

of the Spirit or is appointed by the Spirit or is granted a spiritual gift that has some connection with the laying on of hands.[106] The only clear examples of the laying on of hands in a congregational setting are specific, one-off events that do not reflect a repeated practice.[107]

Each of the passages involved gives us a *different* model of 'proto-ordination'. None of them defines plainly the office or function for which the imposition of hands is used. The central point in all of them is the commissioning of God by the Holy Spirit.

No biblical text commands or illustrates ordination as it is practised by the Seventh-day Adventist Church today. There are certain principles that can be deduced from the Bible, but these depend on a rather complex process of interpretation and are not easily identified – thus, consensus on those details will continue to be difficult to achieve.

No example is found in the New Testament of the imposition of hands on a woman in order to confirm her function as a servant-minister of God. In fact, neither is there any instruction in the New Testament to ordain male servants-ministers with or without the imposition of hands. However, there is no instruction or even definition in the New Testament regarding commissioning-ordination that excludes women.

The four instances with the imposition of hands in what might be a commissioning-ordination scenario are all more or less dependent on Jewish customs and Old Testament rituals that are rooted in a concept of 'leaning on of hands' in order to produce a substitute or representative. This is not how the Seventh-day Adventist Church understands the rite, however. Its understanding of the imposition of hands derived from the evangelical churches from which the early

---

[106] See 9.3.3 and 9.4.2 above.
[107] Acts 6.1-6; 13.1-3.

Adventists came[108], and in these circles, over centuries, the original Jewish significance of the rite had been forgotten.

The laying on of hands in the New Testament proto-ordination passages has been transformed by the Christian church into an ecclesiastical practice – without recognition of the original Old Testament and Jewish meaning of 'laying on of hands'. This practice was adopted in the nearly two-thousand-year-old Christian tradition of ordination. The KJV translation of 1611, where 'ordain' is a key word for many different simple Greek words for 'appoint', created the possibility of making wide connections between passages that dealt with different things. It was also an ecclesiastical translation reflecting the position of the Anglican Church. Thus, King James gave the translators instructions designed to guarantee that the new version would conform to the ecclesiology of the Church of England.[109] Certain Greek and Hebrew words were to be translated in a manner that reflected the traditional usage of the Church.[110] The new translation would reflect the episcopal structure of the Church of England and traditional beliefs about ordained clergy.[111]

Returning to Christ and His Spirit-Filled Ministry

The work of the Spirit in the New Testament church challenges and overrules any human and culturally determined view. Many women were involved in ministry. This was based on Jesus' inclusion of women in his ministry, on their faithfulness to Jesus at his death, burial and resurrection (which surpassed that of the male disciples), and on the subsequent work of the Holy Spirit in the early church from Pentecost. This primary work of the Spirit is the reason why formal ordination ceremonies are hardly evidenced and applied in the New Testament. *They were not needed at the time.* What was needed was the

---

[108] See chap. 2 above.
[109] D. Daniell, *The Bible in* English, 2003, p. 439.
[110] Ibid.
[111] Ibid.

work of God, through Christ and the Spirit, and the demonstration of God's power in the ministry of his servants, regardless of gender.

The 'whole body' that is 'tied together by every ligament with which it is equipped' recognises and does not shut out others from the ministry of Christ, but allows the Head of the church, Christ, to decide who is worthy of serving him. Christ shows his decision by the spiritual gifts he provides to women and men, and the role of the church institution is to acknowledge that those gifts are there.

As the whole body 'clothes itself with Christ […] there is no longer male and female; for all of you are one in Christ Jesus'.[112] Unity in the church will never be achieved unless all recognise other members' equal right to serve the Lord, including as ministers and leaders.

This is the new Israel that the prophets foretold in the Old Testament. The prophecy in Joel 2.28-29 was read by the apostle Peter on the Day of Pentecost when the Holy Spirit was poured out on the believers: 'Upon my servants, both men and women, in those days I will pour out my Spirit; and they shall prophesy'.[113] The prophet Isaiah foretold a new Israel where God will call men and women[114] 'priests of the Lord' and 'ministers of our God',[115] both of which were offices that required formal ordination in Israel.[116]

And this means to return to the Garden of Eden, where men and women were equal as God's servants as they mediated his glory to the world and served him as priests and ministers. This is why men and women are priests, servants, and rulers in John's end-time vision of the church as it goes through the last struggles on the way to the new

---

[112] Galatians 3.27-28.
[113] Acts 2.18.
[114] Note Ellen White's application of this passage to all men and women workers in the church who serve as God's helping hands (TED-TOSCR, 2013, section 4.6.2.4).
[115] Isaiah 61.6.
[116] See 7.2.2 above.

heaven and the new earth that God is preparing in fulfilment of his mission.[117]

The End-Time Church

As the church moves towards God's final accomplishment of his mission,[118] God intensifies the role of men and women as his servants and priests. Three times, at crucial places in the structure of the book of Revelation, John records the biblical vision of men and women as pastoral servants:

> *Revelation 1.6.* Christ has made the church to be 'a kingdom and priests to serve his God and Father'. He has made men and women in the church *ministers* or *servants* of God. The reference to the second advent of the Lord[119] underlines that the priesthood of men and women is a characteristic of the end-time church.
>
> *Revelation 5.9-10.* John sees in vision the throne of God in heaven and the Lamb who alone is 'worthy' of taking the scroll and opening its seven seals.[120] The worthiness of the Lamb is defined in a song by the four creatures and the twenty-four elders: 'For you were slaughtered and by your blood you ransomed for God from every tribe and language and people and nation'.[121] All men and women in the persecuted end-time church are declared to have been made by Christ 'a kingdom and priests serving our God, and they will reign on earth'. The role of ministering as priests has *already* been given to men and women in the church, and the function as rulers *will* be given them by Christ in the world to come.
>
> *Revelation 20.6.* The gender-inclusive ministry is confirmed in the final end-time events: 'Blessed and

---

[117] Revelation 1.6; 5.10; 20.6.
[118] Defined and summarised in Revelation 21.1-5.
[119] Revelation 1.7.
[120] Revelation 4.5.
[121] Revelation 5.9; cf. 14.6. The object of the Greek word for 'ransomed', which is often inserted by the translations ('men' in NIV; 'saints' in NRSV; 'us' in NKJV), is not found in the text; see R. Stefanovic, *Revelation of Jesus Christ: Commentary on the Book of Revelation*, 2009, pp. 199-200, 204, 212.

holy are those who share in the first resurrection. Over these the second death has no power, but they will be priests of God and of Christ, and they will reign with him for a thousand years.'

The priesthood of man and woman in creation, of men and women in Israel, of men and women in the church, will be an *eternal institution*, as intended by God at the creation. As the new Jerusalem, the sanctuary-city of God, descends upon the new earth, 'God will dwell with his people and be their God',[122] and they will serve him as priests and rulers. They will have access to the water of life and the tree of life and the expulsion from Eden will be reversed.

On the basis of what the Bible teaches regarding the end-time church, the biblical vision of the inclusive ministry of men and women sends a special message to Bible-oriented Christians: Return to Creation! Bring men and women into the ministry on equal terms! Free the hands of all to take part in the gospel ministry to the world! Because God's mission is soon to be fulfilled: he will dwell with human beings and live with them, and 'they will be his people and God himself will be with them and be their God'.[123]

10.2 *The Bible, the Church, and the Mission of God*

There are cultural settings in the world today where the ordination of both men and women to the gospel ministry is required for the success of the mission of God through the mission of the church. The decision to allow for this belongs to the church because Scripture does not resolve the practical issue – a fact that is well attested by the lack of consensus among Seventh-day Adventist scholars and administrators since the 1970s. The question now, therefore, is if the institution of the ordained gospel ministry in the Seventh-day Adventist Church is to continue to discriminate against women or become gender-inclusive.

---

[122] Revelation 21.3; cf. 21.9-22.5.
[123] Revelation 21.3-4.

Because of the very limited information in the Bible, the Church needs to decide if it wants to follow the expressed teaching of the Bible or follow James White's principle of accepting any practice for the promotion of the *mission of the church* that does *not contradict the Bible and sound sense*.[124] However, if that principle is applied to the institution of offices for which ordination is required (which is not defined in the Bible) and to the format and significance of ordination itself (which is not defined in the Bible), then the Church may also accept the ordination of women for the gospel ministry (which is not prohibited in the Bible).

The biblical vision of the church as 'a kingdom and priests to our God' tells us that more is needed than study and knowledge in order to change a long-held view among believers. In patience and Christian love, the good of the church body as a whole should be the common aim. Ellen White counselled: 'We cannot then take a position that the unity of the Church consists in viewing every text of Scripture in the very same light. Nothing can perfect unity in the church but the spirit of Christ-like forbearance.'[125]

The equal value of each member of the body of Christ is deeply embedded in Seventh-day Adventist beliefs. Fundamental Belief #14 on 'Unity in the Body of Christ' states that 'distinctions of race, culture, learning, nationality, and differences between high and low, rich and poor, male and female, must not be divisive among us. We are all equal in Christ, who by one Spirit has bonded us into one fellowship with Him and with one another. We are to serve and be served without partiality or reservation.'

Based on this common conviction, the General Conference has established policies that regulate employment practices for women in leadership functions (see *GC Working Policy* BA 60). The Church has

---

[124] See the summary in TED-TOSCR, 2013, section 2.1; G. R. Knight, 'Ecclesiastical Deadlock: James White Solves a Problem That Had No Answer', 2014, pp. 9-13.

[125] E. G. White, *Manuscript Releases*, 1981-1993, vol. 11, p. 266.

decided to allow for the ordination of deaconesses and female local church elders and the commissioning of female pastors. Although these church policies are implemented differently throughout the world field, the Church has remained a unified, worldwide organisation pressing together in mission and message.[126]

The Bible teaches that church practices should be adapted to the needs of the people it seeks to reach – and this is also strongly advocated by Ellen White. As was the case in the New Testament church, growth calls for practical adaptations in order to bring the gospel to all successfully.

For example, as leader of the new-born Christian church, James, who may have been the brother of Jesus, solved the issue at the Jerusalem Council according to Acts 15: 'We should not trouble those Gentiles who are turning to God' (Acts 15.19). The Seventh-day Adventist Church can do the same by accepting that 'division executive committees, as they may deem it appropriate in their territories, make provision for the ordination of women to the gospel ministry'.

Such an affirmation will greatly enhance the work in many countries. Excluding women from spiritual and pastoral leadership breaks down trust in the Church and the gospel, because gender equality is today a widely accepted ethical value. Where this is not yet the case, it will be in the future.

Women's ordination is an ethical issue also for the Seventh-day Adventist Church, but it is more than that. It is a matter of faithfulness to God, his word, and who he is.[127] God shows 'no partiality' (Acts 10.34; Romans 2.11; Galatians 3.28; Ephesians 6.5-9; James 2.2-9; 3.17; I Peter 1.17), and giving him glory is to reflect him also in the church *procedures*.

---

[126] GC-TOSCR, 2014, pp. 123-124.
[127] See R. Dudley, 'The Ordination of Women in Light of the Character of God', 1998, pp. 399-416.

The biblical vision of men and women in a shared pastoral ministry concerns the full participation of the church in the mission of God. Faithfulness to this mission requires constant adaptation of church policies to the Bible. This is part of the very identity of the Seventh-day Adventist Church. It combines radical faithfulness to the word of God with practical means of carrying out the mission of God in a diverse, multi-cultural, worldwide setting.

APPENDIX
Considerations for the Church in Its Ordination Policies

The present study of ordination invites the Seventh-day Adventist Church to consider the following actions:

1. Focus on the mission of God with all believers serving as his ministers for the salvation of the world. Ordination is the installation of men and women into a Christian leadership body without discrimination. This body welcomes other pastoral leaders to achieve God's ultimate purpose for the world, submitting themselves to the Creator who shares himself (Genesis 1-2) and is the God of new beginnings and communion (Revelation 21.1-5). Such a concept of ordination will *revive* the doctrine of the Priesthood of All Believers and the biblical theology of mission and ministry. It will remove the dichotomy between clergy and laity, releasing and inspiring a united and active church in mission.

2. Remove the distance between clergy and laity and the levels of ordination. A biblical church should reform ordination according to truly biblical principles, for example by the following actions:

(a) Admit that there is no biblical command to ordain anyone by the imposition of hands and that there is no consistent biblical formula for how a leader is inducted into office in the Christian church.

(b) Find ways of visibly including the role of lay people in the ordination ceremony.

(c) Remove from the ordination policy any idea of '(apostolic) succession'.

(d) Remove the idea that ordained clergy are a separate class of members with higher rank in the church than others.

(e) Remove the levels of ordination between different 'ministers' and apply one concept of the servanthood of Christ for all.

(f) Let distinctions of responsibilities be based on a clearer understanding of spiritual gifts and document levels of responsibility in written employment contracts.

(g) Remove the ranking differences between various levels of ministry, such as the licensed versus the ordained minister, the commissioned versus the ordained minister, the licensed minister versus the local church elder, the pastor versus the local church elder, and so on, and focus on developing servants of Christ who have been called by him and concentrate on building team ministry between equals.

3. Create an inclusive pastoral ministry. The biblical church has an inclusive pastoral ministry that does not discriminate against race or gender. If the system of issuing credentials is retained in the Seventh-day Adventist Church, such recognition is to be granted to men and women on equal terms.

This requires the removal of all gender distinctions in the *Working Policy* related to the ministry and thus the fulfilment of the biblical intent of *Working Policy* BA 55 on Human Relations. If this change cannot be implemented across the world at the same time, the Church should begin by allowing it where unions/divisions request permission to do so.

This will mean that, in connection with calls or service requests, the regional recognition of an ordained pastor is merely complemented by the authorising vote of the receiving ecclesiastical body that effectuates the call or service request. This is in essence what is done today, but the written policy text will need a few verbal adjustments.

4. Teach members the biblical theology and practice of ordination. There should be an on-going teaching of church members regarding the mission of God, the nature of the church, and the biblical function of ordination.

The Roman Catholic Church has extensive catechetical teachings about 'Orders', which is one of seven sacraments and lays the foundation for the priesthood and the right to determine a person's salvation or condemnation. 'Orders' are part of even brief and popular Catholic Catechisms, but in the Seventh-day Adventist Church, almost nothing is said about ordination to the members. This deficit has generated bias and unwarranted traditions that have predisposed members' opinion on both ordination in general and women's ordination in particular.

5. Consider the best terminology. Careful consideration is to be given to the use of the term 'ordination', which is ambiguous and loaded with ecclesiastical meanings acquired over time that are not necessarily biblical. The origin of the term 'ordination' in the pagan Roman imperial administration, its laws and idol worship, and in the unbiblical ecclesiology introduced by Tertullian and Cyprian and others after them, gives discomfort among strongly Bible-oriented Christians. Examples of terms that are closer to the biblical terminology are 'appointment', 'commissioning', or 'dedication'.

6. Remove ritualistic and sacrament-like flavour. Seeing how commissioning-ordination is treated in the New Testament – which is where Bible-oriented Christians find their guidance on Christian ministry – any ritualistic and sacrament-like flavour of the act of ordination should be removed from policy and practice.

7. Make the imposition of hands optional. While an installation ceremony is a positive and needed feature in church life, the imposition of hands should be an optional part of the ceremony. In the New Testament, the apostle, servants/ministers, overseers/elders are nowhere 'ordained' by the imposition of hands. The practice probably has a Jewish origin in the first century which goes back to the Old Testament concept of making a substitute (Levites, Joshua). For inductions into office, there is a clear biblical ground for celebrating the Lord's appointment in the fellowship of the congregation, but prayer should be the central element in the ceremony, as was the case in the blessings of Christ.

8. Let the ceremony emphasise God's calling, equipment with spiritual gifts and blessing in the setting of self-sacrificing ministry. The Church should *confirm* the candidate's call and spiritual gifts from God, *publicly recognise* the candidate, and *invoke* God's blessing.

9. Give careful study to the influence of non-biblical ordination practices that have roots in church tradition.[1] Such influences may blind the eyes to the biblical vision of men and women in pastoral ministry and Church leadership.

---

[1] See TED-TOSCR, 2013, section 4.6.5. Cf. M. Warkentin, *Ordination: A Biblical-Historical View*, 1982.

Abbreviations

BRI	The Biblical Research Institute of the General Conference
EGWE	The Ellen G. White Encyclopedia
ESCM	The Encyclopedia of the Stone-Campbell Movement
ESV	English Standard Version
GC	The General Conference of Seventh-day Adventists
GCSM	General Conference Session Minutes
GC-TOSC	The General Conference Theology of Ordination Study Committee
GC-TOSCR	The General Conference Theology of Ordination Study Committee Report
HSDAT	Handbook of Seventh-day Adventist Theology
IDB	Interpreter's Dictionary of the Bible
KJV	The King James Version
NAD	The North American Division of the General Conference of SDAs
NAD-TOSCR	Theology of Ordination Study Committee Report, North American Division
NASB	The New American Standard Bible
NKJV	The New King James Version

NRSV	The New Revised Standard Version
R&H	The (Advent) Review and (Sabbath) Herald
RSV	The Revised Standard Version
SDA	Seventh-day Adventist
TED	The Trans-European Division of the General Conference of SDAs
TED-TOSCR	Theology of Ordination Study Committee Report, Trans-European Division
THAT	Theologisches Handwörterbuch zum Alten Testament
ThDNT	Theological Dictionary of the New Testament
ThDOT	Theological Dictionary of the Old Testament

Selected Bibliography

Note that (a) in the list of books by Ellen G. White only the year of the first edition is included for convenience, and (b) the asterisk sign (*) means that the entry is found at *http://www.adventistarchives.org/gc-tosc*.

Abba, R., 'Priests and Levites', *IDB*, vol. 3, pp. 876-889.

Ahn, K., 'Hermeneutics and the Ordination of Women', in: The Theology of Ordination Study Committee Report of the North American Division, November 2013, pp. 22-31.*

Alexander, L., 'Mapping Early Christianity: Acts and the Shape of Early Church History', *Interpretation*, April, 2003, pp. 163-173.

Arnold, C. E., 'Jesus Christ: "Head" of the Church (Colossians and Ephesians)', in: *Jesus of Nazareth: Lord and Christ,* ed. J. B. Green and M. Turner, Grand Rapids, MI & Carlisle: Eerdmans & Paternoster, 1994, pp. 346-366.

Barna, J., *Ordination of Women in Seventh-day Adventist Theology: A Study in Biblical Interpretations*, Belgrade: Preporod, 2012.

----- 'Towards a Biblical-Systematic Theology of Ordination: What the Theological Constructive Task Cannot Neglect', in: *Faith in Search of Depth and Relevance, Festschrift in Honour of Dr Bertil Wiklander*, ed. by R. Bruinsma, St Albans, UK: Trans-European Division of the General Conference of Seventh-day Adventists, 2014, pp. 97-112.

Barnes, A., *Notes on the Acts of the Apostles*, Grand Rapids, MI: Baker Book House, 1975.

Barth, M., *Ephesians*, Anchor Bible, vol. 2, Garden City, NY: Doubleday, 1974.

Bauckham, R., *Gospel Women: Studies of the Named Women in the Gospels*, Grand Rapids, MI: Eerdmans, 2002.

Bauer, W., *A Greek-English Lexicon of the New Testament and Other Early Christian Literature*, trans. and adapt. by W. F. Arndt and W. F. Gingrich, second edition, ed. and rev. W. F. Gingrich and F. W. Danker, Chicago, IL: University of Chicago Press, 1976.

----- *Griechisch-Deutsches Wörterbuch zu den Schriften des Neuen Testaments und der übrigen urchristlichen Literatur*, Berlin: Verlag Alfred Töpelmann, 1963.

Baugh, S. M., 'A Foreign World: Ephesus in the First Century', in: *Women in the Church: A Fresh Analysis of 1 Timothy 2:9-15*, edited by A. J. Körstenberger, T. R. Schreiner and H. S. Baldwin, Grand Rapids, MI: Baker, 1995, pp. 13-63.

Belleville, L. L., 'Teaching and Usurping Authority: 1 Timothy 2:11-15', in: *Discovering Biblical Equality: Complementarity without Hierarchy*, ed. by R. W. Pierce and R. M. Groothuis, Downers Grove, IL: InterVarsity, 2004, p. 205-223.

Berryhill, C. M., 'Common Sense Philosophy', *The Encyclopedia of the Stone-Campbell Movement*, ed. by D. Foster and others, Grand Rapids, MI: Eerdmans, 2004, pp. 230-231.

Bertram, G., '*hybris*' etc., *ThDNT*, vol. 8, pp. 295-307.

Beuken, W. A. M., '*rosh*' etc., *ThDOT*, vol. 13, pp. 248-259.

Beyer, H. W., '*diakonos*', *ThDNT*, vol. 2, pp. 88-93.

Bilezikian, G., *Beyond Sex Roles: What the Bible Says about a Woman's Place in Church and Family*, 3rd edn, Grand Rapids, MI: Baker Academic, 2006.

Blank, S. H., 'Wisdom', *IDB*, vol. 4, pp. 852-861.

Blenkinsopp, J., 'The Structure of P', *Catholic Biblical Quarterly* 38, 1976, pp. 275-292.

Bockmuehl, M., *Jewish Law in Gentile Churches: Halakhah and the Beginning of Christian Public Ethics*, Edinburgh, T&T Clark, 2000.

Boring, M. E., 'Interpretation of the Bible', *The Encyclopedia of the Stone-Campbell Movement*, ed. by D. Foster and others, Grand Rapids, MI: Eerdmans, 2004, pp. 81-87.

Brooten, B. R., 'Junia ... Outstanding among the Apostles (Romans 16:7)', in: *Women Priests*, ed. by L. and A. Swidler, New York: Paulist Press, 1977, pp. 141-144.

Brown, R., 'Role of Women in the Fourth Gospel', in: *The Community of the Beloved Disciple*, New York: Ramsey & Toronto: Paulist, 1979, pp. 183-198.

Bruce, F. F., *1 & 2 Corinthians*, The New Century Bible Commentary, Grand Rapids, MI & London: Eerdmans & Marshall, Morgan & Scott, 1980.

Bultmann, R., '*ginosko, gnosis* etc.', *ThDNT*, vol. 1, pp. 689-719.

Burer, M. H. and Wallace, D. B., 'Was Junia Really an Apostle? A Re-examination of Rom 16:7', *New Testament Studies* 47, 2001, pp. 78-84.

Camp, C. V., '1 and 2 Kings', *The Woman's Bible Commentary*, ed. by C. A. Newsom and S. H. Ringe, London: SPCK Press, 1992.

Carcopino, J., *Daily Life in Ancient Rome: The People and the City at the Height of the Empire*, ed. by H. T. Rowell, (1st French edn: *La vie quotidienne à Rome a l'apogée de l'empire*, Paris: Libraire Hachette, 1939), London: Penguin, 1991.

Cervin, R. S., 'Does *Kephale* Mean "Source" or "Authority Over" in Greek Literature? A Rebuttal', *Trinity Journal* 10 NS, 1989, pp. 85-112.

----- 'A Note regarding the Name "Junia(s)" in Romans 16:7', *New Testament Studies* 40, 1994, pp. 464-470.

Chadwick, H., *Early Church*, Grand Rapids, MI: Eerdmans, 1967.

Clines, D. J. A., *The Theme of the Pentateuch, Journal for the Study of the Old Testament*, Supplement Series 10, Sheffield: The University of Sheffield, 1984.

Cohick, L. H., *Women in the World of the Earliest Christians: Illuminating Ancient Ways of Life*, Grand Rapids, MI: Baker Academic, 2009.

Collins, J. N., *Diakonia: Re-interpreting the Ancient Sources*, Oxford: Oxford University Press, 1990.

Conzelmann, H., *1 Corinthians: A* Commentary, Hermeneia, Philadelphia: Fortress Press, 1975.

Cook, J. E., 'Women in Ezra and Nehemiah', *The Bible Today* 37, 1999, pp. 212–216.

Cossaert, C. P., 'Paul, Women, and the Ephesian Church: An Examination of 1 Timothy 2:8-15', Paper Presented to the TOSC on 23 July 2013.*

Culver, R. D., '*Mashal* III', *Theological Wordbook of the Old Testament*, vol. 1, ed. by R. L. Harris, G. L. Archer and B. K. Waltke, vol. 1, Chicago, IL: Moody Press, 1980.

Damsteegt, P. G., 'Eve, a Priest in Eden?', in: *Prove All Things: A Response to Women in Ministry*, ed. by M. H. Dyer, Berrien Springs, MI: Adventists Affirm, 2000, pp. 123-128.

Daniell, D., *The Bible in English: Its History and Influence*, New Haven, CT: Yale University Press, 2003.

Daube, D., *The New Testament and Rabbinic Judaism*, The Jordan Lectures 1952, Eugene, OR: Wipf & Stock, 2011 (1st edn 1956).

Davidson, J. A., 'Women in Scripture: A Survey and Evaluation', in: *Women in Ministry: Biblical and Historical Perspectives*, ed. by N. Vyhmeister, Berrien Springs, MI: Andrews University Press, 1998, pp. 157-186.

Davidson, R. M., 'Headship, Submission, and Equality in Scripture', in: *Women in Ministry: Biblical and Historical Perspectives*, ed. by N. Vyhmeister, Berrien Springs, MI: Andrews University Press, 1998, pp. 259-295.

----- 'Biblical Interpretation', *Handbook of Seventh-Day Adventist Theology*, Commentary Reference Series, vol. 12, ed. by R. Dederen, Hagerstown, MD: Review and Herald, 2000, pp. 58-104.

----- 'Interpretation of Bible', *The Ellen G. White Encyclopedia*, edited by D. Fortin and J. Moon, Hagerstown, MD: Review and Herald, 2013, pp. 650-653.

----- 'Should Women Be Ordained as Pastors? Old Testament Considerations', Paper Presented to the TOSC on 24 July 2013.* The paper is also found in: Theology of Ordination Study Committee Report of the North American Division, November 2013, pp. 38-95.*

Dawes, G. W., *The Body in Question: Metaphor and Meaning in the Interpretation of Ephesians 5:21-33*, Biblical Interpretation 30, Leiden: Brill, 1998.

Dennis, T., *Sarah Laughed: Women's Voices in the Old Testament*, Nashville, TN: Abingdon, 1994.

Dolson, L. R. van, *Elder J. B. Frisbie – S.D.A. Pioneer in Michigan*, A Term Paper Presented in Partial Fulfilment of the Requirements for the Course C580 Studies in SDA History, April, 1965, Andrews University, the SDA Theological Seminary. http://www.andrews.edu/library/car/cardigital/digitized/documents/b14409367.pdf.

Donkor, K., 'Sola Scriptura Principle and the Reformation', *Reflections*, The BRI Newsletter, No. 40, October 2012, pp. 7-12. https://adventistbiblicalresearch.org/newsletters.

----- 'Contemporary Responses to Sola Scriptura: Implications for Adventist Theology', Reflections, The BRI Newsletter, No. 41, January, 2013, pp. 5-8. https://adventist biblicalresearch.org/newsletters.

Doukhan, J., Women Priests in Israel: A Case for their Absence', in; Women in Ministry: Biblical and Historical Perspectives, ed. by N. Vyhmeister, Berrien Springs, MI: Andrews University Press, 1998, pp. 29-43.

Dozeman, T. B., Holiness and Ministry: A Biblical Theology of Ordination, Oxford: Oxford University Press, 2008.

Dudley, R., 'The Ordination of Women in Light of the Character of God', Women in Ministry: Biblical and Historical Perspectives, ed. by N. Vyhmeister, Berrien Springs, MI: Andrews University Press, 1998, pp. 399-416.

Easton, B. S., The Apostolic Tradition of Hippolytus, Cambridge University Press/ Archon Books, 1962.

Ehrhardt, A., 'Jewish and Christian Ordination', Journal of Ecclesiastical History 5, 1954, pp. 125-138.

Ehrman, B. D., Lost Christianities: The Battles for Scripture and the Faiths We Never Knew, Oxford: Oxford University Press, 2005.

Ellis, E. E., 'The Silenced Wives of Corinth (1 Cor. 14:34-35)', in: New Testament Textual Criticism: Its Significance for Exegesis, ed. by E. J. Epp and G.D. Fee, New York: Oxford University Press, 1981, pp. 213-220.

Eskenazi, T. C., 'Out from the Shadows: Biblical Women in the Postexilic Era', Journal for the Study of the Old Testament 54, 1992, pp. 25–43.

Evans, M. J., Women in the Bible: An Overview of All the Crucial Passages on Women's Roles, Downers Grove, IL: InterVarsity Press, 1983.

Fee, G. D., The First Epistle to the Corinthians, New International Commentary on the New Testament, Grand Rapids, MI: Eerdmans, 1987.

Ferguson, E., 'Jewish and Christian Ordination: Some Observations', Harvard Theological Review 56:1, 1963, pp. 13-19.

----- 'Selection and Installation to Office in Roman, Greek, Jewish and Christian Antiquity', Theologische Zeitschrift 30, 1974, pp. 273-284.

Fitzmyer, J. A., 'Another Look at *Kephale* in 1 Corinthians 11.3', *New Testament Studies* 35, 1989, pp. 503-511.

----- '*Kephale* in 1 Corinthians 11:3', *Interpretation* 47, 1993, pp. 52-59.

Foerster, W., '*kyrieuo*', *ThDNT*, vol. 3, p. 1097.

----- '*eusebeia*' etc., *ThDNT*, vol. 7, p. 175-185.

Fortin, D., 'Ordination in the Writings of Ellen G. White', in: *Women in Ministry: Biblical and Historical Perspectives*, ed. by N. Vyhmeister, Berrien Springs, MI: Andrews University Press, 1998, pp. 115-133.

----- 'Ellen White, Women in Ministry, and the Ordination of Women', in: The Theology of Ordination Study Committee Report of the North American Division, November 2013, pp. 96-119.*

----- 'What Did Early Adventist Pioneers Think about Women in Ministry?', *http://www.memorymeaningfaith.org/archives/*. April 8, 2010.

----- 'Ellen G. White's Role in the Development of Seventh-day Adventist Doctrines', *The Ellen G. White Encyclopedia*, edited by D. Fortin and J. Moon, Hagerstown, MD: Review and Herald, 2013, pp. 774-778.

----- 'Ordinances', *The Ellen G. White Encyclopedia*, edited by D. Fortin and J. Moon, Hagerstown, MD: Review and Herald, 2013, pp. 1010-1011.

----- 'Ordination', *The Ellen G. White Encyclopedia*, edited by D. Fortin and J. Moon, Hagerstown, MD: Review and Herald, 2013, pp. 1011-1014.

Frei, H. W., *The Eclipse of Biblical Narrative: A Study in Eighteenth and Nineteenth Century Hermeneutics*, New Haven & London: Yale University Press, 1974.

Frere, W. H., 'Early Forms of Ordination', in: *Essays on the Early History of the Church and the Ministry*, Macmillan: London, 1918, pp. 263-312.

Friedrich, G., '*euangelion*', *ThDNT*, vol. 2, pp. 721-737.

Friedrich, G. and others, '*profetes* etc.', *ThDNT*, vol. 6, pp. 781-861.

Frisbie, J. B., 'Church Order', *R&H* 6:20, 9 January 1855, pp. 153-155.

----- 'Church Order', *R&H* 8:9, 26 June 1856, pp. 70-71.

Garland, D. E., *1 Corinthians*, Baker Exegetical Commentary on the New Testament, Grand Rapids, MI: Baker Academic, 2003.

Gerhardsson, B., *Memory and Manuscript: Oral Tradition and Written Transmission in Rabbinic Judaism and Early Christianity*, Acta Seminarii Neotestamentici Upsaliensis 22, Lund: Gleerup, 1963.

Gesenius, W. and E. Kautzsch, *Gesenius' Hebrew Grammar*, Oxford: Clarendon Press, 1978.

Gielen, M., *Tradition und Theologie neutestamentlicher Haustafelethik*, Bonner Biblische Beiträge 75, Frankfurt am Main: Anton Hain, 1990.

Gill, D. W. J., 'The Importance of Roman Portraiture for Head-Coverings in 1 Corinthians 11:2-16', *Tyndale Bulletin* 44:2, 1993, pp. 317-330.

Gombis, T. G., 'A Radically New Humanity: The Function of the *Haustafel* in Ephesians', *Journal of the Evangelical Theological Society* 48, 2005, pp. 317-330.

Gorman, F. H., Jr, 'Priestly Rituals of Founding: Time, Space, and Status', in: *History and Interpretation: Essays in Honour of John H. Hayes*, ed. by M. P. Graham, W. P. Brown and J. K. Kuan, Sheffield: Sheffield Academic Press, 1993, pp. 47-64.

Gross, H., '*mashal* II', *ThDOT*, vol. 9, ed. by G. J. Botterweck, H. Ringgren and H.-J. Fabry, Grand Rapids & Cambridge: Eerdmans, 1998, pp. 69-71.

Grudem, W., 'Does *kephale* (Head) Mean "Source" or "Authority over" in Greek Literature? A Survey of 2,336 Examples', *Trinity Journal* 6 NS, 1985, pp. 38-59.

----- 'The Meaning of *Kephale* ("Head"): A Response to Recent Studies', in: *Recovering Biblical Manhood and Womanhood*, ed. J. Piper and W. Grudem, Wheaton, IL: Crossway, 1991, pp. 425-468.

----- 'The Meaning of *Kephale* ("Head"): An Evaluation of New Evidence, Real or Alleged', *Journal of the Evangelical Theological* Society 44:1, 2001, pp. 25-66.

Gulley, N. R., *Systematic Theology: Prolegomena*, Berrien Springs, MI: Andrews University Press, 2003.

Gundry-Volf, J. M., 'Gender and Creation in 1 Corinthians 11:2-16: A Study in Paul's Theological Method', in: *Evangelium, Schriftauslegung, Kirche, Festschrift für Peter Stuhlmacher*, ed. J. Ådna, S. Hafemann, and O. Hofius, Göttingen: Vandenhoeck & Ruprecht, 1997, pp. 151-171.

Haloviak, B., 'A Place at the Table: Women and the Early Years', in: *The Welcome Table: Setting a Place for Ordained Women*, ed. by P. A. Habada and R. Frost Billhart, Langley Park, MD: TeamPress, 1995, pp. 27-44.

----- 'A Response to Two Papers by David Trim: "Ordination in Seventh-day Adventist History", Paper presented to TOSC, January 2013 & 'The Ordination of Women in Seventh-day Adventist Policy and Practice', Paper presented to TOSC, July 2013 (Unpublished paper circulated to the members of TOSC on 30 October 2013).

Haloviak, K., 'Is *Headship* Theology Biblical?', in: The Theology of Ordination Study Committee Report of the North American Division, November 2013, pp. 120-126.*

Hammet, J. S., *Biblical Foundations for Baptist Churches – A Contemporary Ecclesiology*, Grand Rapids, MI: Kregel Publications, 2007.

Hanna, M. and C. Tutsch, (eds), *Questions and Answers about Women's Ordination*, Nampa, ID & Oshawa, Ontario, Canada: Pacific Press, 2014.

Hanson, A. T., *The Pastoral Epistles*, New Century Bible Commentary, Grand Rapids, MI: Eerdmans, 1982.

Hasel, G. F., 'Man and Woman in Genesis 1-3', *Symposium on the Role of Women in the Church*, ed. by G. M. Hyde, distributed by the Biblical Research Committee of the General Conference of Seventh-day Adventists, 1984, pp. 9-22.

Hodge, C., *An Exposition of the First Epistle to the Corinthians*, Grand Rapids, MI: Eerdmans, 1965.

Hodgin Gritz, S., *Paul, Women Teachers, and the Mother Goddess at Ephesus*, Lanham, NY: University Press of America, 1991.

Holladay, W. L. *A Concise Hebrew and Aramaic Lexicon of the Old Testament*, Grand Rapids, MI: Eerdmans, 1976.

Hull, D. B., 'Women in Ministry: 1. Nineteenth Century', *The Encyclopedia of the Stone-Campbell Movement*, ed. by D. Foster and others, Grand Rapids, MI & Cambridge, UK: Eerdmans, 2004, p. 776-777.

Hurowitz, V., 'I Have Built You an Exalted House', *Journal for the Study of the Old Testament*, Supplement Series 115, Sheffield: Sheffield Academic Press, 1992.

Instone-Brewer, D., *Divorce and Remarriage in the Bible: The Social and Literary Context*, Grand Rapids: Eerdmans, 2002.

Jankiewicz, D., 'The Problem of Ordination: Lessons from Early Christian History', Paper Presented to the TOSC on 16 January 2013.*

----- 'Phoebe: Was She an Early Church Leader?', *Ministry*, April 2013, pp. 10-13.

Jeremias, J., *Jerusalem in the Time of Jesus*, London: SCM Press, 1982.

Johnson, A. F., 'A Review of the Scholarly Debate on the Meaning of "Head" (*kephale*) in Paul's Writings', *Ashland Theological Journal*, 2009, pp. 35-57.

Josephus, F., *Jewish Antiquities*, Loeb Classical Library 242, Book 4, Cambridge, MA & London: Harvard University Press, 1995 (reprint of the 1930 edn).

Just, R., *Women in Athenian Law and Life*, London: Routledge, 1991.

Keller, C. A., '*barak*, segnen', sections I-III, *THAT*, vol. 1, cols. 353-367.

Kimberley, D. R., '1 Tim. 2:15: A Possible Understanding of a Difficult Text', *Journal of the Evangelical Theological Society* 35, 1992, pp. 481-486.

Knight, G. R., *Reading Ellen White: How to Understand and Apply Her Writings*, Hagerstown, MD: Review & Herald, 1997.

----- 'Early Seventh-day Adventists and Ordination, 1844-1863', in: *Women in Ministry: Biblical and Historical Perspectives*, ed. by N. Vyhmeister, Berrien Springs, MI: Andrews University Press, 1998, pp. 101-114.

----- *Organizing to Beat the Devil: The Development of Adventist Church Structure*, Hagerstown, MD: Review and Herald, 2001.

----- 'Ecclesiastical Deadlock: James White Solves a Problem That Had No Answer', *Ministry*, July 2014, pp. 9-13.

Kooy, V. H., 'First-Born', *IDB*, vol. 2, pp. 270-272.

----- 'Hospitality', *IDB*, vol. 2, p. 654.

Lampe, P., 'Iunia/Iunias: Sklavenherkunft im Kreise der vorpaulinischen Apostel (Röm. 16:7)', *Zeitschrift für die Neutestamentliche Wissenschaft* 76, 1985, pp. 132-134.

------ *Die Städtrömischen Christen in den ersten beiden Jahrhundert*, Wissenschaftliche Untersuchungen zum Neuen Testament 2/18, Tübingen: Mohr (Siebeck), 1987.

Land, G., *Historical Dictionary of the Seventh-day Adventists*, Lanham, MD: The Scarecrow Press, 1995.

Levenson, J. D., 'The Temple and the World', *Journal of Religion* 64, 1984, pp. 275-298.

Lightman, M. and W. Zeisel, 'Unavira: An Example of Continuity and Change in Roman Society', *Church History* 46, 1977, pp. 93-104.

Lockyer, H., *All the Kings and Queens of the Bible*, Grand Rapids, MI: Zondervan, 1961.

Lohse, E., *Die Ordination im Spätjudentum und im Neuen Testament*, Göttingen: Evangelische Verlagsanstalt, 1951.

----- '*cheir*' etc., *ThDNT*, vol. 9, pp. 424-437.

Longenecker, R. N., *Biblical Exegesis in the Apostolic Period*, Grand Rapids, MI: Eerdmans, 1975.

Lorencin, J., *Priestly Ministry in the Old and New Testament: Should Women Be Ordained?*, Belgrade: Preporod, 2012.

Lumby, J. R. *The Acts of the Apostles*, Cambridge: The University Press, 1912.

McDonald, M. Y., 'Was Celsus Right? The Role of Women in the Expansion of Early Christianity', in: *Early Christian Families in Context: An Interdisciplinary Dialogue*, ed. by D. L. Balch and C. Osiek, Grand Rapids, MI: Eerdmans, 2003, pp. 157-184.

Macy, G., *The Hidden History of Women's Ordination: Female Clergy in the Medieval West*, Oxford: Oxford University Press, 2007.

Malbon, E. S., *In the Company of Jesus: Characters in Mark's Gospel of Jesus*, Louisville: Westminster John Knox Press, 2000.

Malina, B. J., *The New Testament World: Insights from Cultural Anthropology*, 3rd edn, Louisville, KN: Westminster John Knox Press, 2001.

Marsden, G. M., *Fundamentalism and American Culture*, 2nd edn, New York: Oxford University Press, 2006.

Mattingly, K., 'Laying on of Hands in Ordination: A Biblical Study', *Women in Ministry: Biblical and Historical Perspectives*, ed. by N. Vyhmeister, Berrien Springs, MI: Andrews University Press, 1998, pp. 59-74.

Maurer, C., '*epitithemi*', *ThDNT*, vol. 8, pp. 159-161.

Meyers, C. L., *Rediscovering Eve: Ancient Israelite Women in Context*, Oxford: Oxford University Press, 2013.

----- '"Eves" of Everyday Ancient Israel', *Biblical Archaeological Review* 40:6, 2014, pp. 50-54, 66-67.

Middleton, J. Richard, *The Liberating Image: The imago Dei in Genesis 1*, Grand Rapids, MI: Brazos Press, 2005.

Miletic, S. F., *'One Flesh': Eph 5.22-24, 5.31. Marriage and the New Creation*, Analecta Biblica 115, Rome: Pontifical Institute Press, 1988.

Moon, J., '"A Power That Exceeds that of Men": Ellen G. White on Women in Ministry', in: *Women in Ministry: Biblical and Historical Perspectives*, ed. by N. Vyhmeister, Berrien Springs, MI: Andrews University Press, 1998, pp. 187-209.

Moskala, J., 'Back to Creation: Toward a Consistent Adventist Creation – Fall – Re-Creation Hermeneutic: Biblical-Theological Reflections on Basic Principles of Biblical Hermeneutics Applied to the Ordination of Women', 2013. Paper Presented to the TOSC on 23 July 2013.*

----- 'Back to Creation: An Adventist Hermeneutic', in: The Theology of Ordination Study Committee Report of the North American Division, November 2013, pp. 154-175.*

Murphy-O'Connor, J., 'Sex and Logic in 1 Corinthians 11:2-16', *Catholic Biblical Quarterly* 42, pp. 482-500.

----- '1 Cor. 11:2-16 Once Again', *Catholic Biblical Quarterly* 50, 1988, pp. 265-274.

Neil, W., *Acts*, New Century Bible Commentary, Grand Rapids, MI: Eerdmans, 1981.

Neufeld, D. F., 'Biblical Interpretation in the Advent Movement', in: *A Symposium on Biblical Hermeneutics*, ed. by G. M. Hyde, Washington D.C.: Review and Herald, 1974, pp. 109-125.

Norskov Olsen, V., *Myth and Truth about Church, Priesthood and Ordination*, Riverside, CA: Loma Linda University Press, 1990.

----- *The New Relatedness for Man and Woman in Christ: A Mirror of the Divine*, Loma Linda, CA: Loma Linda University Centre for Bioethics, 1993.

Oepke, A., '*pais/teknon*', *ThDNT*, vol. 5, pp. 636-654.

Payne, P. B., 'Libertarian Women in Ephesus: A Response to Douglas J. Moo's Article "1 Timothy 2:11-15: Meaning and Significance",' *Trinity Journal* 2, 1981, p. 169-197.

----- *Man and Woman: One in Christ: An Exegetical and Theological Study of Paul's Letters*, Grand Rapids, MI: Zondervan, 2009.

Pedersen, J., *Israel: Its Life and Culture*, Parts 3-4, London: Oxford University Press, 1963.

Perriman, A. C., 'What Eve Did, What Women Shouldn't Do: The Meaning of *authentein* in 1 Tim. 2:12', *Tyndale Bulletin* 44, January, 1993, pp. 127-142.

----- 'The Head of a Woman: The Meaning of *kephale* in 1 Corinthians 11:3', *Journal of Theological Studies* 45:2, 1994, pp. 602-622.

Piper, O. A., 'Knowledge', *IDB*, vol. 3, pp. 42-48.

Pritchard, J. B., (ed.), *Ancient Near Eastern Texts relating to the Old* Testament, 3rd edn with supplement, Princeton, NJ: Princeton University Press, 1969.

von Rad, G., *Weishetit in Israel*, Neukirchen-Vluyn: Neukirchener Verlag, 1970.

Reid, G. W. (ed.), *Understanding Scripture: An Adventist Approach*, Biblical Research Institute Studies, vol. 1, Silver Spring, MD: Biblical Research Institute of the General Conference of Seventh-day Adventists, 2005.

Rengstorf, K. H., '*doulos*' etc., *ThDNT*, vol. 2, pp. 261-280.

----- '*hyperetes*', *ThDNT*, vol. 8, pp. 542-543.

Richards, L., 'How Does a Woman Prophesy and Keep Silence at the Same Time? (1 Corinthians 11 and 14)', in: *Women in Ministry: Biblical and Historical Perspectives*, ed. by N. Vyhmeister, Berrien Springs, MD: Andrews University Press, 1998, pp. 313-333.

Richardson, H. N., 'Some Notes on 1QSa', *Journal of Biblical Literature* 76, 1957, pp. 108-122.

Robertson, A. T., *A Grammar of the New Testament Greek in Light of Historical Research*, Nashville, TN, 1934.

Rodriguez, A., (ed.), *Message, Mission and Unity of the Church*, Biblical Research Institute Studies in Adventist Ecclesiology 2, Silver Spring, MD 20904: Biblical Research Institute, 2013.

Rylaarsdam, J. C., 'Nazirite', *IDB*, vol. 3, New York & Nashville: Abingdon Press, 1962, pp. 526-527.

Schlier, H., '*kefale*', *ThDNT*, vol. 3, pp. 673-682.

Schneiders, S. M., 'Women in the Fourth Gospel and the Role of Women in the Contemporary Church', *Biblical Theology Bulletin*, vol. 12, 1982, pp. 35-45.

Schuller, W., *Frauen in der römischen Geschichte*, 2nd edn, Munich: Piper, 1992.

Schürer, E., *The History of the Jewish People in the Age of Jesus Christ (175 B.C.-A.D. 135)*, vol. 2, Edinburgh: T & T Clark, 1979.

Seim, T. K., *The Double Message: Patterns of Gender in Luke-Acts*, Nashville, TN: Abingdon & Edinburgh: T & T Clark, 1994, pp. 11-24.

Shepherd, M. H., 'Apostle', *IDB*, vol. 1, Abingdon Press: Nashville, 1982 (1st edn, 1962), pp. 170-172.

'Laying on of Hands', *IDB*, vol. 2, Abingdon Press: Nashville, 1982 (1st edn, 1962), pp. 521-522.

Soggin, J. A., '*mashal*/herrschen', *THAT*, vol. 1, cols. 930-933.

Stefanovic, R., *Revelation of Jesus Christ: Commentary on the Book of Revelation*, 2nd edn, Berrien Springs, MI: Andrews University Press, 2009.

Stegemann, E. W. and W. Stegemann, *The Jesus Movement: A Social History of its First Century*, Minneapolis, MN: Fortress Press, 1999.

Stott, J., *Romans: God's Good News for the World*, Downers Grove: InterVarsity, 1994.

Szikszai, S., 'Anoint', *IDB*, vol. 1, pp. 138-139.

Tengström, S., 'Man och kvinna i Genesis 2-3', *Svensk Exegetisk Årsbok* 70, 2005, pp. 281-285.

The Encyclopedia of the Stone-Campbell Movement, ed. by D. Foster and others, Grand Rapids, MI: Eerdmans, 2004.

The General Conference of Seventh-day Adventists, *General Conference Session Minutes 1863-1888*, General Conference, Office of Archives, Statistics, and Research, n.d. (http://documents.adventistarchives.org/Periodicals/GCSessionBulletins/GCB1863-88.pdf).

----- *General Conference Theology of Ordination Study Committee Report*, Silver Spring, MD: The General Conference of SDAs, 2014.*

----- *Seventh-day Adventist Church Manual*, 18th edn, rev. 2010, Hagerstown, MD: Review and Herald, 2010.

----- *Seventh-day Adventist Minister's Handbook*, Silver Spring, MD: General Conference of SDA Church, Ministerial Association, 2009.

----- *Working Policy of the General Conference*, 2012-2013 edition, Washington DC & Hagerstown, MD: Review and Herald, 2012.

The Mishnah, trans. by H. Danby, Oxford: Oxford University Press, 1933.

The North American Division of the General Conference of Seventh-day Adventists, Theology of Ordination Study Committee Report of the North American Division, 2013.*

The SDA Bible Commentary, ed. by F. D. Nichol and others, Washington DC: Review and Herald, vol. 1 (1978); vol. 5 (1956); vol. 6 (1957); vol. 7 (1957).

The Trans-European Division of the General Conference of Seventh-day Adventists, *Working Policy of the Trans-European Division*, 2012-2013 edn, Warsaw, Poland: Znaki Czasu, 2013.

----- Theology of Ordination Study Committee Report of the Trans-European Division, 2013.*

Thiselton, A. C., *The First Epistle to the Corinthians: A Commentary on the Greek Text*, The New International Greek Testament Commentary, Grand Rapids, MI & Cambridge: Eerdmans, 2000.

Thompson, J. A., 'Ointment', *IDB*, vol. 3, pp. 593-595.

Thompson, S., 'The Boundaries of Christian Hospitality in a Postmodern Setting', in: *Exploring the Frontiers of Faith: Festschrift in Honour of Dr Jan Paulsen*, ed. by B. Schantz and R. Bruinsma, Lueneburg: Advent-Verlag, 2009, pp. 325-340.

Thorley, J., 'Junia, a Woman Apostle', *Novum Testamentum* 38, 1996, pp. 18-29.

Torrance, T. F., 'Consecration and Ordination', *Scottish Journal of Theology 2*, 1958, pp. 225-253.

Trim, D. J. B., 'Ordination in Seventh-day Adventist History', Paper presented to the TOSC on 16 July 2013.*

----- 'The Ordination of Women in Seventh-day Adventist Policy and Practice', Paper presented to the TOSC on 22 July 2013.*

Turner, L., *Genesis*, Sheffield: Sheffield Academic Press, 2000.

de Vaux, R., *Ancient Israel: Its Life and Institutions*, London: Darton, Longman & Todd, 1973.

Vine, C., 'Listening to the Spirit: Lessons in Decision-Making from the Book of Acts', *Adventist Review*, October 18, 2012, pp. 14-16.

Vogels, W.,

'Cultic and Civil Calendars of the Fourth Day of Creation', *Scandinavian Journal of the Old Testament* 11, 1997, pp. 163-180.

----- '"Her Man with Her" (Gen 3:6b)', *Eglise et Théologie* 28, 1997, pp. 147-160.

Vyhmeister, N., 'Proper Church Behaviour in 1 Timothy 2:8-15', in: *Women in Ministry: Biblical & Historical Perspectives*, ed. by N. Vyhmeister, Berrien Springs, MD: Andrews University Press 1998, pp. 335-354.

----- 'Ordination in the New Testament?', *Ministry* 2002:5, pp. 24-27.

----- 'Junia the Apostle', *Ministry* 2013:7, pp. 6-9.

Walton, J. H., 'Creation in Genesis 1:1-2:3 and the Ancient Near East', *Calvin Theological Journal* 43, 2008, pp. 48-63.

----- *The Lost World of Genesis One: Ancient Cosmology and the Origins Debate*, Downers Grove, IL: InterVarsity Press Academic, 2009.

Warkentin, M., *Ordination: A Biblical-Historical View*, Grand Rapids, MI: Eerdmans, 1982.

Westermann, C., '*ebed*', *THAT*, vol. 2, cols. 182-200.

Westphal Wilson, H., 'The Forgotten Disciples: The Empowering of Love vs. the Love of Power', in: *The Welcome Table: Setting a Place for Ordained Women*, ed. by P. A. Habada and R. Frost Brillhart, Langley Park, MD: TeamPress, 1995, pp. 179-195.

Wheeler, F., 'Women in the Gospel of John', *Essays on Women in Earliest Christianity*, Joplin, MO: College Press, 1995, vol. 2, pp. 216-217.

White, A. L., *The Ellen G. White Biography*, vol. 6, The Later Elmshaven Years, 1905-1915, Hagerstown, MD: Review and Herald, 1986.

White, E. G., 'E. G. White to Brother Johnson', Letter 33, 1879, *Manuscript Releases*, vol. 19.

----- 'Search the Scriptures', *R&H* 60:40, 9 October 1883, pp. 625-626.

----- 'Search the Scriptures', *R&H*, 69:30, 26 July, 1892, p. 466.

----- 'Remarks concerning the Foreign Mission Work', Manuscript 75, 1896 (unpublished).

----- 'The Tasmanian Camp Meeting', *R&H* 73:6, 11 February 1896, pp. 81-82.

----- 'The Laborer is Worthy of His Hire', Manuscript 43a, 22 March 1898, *Manuscript Releases*, vol. 5, pp. 323-324.

----- *Early Writings of Ellen G. White*, 1882.

----- *Supplement to the Christian Experience and Views of Ellen G. White*, Published on 1 January 1854, reprinted in: *Early Writings of Ellen G. White*, 1882.

----- *The Desire of Ages*, 1898.

----- *Christ's Object Lessons*, 1900.

----- *Education*, 1903.

----- *The Acts of the Apostles*, 1911.

----- *The Great Controversy between Christ and Satan*, 2nd rev. edn, 1911 (1st edn 1888).

----- *Gospel Workers*, 1915.

----- *Testimonies to Ministers and Gospel Workers*, 1923.

----- *Counsels to Editors and Writers*, 1946.

----- *Evangelism*, 1946.

----- *Selected Messages*, vol. 1, 1958.

----- *In Heavenly Places*, 1967.

----- *Manuscript Releases from the Files of the Letters and Manuscripts Written by Ellen G. White*, Silver Spring MD: Ellen G. White Estate, 1981-1993, 21 vols.

White, J. S., 'Eastern Tour', *R&H* 4:11, 20 September 1953, p. 85.

----- 'Gospel Order', *R&H* 4:22, 6 December 1853, p. 173.

----- 'Gospel Order', *R&H* 4:23, 13 December 1853, p. 180.

----- 'Gospel Order', *R&H* 4:24, 20 December 1853, pp. 188-190.

----- 'Gospel Order', *R&H* 4:25, 27 December 1853, pp. 196-197.

----- 'Making Us a Name', *R&H* 15:23, 26 April 1860, pp. 180-182.

----- 'Report from Brother White', *R&H* 30:9, 13 August 1867, pp. 136-137.

----- *Life Incidents*, with an Introduction by Jerry Moon, Adventist Classical Library, ed. by G. R. Knight, Berrien Springs: Andrews University Press, 2003, (1st edn published in 1868).

Whidden, W. W., '*Sola Scriptura*, Inerrantist Fundamentalism, and the Wesleyan Quadrilateral: Is "No Creed but the Bible" a Workable Solution?', *Andrews University Seminary Studies*, vol. 35:2, 1997, pp. 211-226.

Wiklander, B., *Prophecy as Literature: A Text-Linguistic and Rhetorical Approach to Isaiah 2-4*, Coniectanea Biblica, O.T. Series 22, Stockholm: Liber Tryck, 1984.

----- 'The Mission of God and the Faithfulness of His People: An Exegetical Reading of Revelation 14:6-13', in: *Exploring the Frontiers of Faith: Festschrift in Honour of Dr Jan Paulsen*, ed. by B. Schantz and R. Bruinsma, Lueneburg: Advent-Verlag, 2009, pp. 277-298.

Wildberger, H., '*tselem*/Abbild', *THAT*, vol. 2, cols. 556-563.

Williams, C. S. C., *A Commentary on the Acts of the Apostles*, New York: Harper & Brothers, 1957.

Williams, J. F., *Other Followers of Jesus: Minor Characters as Major Figures in Mark's Gospel*, Sheffield, JSOT Press, 1994.

Winter, B. W., *Roman Wives, Roman Widows: The Appearance of New Roman Women in the Pauline Communities*, Grand Rapids, MI: Eerdmans, 2003.

Wisbey, R. R., 'SDA Women in Ministry 1970-1998', in: *Women in Ministry: Biblical and Historical Perspectives*, ed. by N. Vyhmeister, Berrien Springs: Andrews University Press, 1998, pp. 235-255.

Witherington III, B., *Women in the Earliest Churches*, Society for New Testament Studies, Monograph Series, Cambridge: Cambridge University Press, 1988.

Wolff, H. W., *Anthropology of the Old Testament*, London: SCM Press, 1974.

Wright, C. J. H., *The Mission of God: Unlocking the Bible's Grand Narrative*, Downers Grove, IL: IVP Academic, 2006.

Wuest, K. S., *The Pastoral Epistles in the Greek New Testament*, Grand Rapids, MI: Eerdmans, 1953.

Zerwick, M. and M. Grosvenor, *A Grammatical Analysis of the Greek New Testament*, Rome: Editrice Pontificio, Istituto Biblico, 1996.

Zobel, H. J., '*radah*', *ThDOT*, vol. 13, pp. 330-336.